HIGH
PRIEST

© Tymn Urban

About the Author

Jason Mankey is a third-degree High Priest and prolific Witchcraft author (ten books and counting). A bit of a nomad in his younger years, Jason has lived in both the Midwest and the American South, and currently resides in California's Silicon Valley, where he helps run two local covens with his wife, Ari. Jason has spent the last twenty-five years of his life researching the Horned God, Witchcraft and magickal history, and the occult influences in rock and roll music. He regularly lectures and leads rituals at Pagan and Witchcraft events in both North America and the United Kingdom. When not practicing, writing about, or studying the Craft, Jason can be found spending time with his cats, whisky tasting, and listening to Led Zeppelin. Jason's books include *The Witch's Book of Spellcraft*, *Modern Witchcraft with the Greek Gods* (with Astrea Taylor), *The Horned God of the Witches*, *Transformative Witchcraft*, and *The Witch's Book of Shadows*.

HIGH PRIEST

RAYMOND BUCKLAND

THE FATHER OF AMERICAN WITCHCRAFT

Jason Mankey

LLEWELLYN
WOODBURY, MINNESOTA

FIRST EDITION
First Printing, 2025

Book design by Donna Burch-Brown
Cover photograph courtesy of Llewellyn Worldwide
Cover design by Shira Atakpu
Interior art and photo credits appear on page 351

Photography is used for illustrative purposes only. The persons depicted may not endorse
 or represent the book's subject.

Llewellyn Publications is a registered trademark of Llewellyn Worldwide Ltd.

Library of Congress Cataloging-in-Publication Data

Names: Mankey, Jason, author.
Title: High priest : Raymond Buckland, the father of American witchcraft /
 by Jason Mankey.
Description: First edition. | Woodbury, Minnesota : Llewellyn Worldwide, 2025. | Includes bibli-
ographical references and index. | Summary: "Explore the life of Raymond Buckland, the father of
American Witchcraft, in this extensively researched biography based on his own unpublished memoirs. Known for bringing Wicca to America and sharing it through his writing, Buckland penned more
than sixty titles, placing him among the most prolific occult authors of all time. Drawing on exclu-
sive access to Buckland's unpublished memoirs, personal letters from Gerald Gardner, and firsthand
accounts, Jason Mankey reveals intimate details of Buckland's remarkable journey. Includes a twelve-
page color insert featuring photos of Buckland, his family, and memorabilia"— Provided by publisher.
Identifiers: LCCN 2024060871 (print) | LCCN 2024060872 (ebook) | ISBN
 9780738769691 (paperback) | ISBN 9780738770376 (ebook)
Subjects: LCSH: Buckland, Raymond. | Wiccans—United States—Biography. |
 Witchcraft—United States—History.
Classification: LCC BF1408.2.B83 A3 2025 (print) | LCC BF1408.2.B83
 (ebook) | DDC 133.4/30973—dc23/eng/20250219
LC record available at https://lccn.loc.gov/2024060871
LC ebook record available at https://lccn.loc.gov/2024060872

Llewellyn Worldwide Ltd. does not participate in, endorse, or have any authority or responsibility
concerning private business transactions between our authors and the public.
 All mail addressed to the author is forwarded but the publisher cannot, unless specifically instructed
by the author, give out an address or phone number.
 Any internet references contained in this work are current at publication time, but the publisher cannot guarantee that a specific location will continue to be maintained. Please refer to the publisher's
website for links to authors' websites and other sources.

Llewellyn Publications
A Division of Llewellyn Worldwide Ltd.
2143 Wooddale Drive
Woodbury, MN 55125-2989
www.llewellyn.com

Printed in the United States of America

Other Books by Jason Mankey

The Book of Cernunnos
(coedited with John Beckett,
ADF, 2023)

Modern Witchcraft with the Greek Gods
(cowritten with Astrea Taylor,
Llewellyn, 2022)

The Witch's Book of Spellcraft
(cowritten with Matt Cavalli, Amanda Lynn & Ari Mankey,
Llewellyn, 2022)

The Horned God of the Witches
(Llewellyn, 2021)

Llewellyn's Little Book of Yule
(Llewellyn, 2020)

Witch's Wheel of the Year
(Llewellyn, 2019)

Transformative Witchcraft
(Llewellyn, 2019)

The Witch's Altar
(cowritten with Laura Tempest Zakroff, Llewellyn, 2018)

The Witch's Book of Shadows
(Llewellyn, 2017)

The Witch's Athame
(Llewellyn, 2016)

I can do almost all things through Ari,
who strengthens me!

This book is dedicated to my wife, Ari.
Thank you for everything.

Contents

 **Introduction**

I met Raymond Buckland once in the late 1990s. Buckland was the headliner at a local event near Lansing, Michigan, called Festival of the Spirit, sponsored by our local metaphysical shop, Triple Goddess Bookstore. I was in my mid-twenties at the time but most definitely still felt like a kid. For most of the festival, Buckland sat behind a table next to the event's vendor room, where he happily spoke with whoever came by and signed copies of *Buckland's Complete Book of Witchcraft*, better known to my friends and me at the time (and possibly to you, too!) as *Buckland's Big Blue Book*.

I have always tended to fanboy the influential Pagan and Witchcraft figures I've met over the years, and Buckland was no exception. I remember being scared to meet him and actually going out of my way to avoid him during the first day of the event. But when all my friends told me just how nice Buckland was, I acquiesced and marched over to his table and took the opportunity to say hello. He was just as friendly as my friends had described him, and over the course of writing this book, most everyone else has described Raymond Buckland the same way to me.

Raymond Buckland wasn't anything like I expected him to be. As someone whose early years as a Witch were spent reading *Witchcraft from the Inside*, *Practical Candleburning Rituals*, and (of course) *Buckland's Complete Book of Witchcraft*, I expected someone a bit more austere. Buckland's books always felt so *serious* to me, and I expected him to be a large, imposing, remote, no-nonsense kind of guy. Upon seeing him for the first time, I immediately felt like all those Llewellyn publicity photos over the years had been lying to me. Buckland was much shorter than I had anticipated, but perhaps most importantly, he seemed to smile a lot. Buckland was the exact opposite of what I had expected: He was easily approachable and humble, and he just seemed like a nice dude.

Over the next fifteen years, I found myself in proximity to Raymond Buckland several more times, but I never again got to look him in the eye. Those "close but not quite" moments all happened in Lily Dale, New York, a Spiritualist community in Western New York State. Western New York is home to several groups that participate in what the wider world might call "alternative spiritualities," and not far from Lily Dale, in Sherman, New York, lies the Brushwood Folklore Center, a Pagan campground. On trips to Brushwood, my friends and I would often travel to Lily Dale, where Buckland spent many of his later summers working as a spirit medium.

On one of those trips, we came across Buckland's corvette, complete with "Buckland" on the vanity license plate. To my friends and me, being able to walk up to Buckland's car was more exciting than anything else we encountered at Lily Dale that day. We were touching Raymond Buckland's car! (And yes, I really touched his car. I have no regrets.) I never got to touch a car belonging to Gerald Gardner or Doreen Valiente,[1] but I did get to touch Buckland's! I was even able to snap a few pictures of the car before my cell phone ran out of battery life that afternoon. To this day, it is one of the coolest random pictures I've ever taken.

A few years after running into Buckland's car, I woke up to the news that the great man had passed away. Buckland died on September 27, 2017, and I heard the news the following morning while preparing to board a flight back to California from the American Midwest. Even though I didn't *know* Raymond Buckland, I still felt like I *knew* Raymond Buckland. I didn't cry or anything like that, but I felt a hollowness inside me upon hearing the news. Buckland was one of the primary architects of the modern Witchcraft movement, particularly in the United States. Certainly Witchcraft would still be a living and growing movement had Buckland never been born, but I think it would be less than what it is today, diminished somehow.

---

1. I feel like I should point out here that Valiente never even owned a car.

My sadness at Buckland's passing was due in large part to just how intimate the experience of reading a book can be. When we curl up with a book, we find ourselves alone with the author, the only thoughts in our head the words on the page and the feelings and emotions those words bring to the surface of our awareness. Because of the intimate nature of reading, we often feel as if we know authors, especially in the magickal community. Since the 1950s, Witch authors have been sharing history, knowledge, spellcraft, and personal experiences in books. When reading books about the Craft, we tend to run into a lot of "I's," with the writer sharing what they have done and what their practice means to them. In many ways, it's like speaking to an old friend.

Unlike the folks in many other spiritual communities, those of us in the Pagan and Witchcraft worlds don't have much in the way of celebrities or spiritual leaders. The Witchcraft world especially has always been decentralized, and despite the claims of some, Witchcraft has no kings or queens, but just a myriad assortment of individuals all trying to do the best they can. There are certainly High Priestesses and High Priests and other officiants, but the "power" of those individuals rarely goes beyond one coven or organization.

Many of us also start out as solitary practitioners. For several years, the only other Witches I knew were the names that appeared on the spines of the books in my library, and I don't think my experience was unique. Because of this, writers such as Raymond Buckland quickly went from "Buckland" to "Raymond," and eventually to "Ray" and even "Uncle Bucky."[2] Using first names and nicknames is not a sign of disrespect; it's a sign of familiarity and affection, the ultimate compliment one can pay to an author of Witchcraft books.

Due to my own personal affection for Raymond Buckland, I find myself often referring to the man as "Raymond" or even "Ray" throughout this book. Some of that is a matter of clarity—Buckland's wives all shared his last name (wives, plural—he was married three times), so it's important to specify just which *Buckland* I'm referring to in the text—but mostly it's just because I like him. I might have thought he was stuffy and serious before meeting him, but

---

2. A lot of us who loved Ray's work use the name "Uncle Bucky," but Uncle Bucky was most definitely *not* among Ray's favorite nicknames.

now, after writing about him for a couple of years, I find the man warm and friendly, a feeling backed up by the many people who truly knew Ray when he was here with us.

During his lifetime, Buckland wrote more than forty books, making him one of the most prolific Witchcraft authors of all time. There are writers who have written more books, but few writers in the magickal genre have a more varied catalog. Most of you are probably familiar with his Witchcraft and/or spirit communication books, but he also wrote fiction and was comfortable exploring other facets of the occult, spellwork, and the unexplained. Once Buckland began writing, he averaged a book a year for most of his life.

And then there's all the writing not in his official bibliography. There are the pamphlets he sold at various times in his life, and there's the magickal correspondence course that occupied him for nearly half a decade. Buckland truly enjoyed public speaking, and many of his later lectures and presentations have been preserved digitally, much of the material so well-thought-out that it could very well be published as yet another book. Perhaps the greatest treasure of all in his myriad private writings was an unpublished memoir that I had access to courtesy of his widow, Tara Buckland.

Sadly, Buckland's memoir was really just a starting point for his life story and not the ending he probably wanted it to be. Book editors do more than correct mistakes; they also help shape and sharpen a manuscript. Buckland never got to that stage with his memoir, which is why it will likely remain unpublished. For those of you who might be saddened by not having the opportunity to read Buckland's unpublished memoir, take heart, because you are still getting a version of that work here. Much of this book was shaped and influenced by Buckland's personal account of his life, and many of the more interesting bits from that unpublished work have ended up in these pages.

Although there are some fascinating insights in Buckland's memoir, much of it reads like a collection of a man simply moving from point A to point B. It's nice to know that he talked about Witchcraft on several local radio programs, but a list of the names of every one of those programs doesn't make for scintillating reading, and that information is probably not of much interest to most people. Buckland also really liked cars, and I mean *really liked* cars, and his memoir is as much about his life as a Witch as it is about the cars he drove over the years and how those cars handled on the road. (One of history's most famous Witches was also something of a gearhead!)

Despite being a rather famous personage in the worlds of Witchcraft and Spiritualism, Raymond Buckland lived a life that was rather ordinary in many ways. Buckland didn't become a full-time writer for decades and worked a variety of mundane jobs in the interim. He held office jobs, appraised houses, helped run a resume-writing service, and worked in a print shop. It was this nine-to-five work (and not the proceeds from *Practical Candleburning Rituals*) that paid the bills to keep a house over his head. Despite what many people think, writing Witchcraft books is not particularly profitable, and anyone who does write Witchcraft books generally does so out of a love for the Craft.

Hi, I'm Jason (I feel like I should introduce myself!), the writer of this book and most definitely someone who writes out of love for the Craft. Over the last ten years, I've written (and/or coauthored) nine books for Llewellyn (the publisher of this book), and many of them have a lot of history in them. But I am most certainly not a trained historian, and I am most certainly not a trained biographer. Writing Raymond Buckland's biography has been an honor and an absolutely frightening experience all at the same time.

In the end, I decided to focus on the highlights of Ray's life, focusing on the books he is remembered for and sharing the stories that I think are interesting, along with some of the stories that were certainly important to Raymond Buckland the man. That doesn't mean I included all the stuff about the cars, but Buckland also loved flying small aircraft, so I thought that was worth including. What's not in the book are lists of every TV show he was on and every magazine he was in. Biographies tend to be either shorter and more manageable or very long. I chose shorter and more manageable.

Another choice I made was not to psychoanalyze Raymond Buckland while I was writing about him. Ray wrote books about the occult, Witchcraft, and Spiritualism because he loved those topics and wanted to enlighten his readers on those subjects. He also wrote books for money, because he needed money to eat and keep a roof over his head. Those are the usual reasons those of us who write books choose to write books. I'm here to tell a story, not speculate.

Part of that story is setting Raymond Buckland in the context of the times in which he lived. The Witchcraft world of 1971 was very different from, say, that of 1991, and certainly that of 2025, and in many ways Buckland grew alongside the Witchcraft he loved so much. There were certain ideas about the Craft that Buckland would take with him to the grave, but he was also capable of change and adaptation. That's one of the things I really love about Ray: His Witchcraft circle only became larger with time. His worldview was one of growth, not contraction.

Beginning in the mid-1960s, Raymond Buckland chose to live his life as a public Witch. Not every Witch who was a part of Buckland's life made the same choice. For that reason, there are several instances in the text where I've chosen to forgo the use of legal names, instead using magical names and/or aliases. This might be frustrating for some, especially history nerds like me, but my publisher cannot afford to be sued and neither can I. I'm sorry for having to make this choice, but just know that it was not made lightly.

Many of the ideas we take for granted in the Witchcraft world today come directly from Raymond Buckland, and many of those things are so commonplace that the great majority of people don't realize that Ray was their architect. Those ideas get some extra space in the text, as do some extended looks at a few of Ray's most well-known and loved books. While I have tried hard to quiet my inner critic while writing this book, it does come out when discussing some of Ray's published work. While a lot of that work has aged well, some of it has not, and it's worth sharing why.

In addition to Ray's words and my own words about Ray, I have enlisted a few other folks to write some remembrances of Ray, which are interspersed throughout the text. Despite my one-off introduction to Buckland, I never really got to have much in the way of personal interactions with him. It's nice to hear from some people who had those experiences.

At the end of most of the chapters are some excerpts from Ray's books. Raymond Buckland will be remembered as one of the preeminent writers of the modern occult revival, so sharing some of those writings is a way to share a bit more of Raymond Buckland with you, the reader. I also think Ray liked his books to be practical. Including some spellwork and rituals makes this book much more practical than it might otherwise be!

This is not a gossipy book, but it does address some thorny issues. Buckland wrote several things over the years that probably were not true, and like many of the Witches before him, he was not above embellishing his credentials. I felt bad writing about some of the inconsistencies in the things Buckland said over the course of his life, but I believe that's all part of the story, too. I hope that the more controversial stuff is not what people take away from this book, but instead that readers salute the vast amount of good that Raymond Buckland did for the Witchcraft world.

Having Buckland's memoir available while writing about his life often made it feel like Ray was close at hand. If a story was in his memoir (and wasn't about a car), I felt like it should probably go in this biography. If he thought it was important enough to write about extensively, I tended to concur. Besides, it's Ray's story; I'm just here to bring it to life. When I quote Ray without providing a source, I'm quoting from his memoir.

Raymond Buckland was one of the most important Witches of the last seventy years, and in one hundred years I think people will still be talking about him. In addition to talking about Ray, they will also be reading the *Big Blue Book*, just like so many of us have done since the mid-1980s. While working on this text, I became quite fond of Raymond Buckland, and I think you will feel that way too.

—Jason W. Mankey
October 2023

Chapter One
Beginnings

Raymond Buckland was born on August 31, 1934, at Queen Charlotte's Hospital in London, England. He was born in the late evening, between 8:00 and 8:30 p.m., but as no one was keeping track of birth times in 1934, his exact time of birth is unknown. When asked by astrologers to share his time of birth, Buckland tended to split the difference and claim the time of 8:15 p.m., but of course he could have been born earlier or later. We will never know for sure.

Buckland's father, Stanley Thomas Buckland, was an executive officer in the United Kingdom's Ministry of Health in Westminster. Buckland's mother, Eileen Lizzie (Elizabeth) Wells, worked as a seamstress prior to her marriage to Stanley, but once married, she became a stay-at-home mom. Eileen's legal middle name was Lizzie, but she so despised the name that she claimed she had been born Eileen Elizabeth. Raymond Buckland had an older brother, Gerard Stanley (Stan) Buckland. Gerard took after his father in the looks department, inheriting his father's darker Romani complexion. Raymond was fairer-skinned, taking after his mother.

Buckland's early childhood was comfortable, though not particularly memorable for young Raymond. Buckland's earliest memories revolve around dares made by his brother, Gerard, and giving pretend pony rides in a large, old baby stroller. Young Buckland and his friends would pretend to be either a horse or a rider, with one of the boys pulling the stroller and the other along for the ride. In his memoir, Buckland recalls being infatuated with a golden brass firefighter's helmet and staring at the replica toy version

A very dapper-looking
Stanley Buckland
(Raymond's father)

Eileen Lizzie Wells
(Raymond's mother)

at a local department store. Unfortunately, Buckland never received that helmet due to the onset of World War II.

The United Kingdom entered the war just a few days after Raymond's fifth birthday, and the rest of Buckland's earliest childhood memories would revolve around bombings and the war effort. Due to the war, the Bucklands moved to Nottingham, England, where Stanley worked as a hospital administrator. Stanley Buckland would also work as an air raid warden during the family's time in Nottingham.

The move to Nottingham did not spare the Bucklands from German bombs. As the home of pharmaceutical company Boots the Chemist (today known as Boots), Nottingham was a frequent target of German bombers and, later, V-1 and V-2 rockets. Buckland found the V-2 rockets especially frightening. He described them as "pilot-less airplanes" driven by rockets that would suddenly run out of fuel and drop to the ground. As a child, he would listen to the sound of the V-2 engines, and if that engine sound suddenly stopped, he and everyone around him would immediately dive for shelter.

The skies above Nottingham were also home to dogfights as British and German aircraft battled for supremacy over the air. Downed German aircraft were occasionally displayed in the middle of Nottingham, allowing the locals to see the enemy's aircraft up close. Also on display were British bombs, and citizens were encouraged to write messages to Hitler on the bomb of their choice in chalk. With the threat of death and destruction ever near, the Bucklands built a bomb shelter in their backyard.

In June of 1944, young Buckland witnessed the buildup of aircraft leading to the invasion of Normandy. One spring day he saw "squadron after squadron" flying over Nottingham, including dozens of troop-carrying gliders towed by other aircraft. The planes overhead all bore white stripes on their wings, signifying they were UK planes, so there was no risk of a bombing, but the sight was still unsettling. In his memoir, Buckland describes a sky "black with airplanes...for hours," a feeling that was both stirring and chilling.

Despite the war, Raymond Buckland and the other children in Nottingham still had to go to school. In his memoir, Ray recounts his walks to school during the period:

Gerard and I would walk to school—about two or three miles—noting which buildings had been bombed the previous night, and sometimes climbing through the rubble. We had been instructed that if the air raid siren sounded when we had already started for school in the morning, then we should either go back home or go on to school; whichever was closest. We always went to school even if we hadn't yet reached the end of our road, because at school, in the shelters, they passed out candy.

Even in this photo of him at a young age, one can see this is clearly Raymond Buckland.

Not every moment of Buckland's childhood was spent worrying about war and its consequences. There was a tall cliff with a large field at its top behind the Buckland house that Raymond and the other area boys would play in. The field was owned by a local coal merchant who kept two horses on the property. One of the horses was old and docile, but the other was young and aggressive, and when the young horse was riled up, he would chase the child interlopers in *his* field. Buckland describes the horse's eyes as "evil" and recalls diving over a fence to escape. To a child, the experience might have felt like certain death.

Despite the field's dangers, Buckland liked to visit because he had grown attached to a tree on the property. In the high branches of an old hawthorn tree, Buckland could look out over his neighborhood and pretend for a few moments that the world was a more normal place. The hawthorn tree also offered a quiet place to read and spend some time alone. I can't help but wonder if young Buckland felt the protective energy of that old hawthorn tree while surrounded by the signs of World War II.

There was very little respite from the realities of the war, even for a young boy. Food was rationed and people carried gas masks with them wherever they went. Even on a warm summer night, every house was required to draw their blackout curtains shut to discourage German bombs from raining down upon them. According to Buckland's memoir, as an air raid warden, Stanley Buckland was required to go out in the thick of a bombing attack to make sure every home had their curtains drawn.

Outside of outdoor games and tree-climbing adventures, there was very little for Raymond Buckland to look forward to in World War II Britain, with the exception of candy. Every month during the war, Raymond would save up his candy coupons and splurge on sweets. During the summers, the Bucklands would visit Eileen's parents, who would save up their "sweet coupons" during the year for Raymond and Gerard. Even better, Grandpa and Grandma Wells lived next door to a candy shop.

Despite some hardships, the Bucklands were incredibly fortunate during the war. While Stanley technically held an officer's rank in the Royal Air Force during the war, he went to and from work each day in a business suit and was able to sleep in his own bed at night. Some of Raymond's childhood companions were much less lucky. Their fathers served overseas, and at least one spent much of the war as a prisoner in a Japanese concentration camp and forced to work on the Burma Railway.

Stanley Buckland was an avid gardener, which helped the Buckland family stretch their wartime rations. Even in the midst of war, Stanley Buckland was able to grow "heaps" of vegetables, helping to keep his two growing boys well-fed. The Bucklands also raised chickens for the birds' eggs, a luxury many in the UK went without. Chickens weren't the only birds kept by the Bucklands; Gerard and Raymond also raised pigeons for a time, until one of their birds flew down a neighbor's chimney, covering the living room in soot.

The end of the war was a time of celebration for both children and adults in the United Kingdom, and this period resulted in several happy memories for young Raymond. There were block parties celebrating the victories in Europe and Japan, with Ray dressing up as a cowboy for the former. There was also the evening when "the lights came on again," an event truly worthy of celebration. The exterior lights of the local shops had been turned off during the war, and when the lights were finally turned back on six years later, the sight resulted in gasps from Ray and everyone else in Nottingham who had come to witness the town's relighting.

A certificate of merit presented to young Raymond for swimming one (whole) width!

Raymond Buckland's first brush with notoriety, or at least journalists, happened shortly after the war when a German journalist came to live with the Bucklands. The Germans were having trouble adapting to rationing, so six German journalists were sent to live with six UK families to see how an average British family lived on and adjusted to rationing. Buckland says that local photographers would stick "their cameras through the windows" of the Buckland home to capture images of the exotic German journalist eating with his family.

Humorously, one morning Stanley Buckland commented on the large number of eggs present at breakfast. Eileen then casually mentioned that she had received a dozen eggs from a neighbor whose sister lived on a farm. Stanley then pointed out that receiving eggs from a neighbor was akin to getting food on the black market! The point of this whole exercise was to show the Germans that they could live on what was given to them without needing to find additional sources of foodstuffs.

Buckland was an avid reader throughout his life, a passion he picked up at a young age. In 1948 Buckland read his first occult-adjacent book, *The Apparitions of Borley Rectory*, a chronicle of the ghostly activities at Borley Rectory, thought to be one of the most haunted spots in all of England for a time (the rectory was torn down in 1944). In addition to reading, Buckland also began actively writing and drawing. We are all familiar with Buckland the writer, but Ray was also a talented artist, and many of his books would also feature his illustrations. Buckland lists his early interest in art as "cartooning," as both he and Gerard were comic book (and strip) fans. Buckland even put together a few of his own comics during this period.

But if there's one hobby that Buckland loved more than the others, it was acting. Ray's father, Stanley, was both a playwright and an actor, often directing and producing local productions in Nottingham, so it may have very well been in young Raymond's blood. Plays were a family affair in the Buckland household, with Eileen often acting as wardrobe mistress. Buckland made his stage debut in October of 1945 and just a few months later starred as Harold Rabbit alongside his father in an adaptation of *Toad of Toad Hall* (with the elder Buckland playing Toad). Over the next several years, more local plays followed, and much of Buckland's time away from school during this period was spent either rehearsing or performing.

In February of 1949, Buckland secured his first paid acting gig, a small part in the Nottingham Repertory Company's production of Shakespeare's *Twelfth Night*. Though "Nottingham Repertory Company" might sound like rather small potatoes, the company's production of *Twelfth Night* featured several well-known (at the time) actors, making it a pretty big deal for young

Raymond! The play ran for three weeks and required Raymond to take time off from school. He was paid one pound per week for his acting efforts. In addition to acting, Raymond was also branching out into directing. His second directing project, a one-act play, was even reviewed positively in a few local papers.

The year 1949 would be a high-water mark for Raymond Buckland's time in Nottingham, as the Buckland family moved back to London at the end of July that year. The move back to London meant a new school and more time in the classroom. In Nottingham, Buckland had attended school six days a week, but with only half days on Thursday and Saturday. Students at King's College School in Wimbledon met six days a week, with no half days. It also meant an hour commute to and from school. Even with the increased amount of time at school, Buckland still found time to perform on stage and, now living in the "big city," had even more opportunities for theater-related activities.

Buckland was mostly a good student but had trouble with a few subjects. Though he loved foreign languages, Raymond never quite got the hang of Latin and was dismayed when King's College required anyone taking German language courses to also take Latin classes! Buckland ended up in French class. Strangely, considering how much of it would show up later in his books, Buckland was an indifferent history student. Not surprisingly, he did well in his grammar, literature, and art classes.

Stan Buckland's business card

During their first year back in London, the Bucklands rented a large apartment in East Twickenham, London. The passing of Raymond's grandfather, Herbert Alfred Buckland, in 1950 resulted in the family moving into the home of Raymond's grandmother, Alice Florence Buckland, also in Twickenham. Moving in with her meant more room for the family, as Alice and Herbert owned their own home. Buckland's grandmother could be quite cantankerous to outsiders (including Ray's own mother, Eileen), but "Nana" Buckland got along quite well with young Raymond. Raymond used to sit with his grandmother at the request of his mother as a sort of buffer between the two women.

The Bucklands' return to London also meant Raymond and Gerard got to spend more time with their Uncle George and Aunt Doris. Not having children of their own, George and Doris spoiled the Buckland boys as much as possible. In many ways, I think George served as a source of inspiration for young Raymond. Both George and Doris had a very real sense of adventure and had moved to the United States for several years, along with Eileen's brother Charles and his wife, Peggy (who ended up staying in the United States long term).

Ray's Uncle George Buckland

In his memoir, Buckland writes that George "had an eye for the ladies" and was rather short in stature (a physical trait shared by Ray). Ray's father used to joke that George always carried a brick around with him as a step stool so he would be able to kiss the much taller women he was attracted to. Raymond Buckland never carried a brick around with him, but early in life he was something of a ladies' man too, with several girlfriends going back to his days in Nottingham. George was also an artist and encouraged his nephew's interest in art.

Buckland's parents, along with his aunts and uncles (George, Charles, Doris, and Peggy), had conducted séances together in their early days before George, Charles, Doris, and Peggy ran off to the United States. Most of the séances involved the use of Ouija boards, but not exclusively. For Buckland's parents (along with his Aunt Peggy and Uncle Charles), séances were a passing fancy, but for George and Doris, it became a way of life. The couple became seriously involved in the Spiritualist community, attending a Spiritualist church and attending healing demonstrations.

Despite an earlier interest in ghosts, Buckland credited his Uncle George with his interest in the occult. George lent Raymond books on Spiritualism, which led to Ray visiting his local library for similar titles. Due to the UK's use of the Dewey decimal system in public libraries, books on Spiritualism at the library were housed alongside titles on ESP, the occult, magick, and Witchcraft. Without knowing it, Uncle George opened a door that would lead his nephew to become one of the most famous Witches in the world.

The occult intrigued young Buckland, but during this period his heart remained in the theater. After moving back to London, he found himself on stage within just a few months in a variety of different productions. During this period of time, Buckland started working on solo material, writing and starring in a comedy production he titled *Le Ballet Egyptian*. *Ballet* even earned a write-up in a local paper, with Buckland's performance being called "superb." He performed *Ballet* several times over the next three years at small theaters, weddings, parties, and Masonic lodges.

Buckland conceived and performed several more solo showcases for himself, including a Shakespeare parody titled *King Richard XIII*. He also conceived a spiritual sequel of sorts to *Ballet*, but this time he focused on the foreign destination of Russia. A local paper called it an "uproarious burlesque of a dance…with a ventriloquial turn." Yes, in addition to dramatic and comedic acting, Buckland had taken an interest in ventriloquism. Never one to hold back when finding a new hobby, Buckland produced an entire evening's worth of ventriloquism for the stage by his seventeenth birthday and performed this particular act in a couple of local clubs.

Raymond Buckland
(Cartoonist, Ventriloquist, Entertainer.)

37, Godfrey Ave,
Whitton,
Twickenham,
POPesgrove 8620   Middlesex.

Early business card highlighting the many talents of young Mr. Buckland

Acting also allowed Raymond more time to bond with his father, Stanley. Shortly after Raymond began acting in plays in London, his father began directing them, and not surprisingly, Stanley's directing forays involved his youngest son. For both Bucklands, involvement in local theater productions meant having to do nearly everything involved with a production themselves, including stage makeup. Both Bucklands won awards during this time for best stage makeup in various competitions, once placing first and second, with the elder Buckland just narrowly beating out his progeny. In his memoir, Buckland refers to his father during this period as more of a best friend than a father.

During his time in both Nottingham and London, Buckland was an active member of the United Kingdom's Army Cadet Corps, but when King's College announced it was starting up an air force branch in the corps, Buckland went with the new group. Even before joining the air force branch of the corps, Buckland was in love with airplanes, but the Air Force Corps provided new opportunities to see aircraft up close and fly in one. There were school trips to air force bases and a week at an officer training station. At the training station, Buckland would get a chance to sit in a cockpit as a student pilot.

Buckland enjoyed school, but university life was not for him. After finishing his time at King's College, Raymond went straight into the workforce. Surprisingly, Buckland chose not to go into the arts and instead had dreams of becoming an architect. Unable to find an apprenticeship at an architectural firm, Buckland joined a consulting engineering firm, Rendel, Palmer & Tritton (which is still in business today), as an apprentice draftsman. Buckland worked behind a drafting table at Rendel, Palmer & Tritton (RP&T) for five years, allowing him to defer Britain's then mandatory draft for five years.

Buckland's apprenticeship did not stop him from acting, and with his father, he continued acting in local plays. But over the next couple of years, Raymond would choose to focus on solo pieces. The most interesting might have been *Bumpalong Buckland*, a cowboy-themed skit based on Hopalong Cassidy. Buckland even learned to play some guitar for *Bumpalong*, ending the sketch with a parody song. During this period of time, Buckland was prone to answer yes to any theater company needing someone to fill some stage time. In his memoir, Buckland confesses that much of the reason for this was an attempt to get over his natural shyness. Once he had committed to something, no amount of stage fright would keep him from performing.

That is one scary-looking dummy.

Guitar would not be the only instrument Buckland learned to play during this period. A lover of jazz, Buckland also took up the trombone. Buckland played in local jazz ensembles and did some busking (street performing) in London. Buckland's first busking experience earned him enough money to buy a case for his used (and caseless) trombone. Buckland's love of jazz would be unceasing throughout his life, and he took every opportunity to share jazz with anyone who would listen. He even started a jazz club at RP&T, the engineering firm he worked for.

In post–World War II Britain, housing and cars all came at a premium, and during this period, Buckland continued to live with his parents. Even after the death of his grandmother, he stayed with his family after his parents bought a new home. Buckland's salary from RP&T did provide him with a bit of discretionary income, and shortly after starting work there, Buckland bought his first motor vehicle, a motorcycle. Buckland didn't like riding a motorcycle, but it was all he could afford. Buckland's first car was a BSA three-wheeler (imagine a classic 1930s coup but with only one back wheel). Buckland loved this car, but by the time he was driving it in 1953 at the age of nineteen, the car was already old and not long for this world.

Buckland's early years set up much of what he would accomplish later in life. His welcoming personality and interest in the arts would prepare him well both for leading Witch rituals and for being on talk shows and giving presentations. With his introduction into the world of Spiritualism, Buckland's interest in the occult was primed and would only continue to grow. The man's love of cars, airplanes, and jazz would never abate and played a large role in his future social endeavors. Buckland never became an architect, but he did meet someone at RP&T who would profoundly change his life. Her name was Rosemary Moss.

Exercise 1: Raymond's Stars
By Ivo Dominguez Jr.

Ray Buckland was uncertain of the exact time of his birth to calculate his natal chart. He stated that it was sometime between 8:00 and 8:30 p.m. Having examined several versions of his possible charts and their meanings, I estimate that he was born at 8:05 p.m. Birth charts can illuminate many aspects of a person's life. This is a look at his chart and what it suggests about his life and his impact on the world. We'll start by considering his Sun, Moon, and Rising sign from two different perspectives and then touch on two more placements.

Sabian Symbols

There are 360 Sabian Symbols, one for each degree of the zodiac. The term Sabian Symbols is a bit of a misnomer, as they are more accurately descriptions of each degree with imagery that is reminiscent of tarot or oracle cards. The Sabian Symbols were created/channeled in 1925 by clairvoyant Elsie Wheeler and organized/clarified by astrologer Marc Edmund Jones. Many others, including the famed Dane Rudhyar, have expanded the Sabian Symbols and their uses. The following are the Sabian Symbols for Ray's big three placements.

Sun at 7° 39' Virgo

The Sabian Symbol for the degree of Raymond's Sun (7°–8° Virgo) is "a first lesson in dancing with a teacher of the art and discipline." The goal of the student is to learn it well enough to become the teacher. Dance joins mind, body, and spirit with the music, other dancers, in the infinite possibilities of self-expression.

Raymond's movement from student to teacher to being the torchbearer for witchcraft in the United States is suggested by his Sun's Sabian imagery. Dance is also much like ritual in that inner and outer experiences join with visible and invisible powers.

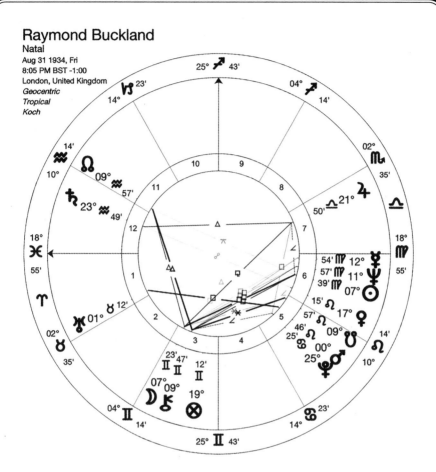

Raymond Buckland
Natal
Aug 31 1934, Fri
8:05 PM BST -1:00
London, United Kingdom
Geocentric
Tropical
Koch

Moon at 7° 23' Gemini

The Sabian Symbol for the degree of Raymond's Moon (7°–8° Gemini) is "workers striking at a factory against injustice." This is self-assertion but with a collective goal of greater dignity and opportunity, which is work toward the great work. When external conditions stifle the needs of the spirit, change must be sought.

When we look at Raymond's work as a Gardnerian in green-lighting the idea of outer courts and as the founder of Seax-Wica, it is clear that he wished to create broader access to witchcraft. Moreover, he embraced the role of being a publicly known witch that had been thrust upon him and became a vanguard in the burgeoning pagan movement.

Rising Sign at 18° 55' Pisces

The Sabian Symbol for the degree of Raymond's Rising Sign (18°–19° Pisces) is "a great teacher passing on the mysteries to their student." This is the transmission of a lineage, a spiritual current, that refines the student, the teacher, and the teachings.

Through his writings, his one-on-one teaching, his creation of a tradition, and his Museum of Witchcraft and Magick, Raymond lived the meaning of this Sabian Symbol.

Ray's Big Three

The Sun in Virgo is mutable earth, which is adaptable and always sprouting new possibilities. Raymond was prolific in his literary output and reinvented himself regularly. Virgos often want to do work that matters, betters the world, and shows their strength and capacities. They are one of the civilization-focused signs. Of all the earth signs, Virgo witches tend to have the strongest interest in upholding and creating traditions. There is no doubt that this describes Ray's prime motivation in life.

The Moon in Gemini gave Ray a second helping of mutability and another dose of Mercury as a ruling planet. No wonder he was an eternal student and a teacher and an exceptional communicator. This Sun-Moon combination often grants a wide range of magickal gifts and nuanced control of auric energy. Raymond wrote on many topics, and he practiced all of them.

Ray's Pisces Rising amplified his psychism and made it easier for him to connect with the energy of others for ritual work or readings. This Pisces energy also helped to balance his Virgo logic with ample intuition. His Rising Sign helped him have deep roots in the earth and branches that touched the heavens.

Lunar Nodes and 1st House Uranus

Raymond's North Node is in Aquarius in the 11th house, with his South Node in Leo in the 5th house. The polarity between these nodes in Aquarius and Leo is reinforced because they are in the houses they rule. This South Node placement is about creative self-expression, and this North Node placement is about working in organizations and communities. This combination also encourages a focus on non-mainstream pursuits as a life path.

Raymond has Uranus in Taurus in the 1st house, which makes a person stand out as different and unusual even when they are trying to blend in. People with this placement are often creative innovators who try to keep the best of the old as they add new ideas. Uranus in Taurus tends to steer their zeal into practical and lasting changes in the world. When you combine this Uranus placement with his nodal axis, it indicates the potential to be the voice for communities and movements. Raymond was one of the most important spokespeople for the witchcraft communities for many decades.

We each make our own choices, but a birth chart, like our genetics, shifts the odds in favor of certain circumstances and traits. Raymond Buckland's birth chart has many additional indicators beyond the ones mentioned here that call him to be psychic, a teacher, a creative, and a walker between many worlds. May he be reborn again among those who will know and love him, and with a chart that brings forth his gifts and memories.

Ivo Dominguez Jr. *has been a witch since 1978 and is one of the founders of the Assembly of the Sacred Wheel. He is the anchor author of Llewellyn's twelve-book Witch's Sun Sign series and the author of* The Four Elements of the Wise, Keys to Perception, Casting Sacred Space, Practical Astrology for Witches & Pagans, *and* Spirit Speak.

Chapter Two
Rosemary & To America

In early 1954, Raymond Buckland began dating Rosemary Moss, a coworker at Rendel, Palmer & Tritton (RP&T). Buckland describes her as looking like Audrey Hepburn, a comparison that is not without merit. Raymond and Rosemary were well suited for each other when they began dating, sharing an interest in jazz and the theater. Rosemary was also musically inclined, eventually taking up the guitar during her time with Ray. She also shared a stage with her then boyfriend a couple of times, with the young Moss finding roles to play in the various variety shows the Buckland family were involved with throughout London.

By March of 1955, Buckland and Moss were engaged, announcing their engagement at the wedding of Raymond's brother, Gerard, on March 19, 1955. Not surprisingly, Ray was the best man at his brother's wedding, while Rosemary was one of the bridesmaids. In order to buy what Raymond describes as a "suitable" engagement ring, Ray sold his accordion. The couple married on November 19, 1955. Raymond Buckland was just twenty-one years of age. The couple quickly moved into a ground floor apartment (secured by Rosemary's parents) near Chelsea. It was Raymond's first time living without his parents.

By 1956 Raymond had been playing jazz for several years, but never in a dedicated group. That changed with the establishment of Count Rudolph's Syncopated Jass Men (named after Raymond, whose nickname was Rudolph, and featuring a stylized spelling of *jazz*). Practices took place in a large social room at RP&T, and for a short period of time Rosemary played guitar in the band. Count Rudolph's band was playing semi-regular gigs by February, and by the summer of 1956 had become a rather proficient unit, capable of playing for three and a half hours at a time, with people still wanting an encore afterward.

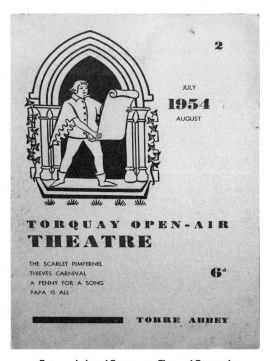

Raymond played Gustave in *Thieves' Carnival.*
Stanley Buckland (Raymond's father) was also in the play.

Beginning in March 25, 1956, the Bucklands and a few friends started participating in a regular séance circle at the Bucklands' apartment. Gatherings varied, with some nights focused on the use of Ouija boards and others revolving around activities such as spirit writing and table tipping. Buckland writes that those meetings gave the participants "information of an evidential nature confirming the continuance of life of the spirit, after death of the physical being." Buckland had previously been interested in occult activities prior to his séance group, but the séance group provided an opportunity to have actual occult experiences.

Ray with his trombone (*center-left*) and Count Rudolph's Syncopated Jass Men

At the group's initial meeting, a spirit reached out directly to Raymond. That spirit claimed to be Ray's brother, with the spirit explaining that he had died at birth. This was nothing Ray had ever heard before, and when he asked his Uncle George about it, George confirmed that Ray's mother had had a stillbirth about two years before Gerard was born. This information was unknown to Ray, and clearly unknown to everyone else participating in the séance that night. Ray downplays this moment in his memoir, but I have to think it marked a turning point in his life. After this encounter, Buckland's readings on Spiritualism and related topics increased considerably.

In his memoir, Buckland writes about another occurrence nearly as extraordinary as his meeting with his deceased brother:

Another time we had an interesting exchange with a spirit who claimed to have been buried in a certain churchyard in London on a particular date. The following weekend we all set out to find the churchyard. Such a church did indeed exist, we found, but although we searched among the tombstones, we couldn't find the name we were looking for. However, during the war the church and its cemetery had been bombed. I therefore got in touch with the minister to ask him about the named person. I gave the excuse that I was involved in genealogical research. The minister came back with the news that all the church records had been put in safe keeping for the duration of the war. Going through them, he was able to confirm that the name we were looking for was indeed there, and the burial was on the date we said.

It's rather surprising that Buckland didn't get more involved with the occult during this period. Certainly there were active Witches in London in the late 1950s, and various other esoteric and occult groups and orders. The hesitation to dive into the occult's deep end might have been the result of being a twenty-one-year-old newlywed, and as we shall see later, Rosemary didn't always quite share her husband's interest in esoteric matters. Another reason for Buckland not getting more involved in the occult during this period might have been because he was preparing to join the military.

Enacted after World War II in 1948, the British National Service Act required every British male to serve in the armed forces for a minimum of eighteen months. In 1950 the service period was extended to two years because of British involvement in the Korean War. (Britain's mandatory enlistment would eventually end in 1960.) Most young men began their service at the age of eighteen, but Buckland's service had been deferred for five years due to his apprenticeship at RP&T. With his apprenticeship ending in February of 1957, Buckland reluctantly enlisted and began interviewing with various military branches to determine where he would be stationed. Before being sent to basic training, Buckland performed one last show with his jazz band and was then officially drafted on February 11, 1957. He was instructed to report to the Royal Air Force station in Bridgnorth (slightly northwest of Birmingham) the following week.

Taking a page from J. R. R. Tolkien's *Lord of the Rings*, Buckland thought of the military as his own Mount Doom. While he was relieved to be serving with the Royal Air Force, given his love of motor vehicles, he did not look forward to his military experience. Prior to heading to basic training, Buckland shaved off his short beard and cut his (for the time) longish hair uncomfortably short. The only upside to this "preemptive grooming" was that it allowed Buckland to keep at least some of his hair upon arriving at RAF

Bridgnorth. All the other recruits with any hair length outside of a crew cut had their locks completely shorn.

Ray looking dapper in uniform and sporting quite the mustache

Conditions at boot camp were less than ideal. Recruits were given seven hours and forty-five minutes of rest every night, with the new recruits near the barrack's stove (the only source of warmth) sweating profusely as they tried to fall asleep while those farthest away shivered uncomfortably. Buckland describes boot camp activities as "mindless regimentation" and "unthinking actions to follow." Clearly, he was not a fan.

Despite the difficult conditions, Buckland kept his sense of his humor at Bridgnorth. In one instance, Buckland, along with some of the other trainees, slipped into their drill instructor's private sleeping quarters and "short-sheeted" his bed. (Short-sheeting involves folding the top sheet of a bed to look like both the top and bottom sheets. When a person then decides to get into the bed, their legs are not allowed to stretch out fully because of the fold in the sheet. It's a harmless prank, but an annoying one!) After a late-night card game, Buckland's drill instructor was enraged to find his sleeping quarters messed with and proceeded to berate and yell at his entire unit in the middle of the night, promising to rain fire and brimstone on them. The drill instructor demanded that the perpetrators step forward, not really thinking anyone would claim responsibility. Buckland and his two accomplices surprised the DI by stepping forward and were "rewarded" with extra duty going forward.

But Buckland says his confession led to a changing of his fortunes in the RAF. His drill instructor gave him a kind of begrudging respect after confessing to the prank and even found a use for Ray's artistic skills. Buckland was commissioned to draw a caricature of another drill instructor, with the result being goodwill from both DIs. And just a month into boot camp, Buckland found himself back on stage, writing, directing, and starring in sketches for a March Madness show to welcome new recruits to Bridgnorth. His willingness to get involved in base activities and take responsibility for his mistakes ended up getting Buckland labeled "Potential Officer Material." Becoming an officer meant extra financial burdens that Buckland was not prepared for (uniforms, officer's clubs, etc.), and he ended his time at boot camp as an aircraftman, second class. Buckland would end up as an air wireless mechanic, servicing radio and radar equipment. Buckland would be stationed at RAF Yatesbury in Wiltshire, close to many of England's most well-known spiritual sites, including Avebury, Silbury Hill, and Stonehenge.

Royal Air Force trade school was much like going back to school. There were classes on electrical theory and the use, operation, and repair of various radio and radar equipment. Buckland never quite grasped it all, but he did well enough to get by and avoid any major hassles during his two years of service. Perhaps most importantly, trade school offered a bit more downtime, and Buckland quickly joined the station band. It wasn't easy going from the free-form style of jazz to the more regimented style of a military base band, but Buckland relished the opportunity to keep playing music. It also provided opportunities for travel, as the Yatesbury base band visited other stations and played the occasional officers' dance.

When Buckland returned to London on his first forty-eight-hour pass, he was dropped off at Hyde Park, where he and Rosemary had planned to meet up. When Buckland saw his new bride, he grinned and picked up his walking pace to get to her as soon as possible. Upon reaching Raymond, Rosemary took one glance at the beardless, short-haired military man in the all-blue uniform and kept walking! "Air Force Raymond" was a man Rosemary didn't quite recognize. Upon Ray calling her name, the couple eventually reunited and embraced, and probably laughed about the incident.

When Buckland finished trade school, he was assigned to a base near Yorkshire and was quite disappointed. If Buckland was going to be forced to serve in the military, he had hoped that it would at least lead to an assignment outside of Great Britain. But married servicemen were typically stationed in-country, which is how Buckland ended up near Yorkshire. Buckland was stationed at Lindholme, the Royal Air Force's bomber command station and a training ground for bomber pilots. The base featured several old airplanes from World War II that were used for training purposes, and Buckland enjoyed the chance to get to see such aircraft up close.

But most importantly, Lindholme had both a drama society and a station band. Buckland's band experience did not start smoothly. Due to a plethora of trombone players, Buckland was forced to take up the cornet (similar to a trumpet), an instrument he didn't even play, to secure a place in the band. He had practiced with a trumpet in the past, and just assumed he'd be able to play the cornet well enough to not get kicked out of the band. Buckland's assumption was correct, and he quickly moved from fourth cornet in the band to second, and when an opening in the trombone section opened up, he jumped at the chance. Buckland would also meet a few other jazz fans on base and eventually form a loose jazz quartet that played in the base's cafeteria on occasion. It wasn't ideal, but Buckland found the experience better than the alternative, which was no jazz at all.

Two months after being stationed at Lindholme, Buckland participated in his first theater production in October of 1957. More plays followed, and the Lindholme troop was accomplished enough that they visited other Royal Air Force stations in the area. Buckland was very much an anomaly in the Lindholme theater group, as most of the other performers (or their wives) were commissioned officers. What involvement there was by non-officers tended to be in offstage roles, such as props, painting, or building scenery.

When Buckland wasn't performing on stage or with the base's band, he was a part of the Airborne Radio/Radar Servicing Unit. But instead of servicing radar and radio units, Buckland ended up as an inventory specialist for his unit, a job that gave him a great deal of freedom. Part of maintaining his base's inventory meant traveling to other RAF bases to exchange radio/radar parts. This was a type of freedom uncommon in the British military, and Buckland relished the opportunities he got to leave Lindholme and strike out on his own, if only for a couple of hours at a time.

The business of an RAF base, even in peacetime, is a twenty-four affair, and once a month Buckland would be required to work an overnight shift, recording base activity in a unit logbook. When there was nighttime activity, it most often consisted of "check-ins" with bomber units out for training. With little going on, Buckland turned his overnight shifts into an exercise in creative writing. He would spend several paragraphs describing an "odd blip" on a radar screen that could ultimately be explained away. When speaking with bomber pilots, Buckland would note the accent coming in over the radio and finish up his evenings by waxing eloquent about the beauty and color of that morning's sunrise.

Buckland would often fill several pages of the base's logbook with such nonsense on the nights he was required to provide monitor duty. Eventually, the shift that followed his would make a run for the logbook after Buckland had worked just to laugh at what he had come up with. Even some of Buckland's superiors got a good chuckle out of his silliness, but eventually an even higher-ranking official went through the logbook and was not amused. Though unable to find any real fault with what Buckland had done, the officer firmly requested that Buckland make briefer notes in the future.

Until he embraced Witchcraft, Buckland was never really one for religion. During his time at trade school for the Royal Air Force, all recruits were required to attend a religious service on Sunday mornings. Buckland opted for the Roman Catholic services because the Catholics had the best collection of tea and pastries after services. At Lindholme, Buckland's irreligiousness reached new heights. When forced to include his religious preference on the identification card affixed to the top of his personal locker on base, Buckland chose to write "Traditional Jazz." The joke went unnoticed for a couple of weeks, but eventually Buckland was hauled into his squadron leader's office and asked to explain himself. Attempts to equate jazz with religion met with failure, and at the end of the meeting Buckland was strongly encouraged to pick a recognized faith to include on his card.

Perhaps the funniest prank played by Buckland and his contemporaries during his tenure at Lindholme occurred on Battle of Britain Day (September 15) in 1958. Crowds had gathered at Lindholme that day for an air show, but suddenly the base's speakers announced that a runaway bride and her groom had found their way onto the base and were now being chased by the bride's father, who was waving a shotgun. Suddenly two Land Rovers came into view on the runway, one with a young airman dressed in drag in a bridal gown and his groom, and the second featuring the gun-brandishing father. The couple's Land Rover pulled up to a small plane that had just landed on the runway, and the bride and groom quickly climbed aboard. The small plane then wheeled around and looked to take off once more, all while the angry father chased the plane in hot pursuit. Spectators at the base didn't know what to think that day, with many wondering if what they had seen was real.

Being stationed at Lindholme did have one advantage: Buckland was able to visit Rosemary in London with some frequency. And on one of those visits Buckland learned that Rosemary was pregnant with their first child. Robert Charles Honoré Buckland was born on March 19, 1958, just thirteen months after Raymond Buckland was forced to join the Royal Air Force. On those rare visits back home, Buckland also continued with the séance group that he had started with Rosemary, and eventually experimented with trance mediumship for a short time.

Buckland did not enjoy his time in the military, but despite the pranks, he was well-thought-of by his commanding officers. He eventually reached the rank of leading aircraftman, which didn't give him any additional responsibilities but did mean an increase in pay. On February 10, 1959, Raymond Buckland was officially "demobilized" and by the end of February had completely returned to civilian life. Before leaving Lindholme, Buckland did participate in one last large theater production there, securing the starring role in *The Duke in Darkness*. The part required Buckland to be on stage as the duke for the entire play. The play was well received, and Buckland thought it was a fitting end to his time in the military.

There was little time to enjoy the return to civilian life after two years in the RAF, as Buckland had a family to support, with a second child already on the way. A new job would have to be found, and quickly. Buckland was not interested in a return to RP&T and instead searched in vain for a job that would allow him to break into animation. Several visits to London studios were met with disappointment, and evening art classes did little to help Buckland's job prospects. Eventually Buckland found some work as a freelance commercial artist. "Rudolph Cartoons" succeeded in selling some cartoons to newspapers and magazines but mostly did posters and promotional materials.

RUDOLPH
CARTOONS
Commercial Artists

79 GLOUCESTER STREET . LONDON . S.W.1

Showcards, Letterheads
Illustrations, Designs   Presented by R. B. BUCKLAND

Fancy a cartoon?

Buckland eventually ended up working at James Brodie Ltd., an educational publisher, as their retail manager. The job at James Brodie allowed Buckland to use his artistic ability, and he ended up illustrating some books for the publisher and did art for a few educational filmstrips. Buckland worked at James Brodie for a little over two years, starting in the late spring of 1959 and staying at the publisher until 1962, the year he and his family moved to the United States. Brodie's offices were located at the edge of Soho and near the famous Foyles bookstore. It might not have paid as much as he wanted, but Buckland enjoyed the job. The location also allowed him to keep reading occult books, and by this period he had begun to read his first books about magick and English occultist Aleister Crowley.

It was a good thing Buckland ended up at James Brodie. He welcomed his second son, Regnauld (Renny) Hugh Cherrington Buckland, just a few months later, on September 1, 1959. Regnauld was born two months premature, and both Regnauld and Rosemary spent two extra weeks at the hospital as a result. Due to Britain's National Health Service, mother and son received excellent care. Their doctor was Sir John Batten (1924–2013), who would later go on to serve as Queen Elizabeth II's personal physician from 1974 to 1989.

Buckland was a devoted father and was actively involved in the lives of his sons, but as this book is about their father, they do not appear as frequently in these pages as perhaps they should. By the time of Raymond Buckland's passing in 2017, he had six grandchildren and one great-grandchild, which brought him great joy. Sadly, Regnauld passed away on April 21, 2003, at the age of forty-three.

In addition to Renny being born, there were a lot of other positives for the Bucklands during this time period. Buckland's growing family (and slightly bigger paycheck) allowed the family to move into a larger apartment in London's Westminster area. Buckland also reconnected with his compatriots in his old jazz band. Rehearsals soon resumed at RP&T's social room, and more gigs followed.

But there was also sorrow. Five months after Renny was born, on February 1, 1960, Raymond's father, Stanley Thomas Buckland, died of a heart attack. The heart attack occurred while Stanley was attempting to board a subway car on his way home from work. London's bus drivers were on strike during this period, which meant everyone was taking the subway, and Stanley's heart gave out amid the stress and crush of people around him. While 1960 doesn't sound that long ago, at the time Raymond and Rosemary were without phone service, and when Raymond got home, he was given instructions by his local grocer to call his mother. The news of Stanley's death was given to Raymond by his brother, Gerard, over the grocer's phone.

Stanley and Raymond had been quite close, especially during the years after World War II when father and son got to work together on various theater productions. While he would never achieve the heights of his second son, Stanley was also a prodigious writer, composing not just plays but also poetry and musical pieces. Stanley was also very clearly a people person and, like Raymond, had a wide circle of friends. Raymond Buckland would have been hard-pressed to find a better mentor than his father.

The loss of a parent is never easy, but over the next twelve months Raymond was presented with several unique opportunities. Between shows with Count Rudolph's Syncopated Jass Men, Raymond immersed himself in the theater world once more, focusing mostly on solo comedy pieces. During a performance at the Thames Valley Review Club, Raymond bumped into an old acquaintance who had become the club's resident comedian. Ray's old friend suggested that the two of them team up and write a script for the weekly Independent Television series *The Army Game*.

The Army Game ran for four seasons (1957–61) and followed the exploits of Hut 29, a group of disorderly conscripted English soldiers. Buckland had never seen the show before, but poking fun at the military just feels like something Buckland would have enjoyed doing. Surprisingly, the pair's script was picked up after revisions from the show's regular writing staff. Buckland then became a regular visitor at tapings of *The Army Game*. (This is according to Buckland's memoir. I was unable to find any episodes of the show specifically attributed to Buckland, though there are a few episodes without listed writers.[3])

Buckland's presence on the set led to a friendship with comedian Ted Lune (1920–68), who starred on the show. Between tapings of *The Army Game*, Lune was a frequent guest on a variety of radio shows and in constant need of new material. Taking a shine to Buckland and his compatriot, Lune asked the pair to write for him. Writing for Lune was not a regular nine-to-five job (Buckland still worked for James Brodie during this period), and writing sessions with Lune took place in the private room of a local pub, with Guinness (beer) always nearby.

During broadcasts featuring Lune, Buckland would tune in and count the number of laughs from the studio audience. When broadcasts happened while Buckland was at his day job, his boss there would call him into the office and the two would listen to the broadcast. Buckland recorded some of the performances with a handheld tape recorder. Sadly, there wasn't a lot of money in writing for Lune, but Buckland loved the experience.

Raymond and his friend continued to work together and developed a bit for Lune and fellow comedian Mario Fabrizi (1924–63) featuring the two comics as prisoners of Rome about to be thrown to the lions. The duo also developed a television pilot specifically for Lune called *The Mayor's Nest*, about the mayor of a small English town. Buckland also wrote a pilot of his own for the BBC, *Sly Digs*, about the denizens of a London boarding house. Neither of Buckland's pilots got picked up, but the experience did allow him

---

3. Internet Movie Database (IMDb), "The Army Game (1957–1961): Full Cast and Crew."

to become a card-carrying member of the Television and Screen Writers Guild.

Buckland's short career writing for television presents a very interesting "what might have been." It's no surprise to any of us familiar with the work of Raymond Buckland that he was a capable writer, but in his Witchcraft and occult books his sense of humor rarely shines through. Raymond Buckland was funny, and with the right lucky break, he could have gone into writing for the screen full-time.

Ray's Uncle Charles the ventriloquist in 1927

While Buckland was flirting with a future in television, he met his Uncle Charles for the first time (Charles being the brother of his mother, Eileen). Buckland calls their meeting a "turning point" in his life. While stories of Charles and his wife, Peggy, had been commonplace in the Buckland household while Raymond was growing up, he had never met his uncle in the flesh before. Charles and Peggy moved to the United States in 1927, and their trip back to England in June of 1961 was their first trip "back home" since they had left all those years before. Upon their initial meeting on June 11, Buckland talked to his uncle about ventriloquism, stage magic, and America. Over the next few weeks, the conversations about America deepened, with Raymond asking about what it was like to live there. Raymond concluded that there were opportunities awaiting his family in America that were just not present in the England of 1961. He and Rosemary soon decided that they would emigrate.

It took Raymond and Rosemary Buckland about nine months to complete the emigration process to the United States. There were required medical examinations and an endless sea of paperwork. Newcomers to the United States were also required to either have a job waiting for them in America or have a sponsor. Sponsors acted as "support" for the recent immigrants, and sponsors entered the process with the understanding that they would help support their charges if those charges were unable to find a job. Buckland writes that during the emigration process, he was in constant communication with his Uncle Charles and Aunt Peggy.

The financial costs of moving were also considerable, and the Bucklands worked hard to save as many pennies as possible for their move. Luckily for the family, Raymond sold a lot of commissioned artwork over this period. Most of it came from James Brodie, but all the work he picked up was in addition to Ray's usual job and salary. The biggest moneymaker during this period was the opportunity to illustrate a junior school science encyclopedia, which required 365 illustrations. There was also some money picked up from selling personal items and the family car.

Moving "across the pond" was a major step for the Bucklands. It required leaving behind family, most notably Raymond's now widowed mother. The Buckland boys were both young enough that they weren't leaving behind dozens of friends, but for children, such an absolute change in culture and circumstance had to have been jarring. It also meant that Raymond was leaving behind his theater opportunities and, of course, his Jass Men. There was a tremendous amount of courage involved in Raymond and Rosemary's decision to move to the United States.

Instead of flying to the United States, the Bucklands chose to travel by boat. The trip would take longer this way (eight days instead of just six hours), but it allowed the Bucklands to travel with more of their personal possessions. Raymond would depart before the rest of his family, securing housing and a job before Rosemary arrived a few months later with the boys in tow. Both the SS *America* and SS *United States* were older vessels, built in 1939, but they were nice ships with dining rooms, bars, and outdoor pools on their decks. The Bucklands couldn't afford the height of luxury, but the boats that took them to America were a fun way to make the trek overseas.

Raymond Buckland departed for the United States on February 26, 1962, taken to the docks by his brother, Gerard. Raymond's trip across the Atlantic Ocean was marred by bad weather, and the captain remarked that this particular crossing had been the roughest since the boat started the London–New York route in 1946. This resulted in Raymond spending several days in his cabin dealing with seasickness. The crew of the *America* also had to secure ropes across staircases and passageways so that the ship's passengers would have something to hold on to due to the bumpy seas. The bad weather was a constant on the voyage, not letting up until the ship was in sight of Long Island, but Raymond recovered enough that by the end of the voyage he was playing his trombone with the ship's band.

The weather had finally broken by the time Buckland reached the shores of the United States on the morning of Monday, March 5, 1962. When he was finally allowed to disembark from the SS *America* several hours after the ship had docked, he did so with just fifteen dollars in his pocket. Luckily for Raymond, his Uncle Charles and Aunt Peggy were there to greet him at customs and had extended an open-ended invitation to their nephew to stay at their house on Long Island until he secured work and a place to live.

New York City was unlike anything Buckland had ever seen before. 1960s London lacked the skyscrapers that make up its skyline today, and Buckland found their presence in the United States "totally alien" as an Englishman. He was also taken aback by the sheer number of adult bookstores and neon signs. Reading about the sights in New York City was not the same as seeing them up close. Charles and Peggy lived outside of New York City in the small city of New Hyde Park on Long Island, and it was at their house that Raymond Buckland would spend most of his first two months in America.

There are many books that claim Raymond Buckland moved to the United States due to his job with British Overseas Airways (later called just British Airways). But as we have seen, Buckland entered the United States jobless and was not employed by the airline prior to moving to the United States. Buckland ended up working for British Airways by chance; at the time, it was the only company comfortable hiring him! Before heading to the United States, Buckland had secured a job with the British Book Company at a salary of eighty-five American dollars per week. He was advised by a family member that he was shortchanging himself and would have the opportunity to make quite a bit more money in the United States, so Buckland turned down the job. Upon arriving in America, Buckland began the long and frustrating search for a new job.

After being advised that he was missing out on employment opportunities due to his beard (beards just weren't popular at the time), Buckland shaved off all his facial hair. Shortly thereafter, he secured a job with British Airways—at eighty-five dollars a week! Shortly after Buckland was hired, British Airways told him they had no issue with an employee having a beard, so he quickly regrew the facial hair.

Buckland worked in the reservations services department at British Overseas Airways Corporation (BOAC) on Fifth Avenue in NYC. Buckland's department provided information to the individuals selling seats on BOAC. Buckland himself worked at the airline's status desk and helped to update the airline's charts that indicated how many passengers were on each flight and where they were sitting. In a short period of time, Buckland would be promoted to assistant to the reservations manager and would receive his own office, allowing him to come and go as he pleased. Buckland did whatever was required of him at British Airways, including working as a baggage handler at Kennedy Airport for a few days during a strike by airport personnel. Buckland would work at BOAC for nearly ten years, leaving the company in 1971. During his time at the company, BOAC would change its name to the better-known British Airways, which is why many online biographies list British Airways as his initial employer in the United States.

BOAC wasn't Buckland's only early employer in the United States; he also spent weekends selling shoes at the store managed by his Uncle Charles. Buckland described his shoe-selling experience as "interesting," but I didn't get the feeling that he particularly liked it. However, he did get some good stories out of the experience:

> I remember one time when we had an irritating customer who would not be satisfied. He complained that not a single pair of shoes would fit; they were all too tight. Uncle Charles soothed him, saying: "Don't worry. This is a common problem. I'll take them in the back and put

them in the expander." We'd then go into the back room and bang two pieces of wood together. Bringing back exactly the same pair of shoes, the customer would try them on and be delighted with the "much better fit"!

By the time Rosemary and the boys arrived in the United States, Raymond had secured a ground floor apartment for his family in Floral Park, New York, also on Long Island. With money being tight, Raymond furnished the apartment with thrift shop finds and donations from his Uncle Charles's neighbors, who had been intrigued to find a young Englishman living in the home of Peggy and Charles. Outside of the Buckland family's new apartment was a bus line that took Raymond to the local train depot, and from there into Manhattan.

Life for the Bucklands soon entered a comfortable routine after Rosemary's arrival in America. Monday through Friday, Raymond would rise early and head off into the city for his job at British Airways while Rosemary raised the boys and turned their apartment into a home. That might have been enough for most people, but by the summer of 1962, Raymond Buckland had stumbled across two books that would change his life forever: *Witchcraft Today* and *The Meaning of Witchcraft*. Try as he might, Buckland couldn't stop thinking about those books and their assertion that Witchcraft was a religion. The idea intrigued Buckland enough that he felt compelled to send a letter to the books' author, Gerald Gardner.

Exercise 2: Automatic Writing

In March of 1956, Raymond and Rosemary Buckland got together with some friends and hosted their first séance. Over the next six years, the Bucklands would host several more séances and begin to experiment with various kinds of spirit communication. Trance mediumship is the most well-known form of spirit communication, but the Bucklands (along with their friends) also investigated table tipping, spirit boards, and automatic writing.

Automatic writing might be the easiest way to communicate with the spirit world. As Raymond Buckland writes in his 2011 book *Solitary Séance: How You Can Talk with Spirits on Your Own*, "The doodle is the most basic form of automatic writing,"[4] and most of us have doodled at least a time or two in our lives. Though we will never know if Raymond Buckland conducted solitary investigations into spirit communications in the late 1950s, if he did, he most likely would have engaged in automatic writing. There's a part of me that likes to imagine Ray sitting in his cabin on the SS *America* with a pen in hand opening himself up to spirit and asking the question "Just how will my family and I fare in the United States?"

The following excerpt from *Solitary Séance* illustrates much of what made Raymond Buckland one of the most popular Witchcraft and paranormal authors of the last fifty years. Ray makes it easy! And he doesn't fuss about a lot of things. There are entire books dedicated to automatic writing, but in this short excerpt,[5] Buckland shares how to do it in just a few paragraphs!

Automatic Writing/Drawing/Painting/Doodling

Do you doodle? Consciously or unconsciously? To doodle consciously is to be thinking about what you are doing (though probably not with all of your concentration, since you usually doodle when on the phone or talking

---

4. Buckland, *Solitary Séance*, 80.
5. Buckland, *Solitary Séance*, 79–83.

to someone). For example, you might scribble the outline of a flower, then go on to add petals, and then more flowers, and then to make it into a bouquet … that sort of thing. But to doodle unconsciously is when you are caught up in your conversation, or whatever the activity, to the point that you are scribbling on a piece of paper without looking at it and have no idea what you are drawing until you finally look down when the conversation ends. It's this unconscious doodling that ties in with spirit communication, and is frequently guided by spirit.

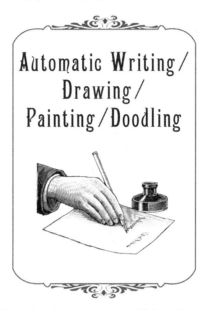

Automatic Writing/ Drawing/ Painting/Doodling

Original art from this excerpt of *Solitary Séance*

When you find that you have doodled without thinking about it, closely examine the scribbling. Turn the paper around and view it from all directions. See if you can make out any letters, numbers, or symbols. Occasionally, even though you have not been paying attention to what your hand was writing, you will find that you have written someone's name, a number or series of numbers, or have drawn a recognizable sign or symbol. If you know you are going to doodle, it's a good idea to have a large piece of paper available so that—as can happen—if spirit has a long message to deliver to you, then there is the opportunity to do so. Yes, what starts as a doodle can develop (again, unconsciously) into a lengthy message from spirit.

The problem is that when you become aware of the fact that your hand is doodling, is scribbling on the paper, then it is human nature to look and see what you are producing. Fight this temptation. If you suddenly become aware that you are doodling, then keep your focus on the conversation, or whatever, and make a point of *not* looking or trying to sense what your hand is doing.

[…]

The doodle is the most basic form of automatic writing and drawing. In itself, it can be a wonderful way of communicating with spirit. At least it can be a great introduction to the more detailed automatic writing and/ or drawing.

If you are going to set out to do automatic writing, then prepare ahead of time by getting as large a piece of paper as possible. It's possible to work with just a simple writing pad, but most automatic writing becomes extensive and if you can keep from having to turn pages, you will be better able to preserve the flow of the communication. I often suggest getting an old roll of wallpaper and using the back of it. It's also possible to get leftover cutoffs from printing runs at newspaper offices. Even large rolls of wrapping paper will suffice.

Sit comfortably at a table, which may be in front of you or to one side. Hold a pen or pencil in your hand and let your hand rest slightly on the paper. Then focus your attention on something else. That "something else" can be reading a book, talking on the phone, watching television, talking to a friend who is with you, or anything similar—anything that will hold your attention for a period of time so that you don't have to look down at what your hand is doing on the paper.

Beforehand, as with other exercises given in this book, you can invite spirit to make contact. Go through your meditation and white-light building, ending with an invitation to spirit to make contact. Then forget all about automatic writing and get into your conversation, reading, or television watching. Ignore your hand. But after a relatively short while, you may notice that your hand starts to move of its own volition. It will feel like a nervous movement; your hand will start to scribble rapidly on the paper. Continue to ignore it, and it will continue scribbling.

What happens is that the scribbling slowly changes from a rapid (and it can be extremely rapid) up and down movement into a swirling: the making of loops and circles. This, in turn, will gradually give way to loops and swirls similar to writing. Then again, in turn, this will become actual writing: actual letters formed and written, very, very fast. When this has been going on for some considerable time, take the opportunity to break your attention and focus and look at the paper. You will be surprised to find that your hand has written words. They may not be easy to make out at first, but the more you continue with the experiment, the clearer will the writing become.

Usually the writing is nothing like your own handwriting. You may possibly recognize it as the hand of a deceased loved one—the spirit making contact. There are even records of the writing coming through in a foreign language, one with which the writer was not familiar. There have also been records of an automatic writer producing two different documents at the same time, in two different handwritings: one from the left hand and one from the right. It's unlikely that you'll do that in the early stages of experimenting, though don't rule out anything!

It can also be that, rather than producing writing, spirit comes through to draw or even paint (if you have the materials available). Some communicators who could never draw anything, by their own admission, have produced wonderful drawings and paintings directed by spirit.

Automatic writing is one of the more immediate forms of spirit communication, in that, once it has been established—in other words, once you have accepted that spirit is in command and it is not you who are controlling what is written—you can begin to have a "conversation" with spirit, asking questions and receiving written answers. Long conversations and discussions have been recorded in this way.

In the past, Jane Roberts received many of the teachings of "Seth" through automatic writing.[6] Also, the majority of the multi-volume works of Patience Worth were received by Pearl Curran through automatic writing.[7] There were approximately 2,500 poems, short stories, plays, and allegories, as well as six full-length novels, authored by that spirit!

---

6. Jane Roberts was a spirit medium best known for channeling the entity Seth beginning in the late 1950s. Roberts is considered one of the most important figures in the founding of the modern New Age movement.

7. Patience Worth was the name of a spirit channeled by medium Phyllis Curran starting in 1913 until Curran's death in 1937.

Chapter Three
Initiation into the Witch-Cult

Gerald Brosseau Gardner (1884–1964) was the first modern public Witch. In July of 1951 in an article in London's *Sunday Pictorial*, Gerald Gardner was announced as the "resident witch" at the soon-to-be-opened Museum of Magic and Witchcraft on the Isle of Man.[8] Today there are millions of self-identified Witches throughout the world, but back in 1951, publicly acknowledging oneself to be a Witch was a rather revolutionary act. Many people have been called Witches over the centuries, and some no doubt embraced the term, but in the modern era Gardner was the first person to publicly (and often loudly) self-identify as one.

Today the Witchcraft shared with the world by Gerald Gardner is more commonly known as Wicca, though *Wicca* (especially with two *c*'s) is not a term Gardner would have identified with. In his published writings, Gardner talks of "the Wica," a turn of phrase that simply means "wise ones." Witches, in other words, were the "wise ones," and the wise ones practiced Witchcraft and were part of a "Witch-cult." Gardner himself did not claim to be the first Witch or the only Witch; in fact, he always left the door wide open for other Witches to come forward. And there very well might have been other modern Witches before Gerald Gardner in the United Kingdom, Canada, and the United States. But we will never know for sure, because if there were self-identified Witches before Gardner, they kept to the shadows and only came out of the broom closet after Gardner had done so.

---

8. Heselton, *Witchfather, Volume 2*, 444.

Gardner's "Witch origin story" is not all that extraordinary. According to Gardner (and Gardner remains our only source for these tales), he was initiated into a coven of Witches in an area of England known as the New Forest in September of 1939. Nearly a year later, in August of 1940, Gardner recounts that his coven (and others) participated in a rite known as Operation Cone of Power, designed to stop Hitler's German forces from invading the United Kingdom. Gardner's initiation and Operation Cone of Power are the only two rituals Gardner ever publicly admitted to participating in with the New Forest Coven.[9]

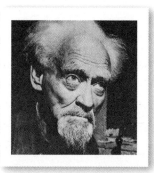

This photo of Gerald Gardner was used by Ray in *Buckland's Complete Book of Witchcraft*.

It's not surprising that Gardner and the rest of the New Forest Coven might have been too busy to engage in a coven Witchcraft practice during World War II, but it's Gardner's activities immediately after the war that seem a bit strange. Instead of jumping back into Witchcraft, Gardner instead dabbles with a variety of other esoteric groups, at one point preparing to take over Aleister Crowley's Ordo Templi Orientis (O.T.O.). By the end of the decade, the pull of Witchcraft must have been too hard to resist, and Gardner publishes the novel *High Magic's Aid* in 1949 (under his Witch name, Scire), which presents a fictionalized version of the Witchcraft that Gardner was initiated into in the New Forest. Gardner claims that his initiators would only allow him to write a fictional novel about the Craft, and he bases

---

9. This very brief version of Gardner's biography comes from the timeline found on pages 31–34 of my book *Transformative Witchcraft*, published in 2019 by Llewellyn. For more on Gardner, see the bibliography.

the magickal system in his novel around *The Key of Solomon*, a fourteenth-century grimoire.

The same year *High Magic's Aid* was released (1949), Gardner began putting together his own magickal grimoire, possibly attempting to re-create the rituals he was first exposed to by the New Forest Coven. That work today is known as *Ye Bok of Ye Art Magical* and for Gardner served as a prototype for his later Book of Shadows. (A Book of Shadows is a private book of Witch rituals and spells.) By 1950 Gardner had begun initiating people into his version of Witchcraft and opened up a Witchcraft museum a year later with a man named Cecil Williamson (1909–99).

Gardner and Williamson would have a falling-out in 1953/54, with Gardner buying out his now former partner in 1954. Free of Williamson, Gardner changed the name of the Folklore Centre of Superstition and Witchcraft to the Museum of Magic and Witchcraft. Gardner's museum would remain in operation until 1970. Williamson opened a competing museum, the Museum of Witchcraft, on English soil in 1954, and in 1960 the museum moved to Boscastle, England, where it still operates today as the Museum of Witchcraft and Magic.

Three years after the opening of the Witchcraft museum, Gardner released his first nonfiction book about Witchcraft, titled *Witchcraft Today* (1954). *Witchcraft Today* focuses mostly on regurgitating Witch history as previously written about by the anthropologist Margaret Murray (1863–1963) in her books *The Witch-Cult in Western Europe* (1921) and *The God of the Witches* (1931). In her Witch books, Murray writes that the individuals executed for Witchcraft in the early modern period were a part of an organized and underground Witch-religion that could be found across Europe. Gardner heavily implied that his Witch-religion was descended from the Witch-cult written about by Murray (and Murray actively blessed this idea by writing the foreword to *Witchcraft Today*). The ideas of Gardner and Murray had a profound impact on Buckland, and he would repeat many of them for the rest of his life.

Gardner tirelessly promoted his version of Witchcraft throughout the 1950s until his death in 1964. Gardner initiated dozens of individuals, including some of Witchcraft's best-known priestesses, such as Doreen Valiente (1922–99), Patricia Crowther (1927–present), Lois Bourne (1928–2017), and eventually one of Buckland's own initiators, Monique Wilson (1923–82). Gardner spent his summers on the Isle of Man running his Witchcraft museum and giving interviews to anyone who asked. Gardner was never shy about publicity, making him the most well-known Witch in the world, and thanks to his museum, he was easy to contact. All one had to do was send a letter to the museum. Gardner's second and final Witchcraft book, *The Meaning of Witchcraft*, would be released in 1959. (A biography about Gardner, produced with Gardner's cooperation and titled *Gerald Gardner: Witch*, was released in 1960.)

It's worth mentioning that Gardner's Witchcraft was radically different from what most of us encounter today. Gardner's Witchcraft was initiatory, meaning the only way to become a Witch was to be initiated by another Witch. (We will see those barriers break down over the course of this book.) Rituals were kept secret (they could only be accessed by initiates, with the exception of a few ritual lines in Gardner's books), as were some of the working tools. Covens were also designed to be run by a High Priestess (though Gardner himself violated this rule with some frequency).

This was the world Buckland was entering when he sent his first letter to Gerald Gardner in 1962. To become a Witch, he would have to be initiated, and that initiation would have to be facilitated by a High Priestess. Gardner's books revealed certain secrets about the Craft, but to truly become a part of the Witch-cult, Buckland would have to venture back to his homeland, as there were either no public Witches in North America or no self-identifying Witches there at all.

· · · · · · · ·

We don't know all of what was in the letter Raymond Buckland sent to Gerald Gardner in 1962, but we do know how Gardner replied. Buckland kept a great deal of his correspondence over the years, and luckily for us, some of it features Gerald Gardner and Buckland's eventual initiators, Monique and Campbell "Scotty" Wilson. In his memoir, Buckland suggests that he had a rather warm and friendly correspondence with Gardner. The surviving letters suggest otherwise, though it's possible that several more personal letters have been lost.

Judging by Gardner's response to Buckland's initial letter, Buckland must have asked Gardner about Witch groups in the United States. Buckland also must have mentioned his Romani heritage, and possibly something about a family member being cremated in a private ceremony outside of a licensed crematorium. Gardner's typed response is rather matter-of-fact and contains several misspellings, which were commonplace in his letters. Gardner signs his letter with his first two initials and his last name in blue ink. Gardner's response is worth sharing in full:

Dear Mr Buckland

Now, I am very sorry, I don't know of any witch Coven in the States anywhere. I have heard rumours that there is one in New York. but cant find out where. but I am told it issent real, just some people who like dancing nude etc. have formed a little secret society. calling themselves witches, in hops of frightening the Police away. I am afraid that unless you are in England. or Brettiany. or Italy. thers not much chance for you,

I should suggest that you should also read Marggret Murrays "The witch cult inwestern Europe" and my. "The Meaning of Witchcraft" & High Magics AiD. I think they would interest you.

My, your luckey being able to travel to all sorts of interesting places cheap, by air. would you be able to come over to London regularly, for instance?

Blessed be,

G.B. Gardner

P.S. I knew it was the custome to burn a Gypseys Caravan whe the owner died, but I thought it was against some English law to burn anyone except in a properly licnced cermatorium. G.B.G.[10]

Buckland most likely followed up his first letter to Gardner with a second, but the remaining response from Gardner among Buckland's saved correspondence repeats much of what was in the first missive. The only real difference between the two letters is that Gardner mentions Buckland's connection to discounted airfares due to Ray's job at British Airways and suggests that

---

10. Gardner, letter to Raymond Buckland, exact date uncertain, 1962.

the two of them meet at Gardner's museum the following summer. Gardner's signature is much more assured in the second letter, looking more like careful calligraphy than a quickly scrawled signature. Gardner's disdain for what he perceives as an American lack of patience is a theme in the letter's first paragraph:

> Dear Mr Buckland
>
> I am sorry to say, I dont know of any Covens anywhere in the U.S.A. I am supprised that no one has take the craft across. but I suppose its partly Americans are not intrested. and also if they are, they expect to turn up at a Coven and demain to beinitiated im ediatly. There many people like that even over here. who think they can come up, put down a shilling and expect to be taken in right away, well, witches never did bus[iness?] like that. There are so many spies who are always trying toget in. so we have to be very sure of people we take them in.
>
> I will be up here from about mid April to September, as far as I know next year, so hope to meet. you can fly from London in less than two hours, and the Airport is about 6 m six minutes in a taxi fro m the air port. If there issent a taxi there. tell the police to you ne½ [*sic*].
>
> Looking forward to meeting you
> Your sincerely
> G.B. Gardner[11]

Gardner's second letter to Buckland was written in November of 1962, and no further correspondence between the two survives. Gerald Gardner's primary biographer, Philip Heselton, has written that Buckland's correspondence with Gardner was much more extensive than what remains and most likely included a typed "correspondence course" that was initially set up to teach a covenless group of Witches in Glasgow, Scotland.[12] However, there are no references to a correspondence course in any of the letters between Buckland, Gardner, and the Wilsons. (Buckland was thorough enough to keep copies of his letters to the Wilsons.) A correspondence course also feels like something Buckland would have kept in his possession over the decades.

---

11. Gardner, letter to Raymond Buckland, November 8, 1962.
12. Heselton, *Witchfather, Volume 2,* 575 and 570.

Gardner would have also been hard to reach post-Yuletide by post, as he generally left England most winters to escape the cold. By February of 1963, Buckland's Witch correspondence had shifted to Monique Wilson (Craft name Olwen, which is how she introduces herself to Buckland), who informs Buckland in a letter dated February 26, 1963, that she is "Dr. Gardner's High Priestess" and has final say over all potential initiates. Wilson also warns Buckland that "witches always work in pair (male-female), with few exceptions we only bring in couples" and that "the woman rules supreme in the Circle."[13]

Wilson's letter also makes her out to be *the* contact person for potential American Witches. In her note she mentions that she has already "approached my contacts in your area" to see if any of them were interested in Buckland as a potential student. Wilson also writes that she hopes to have an American coven in operation by the end of the year, with the caveat that Buckland "will be up then for consideration." Such comments suggest an alternative timeline where Ray and Rosemary were not the first Gardnerian initiates in the United States.

Wilson's tone in her first letter to Buckland is rather remote. She notes that there "is very little" she can tell Buckland at this stage of their correspondence. She also requests a picture, which suggests that perhaps physical appearance was used as a criteria for vetting students. (Later, this would be repeated when Rosemary becomes a part of the correspondence between the Bucklands and the Wilsons.) The most humorous part of Wilson's first letter to Ray is her directive to "destroy the letter." Obviously, this did not happen. Wilson ends her first missive with a hearty "Blessed Be," adding her titles "High Priestess of the WICA and Witch-Queen" below her typed Craft name.

Monique Wilson's ascension to High Priestess, Witch Queen,[14] and confidante of Gerald Gardner was quite rapid. Monique Marie Mauricette Wilson (maiden name Arnoux) was born in French Indochina (later Vietnam) in 1923 and was French by birth, not British. Her husband, Campbell "Scotty" Wilson, was in the British Royal Air Force when he first met Monique Marie in Hong Kong following World War II. After his discharge from the service,

---

13. Monique Wilson, letter to Raymond Buckland, February 26, 1963.

14. There aren't really any "Witch Queens," but some forms of initiatory Wicca use the term Witch-Queen to designate a High Priestess whose initiates have started their own coven.

the Wilsons settled in Perth, Scotland. By 1960 the Wilsons had become interested in Witchcraft and contacted Gerald Gardner, who directed them to Charles Clark (1930–2002), an early initiate of Gardner's who was also living in Scotland.[15]

The Wilsons were likely initiated and elevated to the second or third degree by Clark in 1961. (Second- and third-degree Gardnerians are allowed to initiate others and set up covens.) Shortly after starting their own coven in Perth, there was a falling-out between Clark and the Wilsons, with Clark so hurt by this turn of events that he left the Craft as a result. Monique then became a student of Gardner, who most likely reinitiated her and elevated her to the second and third degrees. During this period of time, she also began assisting Gardner with his correspondence to Witches around the world. In short order, the Wilsons went from being interested in the Craft to running their own coven and acting as an additional voice for Gerald Gardner. Raymond Buckland's rise would be nearly as fast, but with fewer hurt feelings.

Buckland's response to Wilson (dated March 14, 1963) again suggests that his interactions with Gardner were rather limited. Buckland writes that he "was afraid that Dr. Gardner had dismissed me from his thoughts" after not hearing from him in several months. Buckland writes that he "tried hard to impress upon him [Gardner] how sincere" he was in his "wish to join a Coven," apparently without much success.[16]

In his memoir, Buckland writes:

> I shared my enthusiasm with Rosemary, who also read the books. Her reaction was the same; she had similar thoughts and feelings. We determined that we wanted to be a part of what Gardner termed "Wica," the modern expression of Witchcraft.

However, early on, Rosemary was indifferent to the Craft. In that same March letter to Wilson, Buckland writes:

> You say you prefer to accept people into the Cult in pairs. This is a drawback for me at the moment, as I have no one to join with me. My wife is not enthusiastic although encouraging me to do as I wish.

---

15. Heselton, *Witchfather, Volume 2*, 569–70.
16. Raymond Buckland, letter to Monique Wilson, March 14, 1963.

I have got her to read "Witchcraft Today" and "God of the Witches" also one or two articles, but for the present at any rate she is not keen.

Buckland ends this portion of his letter with the hope that Wilson might know "some young lady in a similar predicament" who could be his working partner. (As we will see, Rosemary eventually comes around, but it's a journey.)

Perhaps presaging many of the books Buckland would eventually write in the 1990s, Buckland asks Wilson how the "gipsy's [sic] religious views compare with the Witch Cult."[17] Buckland was convinced very early on that there was a strong connection between the two lines of thought. He closes his letter by asking Wilson's permission to use her expression "Blessed Be," perhaps marking the first time the phrase "Blessed Be" was used by a soon-to-be Witch living in the United States.

Monique Wilson in full Witch-Queen mode.
Buckland originally included this photo in his book *Witchcraft from the Inside*.

Buckland's initial letter to Monique Wilson did not elicit a response, so he writes her again in May, once more expressing his eagerness to become a part

---

17. Today the word *gypsy* is generally seen as a slur, but that was not the case for Buckland in 1963. We will be spending more time with Buckland's Romani roots in chapter 8.

of the Craft.[18] He suggests that he could use this period of time before initiation to gather and make his ritual tools, and he shares a few Witch-related books he has been reading. He also extols the virtues of detached American houses, most of which have large basements and central heating—perfect, he writes, for "nude meetings in the winter!" Buckland's letter is full of pent-up energy and a bit of humor. He closes things with this:

> The witches of old were always looking forward eagerly to their next sabbath,—I am just longing for my first!

Wilson's response (dated June, 5, 1963) to Buckland's May letter is far more welcoming than her earlier missive, but she does seem especially concerned about Buckland's lack of a High Priestess and (female) working partner. She writes:

> Will you be able to form a Coven? Do you have a Priestess in view? I am afraid you will not have much chance to be initiated on your own as we do not care for free-lancers. Anyway you couldn't do a thing by yourself as the Priestess rules the Circle, and you be highly frustrated knowing you were a witch and not being able to even form the Circle. So possess your soul in patience…. The most important is that you should have a Priestess. Write and let me know.[19]

Near the end of her letter, Wilson again tells Buckland that without a Priestess, "You've had it I am afraid."

The most surprising part of the letter is the suggestion that Buckland might have an opportunity for initiation into the Witch-cult quite soon. Wilson suggests that Buckland might be able to celebrate the Autumn Equinox or "at the latest Hallowe'en" in a Witch circle. An autumn initiation for Buckland would have been the result of his initiation being carried out by an American named Robin, in California, who would have been the Wilsons' first American initiate. That alternate timeline did not come to pass, and perhaps Wilson's friendlier tone in this letter was the result of disintegrating trust with Robin. Wilson's letter also suggests that she might be sending a surrogate to the United States to interview Buckland in her stead. Wilson

---

18. Raymond Buckland, letter to Monique Wilson, May 15, 1963.
19. Monique Wilson, letter to Raymond Buckland, June, 5, 1963.

closes with a postscript asking Buckland to "destroy my letters as they have my address," which he again ignores.

In the current era of near instant contact, it's easy to forget just how hard communications could be only sixty years ago. Months between letters, cryptic one-name references to unknown Witches … It was a very different world. The letters being quoted in this chapter are all especially short, too, as every letter from the Wilsons to the Bucklands was sent via British Airmail, which dictated the size of every letter. (Airmail letters were made up of one blue sheet designed to be folded into something the size of a postcard, so the letter writer really only got one and a half pages to type or write a message on.)

Buckland's (undated) response to Wilson's May letter contains a major change of circumstance in Buckland's pursuit of the Craft. He writes:

Well now, I have a Priestess in mind and enclose her photograph. (Incidentally, I took the picture and developed and printed it myself.) She is my wife, Rosemary. Originally, when I first wrote to you, she was rather uncertain of her attitude to the Wica but after intensive reading of Dr. Gardner's and Margaret Murray's books she is quite catching my enthusiasm.[20]

Showing his attention to the small details, Buckland also inquires in this letter about whether joining the Wica requires taking a new name upon initiation. In all her correspondence, Monique Wilson signs her name as Olwen, her Craft name, while listing her return address on the outside of every letter as "Mrs. M. Wilson." Buckland is curious about whether a Craft name is chosen upon initiation or given to a new Witch by their initiators.

Buckland also mentions a wavy knife that he thinks would make a perfect athame. The style of knife he references is a kris (or keris) and coincidently is the subject of the 1936 book *Keris and Other Malay Weapons*, written by Gerald Gardner! Despite Gardner's interest in the kris knife, Wilson writes

---

20. Raymond Buckland, letter to Monique Wilson, exact date unknown 1. Though this letter (and several others) lacks a date, through context clues it's possible to reconstruct the back-and-forth between the Bucklands and Wilsons during this period.

in a letter dated July 28, 1963, that Buckland's wavy knife[21] is not an acceptable athame: "Sorry but it must have a straight blade with cutting edges."[22]

Circumstances in North America have also changed since Wilson's last
letter to the Bucklands. Initiation by the hypothetical California Coven now
feels off the table. Robin's trip to Scotland to be initiated has been postponed,
and Wilson writes that "Rosemary must form her Coven and take charge of
the East Coast." Wilson's July letter also marks the first time the Bucklands are
put in charge of correspondence with potential American Witches, as Wilson
includes the name and address of a local seeker. The correspondence saved by
Buckland during this period also includes a typewritten letter from Gerald
Gardner to an American seeker named "Mr Gunter," which was likely passed
on to Buckland by Monique Wilson. Curiously, there's a written date at the
bottom of the letter, 30/10/66,[23] suggesting that it may have arrived in Buckland's possession several years after it was written. (Gardner died in 1964.)

At this point in their correspondence, there has been no direct communication between Rosemary and Monique Wilson, yet Rosemary is being set
up to manage Witchcraft on America's East Coast. Even sixty years ago, that
would have put the Bucklands in charge of networking with tens of millions
of Americans. Why the sudden and complete acceptance of Rosemary as a
potential High Priestess?

Wilson writes that the photo of Rosemary shared by Raymond "caused
quite a stir in our circles among the males as your photo did among the
priestesses." Physical beauty has never been a prerequisite for initiatory
Witchcraft, but early Witches were conscious of what types of people might
draw more favorable coverage in the press. That's all speculation, of course, as
Wilson's excitement about Rosemary as a High Priestess might have simply
been due to Rosemary being the only potential High Priestess currently corresponding with her.

Raymond wasn't the only Buckland to write Monique Wilson in 1963;
Rosemary had her own questions for the High Priestess. Unlike Ray, Rosemary's questions were mostly of a very practical nature. In the letter she asks,

---

21. A straight blade with two cutting edges and a black wooden handle is traditional for a
    Gardnerian athame, but today such standards aren't enforced so rigidly. My first athame
    was actually a kris.
22. Monique Wilson, letter to Raymond Buckland, July 28, 1963.
23. The date is written in European style, with the day first, followed by the month.

"[H]ow are people of the Wica buried, and married, do they have a civil service[?]," concerned with ceremonies most of us take for granted in today's
Witchcraft/Pagan world.[24] In a reply to Rosemary's undated letter, Wilson
writes that the Wica

> do have a ritual for the dying. We call it "opening the door". Once they
> are dead they are not our concern any more but to theGods [sic]. So
> we leave the funeral service to the Christians.[25]

In her letter to Wilson, it's clear that Rosemary is looking for a religious practice as much as a magickal one. She states that she is looking for a religion
that "I can love and enjoy, and [unintelligible][26] all understand, I feel I can get
this in the Wica." Rosemary also makes a point of asking about children in
the Craft, stating that she would like to raise her "boy's [sic] up in the faith,"
though unsure of how to introduce "3 and 5 year old[s] into it." Monique and
her husband, Scotty, had direct knowledge of young Witchlings, having previously initiated their daughter, Yvette, who took the Witch name Morven.
(The decision to initiate Yvette would have dire repercussions later, which we
will get to.)

Monique Wilson expresses a great deal of joy that the Bucklands plan to
bring their children into the Craft. In her letter, Wilson adds:

> They [children] are brought in as any adult, except that the oath is
> taken on their behalf by the parents of sponsors. Once they have been
> initiated they are brought into as many circles as possible … No work
> is ever done with children in the circle. The meeting usually consists
> of forming the circle, a bit of dancing or singing or both.

Perhaps presaging the trouble to come, Wilson writes that Morven will "start
taking her place in the full circle" between ten and twelve years of age.

Illustrative of just how different the Witch world of 1963 was from that
of the present day, Rosemary writes a bit sympathetically about Christianity, despite professing earlier in her letter that she felt little "warmth" for it:

---

24. Rosemary Buckland, letter to Monique Wilson, exact date unknown.

25. Monique Wilson, letter to Rosemary Buckland, September 13, 1963.

26. Rosemary's letter is quite hard to read, most likely the result of quickly copying a missive for
recordkeeping purposes that she had previously written. Raymond's records of his correspondence are generally typed.

"Do you attend a Christian Church, I sing in the local choir, and the boys go to Sunday School." While there are probably still many Witches who lead double lives when it comes to religion, the easy acceptance of Christianity by Rosemary is a bit striking by modern Witch standards.

Rosemary's first letter to Monique Wilson is notable for one other reason: It's the first documentation of what would become Raymond Buckland's Craft name, Robat. Despite sounding quite mysterious, Robat is simply a Welsh name and means "bright fame."[27] The meaning of Robat is certainly something that Buckland would live up to. Wilson gives her approval to the name Robat in an additional letter to Rosemary and Ray, also dated September 13, 1963, adding that "this name [Robat] will now be used in correspondence with you or with other groups."[28]

In the course of the correspondence between the Bucklands and the Wilsons, it's suggested at one point that Monique and Scotty go to the United States to perform initiations. Monique suggests that a group of people interested in Witchcraft could pay the costs of her travel. (This would have included the Bucklands obviously, but also possibly the members of the hypothetical California Coven.) Later, due to health troubles, Monique herself shoots down this idea, writing that she would not be able to travel again until the spring of 1964. Wilson then brings up the idea of the Bucklands visiting Scotland for initiation in the winter of 1963/64. Knowing that Raymond works for British Airways, Wilson assumes that he would be able to make the trip rather cheaply. She makes this suggestion in the second letter dated September 13, 1963.

In his reply, Buckland reminds Wilson that he and his family have been living in the United States for only eighteen months, and as a result are still trying to establish themselves financially. Buckland adds that the entire family might possibly be able to visit Scotland after Christmas, but then he offers a rather novel solution:

---

27. BabyNamesPedia, "Robat—Meaning of Robat."
28. Monique Wilson, letter to Rosemary and Ray Buckland, September 13, 1963.

The only other possibility ... would be for <u>one</u> of us to come now. But
I guess it wouldn't do much good for one without the other? It seems
so terrible if we have to wait till after Christmas.[29]

Buckland's urgent desire to be initiated is not surprising, but the idea that it
might now be affordable is something new. Perhaps Rosemary's newfound
interest in the Craft changed the Bucklands' timeline?

In a follow-up letter to Monique dated October 23, 1963, Buckland
informs the Wilsons that he's been able to clear his schedule and could arrive
at their doorstop on Saturday, November 23 (leaving the US the previous
day). He adds that he's in a position to stay with the Wilsons for nine days,
needing to return on Sunday, December 1. In the course of sharing his potential travel plans, he does add the caveat that he realizes only one Buckland
might not be enough to guarantee an initiation.[30]

Within days of Buckland mailing his letter to the UK, Wilson responds
(in a letter dated October 28, 1963) that she would be willing to initiate
Raymond in November:

We'll be pleased to have you Robat. We'd prefer to have the both of
you but we'll do with one. We'll bring you in & teach you & you can
bring Rosemary in. It has been done that way before, especially when
great distances are involved & no priestess is available. We'll show you
how.[31]

Things were moving quickly. Buckland would soon be an initiate, and he and
Rosemary would be ready to hit the ground running with their own coven
shortly after he returned from Scotland.

· · · · · · · ·

Even before his initiation, Buckland was busy attempting to network with
other individuals interested in Witchcraft. In his memoir, Buckland writes
that "Gerald [Gardner] started forwarding to me any letters he received from
the United States." While this is probably not exactly true, Monique Wilson

---

29. Raymond Buckland, letter to Monique Wilson, exact date unknown 2.

30. Raymond Buckland, letter to Monique Wilson, October 23, 1963.

31. Monique Wilson, letter to Raymond and Rosemary Buckland, October 28, 1963.

did begin sending Buckland the addresses of other Witches as early as July of 1963 (I assume with the approval of Gardner). The first address received by Buckland was that of a fellow New Yorker who would later adopt the Witch-name Maverick and who had previously been in contact with Monique Wilson.[32] Maverick would later become one of Raymond and Rosemary's first initiates. Her passing along of addresses would continue going forward, even before Buckland was an initiate.

Never one to sit around and wait for things to happen, Buckland wrote a letter to the magazine *Exploring the Unknown* in the late winter of 1963, presenting himself as a potential author looking for background into Witchcraft practices. The time of submission to the time of publication was several months, and Buckland notes he had forgotten about the letter until it appeared in the magazine's August issue. The end result was that Buckland received his first seeker letters independent of Monique Wilson and Gerald Gardner. Out of the initial letters he received, two were from California and one from Texas, not ideal spots for potential Buckland initiates but a sign that there were individuals curious about Witchcraft outside of the East Coast.[33]

The most interesting of those letters received by Buckland is rather cryptic and suggests a New York coven in existence prior to Buckland's initiation:

> I see you are interested in finding the coven of N.Y., undoubtedly you will receive many replies. how-ever if I know witches & warlocks as I think I know them your answer will be either un-answered or false. how-ever I am also interested in the same. If you would like to write me I would gladly answer your letter.
>
> [Name redacted]
>
> P.S. Seek for witch Olymia.[34]

Buckland never did find the "witch Olymia" (nor did he receive very many replies to his *Exploring the Unknown* letter), and his response to the writer of the letter went unanswered.

In these early days, there's a level of deference to Monique Wilson that's worth mentioning. Buckland shares the contents of the letters he's received

---

32. Monique Wilson, letter to Raymond Buckland, July 28, 1963.

33. Raymond Buckland, letter to Monique Wilson, exact date unknown 2.

34. As recounted in Raymond Buckland's letter to Monique Wilson, exact date unknown 2.

from other potential initiates (or those curious about Witchcraft) with Wilson, including their addresses. Wilson seems to trust Buckland by the summer of 1963, but she's slow to share the names and addresses of other potential North American Witches outside of the New York City area. She mentions contacts in Chicago, Kentucky, Colorado, and Canada (Wilson does not specify where in Canada), as well as the previously mentioned Robin in California. It's likely that at least a few of these individuals did in fact meet Buckland in the years to come.

One of the most productive friendships Buckland would establish during this period was with Dr. Joseph Kaster, a professor at the New School for Social Research, a graduate university in New York City. Today Kaster is best known for his works dealing with ancient Egypt, but he was interested in a broad range of mythologies, and at the time of his first meeting with Buckland, he had already published *Putnam's Concise Mythological Dictionary* (1963). With their shared interest in mythology, it's not surprising that Buckland and Kaster would become fast friends in the early 1960s.

Kaster, along with the previously mentioned Maverick, would both attend the first ever Witchcraft-related meeting held at the home of the Bucklands. On October 20, 1963, Raymond and Rosemary hosted a meeting of potential Witches in the New York area to announce that Ray would be heading to Scotland the following month for initiation. Kaster must have liked what he heard that night, as he, too, was one of Buckland's earliest initiates, being initiated in January of 1964. It's unknown how many people were at that historic first Witchcraft meeting in New York, but according to Ray's records, he and Rosemary initiated eight adult Witches in 1964, six of them by April of that year. This suggests that there were more individuals present than just Kaster and Maverick that October night.

Kaster also facilitated Buckland's first ever public lecture on Witchcraft. On November 5, 1963, Buckland was a guest lecturer in Kaster's "Witchcraft and Magic" class. Buckland doesn't mention the topic of his lecture in any of his surviving papers, but it's likely that he talked about Gerald Gardner and Gardner's Witchcraft museum on the Isle of Man. Buckland also mentions that he later accompanied Kaster and his class to Salem, Massachusetts, for a Witchcraft field trip. (In his memoir, Buckland snidely adds that this trip was before the city had become "commercial.")

With a Witchcraft lecture under his belt, pen pals in a couple of different states, and several potential initiates near home, all that was left for Raymond Buckland to do was journey to Scotland and begin walking the path of
the Witch.

• • • • • • • •

Buckland left for Scotland and the Wilsons on either November 18, 1963,
or November 22, 1963. Buckland himself is responsible for this confusion.
In his memoir, he states that he left New York City on November 18. In his
letters to the Wilsons, he tells them that he will be arriving at their home on
November 23. In one letter written by Buckland and dated November 13, he
gives detailed information on his travel plans:

> I shall be leaving here Friday evening (our time) arriving at Prestwick
> Saturday morning at about 7.45a.m. (your time) on BOAC flight
> BA538.[35]

He also asks the Wilsons for additional information about his trip (such as
how often the local trains ran) and offers to bring Monique and Scotty anything they might like from New York. He ends the letter with "See you on
the 23rd."

To me, this letter strongly suggests that he arrived in Scotland on November 23. If he did arrive on November 18, he must have shown up unannounced on the Wilsons' front door! And why would Buckland expect a
response before he left New York if he was arriving in Perth on November
18? It's possible that Buckland misdated his letter and wrote it on November
3, but he is quite adamant about his arrival date in two different spots in the
letter. Buckland's arrival date is important, because a later arrival date suggests that he would have missed seeing Gerald Gardner in person.

Despite the confusion about just when Buckland arrived in Scotland, the
date of his initiation doesn't seem to be in doubt. His memoir states that he
was initiated on November 23, 1963. In his memoir, Buckland doesn't have
much to say about his initiation, but as initiations are oathbound things,

---

35. Raymond Buckland, letter to Monique Wilson, November 13, 1963.

that's to be expected. Like many initiates, Buckland remembered just how meaningful it was, and that he had a little bit of trepidation going into it:

> That Saturday evening, November 23, 1963, I was initiated. It was perhaps one of the most moving experiences of my life; one I would never forget. I didn't know what to expect—there were no details given in Gerald's books, of course, and in those days there were no other books on true Witchcraft. But Olwen was a slight lady about five feet four and I kept telling myself that if she went through it and survived then so could I!

Though Buckland is mostly silent about what went on at his initiation, there are some public things known about initiations in the Gardnerian tradition.[36] All the participants in the rite would have been wearing nothing more than jewelry, as Gardnerian rituals are generally performed skyclad (in the nude). (Scotland is quite cold in the winter, so let's hope that the heater at the Wilsons' house was working properly that evening.) High Priestesses and High Priests often wear circlets or crowns on top of their heads. If Scotty Wilson was wearing one during any of Buckland's initiations or elevations, it would have had horns on top of it. Monique Wilson likely wore a metal cuff on her arm, signifying that other covens could trace their lineage back to her. Monique would also have been the one to initiate Buckland, as the initiation would have been done female (initiator) to male (initiate).

Something truly extraordinary happened between Raymond Buckland and Monique Wilson during his initiation ritual, or perhaps I should write that something truly extraordinary happened between Ray, Monique, and a Witch Goddess. In his memoir, Buckland recounts that at his initiation "Monique changed before my eyes—in good, white [candle]light—from a forty-something-year-old woman into a girl of eighteen or so." He goes on to say that this transformation occurred in other circles, too, and with different High Priestesses. While this feels like a throwaway comment, I believe it to be a revealing look into how Raymond Buckland perceived and experienced the Goddess. (Sadly, this idea is not followed up anywhere else in Buckland's

---

36. There are several books on the market that allegedly contain a traditional Book of Shadows, including the rites for initiations and elevations, but since Buckland honored his oath to keep his initiation private, I have chosen to honor that choice in this book.

writings and is included in his memoir in a section completely unrelated to his initiation.)

The belief among many self-identifying Witches at the time of Buckland's initiation was that "it takes a Witch to make a Witch." With thousands of books now available about how to practice Witchcraft and live one's life as a Witch, such ideas often feel antiquated and out of place today. Certainly, to be a Gardnerian Witch (or a practicing Witch of any other initiatory tradition), one must be initiated. Having a Gardnerian Book of Shadows is not enough to be Gardnerian. Several aspects of the tradition are not written down and are only committed to memory. (In his memoir, Buckland says that he spent many nights on his Scotland trip "being coached by both Olwen and Loic [Scotty Wilson's Witch name]" and memorizing "those things which were never written down.") Initiated Witches can also trace their lineage back to the founder of their tradition. In the case of Gardnerian Witchcraft, all Gardnerians can trace their lineage back to Gerald Gardner.

At the time of his initiation, Buckland would have certainly believed that it took a Witch to make a Witch, but that opinion would change over time. Just ten years after his initiation, Buckland would see self-dedication into Witchcraft as an equally valid ritual for proclaiming oneself a Witch. But even with his acceptance of self-dedications, there was something about initiation that stuck with Buckland over the decades.

The Tree (1974) is the first Buckland book (and first Witchcraft book) to include a self-dedication ritual, but it also includes a coven initiation ritual. *Buckland's Complete Book of Witchcraft* (1986) follows the same pattern, with both types of ritual included in the work. Clearly Buckland still found value in initiation rituals, even after starting a tradition that didn't require them.

Once he was initiated, Buckland says that he spent his remaining days in Scotland participating in ritual every night with the Wilsons. On two of those evenings, Monday, November 25, and Wednesday, November 27, he was advanced to the second and third degrees. During that period of time, Buckland also hand-copied the Wilsons' copy of the Gardnerian Book of Shadows. (Luckily, for the sake of Buckland's hand, the original Gardnerian BoS is not all that long in terms of words or pages.) He also found a suitable athame while in Scotland, and it can be assumed that this knife had straight edges instead of wavy ones. The consecration of that first athame would have been another activity done in the magick circle while Buckland was with the Wilsons.

When Buckland set out for the UK in November of 1963, there was no guarantee of initiation or further elevations. If Monique Wilson had not approved of Buckland, she would not have initiated him and would most certainly not have raised him to the third degree. But Wilson seemed to have liked Raymond upon their initial meeting. Later letters between the Wilsons and the Bucklands show a great deal of affection between the two couples, and that must have started when Raymond Buckland initially impressed Monique Wilson during their first meeting.

While in Scotland, Buckland also met several members of Monique Wilson's coven, though he did not do ritual with them. Much of Wilson's Witchcraft instruction centered around healing techniques. In his memoir, Buckland specifically mentions "the Craft method of laying-on of hands," a practice he was still engaging in forty years later. He also writes that Wilson taught him to scry (a form of divination) using a crystal ball. Buckland flew home on December 1 in his words "mentally exhausted but incredibly elated."

· · · · · · · · ·

One of the most notable absences in both Buckland's unfinished memoir and his letters to the Wilsons post-initiation is any reference to Gerald Gardner. In most books dealing with Witch history, it's assumed that Buckland had a warm and friendly correspondence with Gardner and that Gardner was present at Buckland's initiation. However, neither Buckland's memoir nor the letters to and from the Wilsons suggest that Gardner was present. And in a letter to Gerald Gardner dated December 5, 1963, Monique Wilson comments that "the American group is formed" and that she has sent Robat back to the States as a High Priest. She goes on to comment that Buckland will then "bring in Rowen."[37] If Gardner had been present at Buckland's initiation, wouldn't Gardner have been aware that all this had gone on? Gardner's presence at Ray's initiation also feels like something that Buckland or the Wilsons might have commented on in subsequent letters. Letters to Buck-

---

37. Heselton, *Witchfather, Volume 2*, 632.

land before his initiation also make no mention of Gardner possibly participating, and there is some difficulty with the timeline.

If Buckland did arrive in Scotland on November 18, he most certainly could have seen Gardner, but he would have probably missed out on a chance to engage in ritual with him. According to Patricia Crowther, one of Gardner's High Priestesses, she and her then husband Arnold took Gardner to the port of Manchester on November 21, where he boarded a cargo ship bound for Lebanon that would eventually take him to Tunisia (where he passed away in February of 1964).[38] Gardner boards the ship where he would spend his final months either two days before Buckland's initiation or (perhaps) two days before Buckland's arrival in Scotland. The dates simply don't add up.

It's possible that there could be a mix-up with the dates. Buckland could be wrong in his recounting, but if there was one date he would most likely have wanted to commit to memory during his meeting with the Wilsons, it's the date of his initiation. It's also possible that the Crowthers have their date wrong and Gardner boarded his ship after November 23. Gardner biographer Philip Heselton is confident about the dates supplied by the Crowthers, but it's certainly possible that they might have made a mistake. I don't think the circumstantial evidence backs this up, but it's possible. Just about every Witchcraft origin story from the 1950s/60s has an element of uncertainty about it.

There was also a small issue with the boat. While scheduled to leave on November 23, it actually left port two weeks behind schedule. It's possible that in the interim Gardner made a special trip back up to Perth (he had just visited the Wilsons the week prior to his scheduled voyage), but there are several reasons for that being an unlikely scenario, the most important reason being Gardner's health at the time. He was seventy-nine in November of 1963 and not particularly hearty. Someone would have had to assist him in his travels, but there are no records or recollections of anyone picking up Gardner in late November of 1963 from a train station or airport. He could have hired a private driver, but if he had been in Scotland for Buckland's initiation, it seems likely that someone would have mentioned it.

---

38. Heselton, *Witchfather, Volume 2*, 630.

Buckland does claim to have met Gardner, and his story of their meeting is understated:

> At our one-time meeting I found him truly delightful, with a wicked sense of humor.... He was also very sharp and very knowledgeable on all things to do with religo-magic. I was especially struck by the strength of his voice in ritual; in contrast to his normal speaking voice.[39]

If Buckland was trying to create a fictitious friendship with Gardner, it seems like he would have tried a little harder.

There was another instance where it might have been possible for Buckland and Gardner to cross paths, and this occurred several months before Buckland's November initiation. From March 22 through April 1 of 1963, Buckland found himself once more in his homeland, visiting London for British Airways. By this period of time, Buckland was certainly interested in Witchcraft and had already sent Gardner at least two letters, and he had received his first letter from Monique Wilson only a month prior. Could the two have met in London in the spring of 1963?

Buckland doesn't mention meeting Gardner during that trip in his memoir, but he also doesn't mention meeting Gardner in any other place in it. London's occult world was quite small in 1963, so it's certainly possible that the two ran into each other at an occult bookstore, such as Atlantis or Watkins Books.[40] Buckland could have also found himself at a lecture being given by Gardner, and afterward exchanged a few pleasantries. All that is conjecture, but it could have happened.

In Buckland's recounting of his meeting with Gardner, he makes mention of Gardner's "voice in ritual." Of course, Buckland would not have been able to hear Gardner's voice in ritual without an initiation, and he was not an initiate in the spring of 1963, though it's possible that Buckland heard Gardner quoting a bit of ritual at a public gathering or lecture. (Gardner's books have bits of ritual in them, so obviously he didn't keep every line used in ritual a secret.)

---

39. Heselton, *Witchfather, Volume 2*, 576.
40. Both of these bookstores are still in operation today! If you ever visit London, these are must-visit stores.

Even though Gardner often left England for prolonged excursions abroad during the country's winter months, his only trip overseas in the winter of 1962/63 was a visit to Spain.[41] Spain's proximity to London increases the chance that this visit was not an extensive, months-long trip, and that Gardner could have been in the UK when Buckland visited his old homeland that March. I don't find this argument particularly convincing, but it's certainly possible.

So did Buckland meet Gardner? Ultimately, it doesn't particularly matter, as Buckland was never going to be initiated directly by Gardner anyway, but it is an interesting question. It's also an assertion that gets passed around so often that it's worth bringing up in this book. I think the evidence suggests that they never met, and perhaps Buckland confused Gardner with someone else. It's also possible that Buckland was telling a little fib about meeting Gardner, hoping it would add to his own credibility.

There's a long history of Modern Witches embellishing their credentials and who exactly is in their circle of friends. If Buckland was telling an untrue tale about meeting Gardner, he wouldn't have been the first (and was certainly not the last). The story of Buckland meeting Gardner in November of 1963 is so woven into Witch history (especially for Gardnerian Witches) that Buckland might have been nervous about contradicting the tale!

Physically, Gardner might not have been all that involved with Buckland's initiation, but his spiritual presence seems to loom large over the entire enterprise. Monique Wilson is clearly acting as Gardner's surrogate, a fact that she acknowledges in her correspondence with Buckland, and the initiation of Buckland was certainly done with the consent and approval of Gardner.

Before we close this particular chapter, I think it's important to point out that Buckland clearly had a lot of affection for Gardner. *Buckland's Complete Book of Witchcraft* is partially dedicated to the memory of "Scire and Olwen," Scire being Gerald Gardner's Witch name. Throughout his written works, both published and unpublished, Buckland is always quite reverential toward Gardner. In *The Tree*, Buckland wrote that Gardner's book *Witchcraft Today* was still "the finest work" on the subject of Witchcraft twenty years after its initial publication.[42]

---

41. Heselton, *Witchfather, Volume 2*, 625.
42. Buckland, *The Tree*, 2.

Many of us often feel as if we know celebrities and authors simply because we are fans of them or have read their books. Buckland was most certainly a fan of Gardner and held a great deal of respect for the man. In later years, Buckland would stop actively participating in the Gardnerian tradition, but that respect and admiration for Gardner would continue. Even before his passing in 1964, Gerald Gardner was acknowledged as a trailblazer and larger-than-life figure, which is why we're still talking about him and Raymond Buckland.

Exercise 3: Initiation

Buckland considered initiation an important step for anyone interested in joining a coven. He also believed that initiation rituals were not limited to established traditions. Any group of people could put together an initiation rite for their members, and his initiation rituals in *Buckland's Complete Book of Witchcraft* and *The Tree* are great templates for people interested in creating their own initiation rites.

The coven initiation ritual in *Buckland's Complete* presented here[43] was heavily influenced by Gardnerian Witchcraft and the prevailing beliefs at the time. In the text, male initiates are initiated by a High Priestess, and female initiates by a High Priest. (In the ritual script below, the initiate is female, with the High Priest performing the initiation.) Buckland also suggests that the ritual be performed skyclad, though there are instructions for Witches who wish to work robed. Buckland's initiation rite is designed for five people: the initiate, High Priestess, High Priest, Maiden, and Squire. The Maiden and Squire operate as assistants to the Priestess and Priest, though with their own speaking parts.

Buckland was always true to his oaths of secrecy, so the initiation rituals in his books are very different from the Gardnerian initiation he undertook in November of 1963. However, there are elements between the two rites that might be similar. As an initiated Gardnerian myself, much of the following ritual feels familiar, right down to Buckland's use of archaic-sounding language in the speaking parts. (Gardner did much the same thing!)

What makes this ritual special is the emphasis placed on the coven as family. The initiate here is not just being brought into Witchcraft; they are being brought into a circle of people who love and trust one another. Clearly the Witchcraft phrase "in perfect love and perfect trust" meant something to Raymond Buckland.

---

43. Buckland, *Buckland's Complete Book of Witchcraft*, 68–72.

Coven Initiation

Priestess: "Let there be none who suffer loneliness; now who are friendless and without brother or sister. For all may find love and peace within the Circle."

Priest: "With open arms, the Lord and Lady welcome all."

Squire: "I bring news of one who has traveled far, seeking that which we enjoy."

Maiden: "Long has been her journey, but now she feels an end is near."

Priest: "Of whom do you speak?"

Squire: "Of she who, even now, waits outside our temple, seeking entry."

Priestess: "Who caused her to come here?"

Maiden: "She came herself, of her own free will."

Priest: "What does she seek?"

Maiden: "She seeks to become one with the Lord and the Lady. She seeks to join with us in our worship of them."

Priestess: "Who can vouch for this person?"

Squire: "I can. As her teacher I have shown her the ways; pointed her in the right direction and set her feet upon the path. But she has chosen to take this step and now bids you give her entrance."

Priest: "Can she be brought before us?"

Squire: "Indeed she can."

Priestess: "Then let it be so."

Squire takes Cord and athame; Maiden takes blindfold and candle. They go, clockwise, around Circle to the east and there exit the Circle. They go out of the temple, to the initiate. Maiden blindfolds her while squire binds her (see illustration). With initiate between them, they approach the door to the temple room. Squire bangs on door with handle of athame.

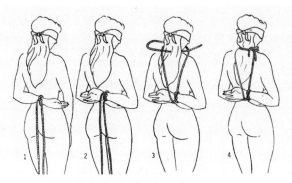

Method of Binding for an Initiation

Priest: "Who knocks?"

Squire: "We return with one who would join our number."

Priestess: "What is her name?"

Initiate: "My name is … (given name) … I beg entry."

Priestess: "Enter this our temple."

The three enter the temple room and stand outside the Circle, in the east. Maiden holds the candle; squire the athame. The bell is rung once.

Priest: "… (Name) …, why do you come here?"

Initiate: "To worship the gods in whom I believe and to become one with them and with my brothers and sisters of the Craft."

Priestess: "What do you bring with you?"

Initiate: "I bring nothing but my true self, naked and unadorned."

Priestess: "Then I bid you enter this our Circle of worship and magick."

Squire admits them to the Circle. They stand just within, still in the east. Priest and priestess move around to them; priest carrying the censer and priestess the salted water.

Priest: "To enter this our Sacred Circle, I here duly consecrate you, in the names of the God and the Goddess."

If initiate is robed, the priestess opens the robe while the priest sprinkles and censes her, then closes it again. Priest and priestess return to the altar, followed by squire, initiate, and maiden. Priest and priestess stand in front of altar, while squire and maiden move around to far side, opposite, with initiate between them. They face priest and priestess. Bell is rung twice.

Priestess: "I speak now for the Lady. Why are you here?"

Initiate: "I am here to become one with the Lord and the Lady; to join in worship of them."

Priest: "I am he who speaks for the Lord. Who made you come here?"

Initiate: "None made me come, for I am here of my own choosing."

Priest: "Do you wish an end to the life you have known so far?"

Initiate: "I do."

Priest: "Then so be it."

With his athame, squire cuts a lock of initiate's hair and throws it on the censer. Squire and maiden lead initiate around Circle to the east.

Maiden: "Hearken, all ye at the east gate. Here is one who would join us. Welcome her and bring her joy."

They move to the south.

Squire: "Hearken all ye at the south gate. Here is one who would join us. Welcome her and bring her joy."

They move on to the west.

Maiden: "Hearken all ye at the west gate. Here is one who would join us. Welcome her and bring her joy."

They move on to the north.

Squire: "Hearken all ye at the north gate. Here is one who would join us. Welcome her and bring her joy."

Squire and maiden lead initiate back to stand behind altar again, facing priest and priestess. Priest and priestess place their crowns on their heads and, taking up their athames, stand side by side with their right arms holding the athames high in salute. Squire rings bell three times.

Maiden: "Now, then, must you face those whom you seek."

Maiden removes initiate's blindfold.

Maiden: "Behold, in these two priests do we see the gods. And in that know that we and they are the same."

Squire: "As we need the gods, so do the gods need us."

Priest: "I am he who speaks for the God. Yet are you and I equal."

Priestess: "I am she who speaks for the Goddess. Yet are you and I equal."

Priest and priestess lower their athames and present the blades to the initiate, who kisses the blades.

Initiate: "I salute the Lord and the Lady, as I salute those who represent them. I pledge my love and support to them, and to my brothers and sisters of the Craft."

Priest: "Know you the Wiccan Rede?"

Initiate: "I do. An' it harm none, do what thou wilt."

Priestess: "And do you abide by that Rede?"

Initiate: "I do."

Priest: "Well said. Let your bonds be loosed that ye may be reborn."

Squire unties cord. Maiden leads initiate around to stand between priest and priestess. Maiden then returns to her place beside squire.

Priestess: "That you may start life afresh it is only meet and right that you start with a name of your own choosing. Have you such a name?"

Initiate: "I have. It is … (Craft name) …."

Priest: "Then shall you be known by that name henceforth, by your brothers and sisters of the Craft."

Priest takes up anointing oil. If initiate is robed, priestess opens robe. Priest anoints (cross, pentagram, and triangle) and says:

Priest: "With this sacred oil I anoint and cleanse thee, giving new life to one of the children of the gods. From this day forth you shall be known as … (Craft name) …, within this Circle and without it, to all your brothers and sisters of the Craft. So mote it be."

All: "So mote it be!"

Priestess: "Now you are truly one of us. As one of us will you share our knowledge of the gods and of the arts of healing, of divination, of magick, and of all the mystic arts. These shall you learn as you progress."

Priest: "But we caution you ever to remember the Wiccan Rede. An' it harm none, do what thou wilt."

Priestess: "An' it harm none, do what thou wilt. Come now, … (name) …, and meet your kindred."

Initiate salutes[44] priest and priestess then moves around to salute and greet all the others in the Circle. If the initiation has been taking place without the other coven members being present, they now return to the

---

44. Note: When one Witch *salutes* another, it is with an embrace and a kiss.

Circle to join the celebrants. If it is the coven custom to present a newcomer with any gift(s), this may be done at this time. Bell is rung three times.

Priest: "Now it is truly a time for celebration."

Feasting and merriment follow until the temple is closed.

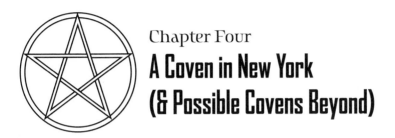

Chapter Four

A Coven in New York (& Possible Covens Beyond)

Writing about Witchcraft, especially in a historical sense, presents a lot of challenges, the biggest one being the rather nebulous definition of the word *Witch*. People have been accused of Witchcraft for hundreds if not thousands of years. (Certainly we've all read about Witchcraft being practiced thousands of years ago, but the word Witch did not exist back then!) Some of those accused of Witchcraft during that period of time practiced magickal traditions that might have dated back hundreds of years. But there's a difference between being called a Witch and self-identifying as a Witch. My own practice of Witchcraft has resulted in me being labeled a Satanist on a number of occasions. I have no argument with Satanists, but I'm most certainly not one, and people calling me a Satanist doesn't make me one either.

By the mid-1950s, due to a changing social climate, Gerald Gardner's books on Witchcraft and their coverage in the press on both sides of the Atlantic most likely led to many people beginning to self-identify as Witches. Some of these people no doubt started traditions and did ritual, but sadly nothing from that era exists today that can be definitively documented. It's not until 1964 that we begin to see magazines and periodicals spring up documenting American Witchcraft when the first American Witch/Pagan periodical goes into print. The brainchild of Joseph "Bearwalker" Wilson (1942–2004), the first edition of *The Waxing Moon* was a scant four pages long, but it was *something* and would pave the way for larger and more ambitious projects in the years to come.

The Fellowship of Hesperides was founded by Frederick McLaren Adams (1928–2008) in 1957 and incorporated a liturgy honoring seasonal festivals.[45] Adams did not call his practice Witchcraft, but it would certainly have looked familiar to modern Witches. In the late 1960s, Adams changed the name of the group to Feraferia and most definitely began hanging out with Witches and other like-minded folks.[46]

Buckland's founding of the New York Coven in 1964 is often written about in Witchcraft books as the official start of the Craft movement in the United States. There likely were precursors, but because those precursors have been largely lost to history, they would end up lacking the influence that Buckland's importation of Gardnerian Craft would have on the American Witchcraft scene. To be influential, a group or practice must either have second- and third-generation adherents and grow outside of a limited geographical area or have its ideas popularized in the press.

It's also quite possible that many of the traditions that today we call Witchcraft were originally called something else and only adopted the Witchcraft moniker in later years. San Franciscan Victor Anderson, cofounder of the Feri Tradition, claimed in 1932 to be an initiate of what he called the Harpy Coven.[47] Anderson typically described the coven as focused on magickal practice, mixing American-style folk magick with practices from the tradition known as Huna. Huna was alleged to be a secret Hawaiian magickal practice, but was actually the creation of an American named Max Freedom Long. Long first wrote about Huna in 1936 in the book *Discovering the Ancient Magic*, four years after Anderson's initiation into the Harpy Coven.

I find it likely that Victor Anderson was initiated into something in the 1930s (though he might have been a little off with his dates), but would its practitioners have called it Witchcraft? In an interview in the 1970s for her book *Drawing Down the Moon* (1979), author and journalist Margot Adler asked Anderson when he decided to form a coven, and his reply was "when

45. Clifton, *Her Hidden Children*, 142.

46. For those interested in Feraferia, I wholeheartedly suggest picking up *Celebrate Wildness: Magic, Mirth, and Love on the Feraferia Path* by Jo Carson. The book includes a breakdown of Feraferian beliefs and a lot of Fred Adams's artwork.

47. Kelly, *A Tapestry of Witches, Volume 1*, 34.

Gerald Gardner put out this book of his, *Witchcraft Today*."[48] Absent a diary or a letter from a member of the Harpy Coven dating back to the 1930s/40s, we will never know for sure if its practitioners truly thought of themselves as Witches. But certainly by the 1950s/60s, thanks to the work of Gardner and others, the word Witch was becoming increasingly acceptable in certain circles.

There is a long history of folk magick practice in the American Ozarks, and in 1947 much of that practice was documented in Vance Randolph's (1892–1980) *Ozark Superstitions* (later published as *Ozark Magic and Folklore*). Randolph's book is of special interest because it possibly references self-identifying Witches who practice magick. I use the word *possibly* here because Randolph contradicts himself several times in the text and casts doubt on the sanity of those who might self-identify as Witches.[49]

Randolph mentions knowing and interviewing twenty-four people who were thought to be Witches in the Ozarks during his time there, three of whom were "lunatics" who had claimed to sell their soul to the Devil. The twenty-one remaining individuals worked magick for good and were called "witch masters, white witches, witch doctors, faith doctors, goomer doctors and conjure folks."[50] Randolph writes that these benign practitioners of magick were "clairvoyants, fortunetellers, seers, mystics, purveyors of medical advice, seekers of lost property," but not Witches as he understood the term.[51]

What makes Randolph's work so interesting is that we have people being called "white witches" who were valued members of their communities. Randolph's work also hints at Witchcraft as a tradition being passed down among practitioners, with transmission typically done female to male (and the reverse) and nude. Certainly there are overlaps here with what Buckland experienced in Perth, but there are major differences, too. In the Ozarks, clothes are to be hung "on an infidel's tombstone"[52] and one's body given to the Devil in sexual intercourse. This all requires saying the Lord's Prayer

---

48. Adler, *Drawing Down the Moon*, 79.
49. Randolph, *Ozark Magic and Folklore*, 265.
50. Randolph, *Ozark Magic and Folklore*, 265.
51. Randolph, *Ozark Magic and Folklore*, 265.
52. Randolph, *Ozark Magic and Folklore*, 267.

backward, too. These types of ideas were common during the era of the Witch Trials, and some of them seem more like superstitions than real practices, but self-identifying Witches in the Ozarks can't be dismissed entirely out of hand as a possibility.

Even if Raymond Buckland was not the first self-identified Witch in North America, he was probably the founder of the first Gardnerian coven in North America. I write *probably* here because for several years there have been rumors of a North American coven that predates Buckland's. The rumor is largely the result of Dayonis, the Bricket Wood coven's High Priestess,[53] marrying and emigrating to Canada in 1959.[54] If Dayonis had wanted to start a coven, she most certainly could have, but she's never claimed to have started one, nor do I know anyone who claims lineage in the Gardnerian tradition through Dayonis via Canada.[55] I think it's likely that there were self-identifying Witches in the United States (and Canada!) before Buckland's initiation, but nearly all those who have claimed a Witchcraft practice before Buckland did so after both Ray's and Rosemary's initiations.

On December 7, 1963, Rosemary Buckland was initiated by Raymond into the Wica and took the Witch name Rowen. The name Rowen had been suggested to Rosemary by Monique Wilson in one of Wilson's letters. Wilson does not elaborate on why she suggested Rowen, and it's possible that Wilson was suggesting the rowan tree, replacing the *a* with an *e*.[56] In modern English, rowen signifies the "second crop of grass or hay in one growing season" and comes from an Old French word meaning "regain."[57] Nearly sixty years after that December night, most Gardnerians in the United States still trace their lineage through Rowen and Robat.

Rosemary was elevated to the third degree in short order, becoming a second-degree Priestess on December 9, 1963, and a third-degree Priestess just ten days later. Much like Raymond's whirlwind elevation to the third

---

53. Bricket Wood was the first coven established by Gerald Gardner, and it still exists today!
54. Heselton, *Witchfather, Volume 2*, 602. Michael Lloyd alludes to the alleged Canadian coven in his book *Bull of Heaven*.
55. Lloyd, *Bull of Heaven*, 15. Lloyd never comes out and says Dayonis started a coven in Canada, but he suggests that a Canadian coven might have existed.
56. Monique Wilson, letter to Raymond and Rosemary Buckland, October 28, 1963.
57. Collins Online English Dictionary, "rowen."

degree while with the Wilsons, this was done so that the Gardnerian tradition could be established as soon as possible in the United States. Today,
Gardnerian Witches often wait a year or more just to be initiated, and then
several more years before being elevated to the second and/or third degrees.

Rosemary's initiations and elevations are notable for another reason:
Raymond Buckland most certainly cast the magick circle that those rites
happened inside of. To most Witches, this is probably not a big deal (who
cares who cast the circle?), but in Gardnerian circles, the identity and gender
of the circle-caster has always been a big issue. In one of her earliest letters to
Raymond, Monique Wilson says that a solo Raymond would not be "able to
even form a circle," and even today in most Gardnerian circles, initiations and
elevations take place inside of a circle cast by the High Priestess.[58] But was
this Wilson's rule or Gardner's?

Gardner himself cast the circle in the initiation and elevation rituals of
one Olive Greene in February of 1959. Like the Bucklands', Greene's ascent
through the three Witch degrees occurred quite quickly. Greene first got into
contact with Gardner in February of 1959, and by the end of the month she
had likely attained all three degrees. Shortly after meeting Greene, Gardner
introduced her to the rest of the Bricket Wood coven, who found her an
unacceptable candidate for initiation. Despite the disapproval of his coven,
Gardner took Greene through the three degrees himself without any other
Witches present. Although Gardner considered a circle cast by the hand of
a High Priest to be acceptable for initiations and elevations, the idea is still
frowned upon by many Gardnerians.[59]

(The tale of Olive Greene is one of early Wiccan-Witchcraft's great soap
operas. Greene was not what she appeared to be and was most likely working as a "spy" for a couple named Charles and Mary Cardell.[60] By August of
1959, Greene had taken to sending Gardner many rather vile and mean letters, which were so cruel that they affected the health and mental well-being
of both Gerald and his wife, Donna. In 1964 Greene provided a firsthand
account of her time with Gerald Gardner and shared much of his Book of

---

58. Monique Wilson, letter to Raymond Buckland, June 5, 1963.

59. Hutton, *The Triumph of the Moon*, 259–60.

60. The Cardells liked to pretend they were brother and sister, while they most definitely were
    not siblings. They were a strange duo.

Shadows in the booklet *Witch*, attributed to Rex Nemorensis, which was a pseudonym used by Charles Cardell.[61] Given the results of Greene's initiation, perhaps High Priestesses have a higher level of discernment than do High Priests.)

According to his biographers and those who knew him over the last fifteen years of his life, Gardner was singularly focused on bringing as many individuals as possible into the Wica. Even by 1959, the number of Wiccan initiates in the United Kingdom was quite small, so ignoring the rules for the opportunity to bring in more new Witches would have appealed to Gardner. In regard to the Bucklands, Gardner was most certainly aware of how they would proceed in the United States and gave the enterprise his blessing. It wasn't following the rules that was important; what was important was sharing the Craft.

While Rosemary immediately became the High Priestess of the New York Coven upon receiving the third degree, she was later "redone" by the Wilsons in July of 1964. Buckland writes that this ceremony "confirmed" her initiation and marked her coronation as "Witch Queen and Queen of the Sabbat." This is significant because some have claimed that Rosemary had simply been appointed "Maiden" of America's inaugural Wiccan coven by Monique Wilson and was not a full-fledged High Priestess. But since Wilson never questioned the validity of the Bucklands' initiates prior to July of 1964, Rosemary must have been seen as a High Priestess in good standing.

The Bucklands could have begun initiating new Witches as soon as December 13, 1963, but Raymond writes in his memoir that

> we took time to adjust to the positions and for Rowen to familiarize herself with the Book of Shadows. Consequently we did not initiate our first coven member until the start of the New Year.

In addition to understanding their new roles as High Priestess and High Priest, the Bucklands also would have had to procure all the tools necessary to perform a Gardnerian ritual. In 1963 many of those tools would have been unfamiliar to them until their initiation.

---

61. *Witch* has long been out of print, but a facsimile version was published by Wishan Books in 2022.

Just a little less than a month after Rowen's ascension to the third degree, the Bucklands brought in their first initiate, the previously mentioned Maverick. Five days later, Joseph Kaster would be initiated and would choose the name Reinhardt. Both Maverick and Reinhardt were brought in as "solo Witches," as the Bucklands didn't seem to care if someone had a "working partner" (of the opposite gender) or not. The focus was not on gender balance, but on bringing in good Witches.

Maverick, Kaster, and the Bucklands operated as a coven of four for several months, meeting most Saturday nights. At those first American coven meetings, the initial members of the New York Coven celebrated the sabbats and mourned the passing of Gerald Gardner, who died in February of that year (1964) while aboard a ship nearing Tunis.[62] (Gardner was then buried in Tunis, and his remains are still there today.) In April, the coven would double in size, with four new initiates. Three of those four initiates were women, and all four initiations occurred over a frantic eight days. (Four initiations in eight days might not sound like much, but initiations are long and involved rites, so that is a *lot* of work.)

The Bucklands' seventh initiate was, surprisingly, another Buckland. In his memoir, Buckland writes about the activities of Robert, his elder son, in the circle:

> One of the people initiated in May of 1964 was my older son, who took the name Puck. He was seven years old at the time, but was ready for it. He had always been a somewhat serious child and had a great interest in all that we did. He was brought in on the understanding that if, at a later age (around puberty), he decided this was not for him, then he was at liberty to leave. Actually this was so for everyone coming into the Craft. No one was forced to stay, if they had a change of heart. But Puck enjoyed the ceremonies. He went through exactly the same ritual initiation that everyone else did, except that his father (myself) took the Oath of Secrecy on his behalf. If, at puberty, Puck decided he wanted to remain in the Craft, he would then take the ceremony again—like a confirmation—but then take the Oath himself.

---

62. Heselton, *Witchfather, Volume 2*, 634.

...On Circle nights, the two [Buckland] boys would be put to bed, but the older one only pretended to sleep. When his brother was asleep, he would slip out of bed and come to join the group. He would be a part of the ceremonies up to what is termed the Cakes and Wine ritual—basically a thanksgiving for the food and drink necessary for life. There were small cakes, or cookies, given to everyone together with a glass of wine. For Puck it was a glass of fruit-juice or even Cool-Aid [sic]. After this Puck would leave the Circle and return to bed while the coven continued with any magical work to be done.

Despite the lack of initiation of Regnauld (the Bucklands' younger son), he did partake in at least one ritual, the end result of which feels almost duplicitous:

There was one memorable night that served to show how suited Puck, my elder son, was to the religion. We had gone through the opening ritual and just got to the Cakes and Wine when we all heard my younger son, in his bedroom upstairs from the basement ritual room, calling out for his brother. For whatever reason he had woken up and wondered where everyone was. I went upstairs and brought him down to join us. As we went in, he stood wide-eyed looking at the candles, the burning incense, the seated people (he knew them all), and especially his brother who was sitting with cookies and Cool-Aid. It took no time for him to join his brother. Shortly after, both boys went back upstairs to bed. The next morning, at breakfast, the younger boy came out with "Hey, are we going to have another one of those things tonight?" His brother looked at him blankly. "What do you mean?" he asked. "You know, that thing with the cookies and Cool-Aid." "Cookies and Cool-Aid?" "Yes. You know. We had it last night." The older boy looked steadily at his brother. "You must have been dreaming," he said.

Luckily the initiation of Puck (and his younger brother's ritual guest appearance) did not result in any legal trouble for the Bucklands. Initiating children into Witchcraft and having them partake in rites in the nude was a rather risqué thing to do in 1964.

Eight initiations in four months seems like a lot of initiations, and in the course of writing this book, I've had people comment to me that "Raymond initiated just about anybody." My response to such an accusation has generally been mild laughter. Raymond and Rosemary were active Gardnerians for a period of approximately eight years (1964–72), and during that time they initiated thirty-five individuals. Many of their initiates took the Craft to new locations. If the Bucklands were going to grow Wiccan-Witchcraft in the United States, they had to initiate individuals who were going to start new covens outside of New York City.

Circumstances were much different in 1964 than today. Most people now who are interested in Gardnerian Witchcraft have been exposed to Witch rituals and ideas for an extended period of time prior to their initiation. Sixty years ago, there were no open circles to visit, either in the flesh or online. There were also no how-to books or even books that included a complete ritual. This meant that people had to either get initiated or create their own practice with the few resources available. In other words, the Bucklands had to initiate individuals if people were going to practice the Craft.

In his memoir, Buckland comments that he and Rosemary were "relatively slow" about bringing people into their circle and were criticized for it. Apparently, there was no way for the Bucklands to win the PR battle on just what the proper number of initiates should be over the course of nearly a decade. In many initiate circles, it's traditional to have potential coven members wait for at least a "year and a day" before being initiated, but most early Witches weren't held to this standard (both Ray and Rosemary were not), and it has always felt rather arbitrary. Early in their lives as initiates, the Bucklands also felt immense pressure (partly from Monique Wilson) to speed up the process as much as possible, but that presented its own challenges.

All covens vet potential members hoping to find great matches and individuals who might measure up to the ideal of "perfect love and perfect trust" within the circle, but vetting was even more important in the 1960s. Many people still operated under the delusion that Modern Witchcraft was a Satanic cult or an excuse for orgies and drugs. All things considered, the Bucklands found a successful middle way between the extremes of keeping the door tightly shut and letting any and all seekers become initiates.

Just a little over seven months after Raymond's initiation, he, Rosemary, and the boys visited the Wilsons on the Isle of Man. It was on this trip that Rosemary's initiation and elevation were "redone" by Monique Wilson. If Rosemary truly had to be "redone" because her initiation and elevations weren't completely valid, wouldn't everyone she had previously initiated also need to be "redone"? I've always found this whole exercise rather silly since those previously initiated by Rosemary and Ray did not get reinitiated, but reinitiating Rosemary most likely served as a measure of control over the Bucklands.

According to Raymond's memoir, on July 13, 1964, Rowen had her "coronation as a Witch Queen and Queen of the Sabbat" during this visit. Typically, the title of Witch Queen is reserved for an individual whose initiates have hived off and started another coven. Perhaps Rosemary was given the title of Queen because she and Raymond were (nominally) in charge of Witch correspondence in North America.

There was another reason for the Bucklands' visit to the Isle of Man. Raymond Buckland seemed to have a genuine affection for both Monique and Scotty Wilson, and they for him. After visiting the Isle of Man, Rosemary seems to have adopted similar feelings. In a letter written on August 4, 1964, just a few weeks after his return to the United States, Raymond writes:

> We can't really express our feelings towards you, but then you probably know them. We keep remembering how fantastically well we all seemed to go together,—it really was amazing.[63]

During their trip to the Isle of Man, Raymond took several photographs depicting Olwen, Loic, and Rowen in various states of witchiness. Among those photos there is one that clearly stands out. Olwen and Rowen are shown standing aside a broom, both skyclad, save for matching bracelets, circlets, and garters on their left legs. Holding a sword and wearing a horned helmet, Loic stands to the left of them, a sly look upon his face (see color photo insert). What's most captivating about the picture is just how joyful everyone seems. Monique Wilson (a figure loathed by many Modern Witches for reasons we will get to later) wears the biggest grin on her face.

---

63. Raymond Buckland, letter to Monique and Scotty Wilson, August 4, 1964.

It's clear in the photographic evidence that these four individuals were deeply in love with Witchcraft during this period.

Many of the witchy photos from this particular trip look as if they might have been taken for more than just the memories; they suggest that someone might have wanted to use them in (possible future) newspaper or magazine articles. Long before Time-Life would professionally capture Witchcraft in the 1970s, Raymond Buckland was doing so by his lonesome in 1964. As the operators of the Museum of Magic and Witchcraft, the Wilsons were getting accustomed to being in the public eye and seemed to like the attention and potential monetary benefits. (In 1965 the Wilsons would pressure the Bucklands into setting up a media tour in the States to talk about Witchcraft. Not surprisingly, given the times, there were few takers.[64])

· · · · · · · ·

Though the initiations undertaken by the Bucklands had all gone off without a hitch, success was not assured. Early in 1964, the Bucklands' first landlord sold the duplex the family lived in, and the new owner, according to Ray, was "antagonistic from the start." Apparently, the new owner was hoping to drive the Bucklands out so that his daughter and her new husband could take over the flat. The new owner's plan to rid himself of the Bucklands found the landlord resorting to tactics expected and unexpected to get rid of his tenants.

The Bucklands' rent nearly doubled when the new owner took over. Raymond refused to pay the increase, beginning what he called "a long battle of wits" with his landlord. Perhaps the most despicable tactic of this new landlord was to turn off the hot water in the Bucklands' apartment. Instead of complaining, Raymond simply went into the basement in the dark of night and turned the hot water on again. The landlord retaliated by removing all the faucet handles on the pipes that ran through the basement, making turning the hot water back on a little more challenging. Undaunted, Ray headed to the basement (again in the middle of the night) with a wrench and restored the hot water. This time his landlord remained in the dark about Ray's handiwork for an extended length of time. Luckily this combative

---

64. Buckland, Raymond, letter to Monique and Scotty Wilson, June 2, 1965.

landlord either was unaware of the Witchcraft going on at the Bucklands' place or was too scared to do anything about it.

A few months after fighting over access to hot water, Raymond Buckland's mother traveled across the pond to visit for several weeks. This led the Bucklands' landlord to suggest that the family was subletting their space, despite this obviously not being true. This was the straw that broke the camel's back (or forced the Witches to pack up their broomstick) and drove the Bucklands to begin seeking a new residence.

Luckily for the Bucklands, the couple's last initiates of 1964, Hu and Herne, turned out to be excellent house-hunters. Hu and Herne encouraged the Bucklands to buy a home in 1964 instead of looking for another place to rent, and guided Raymond and Rosemary through the process of acquiring home ownership. Since the Bucklands had very little in the way of savings, Hu and Herne directed them to a property that had been repossessed by the Veterans Administration and required no down payment. (Witchcraft!) Shortly thereafter, the Bucklands relocated to Brentwood, New York, on Long Island.

Ritual in the Floral Park apartment required the Bucklands to clear their living room most Saturday nights in order to hold a circle. The Brentwood house had a basement that allowed them to set up a dedicated ritual room, complete with carpet, a permanent altar, and candles at the four cardinal points of the circle. The year 1965 wouldn't be quite as prolific in terms of initiations, but at least circle would be easier to set up and tear down. The basement location for ritual also provided an extra degree of privacy. The Bucklands even installed metal shutters on their basement windows to keep out prying eyes.

The move to Brentwood required Raymond to walk two miles to and from the train station in order to reach his job in New York City. The walk kept Ray in good shape, but it did eat up a lot of time and he decided that purchasing a new car was in order. With two children, a mortgage, and not a lot of money, Buckland decided on an unorthodox approach to car ownership: He would buy a used hearse. He reasoned that a used hearse was likely in good condition, with low mileage, and would look a lot like a station wagon with the curtains removed. There's something so cliché and so right about a Witch driving around in a hearse!

Instead of being horrified that their neighbor was driving a hearse, Buckland's neighbors seemed a bit enchanted by it. The family put a used mattress in the back of the hearse and Raymond would take local kids around the block for joy rides. Shortly after buying the car, he picked up his work colleagues for a "hearse warming party," driving from the BOAC (British Overseas Airways Corporation) offices in Manhattan to Long Island. In his memoir, Buckland writes that he passed an actual funeral procession on his way home, surprising mourners who witnessed the arms of his work friends sticking out of the hearse holding champagne glasses.

The hearse was obviously fun to a degree but came with its own set of drawbacks, most notably that it was too long to fit inside the garage. This led to the car being "half in and half out" in the driveway, with the garage door open. The temptation of being able to vandalize such a unique vehicle ended up being too much for the young people of Brentwood, who one night threw a can of green paint on it. A friend helped repair the damage, and Buckland sold the hearse shortly thereafter.

Just a month after moving to Brentwood, Buckland was again sent overseas to London by BOAC for a work trip. He writes that most of his American friends visited Paris when their training was over, but he opted for a different experience: Italy. Much of his motivation for visiting Italy came from his admiration for Gerald Gardner. Gardner wrote about a 1952 visit to Rome in 1954's *Witchcraft Today* and even mentions meeting another Witch in Rome. Witches and ancient Pagan deities? What's not to love!

The most memorable part of Buckland's journey to Rome occurred near Pompeii during a visit to the Villa of the Mysteries, famous for its frescoes depicting a young woman being initiated into a mystery cult. Buckland writes of the experience:

> I rented a buggy and was driven up the orange-tree-lined road to the Villa of Mysteries, in the Street of Tombs. This was set apart from the main town and was where everyone in the country used to go to be initiated into the Dionysian Mysteries.

The main room, or hall, has its walls decorated with frescoes of life-size figures depicting an initiate going through entry into the Orphic Mysteries. What is so interesting to me—as it was to Gerald Gardner—is that the various stages are almost identical to the stages passed through in the initiation into Wica. It shows the same catharsis, the same palingenesis, the same agape, and much more. I took lots of photographs and came away greatly impressed. It had been far more than I had expected, and I had expected a great deal.

· · · · · · · ·

Despite the Bucklands' initial success in finding and initiating new Witches, the couple still played a secondary role to Monique Wilson on the Isle of Man when it came to correspondence. In the early 1960s, anyone interested in Witchcraft, whether in the UK or in the United States, wrote to the museum that Gardner had helped found. This meant that all correspondence went through Wilson, who forwarded letters to the Bucklands and then checked up on them to see if Raymond had been in contact with seekers.

In a letter dated May 24, 1965, Monique expresses a degree of frustration with her American ambassadors:

> Now we know both [of] you have been busy this year, moving out and moving in, but what you done with the correspondence we handed over to you? There are no secrets between us, and there should not be, but when we handed over the American Continent to you last year we did expect more results. We wrote to our contacts telling them that some way or other you would get in touch with them. They have been very patient, but now in trickles comes back the sorry tale that none of them so far have been approached. We did warn you that it was a tough job ... If you can't handle it or don't want to please let me have the letters back....
>
> I do not want to criticize ... but it is nearly a year since these poor people have been waiting.[65]

---

65. Monique Wilson, letter to Rosemary and Raymond Buckland, May 24, 1965.

It's impossible to say if the Bucklands had been neglectful in their duties during the first half of 1965, but with two small boys, a precarious financial situation, and a new house, it feels like correspondence might have rightfully taken a secondary role to other concerns. Initiations in 1965 slowed to a trickle compared to 1964, with only five new initiates being brought into the fold. One of those initiated in 1965 (Thain) was mentioned in the letter quoted above and was initiated two months later.

Theo and Thain, a couple from Kentucky, stayed with the Bucklands that July and over the course of their stay were raised to the third degree.[66] Theo and Thain then became the first Gardnerian Witches outside of the New York area initiated by Raymond and Rosemary (they would also not be the last). Shortly after their initiation, Theo and Thain began their own coven in Louisville, Kentucky, and started a Witchcraft museum there named "The Covenstead." Two of their initiates, Deidre and Modred, would go on to start the magazine *Nemesis*, which later evolved into *The Hidden Path*, a magazine for Gardnerian initiates. Sixty years after Theo and Thain were first initiated, Louisville, Kentucky, remains a hotbed for Gardnerian Witchcraft.

The year 1965 also saw the Bucklands visiting the Isle of Man and the Wilsons for a second consecutive summer. Many outlines of Buckland's life make it appear as if he visited the Wilsons just once or twice and then was left to his own devices when it came to transmitting Gardnerian Witchcraft, but clearly he spent a great deal of time with them. He may have been initiated and elevated rather hastily, but he (and Rosemary) spent a significant amount of time with the Wilsons studying and practicing the Craft.

Samhain season of 1965 would mark the Bucklands' emergence as public Witches in the mainstream media, sort of. Instead of reading about Rosemary Buckland housewife and Raymond Buckland office worker, the readers of New York's newspapers were introduced to Rowen and Robat, High Priestess and High Priest of the Wica. The first of the two articles featuring the Bucklands that Halloween season was published in *Newsday* on October 30.

---

66. In some Craft histories I have seen Thain spelled "Thane." In Buckland's written correspondence he uses the spelling "Thain," so I have chosen to do the same.

The raven-tressed Rowen (Rosemary)

Columnist Mike McGrady's article "Suffolk's Secret Witch" spends a lot of time noting how ordinary Rowen and Robat's existence is. The couple have a "small white house," the lawn is well tended, and of course the couple have "two tow-headed children, scrubbed to a shine." The one exception to this rather ordinary turn of events is the description of Rowen's "raven-tressed" hair—hair so striking that it might inspire poetic verse.[67]

McGrady's article spends very little time on the practice of Witchcraft, though he does dive extensively into the pseudo-history of the Craft that was common in 1965. Robat shares the then popular version of Witch history:

> The Craft has always been an entirely serious religion. It is a religion that has been traced back to Paleolithic times—back to the time when man was a hunter and worshiped a hunting god; he is traditionally pictured as wearing horns or antlers. When agriculture came into being, the goddess came into being. The religion is still tied in closely with nature. It remains a pagan religion and it is a fertility cult; the life force is still worshiped.[68]

---

67. McGrady, "Suffolk's Secret Witch."
68. McGrady, "Suffolk's Secret Witch."

This description of Witchcraft history would be used by Buckland with very little in the way of changes for the next four decades.

The use of the word *pagan* in Raymond Buckland's description of Witchcraft history in the article is worth commenting on. Long before it would become commonplace, Buckland places Wiccan-Witchcraft within the cloak of Paganism. Various individuals have taken credit for first using *Pagan* as an umbrella term for Witchcraft, Druidry, and other magical traditions, but the idea seems more like an organic outgrowth than one person's eureka moment.

The article also curiously quotes Lady Rowen as saying that "we have three covens here and a fourth is being formed. My covens are here, in Kentucky, in Washington and there's still another in Canada."[69] The Kentucky coven is clearly a reference to Theo and Thain, with the Canadian coven a reference to Witches Morag and Ketrin, who would be initiated in 1965 and would go on to start a Gardnerian coven in that country. Like Buckland, Morag had contacted Gerald Gardner in her desire to begin practicing Witchcraft before being directed to Ray and Rosemary. The identities of the High Priest and High Priestess of the Washington coven remain a mystery. Buckland makes no mention of the coven in his memoir, nor of any initiates/potential seekers from Washington State (or the District of Columbia).

McGrady's article also features several pictures of Robat and (especially) Rowen. For a couple still desiring a measure of privacy for their Witchcraft practice, the inclusion of the photographs is especially surprising. Raymond's face never makes the pages of *Newsday*; instead, the back of his head can be seen as he holds a chalice for the symbolic Great Rite—but Rosemary's face is rather clear. In one photograph she appears with her arms crossed, a hint of a smile on her lips, and her long "raven-tressed" hair arranged strategically over her breasts. The only nod to privacy is a small domino mask covering the area above her nose. Anyone who knew Rosemary would have easily been able to tell that she was the Witch in the picture (especially with the smattering of biographical details included in the article).

In his memoir, Buckland comments that he and Rosemary were contacted by Mike McGrady, an odd assertion given that the Bucklands were supposed to be private Witches. In the spirit of Gerald Gardner (who loved publicity),

---

69. McGrady, "Suffolk's Secret Witch."

it's possible that Raymond himself contacted McGrady in an attempt to stir up interest in the Craft in the United States. In the article, Rosemary states that the United States has a "shortage of witches" and that finding High Priestesses is a "major problem."[70] Alternatively, it's possible that McGrady came across the Bucklands through Joseph Kaster at the New School.

While McGrady's article makes some effort to hide the identities of the Bucklands (domino mask notwithstanding), there is less care taken in an article published just one day later in the Long Island Press. Writer Gregory Wynne again uses the names Rowen and Robat, but also provides extra biographical details, such as the ages of the Bucklands and the fact that they both hail from England and arrived in the States four years prior. He also mentions Puck being an eight-year-old initiate of the Witch-cult.[71] (Luckily for the Bucklands, the inclusion of that information had no negative consequences.)

Wynne is much more forthcoming when it comes to what had taken place in the Bucklands' Samhain circle. He mentions the "passing of power from Lady Rowen to Robat" as a highlight of the ritual and how that act signifies how the "man god" will dominate "the next half year."[72] Wynne also mentions that the ritual includes incense and a "strange sounding, pulsating music" that "played an important part in the ceremony."[73] (Aren't you curious what, exactly, the Bucklands chose to play that evening?)

The most striking part of the Long Island Press article is a photo of Raymond and Rosemary in silhouette. Raymond stands straight and tall, the edges of his goatee clearly visible, with Rosemary across from him, presumably meeting his eyes and holding a horned helmet with an ornamental ram in the crown's center. Both Bucklands appear as shadows, and the effect makes them look like graceful cartoons. Despite the attempt to maintain their privacy, the profiles of both Raymond and (especially) Rosemary would have been quite evident to anyone who knew them. Upon first reading the Long Island Press article, I naturally assumed it was the article that outed them as Witches in the New York media.

---

70. McGrady, "Suffolk's Secret Witch."

71. Wynne, "They're Witches, Just Ask 'Em."

72. Wynne, "They're Witches, Just Ask 'Em."

73. Wynne, "They're Witches, Just Ask 'Em." According to Tara, Ray's widow, Ray enjoyed playing Maurice Ravel's Boléro during ritual in the 1960s. Mystery (perhaps) solved!

Raymond Buckland's horned helmet

Despite it being rather obvious that the Bucklands were the Witches described in both articles, most of their friends and colleagues outside of the Craft remained blissfully unaware. The articles did resonate, though. Buckland himself recounts a humorous anecdote that occurred shortly after the pieces were published:

> There was one amusing incident stemming from the article. Rowen could always be counted on to baby-sit neighbors' children, if needed. One person she had frequently babysat for was a close neighbor named Joyce. In fact, Joyce had come to know of our religious beliefs and practices. When the *Newsday* article appeared, Joyce received a phone call from her sister…The sister said, "Joyce! Have you seen? We have Witches in Long Island!" Joyce immediately retorted, "They're not *your* Witches; they're *our* Witches!"

Exercise 4: To Settle a Disturbed Condition in the Home

Buckland's most successful book in terms of sales and influence is undoubtedly *Buckland's Complete Book of Witchcraft* (also known in the community as the *Big Blue Book* and *Buckland's Big Blue Book*), but coming in a close second might be 1970's *Practical Candleburning Rituals: Spells and Rituals for Every Purpose*. First published in 1970 by Llewellyn (and then revised in 1976 and 1982), *Practical Candleburning Rituals* has continuously been in print longer than any of Buckland's other books and remains a popular magickal title into the present day. (It has sold over half a million copies as of 2022.) Not strictly a Witchcraft book, *Practical Candleburning Rituals* contains two versions of every spell: one for Christians and one for Witches.

The spells in the book for Witches are familiar to most modern-day practitioners of the Craft: Light the candles, picture your reason for the spell clearly, and then raise some energy. The Christian spells are far different, with almost all of them containing passages from the Bible, many of which have little to do with the actual purpose of the spell. Such spells might strike Witches as odd, but spells using the Psalms and other parts of the Bible are commonplace in many types of folk magick.

One of the reasons for the ongoing popularity of *Candleburning Rituals* might be the ambiguity of the spells in its pages. Instead of including one hundred very specific spells, most of the spells are for vague purposes, such as luck, fear, and health. This makes them all quite adaptable, and each spell in the book can potentially be used for a variety of different circumstances.

Despite the popularity of *Candleburning Rituals*, Buckland claims that he wrote it simply to get out of a contractual obligation. Buckland's first title for Llewellyn was *Witchcraft from the Inside* (1970), and in his memoir, Buckland writes that his contract for *Inside*

> called for me to offer my next book also to Llewellyn; a not unusual clause. But I thought to myself, "I don't want to just write for this one publisher! I want to do fiction; novels; which Llewellyn doesn't

do [or didn't at that time]." So I thought I'd do a "quick book" to fulfill that part of the contract, and then make sure there was no such clause in future contracts.

Candleburning Rituals was one of my earliest Witchcraft books,[74] but I'll admit that many of the rituals in the book left me a bit cold. The biggest reason for that is that many of the "practical" rituals in the book require half a dozen candles (or more)! I was a poor college student when I picked up this book, and I often didn't have enough money for two candles, let alone six! However, the last few pages of the book have always stuck with me, and as Buckland's biographer, I think they capture him at his best.

In appendix 2, Buckland writes openly and honestly about what magick can and can't do. He does so in the form of a parable featuring two brothers named Eugene and Carlson. Both brothers desire good jobs, but only one reaches his goal. Carlson refuses several jobs, not wanting any position "beneath" him. This makes his job search long and difficult, and he eventually becomes bitter and is forced to take what he can get. Eugene, on the other hand, takes a low-paying job that provides enough extra money for a used car. Eugene is continually promoted and ends up with a brand-new car and a management position just as Carlson finally begrudgingly takes a job he doesn't want. Magick, to work effectively, requires a realistic end goal. Instead of starting with a new car, perhaps it's best to start with simply a car.

Buckland's time in the 1960s and early '70s was one of constant movement. He went from the UK to the US, and from a non-initiate to one of the most well-known Witches in the United States! He was also forced to move a couple of times, and it's easy for me to imagine him doing several of the spells in *Candleburning* while trying to make sense of these changes and to find just the right situation for himself and his family.

Here is the ritual to settle a disturbed condition in the home from Buckland's *Practical Candleburning Rituals.*[75]

---

74. For the curious, the copy I own is a seventeenth printing of 1982's 3rd edition.
75. Buckland, *Practical Candleburning Rituals*, 24–26.

```
┌─────────────────────────────────────────────┐
│   Altar 1        Figure        Altar 2        │
│                  Censer                        │
│                                                │
│                   Pink                         │
│                 Petitioner                     │
│                                                │
│   Light blue                  Orange           │
│                                                │
│   Book                                         │
└─────────────────────────────────────────────┘
```

To Settle a Disturbed Condition in the Home

Light altar candles 1 and 2.

Light incense.

Sit for a moment and meditate, getting clear in your mind just what you want to accomplish.

Light petitioner's candle, thinking hard on the petitioner. Say:

> This candle represents … (name)….
> As it burns, so burns his/her spirit.

Light the light blue, pink, and orange candles, in that order, thinking of peace and tranquility, of understanding and love in the house in question. Then say:

> Here burns happiness about … (name)…,
> it is in his/her house; it is all about him/her.
> There is tranquility in the home.
> Peace and love abound and are with him/her.
> For true happiness now is known.
> Understanding and love are there in abundance;
> discord and chaos are fled.
> For be it ever thus, that as patience and
> love do grow and prosper so barren become
> the fields of doubt and distress.

> *Happiness is the light that burns and*
> *darkness all away is sent.*
> *The home is peace; peace is the home.*

Sit then for three to five minutes concentrating on settling the disturbed condition in the home. Then say again:

> *Here burns happiness about… (name)… ,*
> *it is in his/her house; it is all about him/her.*
> *There is tranquility in the home.*
> *Peace and love abound and are with him/her.*
> *For true happiness now is known.*
> *Understanding and love are there in abundance;*
> *discord and chaos are fled.*
> *For be it ever thus, that as patience and*
> *love do grow and prosper so barren become*
> *the fields of doubt and distress.*
> *Happiness is the light that burns and*
> *darkness all away is sent.*
> *The home is peace; peace is the home.*

Again sit for three to five minutes concentrating on settling the disturbed condition in the home. Then, for the third time, say:

> *Here burns happiness about… (name)… ,*
> *it is in his/her house; it is all about him/her.*
> *There is tranquility in the home.*
> *Peace and love abound and are with him/her.*
> *For true happiness now is known.*
> *Understanding and love are there in abundance;*
> *discord and chaos are fled.*
> *For be it ever thus, that as patience and*
> *love do grow and prosper so barren become*
> *the fields of doubt and distress.*
> *Happiness is the light that burns and*

> *darkness all away is sent.*
> *The home is peace; peace is the home.*

Again sit for three to five minutes concentrating on settling the disturbed condition in the home.

Then extinguish the candles.

This ritual should be repeated on three consecutive nights.

Chapter Five
Public Witchcraft

If the 1965 Samhain articles in *Newsday* and the *Long Island Press* nearly outed Raymond and Rosemary publicly as Witches, 1966 would accelerate the process, and by the end of the decade the name Raymond Buckland would become synonymous with Witchcraft in the United States. Despite being somewhat concerned about being identified publicly as Witches, the couple agreed to take part in a documentary film in March of 1966.

According to Ray's memoir, he and Rosemary became friends with two independent filmmakers in New York City. Those filmmakers were looking to make an "anthology" film about the unexplained, featuring the Bermuda Triangle and Adolf Hitler's occult leanings and then culminating in a segment on Witchcraft that would feature Rosemary, Ray, and their coven engaged in ritual. The ritual was recorded in the Bucklands' basement and no legal names were used, but anyone running across the segment would have most certainly recognized the Bucklands. Sadly, no trace of this film can be found today, though Ray says in his memoir that the film used to show up occasionally on late-night New York television.

Buckland's reasoning for being on film was one of duty:

I had agreed to do this as part of what I had taken upon myself as my responsibility to the Craft and to the memory of Gerald Gardner. I had decided to dedicate myself to straightening the many misconceptions about Witchcraft. This documentary I saw as part of that mission.

Perhaps the best thing to come out of 1966's movie venture was a friendship with the film's producers. Those producers lived with a pet chimpanzee, an arrangement that fascinated Ray. After taking notice of their friend's interest in their chimp, the Bucklands' producer friends presented Rosemary and Ray with a Capuchin monkey to take home. (Capuchin monkeys are native to Central and South America and are most familiar to English-speaking audiences as "organ grinder" monkeys.) Raymond promptly named the new monkey Willy Warlock and drove back to Brentwood with the monkey sitting on his shoulder and holding onto his head. A cage for the monkey was quickly fashioned by fastening chicken wire over a dresser with the drawers removed. A coven member helped to fashion a larger cage for Willy, but his stay with the Bucklands was brief, and within three years Willy was living in New Jersey with several other monkeys. A member of the New York Coven had a neighbor whose basement has been turned into a dedicated monkey playground, which allowed Willy to live happily and cage-free.

· · · · · · · ·

The majority of Raymond and Rosemary's initiates either did great things in the Craft or disappeared into the ether after initiation. But one of their early initiates turned out to be quite problematic. Mary Nesnick (magickal name Dionysia) is not a name uttered with great frequency in Witchcraft circles today, but not for a lack of trying on Nesnick's part.[76] There had been red flags from the start, but the Bucklands proceeded with the initiation anyway. Buckland writes in his memoir:

> When we first met her she'd claimed that she owned a flower shop in lower Manhattan. I guess she didn't realize that I would do some checking, as I did with all would-be initiates. I found that although she had indeed worked at the shop very briefly over one Christmas period, she certainly did not own it and was only an occasional customer there. However, I said nothing to her about it. (She kept up the pretense of ownership for as long as we knew her.)

---

76. Grimassi, *Encyclopedia of Wicca and Witchcraft*, 7.

Initiated in October of 1966, Nesnick stuck around long enough to nick parts of the Book of Shadows that she (most likely) had not been explicitly granted access to. (Buckland is quite adamant that she only obtained the first degree in his coven, despite claims to the contrary from Nesnick.) In those days Books of Shadows were hand-copied, and it's hard to imagine the Bucklands constantly peering over anyone's shoulder to make sure their initiates were on the right page. By 1967 Nesnick had acquired enough material to announce herself as the "Grand High Priestess of the United States and Canada," claiming to be part of a previously unknown Witchcraft tradition.[77] Nesnick was clearly not a "Grand High Priestess," but she was at least creative enough to mix the Gardnerian Craft she had been taught with a bit of Kabbalah to make it a little bit unique.

After proclaiming herself Grand High Priestess of the United States and Canada, Nesnick passed along oathbound information regarding initiation to author Hans Holzer. That material would show up in Holzer's 1969 book *The Truth About Witchcraft.*[78] Her bridges burned in the Gardnerian community, Nesnick wrote to English Witch Alex Sanders (1926–88) in 1970/71 asking if she could change her affiliation to his Alexandrian Tradition. Sanders agreed, and Nesnick was reinitiated as an Alexandrian and helped found the second Alexandrian coven in New York City in 1971.[79]

Hans Holzer in the early 1960s

By all accounts, Nesnick was a rather devoted Alexandrian for a short time and was actively engaged in outreach within that community and with seekers.[80] (To her credit, she also apparently initiated some very good Witches.) But it was not to last, and in 1972 Nesnick founded the Algard tradition, an alleged mix of Gardnerian and Alexandrian practices.[81] The purpose of this is quite strange, since the Alexandrian Book of Shadows is derived from the Gardnerian BoS.

77. Fitch, *A Grimoire of Shadows*, xl.
78. In Holzer's *The Truth About Witchcraft*, Nesnick is referred to as "Mary N."
79. Kelly, *A Tapestry of Witches*, 109–10.
80. Kelly, *A Tapestry of Witches*, 110.
81. Kelly, *A Tapestry of Witches*, 110.

By 1976 Nesnick claimed to have started over fifty covens in the United State. If that was indeed the case, Nesnick spearheaded something that most likely brought joy and fulfillment to a great many people. But that number seems unlikely, and while writing her book *Drawing Down the* Moon in the mid-1970s, Margot Adler (1946–2014) was unable to find *any* Algard covens.[82] (Today the term Algard still shows up occasionally in lists of Wiccan denominations, but in thirty years I've never met anyone who claims to be a practicing Algard.) Nesnick would not be the last person to use the basics of their Gardnerian training and initiation to start a new Witchcraft tradition in the United States, and in that sense she was a pioneer.

The 1963 novel *Sign of the Labrys* by Margaret St. Clair (1911–95, born Eva Margaret Neely) is not spoken about often in Witchcraft circles, but it's the first fiction book (science fiction or otherwise) to utilize concepts taken directly from the Wiccan-Witchcraft of Gerald Gardner. Born in Kansas, St. Clair spent the majority of her life in California and graduated from the University of California at Berkeley in 1932, the same year she married Eric St. Clair. In 1934 Margaret would graduate from Berkeley with a master's degree in Greek Classics. Both she and her husband shared an interest in ceremonial magick and ancient Pagan religions. They were ready-made for Modern Witchcraft.

Margaret St. Clair in 1946

Sign of the Labrys is an unlikely vehicle for the first American novel (or book, for that matter) with Wiccan themes. Most of the book is set below ground; a terrible bacterium (yeast, in the novel) has killed off 90 percent of the world's population and the majority who remain have moved underground. A lot of the story focuses on getting from one level of the underground cave complex to another. As the main characters move from level to level, it almost feels like the plot of a video game.

In the midst of this rather dystopian novel, St. Clair weaves in magick, psychic abilities, reincarnation, and Witchcraft and specifically uses the word Wicca. (It's worth noting once again that Gardner himself didn't spell Wicca with two c's.) St. Clair uses phrasing that feels directly out of that found

---

82. Adler, *Drawing Down the Moon*, 120.

in initiatory Wicca and even hints that some individuals will have a secret understanding of the ritual secrets she writes about. The phrase "blessed be" is used several times, and one of the central characters carries an athame and another uses a ritual scourge.

Even more surprising is the use of the fivefold kiss in one particularly striking scene. Upon meeting the High Priestess figure, the book's male protagonist says:

> Blessed be my feet … that have brought me in these ways … Blessed be my eyes … that have looked on the Lady.[83]

The Horned God shows up too, as a man "with the head of a stag, with great sweeping horns … entirely naked except for a band of leather just under his right knee."[84] St. Clair writes that this individual was the "lord of the gates of death. And life."[85] Reading St. Clair's prose feels very much like being in ritual.

St. Clair's Witchcraft is also a reincarnation cult, an idea alluded to by Gerald Gardner and others. Scenes that feel like dreams are eventually revealed to be memories, and when the main character objects to the idea, saying "nothing like that has ever happened to me," he's met with the rejoinder "I didn't say *when* it had happened. But it was a memory."[86] The Witch characters also *know* one another from past lives and are related through blood. (The idea of "Witch blood" was a popular one sixty years ago.)

What makes *Sign of the Labrys* even more surprising is that St. Clair was not an initiated Witch in 1963, nor did she know any initiated Witches. Every bit of detail in her book about Wicca comes from the work of Gerald Gardner. Gardner's 1950s books on Witchcraft, *Witchcraft Today* and *The Meaning of Witchcraft*, would have been easy enough for anyone living in a large cosmopolitan area like California's Bay Area to secure in the early 1960s. But *Sign of the Labrys* also utilizes material from Gardner's 1949 fiction novel *High Magic's Aid*, which would have required some serious work (or a trip to the UK) to get hold of.

---

83. St. Clair, *Sign of the Labrys*, 65.
84. St. Clair, *Sign of the Labrys*, 63.
85. St. Clair, *Sign of the Labrys*, 63.
86. St. Clair, *Sign of the Labrys*, 70.

Perhaps the St. Clairs were working with some knowledge of Witchcraft gleaned from a past life. Witch Ed Fitch (more on him soon) recounted visiting their home in 1964 and being struck by a triple circle with a pentagram in the center of it carved into their wood floor. He also remembered a ceremonial sword hanging from their wall.[87] Clearly the St. Clairs were practicing some form of Witchcraft before the arrival of Gardnerian Craft in the United States via Raymond Buckland.

Sometime in 1965 or early 1966, the St. Clairs began corresponding with Buckland, and during this period of time Margaret St. Clair sent a copy of *Sign of the Labrys* to the Bucklands, curious about the Craft details she had gotten right and wrong. Decades later, Ray commented that St. Clair had done a very good job given the materials available to her, except for "having a man initiating a man."[88] Despite the rather positive comments on her work after the fact, St. Clair was apparently chided back in the mid-'60s for "giving away too much," though Buckland would recommend *Sign of the Labrys* in his 1970 book *Witchcraft from the Inside*.[89]

Buckland described the St. Clairs as a "dear sweet couple" and "warm and loving," and it's not surprising that the St. Clairs and the Bucklands struck up a friendship. That friendship, and the St. Clairs' interest in the Craft, led to Rosemary and Raymond flying to Northern California and initiating Margaret and Eric on April 15, 1966, with the St. Clairs taking the Craft names Froniga and Wayland. A little over a year later, in June of 1966, the couple was elevated to the third degree.

Sadly, the St. Clairs never did start their own Gardnerian coven on the West Coast, but they became involved in the Bay Area's magical community and continued to practice Witchcraft. As a Bay Area resident myself, I've talked with individuals who knew the St. Clairs, and, like Buckland, those individuals had nothing but praise for Margaret and Eric. The St. Clairs continued to stay in touch with the Bucklands; the crown worn by Rosemary Buckland in *Witchcraft from the Inside* was made by Eric St. Clair.

I can't help but wonder what might have been if the St. Clairs had initiated other Witches, but thanks to *Sign of the Labrys*, thousands were likely

---

87. Clifton, *Her Hidden Children*, 17–18.
88. Clifton, *Her Hidden Children*, 17.
89. Clifton, *Her Hidden Children*, 16.

introduced to Wicca for the first time in the pages of a dystopian sci-fi novel about yeast. Certainly the Bucklands could spot talented Witches, and one of their next initiates would not just introduce thousands to Witchcraft but also change how people found the Craft. His name was Ed Fitch, and he became one of the most important people in the spread of Wiccan-Witchcraft in the United States.

Fitch (1937–2024)[90] found the Bucklands through the St. Clairs. Having long been interested in the occult, Fitch wrote Margaret St. Clair in care of her publisher after reading *Sign of the Labrys*. Over the course of several letters, a true friendship developed, with Fitch visiting the couple in California in 1964. Fitch visited the St. Clairs in between enlistments in the United States Air Force.[91] A graduate of the Virginia Military Institute, Fitch's first run in the air force lasted three years and took him as far afield as Japan.

When Fitch reenlisted in 1967, he was initially stationed in Massachusetts and found the Bucklands through the St. Clairs, who had been initiated the previous year. In Chas Clifton's *Her Hidden Children*, Fitch recounts his initial interactions with the Bucklands:

> They [the St. Clairs] sent a report on me to the Bucklands and said that I was a good material for the Gardnerian Craft. I got a letter from Rosemary, and as soon as I got settled in at the air base, I contacted the Bucklands, went down [to Long Island] to pay them a visit and we were friends instantly.[92]

Fitch didn't have to wait long to be initiated after meeting the Bucklands. He was initiated the same year as their first meeting in August of 1967. Fitch was initiated alongside a then girlfriend, taking the magickal names Ea and Jonvieve, respectively. Fitch spent some of his second enlistment in the United States traveling around the country. During that time he worked for the Bucklands, checking in on various initiates and vetting potential future Witches. Buckland had a great deal of praise for Fitch during this period:

---

90. Sadly, Fitch passed away during the writing of this book in February of 2024.
91. Clifton, *Her Hidden Children*, 18.
92. Clifton, *Her Hidden Children*, 18.

[Fitch's] work involved him traveling about the country and so he became Rowen's "Red Garters." In the Middle Ages, when Witches were having to keep a low profile, the Witch Queen would send out word to her various covens by messenger. So that he would be recognized as bringing word from the Queen, he would wear red garters, and so the position became known as "Red Garters." Ed took on this position (though without the garters!), visiting those who had contacted us but were too far distant to come and visit. He would visit them and then send a report to Rowen and myself. Ea's reports were always very lengthy, with full details, which we very much appreciated. He did a tremendous service.

There is also a note of disapproval regarding Fitch in Buckland's memoir. In that work, Buckland remarks that Fitch performed an initiation "without authority (either from Rowen or by degree)." That initiation was of Donna Cole Schultz (1937–2004, generally known as Donna Cole in Witch circles), a remarkable woman from Chicago who was not only one of America's first Gardnerian Priestesses but also one of the founders of the eclectic Temple of the Pagan Way. According to Cole, Fitch was the High Priest who initially raised her to the third degree, after she had been elevated to the second degree in England by Witches Madge Worthington (1913–2005) and her High Priest, Arthur, themselves initiates of Priestess Rae Bone (1910–2001), one of Gardner's High Priestesses.

If Fitch's only contribution to the Craft had been initiating Donna Cole, then he would still be worthy of mention in this book, but Fitch changed initiatory Witchcraft forever with the introduction of what has come to be known as an Outer Court. Visiting the Bucklands in 1967 shortly after his initiation into the Craft, Fitch found both Ray and Rosemary sullen and angry. Their anger that day was the result of Mary Nesnick's violation of her secrecy oaths and her public sharing of oathbound material. Attempting to improve a bad situation, Fitch brought up the idea of the "Outer Court," a concept Fitch borrowed from English occultist Dion Fortune.

An Outer Court serves as a training ground for individuals interested in an initiatory path, but one that doesn't reveal any secrets or require an initiation. A Gardnerian Outer Court allows a potential initiate the chance to experience Witch ritual without partaking in materials from the Gardnerian Book of Shadows. In Gardnerian parlance, Outer Court rituals are referred to as Pagan Rituals (which is why Donna Cole's tradition was known as the Temple of the Pagan Way), and participants are often called Pagans.

Curiously, Fitch told the Bucklands that he had already started work on the Outer Court idea. This wasn't true, but over the next few months, Fitch would eagerly take up the work. Most histories of the Craft state that Fitch wrote the majority of what would come to be known as *The Outer Court Book of Shadows* and *The Grimoire of Shadows* (later commercially published as *A Grimoire of Shadows* in 1996 by Llewellyn) while stationed overseas in Thailand in 1968, but according to Fitch, he began the work in Massachusetts, where he was initially stationed in the air force. During his writing of the material, he also consulted frequently with Raymond and Rosemary, who told Fitch "what would be usable and what wouldn't."[93] The Bucklands didn't come up with the Outer Court concept or the initial materials used in creating an Outer Court, but they helped shape the idea and the liturgy involved.

When reading books on Wiccan history, the approval and editing of Ray and Rosemary is often left out. In the run-up to this book, most accounts of the development of the Outer Court suggest either that the entire process was exclusively the domain of Ed Fitch or that Ed Fitch and some of Buckland's later initiates were the primary architects of the concept and the execution of it. As important as I believe the development of the Outer Court idea to be, and given that this is a biography of Raymond Buckland, it's important to note that Ray most certainly played a role in the development of the Outer Court. I would argue that without the implicit approval of Raymond and Rosemary Buckland, it would have been several more years before the development and implementation of the Outer Court in initiatory groups.

The material assembled by Fitch for his two volumes might be the first ever Wicca 101 books to be circulated by a wide range of people. Drawing upon Greek and Celtic myth, along with more contemporary sources such as Robert Graves's *The White Goddess* and James Frazer's *The Golden Bough*, Fitch's work is a crash course in Wiccan-Witchcraft. His works contain a lot of ideas found in Gardnerian Witchcraft but none of the words, deity names,

---

93. Fitch, *A Grimoire of Shadows*, xiii.

or ritual practices that make it truly unique. For uninitiated Witches, the materials in Fitch's Outer Court materials probably look more like the Wicca they know than a Gardnerian Book of Shadows!

Fitch had originally envisioned his Outer Court material as something that would be readily passed on to whoever might be interested. But because the material contained its own set of initiation rituals, it was often thought of as something demanding secrecy. In the introduction to the 1996 edition of *A Grimoire of Shadows*, Fitch laments that his words often ended up in "wall safes, behind hidden panels, or into strong steel boxes."[94] The lack of distribution for the original Outer Court material led Fitch to create an entirely new second set of rituals (with Donna Cole and others) that could be easily shared. This material became known as the Pagan Way and is still in circulation today. Most of the Pagan Way material was published in 1978 as *A Book of Pagan Rituals*, with Herman Slater (1938–92), the then owner of the Magical Childe Witchcraft shop in New York City, listed as the author. Fitch also published even more rituals in his periodical *The Crystal Well*. A collection of that material was published as *Magical Rites from the Crystal Well* in 1984.

Eventually Fitch's material traveled outside Gardnerian covens, too, and found its way into the practice of various Witches across the globe. In many cases it was treated as an authoritative text, and covens sprang up that simply used Fitch's material, never realizing it was simply meant to be a gateway into the Gardnerian tradition. Years after the material was released, Fitch recalled instances where he would find someone else reading his words during ritual, with the individuals doing the reading unaware that the author of the materials they were using was standing in the circle with them.[95]

As we have seen previously, many initiatory forms of Witchcraft adhere to (or at least pay lip service to) the idea of "a year and a day," in which prospective initiates are required to wait a year before being initiated. The idea of a year and a day is often bandied about as something of a requirement by many initiates, but the earliest modern Witches certainly didn't adhere to it. Raymond Buckland was initiated within ten months of beginning his correspondence with Monique Wilson. Rosemary Buckland was initiated a few

---

94. Fitch, *A Grimoire of Shadows*, xiv.
95. Fitch, *A Grimoire of Shadows*, xvi.

days after her husband returned from Scotland in 1963. Buckland's earliest initiates had to wait all of a month after the New York Coven was formed. Certainly there were extenuating circumstances in these early cases, but we see the lack of hesitation to initiate in other examples.

Ed Fitch met the Bucklands in 1967 and was initiated in 1967. He was trusted enough by Rowen and Robat to begin work on what would become the Outer Court materials shortly after his initiation. I mentioned earlier that there had been many critics of the Bucklands who suggested they did not initiate enough people and were too cautious, but were they? It certainly doesn't feel like it, and besides, they were just two people. Realistically, how many people can two individuals initiate in a year, all while raising two children, working full-time, and seeing to their own personal needs, both mundane and magickal?

It wasn't until the development of the Outer Court materials that ideas such as "a year and a day" suddenly went from theoretical to practical. Imagine being interested in Witchcraft and then being told there's not much to be done about it, but here are some Gerald Gardner books that will probably take you all of two weeks to read. The development of the Outer Court provided a door into the world of Witchcraft and, better yet, kept people interested in it! With an Outer Court, a prospective initiate can start doing things that look and feel like Wicca right away.

The Outer Court concept also allows for better vetting of potential initiates. You can have people over for as many study sessions and cups of tea as you like, but there's no substitute for actually getting in a circle with someone and participating in ritual. A participatory training program also takes the pressure off potential initiators, as with prospective initiates participating in actual magickal activities, there's less immediate need to initiate them as soon as possible. The Outer Court has become a tremendous asset to initiating traditions, and Ed Fitch's early "open source" material has been providing inspiration to Witches and Pagans for over fifty years now.

Buckland credits an article about the New York Coven by reporter Lisa Hoffman, "The Witch Next Door," in the *New York Sunday News*, dated October 27, 1968, for outing him and Rosemary as Witches. There is very little contempt in Buckland's memoir, but his passage on Lisa Hoffman suggests a great deal of anger:

We accepted another reporter as a visitor to a Circle. She was Lisa Hoffman, writing for the *New York Sunday News*. She came and seemed a very nice person, assuring us of a sympathetic article and promising not to reveal our names or whereabouts. My hope, after all, was to straighten misconceptions about the Craft but I was not looking to publicize myself. On October 27, 1968, her article appeared. In it she equated the Craft with Ira Levin's novel *Rosemary's Baby*, which was about Satanists not Witches (Witches do not believe in Satan). In her article, she included such innuendo as "... the Old English word wicce which, embarrassingly, is also the root of the English word Wicked." Embarrassing to whom, I wondered? Apparently Hoffman was ignorant of the fact that "wicked" itself comes from "witted", i.e. to have wit; to have knowledge. Both wit and Witch come from wicce meaning "the wise ones." But more to the point, perhaps, was the fact that not only did she give my name and Rosemary's, but she also printed our complete address! So much for journalistic integrity.

I expected the worst upon my first reading of Hoffman's article, but it's hardly the character assassination Raymond remembers it as. Hoffman's attitude toward Witchcraft is insulting and condescending, but she stops herself before calling Rowen and Robat Satanists. In the picture of Rosemary and Raymond accompanying the article, the couple's backs are turned to the camera and their faces are not clearly visible. There are several references in the article to *Rosemary's Baby*, which had been released that year, but *Rosemary's Baby* was a very successful movie and was lodged quite prominently in the public zeitgeist in October of 1968. Hoffman does suggest that the ritual she observed was "eerily similar" to *Rosemary's Baby*, an observance most anyone unfamiliar with Witchcraft would have made.

Though there's a skeptical and cheeky tone to the article, Hoffman does make a point to say that Rowen and Robat are

> white, or good witches, possibly because they believe that whatever a human being does in his life will return to him threefold. Under such circumstances, doing evil is hardly practical.[96]

---

96. Hoffman, "The Witch Next Door."

Hoffman does not include the couple's address in the article, but she does offer up a lot of hints as to the identity of Robat and Rowen:

They have the standard white frame home with a mortgage, two sons of grammar school age, a cat, and two dogs.[97]

Perhaps most tellingly, Hoffman mentions that the couple are from England and residing on the South Shore of Long Island. She also adds that Robat works in a Manhattan office. With these hints, it would be pretty easy to figure out that the Bucklands were practicing Witches.

Hoffman also adds that the "Long Islanders are not Satanists" and separates them from Anton LaVey's Church of Satan in California.[98]

Hoffman's article is also interesting historically because it mentions several Witch-related ideas that had (probably) not previously been written about in American newspapers. The first is *handfasting* (which Hoffman calls a "ponderous sermon"[99]), and she mentions that Rosemary and Raymond had been remarried in a handfasting ceremony. She also suggests that Gerald Gardner had conducted the rite himself (and had initiated both Raymond and Rosemary). Hoffman also includes the line "as long as love shall last" in her two paragraphs on handfasting, a common refrain over fifty years later in Wiccan handfasting ceremonies.

Quoting from the Bucklands' Book of Shadows, Hoffman also includes the opening line of Doreen Valiente's *Charge of the Goddess*:

Once in the month, and better it be when the moon is full, gather in some secret place and adore me who am the Queen of all the Witcheries.[100]

This might be the first time that any of Valiente's *Charge*, Witchcraft's best-known piece of liturgy, had been printed in an American periodical or book.

Buckland writes that the aftermath of the Hoffman article presented several difficulties, but it also presented a new opportunity:

---

97. Hoffman, "The Witch Next Door."
98. Hoffman, "The Witch Next Door."
99. Hoffman, "The Witch Next Door."
100. Hoffman, "The Witch Next Door."

During the ensuing weeks after Hoffman's article appeared, we were plagued with unwelcome visitors. One day I arrived home from work to find about twenty or thirty teenagers standing in the road outside, just looking at the house. We had rocks thrown through our windows. We had the front door and screen kicked in. We had a car set on fire. We—my wife and children especially—suffered verbal abuse whenever they went out, all thanks to Ms. Hoffman. One day a group of teenagers was passing the house, walking slowly and singing the latest popular song: "Ding dong, the witch is dead!" It was actually rather amusing. I think they were a little surprised when I opened the door and loudly played that very song on our stereo.

However, Hoffman's cavalier attitude did actually have one positive aspect to it. Now that the cat was out of the bag—or the Witch was out of the broom closet—it meant that I would be able to do far more, for I still believed that it was a duty to persevere with trying to straighten the misconceptions. So now I could do television and radio, and magazine and newspaper articles, without having to worry about my name being given since it was already out there.

The emergence of the Bucklands from the proverbial broom closet was certainly hastened by allowing newspaper coverage of their activities, but Raymond also took steps to accelerate the process. His most noticeable action was establishing a Witchcraft museum in his basement in 1966. (Owning books on Witchcraft and Witchcraft paraphernalia doesn't necessarily make someone a Witch, but it probably does make the neighbors wonder if the people next door are Witches.) The process started innocently enough. Buckland simply started displaying his Witchcraft paraphernalia in front of the books on his bookshelf. Eventually he grew frustrated with having to move the Witchcraft items to get to his books, so he bought a series of bookshelves and display cases to house his Witchcraft collection.

Buckland eventually began letting friends and neighbors view his collection, and when word got out, this was extended to school groups, Boy Scout troops, and other assorted clubs and societies. The collection was eventually named the Buckland Museum of Witchcraft and Magick, and the museum would play a large role in his life for just over the next ten years. Many of the items from the original incarnation of the Buckland Museum can still be seen today in Cleveland, Ohio, the current home of the museum (more on this later).

If you've ever seen pictures of Raymond and Rosemary from the late 1960s, you're already familiar with many of the items that made up the initial collection in the museum. There was the famous horned helmet worn by Raymond in a variety of pictures, along with his athame and wand. There were also items on display once owned by Gerald Gardner.

The museum itself might have been started as an homage to Gardner. Gardner had been the proprietor of his own Witchcraft museum on the Isle of Man, originally with partner Cecil Williamson and then eventually on his own. Monique Wilson was made the caretaker and owner of the museum's contents after Gardner's death and ended up running the museum when Gardner's caretaker passed on the opportunity,[101] and the Bucklands were annual visitors to the museum for several years, assisting Monique and Scotty with running the enterprise in addition to the social nature of their visits.

Some of Ray's magickal tools, including the cuff worn by Rosemary Buckland

---

101. Heselton, *Witchfather, Volume 2*, 632.

In his memoir, Buckland claims that the Gardner-related items in the museum were "given to me by Gerald himself," which seems doubtful. If Gardner and Buckland did meet face-to-face, that meeting was brief and took place far from the museum. It's much more likely that Monique Wilson gave Buckland some of Gardner's effects on one of the Bucklands' trips to the Isle of Man. Wilson certainly had the authority to do so. There is also a cuff at the museum that Buckland claims was made by himself and Gardner for Rosemary,[102] which again seems unlikely. It's far more likely that the cuff was made with the Wilsons.

Taking another cue from Gardner, Buckland got into the Witchcraft writing business in 1966 with *Witchcraft … the Religion*, a small booklet outlining many of Buckland's ideas about Witchcraft. *Witchcraft … the Religion* would include several ideas that formed the backbone of Buckland's subsequent writings on the Craft and would be repeated in many of his best-known works. Many of those ideas feel antiquated today, as Witchcraft has changed over the decades, but they were pretty common into the 1990s.

The first of those ideas, not surprisingly, was that Witchcraft was a religion. Today it's quite common to think of Witchcraft as a magical practice separate from religion, but Witchcraft (especially the Wiccan-Witchcraft practiced by the Bucklands) as a religious tradition was a commonplace idea in the Craft until fairly recently. In Buckland's worldview, magickal practice was certainly open to anyone (and books like *Practical Candleburning Rituals* contain both Christian and Pagan spells), but due to the religious nature of Witchcraft, it was all but impossible to be a Witch and a practitioner of an alternate religion.

Borrowing a page from Margaret Murray and later Gerald Gardner, Witchcraft was also the "Old Religion," a pre-Christian faith venerating a Goddess and a God and honoring the seasons. The period that today we call the Witch Trials was the last gasp of a public Witchcraft religion, with the persecutions of that time period forcing the Craft to go underground until it could reemerge in the middle of the twentieth century. Today there is a great deal of evidence arguing against religious Witchcraft as the "Old Religion" (and certainly Buckland would have been exposed to some of it in the years

---

102. A cuff is a metal bracelet worn on the upper arm, traditionally given to High Priestesses in initiatory Craft traditions.

before his death), but the acceptance of Murray and the idea of the "Old Religion" would continue to show up in his later works.

For example, 2004's *Wicca for One* continues Buckland's strong defense of and advocation for Murray's religious Witchcraft argument. Acknowledging that Murray was a "controversial figure," Buckland goes on to write that "much of what she uncovered … was valid," adding that many of her detractors "are nowhere near as qualified as she was herself," despite many of those detractors having history degrees and specializing in subjects directly related to Witchcraft.[103] I don't believe Buckland was ever intentionally trying to mislead people with rather sketchy history. For much of his writing career, he was simply sharing what was believed at the time. And later in life, it's easy to imagine him having trouble giving up a cherished idea.

Buckland was also adamant about drawing stark lines between Witchcraft and Satanism. The Horned God, in Buckland's worldview, had nothing to do with the Christian Devil, despite many Witches finding inspiration in the folkloric Devil over the decades. (The Devil of folklore has traditionally been a giver of gifts and self-empowerment and less the source of all evil in the world.) Certainly in 1966 it was a smart PR move to disavow any connection between Satanism, the Devil, and Witchcraft.

For the low, low price of one dollar, museum patrons could take home one of the first ever self-published works on Witchcraft in the United States. Despite Buckland blaming Lisa Hoffman for his emergence from the broom closet, Buckland had sold *Witchcraft … the Religion* to his coworkers at British Airways two years before Hoffman's *Sunday News* article, which hardly seems like a good idea if one is trying to hide the fact that they are a Witch! I think it's safe to say that Buckland's emergence as a public Witch had a lot to do with the museum.

Witchcraft … the Religion had a very interesting second life away from Buckland's Witchcraft Museum. In 1969 Buckland's pamphlet was reprinted in the magazine *Popular Medicine*. If an article about Witchcraft and a medical magazine feel like an odd fit, don't worry. *Popular Medicine* was just as much of a tabloid as it was a medical magazine. When going through the archives of *Popular Medicine*, one is more likely to come across articles dealing

---

103. Buckland, *Wicca for One*, 18.

with sex than physical health. Cover stories include "Sex Life of the Modern Teenager" and "The Lonely Sex" and "Natural Sex Stimulants for Men." In one issue of the magazine, twelve articles are listed on the cover, eight of which are about sex and/or relationships. A sex-positive religion practiced in the nude was right up *Popular Medicine*'s alley.

After being approached about reprinting *Witchcraft...the Religion*, Buckland was even kind enough to include a couple of photographs. Unfortunately, *Popular Medicine* made a mockery of Buckland's pamphlet. While the contents of *Religion* were printed in full, without editorial adornment, editor Carlson Wade decided to sensationalize and mischaracterize Buckland's work. A subtitle was added to the work calling Raymond a "Satan Church leader in New York. He worships the Devil and tells why he and his many followers believe in Satan worship." Of course, the contents of the article argue just the opposite.

Although Buckland included captions for the pictures he provided for *Popular Medicine*, they ended up being replaced by those of an editor. The Book of Shadows became the "Official Satan Bible," and a ritual photograph included the text "A salute to Satan—this ceremony commences the worship service of the Devil followers of this New York Church of Satan." Buckland requested a retraction and an apology from the publisher, but unsurprisingly was met with silence.

Popular Medicine was not quite through with the indignities, and in 1970 *Witchcraft...the Religion* was included in an anthology titled *Tales from the Unknown*, edited by Kurt Singer, printed first in the UK and then a year later in the United States. *Tales* is a random collection of ghost stories, tales of the unexplained, and Buckland's booklet. Apparently, *Popular Medicine* had licensed Buckland's work to the English publisher (W. H. Allen) despite the magazine not owning the copyright. The notes about the New York Coven engaging in Satanic activity were included in the book edition, too, this time as footnotes. Hopefully most people who encountered *Witchcraft...the Religion* in magazine and book form read more than the captions and the footnotes!

• • • • • • • •

The Bucklands showing up in the pages of a New York newspaper in 1964 was a pretty big deal, but modern Witches had shown up on American televisions even earlier. On April 13, 1964, America met its first self-identified Witch on the television game show *To Tell the Truth*. The show begins with three middle-aged women cloaked in shadows and wearing capes. The show's announcer then reads Shakespeare's famous lines about Witches from the play *Macbeth*, "Double double toil and trouble, fire burn and cauldron bubble," before adding the zinger "One of these ladies is a Witch!" The announcer then asks the three caped ladies for their names, with all responding, "My name is Sybil Leek!" And with those words, the game begins with host Bud Collyer (1908–69 and the voice of Superman on the radio in the 1940s) and a celebrity panel whose job it is to figure out which of the three women is the real Sybil Leek.

Sybil Leek

Though often overlooked today, Sybil Leek (1917–82) was one of the biggest names in the modern Witchcraft revival back in the 1960s and '70s. And if Leek's 1966 memoir is to be believed, she also lived one of the most incredible lives in human history. When she was a child, not only was science fiction writer H. G. Wells a frequent visitor to her household, but so was English occultist Aleister Crowley. According to Leek, Crowley once cupped his hands around her face and proclaimed, "This is the one who will take up where I leave off,"[104] suggesting that Crowley believed Leek would inherit leadership of the Witchcraft world after his demise (despite Crowley not being an actual Witch!). Later in her memoir, Leek writes of marrying a famous (unnamed) concert pianist, being initiated into a group of French Witches, studying with the Romani, and becoming a widow at the age of eighteen.

Most of the more outlandish claims in Leek's memoir are clearly mistruths or exaggerations, but Leek is the only Witch I'm aware of who was a star on both sides of the Atlantic in Witchcraft's early years. Leek was born in the Midlands in England in 1923 but didn't become a public Witch until

---

104. Leek, *Diary of a Witch*, 31.

1962. Extremely media savvy (Leek had worked both in print journalism and for a TV station), Leek became one of the UK's most well-known Witches in short order. Described by Ronald Hutton as a "jolly, dark-haired woman,"[105] Leek's face seemed to always be stuck in a perpetual grin. Pictures of Leek from the 1960s most often feature her wearing a cape, with her jackdaw, Hotfoot Jackson, perched upon her shoulder.

Despite her effervescent nature, Leek was forced out of her prominent spot in the UK's Witchcraft world in 1964 for being too close to a wave of vandalism inflicted upon English churches. Despite condemning the vandalism, Leek claimed that chalk symbols accompanying the vandalism were dedicated to her,[106] and that was enough to make her *persona non grata* in English Witch circles. But Leek took her banishment in stride, packed her bags, and emigrated to the United States.

Like many other Gardnerian Witches of the time, the Bucklands' attitude toward both Leek and anyone else who claimed to be a Witch without a Gardnerian initiation was dismissive. In a letter to the Wilsons, Buckland mentions Alex Sanders (1926–88), who would go on to become the founder of the Alexandrian tradition with his then wife Maxine, calling him a "male Sybil Leek!!!"[107] Mentions of Leek herself would show up in several letters from the Bucklands to the Wilsons. In a letter dated June 4, 1966, Buckland is both suspicious and dismissive of Leek:

> Afraid Sybil Leek is still flaunting herself on television and in the press here. Her claims range from being the only practicing witch in Britain (!) to being Queen of all the Witches! I don't quite see how she can have it both ways! There is an unpleasant rumour to the effect that she will be returning here towards the end of the year to live permanently.[108]

Raymond and Rosemary Buckland made their first television appearance on the *Alan Burke Show* on May 5, 1967, just a little more than three years after Leek's appearance on *To Tell the Truth*. About five weeks later, Ray was once

---

105. Hutton, *The Triumph of the Moon*, 308.

106. Hutton, *The Triumph of the Moon*, 323.

107. Raymond Buckland, letter to Monique and Scotty (and Yvette) Wilson, February 4, 1966.

108. Raymond Buckland, letter to Monique and Scotty Wilson, June 4, 1964.

again a guest on the *Alan Burke Show*, but this time he was joined by none other than Sybil Leek. In his memoir, Buckland suggests that this was his first run-in with Leek, but in a letter to the Wilsons in December of 1966, Rosemary recounts that Robat "shot her [Leek] down" on television, suggesting that Ray might have been a guest-caller on a call-in television show featuring Leek.[109] (One can only dream of finding the videotape!) Rosemary wrote that Ray's barbs at Leek led to Leek being "hard up" and forced to cast horoscopes for the low price of just one dollar per chart.[110]

Despite the possible past altercation, Leek and Buckland opened the show with a hug, but Ray soon took to the offensive, asking Leek about her many outlandish claims, often with direct quotes. Echoing modern politicians, Leek often responded by claiming she had been misquoted. In Buckland's 1970 book *Witchcraft from the Inside*, he devotes three pages to the various claims made by Leek during the period. He concludes his allegations against Leek by writing that

> it must be said that this woman has said so much nonsense about the Craft; has contradicted herself so frequently, that it is amazing that she is still taken seriously by anyone.[111]

Despite his initial dislike of Leek, Buckland writes in his memoir that "Sybil was indeed a character and she did a lot of good for the Craft, introducing many people to it." And Leek herself didn't suffer any lasting damage from her disagreements with the Bucklands. During her time in the United States, Leek wrote over sixty books, published a magazine with her name on it (*Sybil Leek's Astrology*), and had a nationally syndicated astrology column. After moving to New York, Leek later set up shop in Los Angeles, Texas, and finally Florida, where she passed away from cancer in 1983. Forty-plus years after her death, there are still covens in the United States that can trace their lineage to Sybil Leek.

Though Sybil Leek beat Buckland to television by several years, by the end of the 1960s Raymond had established himself as a frequent presence on both the radio and television airwaves. He also showed up increasingly

---

109. Rosemary Buckland, letter to Monique and Scotty Wilson, December 5, 1966.
110. Rosemary Buckland, letter to Monique and Scotty Wilson, December 5, 1966.
111. Buckland, *Witchcraft from the Inside*, 81–82.

in print, often internationally, and by 1969 had been in newspapers in both Germany and Australia. Buckland sometimes showed up in unexpected places, too, like the pages of *Weight Watchers* magazine. Witchcraft can be used to solve a variety of problems!

• • • • • • • •

First published in 1969 by Doubleday and then as a mass-market paperback in 1971 by Pocket Books, Hans Holzer's (1920–2009) *The Truth About Witchcraft* was one of the first widely available Witchcraft books written by a non-Witch in the United States. Because Holzer was not bound by any oaths of secrecy (unlike most initiated Witches of the period), many of his Witchcraft-related books are more enlightening than those written by actual Witches. In a career that spanned forty-five-years, Holzer wrote nearly a dozen Witchcraft-related books and over a hundred books dealing with UFOs, ghosts, and ESP. As one of the most prominent Witches in the United States, Raymond Buckland features prominently in both *The Truth About Witchcraft* and several of Holzer's later works.

While far from flattering, Holzer's work does paint a vivid picture of the Bucklands in the late 1960s, and hints at the various tensions among US Witches at the time of publication of *The Truth About Witchcraft*. Holzer's descriptions of Raymond and Rosemary come from personal interaction, along with the recollections of Mary Nesnick (discussed previously), whom Buckland had apparently sent to Holzer because of the latter's experience with ESP. Once Holzer made the acquaintance of Nesnick, he moved quickly from ESP to Witchcraft. In *Truth*, Holzer describes himself as "sneaky" in his efforts to get Nesnick to talk about the Bucklands.[112]

Or perhaps that last name was not Buckland, but Bockland, at least according to Holzer. Despite Raymond having introduced Nesnick to Holzer, Holzer chose to spell "Buckland" as "Bockland" in his work. A one-time mistake in the book's original printing would be understandable, but the fact that "Bockland" was never corrected in subsequent editions suggests something a bit more disrespectful. In another odd passage, Holzer refers to Rosemary Buckland as "Mrs. Ray (he calls her Rosemary)."[113] Still, Holzer

---

112. Holzer, *The Truth About Witchcraft*, 86.
113. Holzer, *The Truth About Witchcraft*, 87.

begins his profile of the Bucklands (or is that Bocklands?) by writing that Raymond is a careful ritualist, handsome, and levelheaded. After this rather benign beginning, Holzer writes that Buckland had the belief that "his is the only coven worth knowing in America, while most Witches show more humility toward each other."[114] Certainly in the late 1960s there were tensions between Gardnerian Witches and non-Gardnerian Witches, but Buckland was never the type of person to be completely dismissive of another's religious practice.

The next few pages of Holzer's profile of the Bucklands contain Nesnick's recollections of her initiation ritual (violating her oaths of secrecy) and share her personal grievances against the Bucklands. Nesnick's complaints are especially petty; she expresses disappointment that she wasn't given special treatment and says she was told upon meeting Buckland that she would likely have to wait for at least "a year and a day" before being initiated. Nesnick was also bothered by the idea that the other members of the New York Coven would have to approve of her before she could be initiated. Holzer tries to make this into a bad look for the Bucklands, but if anything, it feels like Raymond and Rosemary are simply trying to be responsible coven leaders.

The fact that Nesnick lays bare the details of Gardnerian initiation suggests that maybe the Bucklands were not cautious enough! In his memoir, Buckland makes a note of this incident and writes that immediately after her initiation, Nesnick "ran off to tell Hans Holzer all the details so he could put them in a book he was working on." Buckland adds that it was "unfortunate" he and Rosemary initiated Nesnick in the first place.

Though Holzer doesn't list the names of any other Witches besides "the Bocklands" and "Mary," he does list the professions of the other members of the New York Coven. Given Buckland's growing media presence by 1969 (though in *Truth* Holzer is writing about Witches from five years previous, back when Nesnick was a coven member), anyone especially interested in just who was in the Bucklands' coven might have been able to figure it out. Holzer lists "a major in the air force, a housewife, a schoolteacher, a college lecturer, a businessman … a hair dresser, a truck driver, another housewife."[115] Holzer's description of the coven makes it sound like a genuine and rather

---

114. Holzer, *The Truth About Witchcraft*, 86.

115. Holzer, *The Truth About Witchcraft*, 90–91.

mundane cross section of America, putting a positive spin on the Craft, but it might also have put good people at risk of having their Witchcraft practice discovered (which would not have been a good idea for many in 1969).

Buckland writes in his memoir that he initially crossed paths with Holzer because Holzer was hoping to attend an esbat or sabbat ritual. Buckland had to inform the author that the answer was no (despite several journalists having sat in on rituals previously), which might be the reason for some of the cattiness in Holzer's writing about the Bucklands. Though Holzer and Buckland apparently reconciled before the former's death in 2009 (Buckland writes that the two became "good friends"), it took several years to reach that point. Holzer was even worse to Raymond in his 1973 book *The Witchcraft Report* (which Ray refers to as "*The Witchcrap Report.*")

Holzer begins this second odd profile of Buckland by emphasizing once again that Raymond and Rosemary were selective about potential coven-mates. Writing about Buckland's Witchcraft Museum, Holzer says that the "museum can be easily seen; it is not so easy to be accepted into Mr. Buckland's coven."[116] By the early 1970s, the idea of potential initiates being forced to wait at least "a year and a day" before initiation was a fairly common one in Witchcraft circles. Why Holzer dwelled on this over the course of several books is an open question.

The most bizarre story in *The Witchcraft Report* involves alleged standards for potential initiates that Holzer describes as "grotesque." According to Holzer, Buckland denied a young man identified as "Gene B. from New Jersey" initiation into the New York Coven because Gene's wedding ring had Hebrew letters engraved on it.[117] That's just not the kind of man Raymond was, and there is nothing in his history to suggest such a thing. Given Buckland's love of the occult, which of course includes the Jewish Kabbalah, a wedding ring with Hebrew characters on it would probably get someone initiated sooner rather than later!

In his memoir, Buckland writes that Gene B. actually was initiated (though he doesn't give a date), making Holzer's story even sillier. Buckland kept a thorough record of all the people he and Rosemary initiated over the years, and there is no Gene on that list; however, Holzer often used alter-

---

116. Holzer, *The Witchcraft Report*, 34.
117. Holzer, *The Witchcraft Report*, 35.

nate names for real people to keep their identity a secret. Hopefully Holzer's descriptions of the Bucklands didn't dissuade too many potential Witches from meeting with the couple!

After appearing in print and on the television airwaves, Raymond decided it was time to write his first book. Witchcraft as the sole book topic would have made a lot of sense, but Buckland chose a broader angle: the occult. Work on what became *A Pocket Guide to the Supernatural* began in 1968 with three sample chapters. Once those were done, Buckland finished up the outline for the rest of the book and sent a book proposal to Ace Books, who quickly offered Ray a contract.

Published as a mass-market paperback, Buckland's first book lived up to its title. It was pocket-sized, but most importantly it contained information about ceremonial magick, mediumship, astrology, Tarot, scrying, hauntings, Witchcraft, and Ouija boards. It was also rather short, clocking in at just 189 pages. In some printings the phrase "Noted Occultist and Lecturer" appears beneath Buckland's name on the front cover. The most striking thing about the cover, from a historical perspective, is the honorific "Dr." appearing before Ray's name on the spine. *A Pocket Guide to the Supernatural* was released in the United States in 1969 and was also available shortly thereafter in Buckland's native Britain, where the book was titled simply *Guide to the Supernatural*. *A Pocket Guide* stayed in print for several years, with printings continuing until at least 1973.

Not surprisingly, Buckland's second book was dedicated solely to Witchcraft. First published in late 1970, with second and third editions in 1975 and 1995, respectively, *Witchcraft from the Inside* began Buckland's nearly fifty-year partnership with Llewellyn Publications (the publishers of this book). Taking a page from Gerald Gardner's approach in 1954's *Witchcraft Today*, Buckland writes about Witchcraft as a scholar, separating himself from the subject to some degree. The references to his museum are the only real evidence that Raymond himself might be a Witch. (My second-edition copy has information about the museum prominently underlined.) Rosemary is simply "Rowen," with no mention of her being the author's wife. A picture of Raymond's famous horned helmet is included in the book, but there's no picture of Ray in action. Instead, the only Witch to appear in photographs is Rosemary (who is unsurprisingly nude, though there's no part of her body showing that would get booksellers from 1970 in trouble).

The first third of *Witchcraft from the Inside* regurgitates the then standard history of Witchcraft as recounted by Margaret Murray and Gerald Gardner. Witchcraft has been practiced for thousands of years, the Horned God and the Great Goddess were the first deities ever worshipped, and anything that looks as if it might have an origin in Pagan antiquity most certainly does. Some of this history is funny in the 2020s, but it was pretty standard stuff in Witchcraft circles circa 1970 (though less so in scholarly ones, but that wasn't the audience Buckland was writing for, despite trying to appear as an unattached observer). There's a noticeable improvement in the book when Buckland begins recounting the last hundred years of magickal history. Here Buckland moves beyond simple retellings of Murray/Gardner and shares one of the earliest accurate histories of the modern Witchcraft movement.

The scope of *Witchcraft from the Inside* is rather limited. By 1970 there were several different varieties of Witchcraft being practiced in the English-speaking world, but Buckland's focus is clearly on the initiatory (Gardnerian) one. A few paragraphs are reserved for withering comments directed at Alex Sanders and Sybil Leek (the loudest non-Gardnerians of the period). Sanders and Leek are not named directly, but anyone familiar with them will instantly pick up on the subtext. For a book so focused on what most today would call Wicca, Buckland never uses the term Wicca to describe the Witch-religion. Witches in Buckland's telling practice a religion called Witchcraft. Sometimes those practitioners are referred to as *the Wica* (again, note the one *c*), but the Wica is a title for a people, not a religion.

Witchcraft from the Inside is largely responsible for the proliferation of what has come to be known as the "Threefold Law" or "Law of Three" in Witchcraft traditions. Buckland writes in *Inside*:

> Mention has been made of the Wica belief in reincarnation…Along with this belief goes another—in retribution in the present life. It is thought that whatever is done returns threefold. If good is done then good will return threefold in the same life; but if evil is done, then that

too will return threefold *in this life*. There is therefore, no inducement for a witch to do any form of evil.[118]

By 1970 Buckland had been sharing something resembling the Threefold Law for a couple of years. In the October 1968 edition of *Beyond* magazine, an article by Raymond tells readers that Witches "believe that whatever we do will return threefold in this life. Do good to someone and you will receive three times as much good in return. But do evil and that too will return triple."[119]

The "threefold rule" is absent from Witchcraft materials pre-Buckland and is probably a misunderstanding on Raymond's part of a sequence in Gerald Gardner's *High Magic's Aid*. In that book, the protagonist, while being initiated, is told, "But mark well when thou receivest good, so equally art bound to return good threefold."[120] Gardner is suggesting that when a good deed is done, the recipient of that deed should share the good energy they've received. That doesn't mean that one has to give away three dollars when one is given a dollar, just that an amount of energy equivalent to three dollars should be shared. Today most of us would call that "paying it forward."

Buckland's interpretation of Gardner's suggestion is completely different, suggesting a cosmic system of rewards and punishments based strictly on behavior. Buckland's Threefold Law was a good public relations move and, judging by its ubiquity in Modern Witchcraft books, a popular idea, but it is rather limiting and has inspired far too many "You can't do that!" types of conversations in the Witchcraft community. Curiously, Buckland completely ignores the Wiccan Rede of "An it harm none, do what you (or ye) will" in *Inside*. It's possible that Buckland was unfamiliar with the Rede, and it's possible that it was never shared with Buckland by the Wilsons. Or perhaps he deemed the Wiccan Rede an "oathbound" rule (despite English Witches having spoken of it publicly since 1964).

By 1994 Buckland would have no doubt been familiar with the Wiccan Rede, but he leaves it out of the third edition of *Witchcraft from the Inside*. Instead, he relates "the one law of Witchcraft: An' it harm none, do what thou

---

118. Buckland, *Witchcraft from the Inside*, 69.
119. Buckland, "I Live with a Witch," 109–10.
120. Gardner, *High Magic's Aid*, 188.

wilt."[121] Here Buckland is clearly combining the Wiccan Rede with English occultist Aleister Crowley's maxim "Do what thou wilt shall be the whole of law" from Crowley's 1909 work *The Book of the Law*. The result is a curious hybrid statement that I've only ever encountered in Buckland's work and is mostly absent from subsequent Witchcraft materials.

While most of *Witchcraft from the Inside* focuses on what would today be labeled "Wiccan-Witchcraft" and related topics (Freemasonry, cunningcraft, ancient Pagan religions), the last chapter in the book is a radical departure. No doubt inspired by Buckland's 1969 trip to Haiti, the book's last chapter is devoted exclusively to Haitian Vodou (often spelled Voodoo in the book). In his memoir, Buckland writes that, while flying into Haiti, he sensed "a tremendous feeling of 'coming home.'" He also adds that if he "hadn't been so involved with Wicca at that time," he might "have become a part of the Vodoun." Here Buckland uses the word Vodoun to refer to a group of individuals within a faith tradition, much like he used the term Wica.

Buckland's interest in Voodoo would crop up in future books and even resulted in a few odd rumors. Back in the 1990s, there were some who claimed that author Ray T. Malbrough was a nom de plume of Raymond Buckland! Malbrough, the author of books such as *The Magical Power of the Saints*, *Hoodoo Mysteries*, and *Charms, Spells, and Formulas*, had studied with Buckland in the 1970s, but he was also a New Orleans native and was well-versed in the magical traditions of Louisiana.

Buckland quickly followed up *Witchcraft from the Inside* with *Practical Candleburning* (later renamed *Practical Candleburning Rituals* in subsequent editions), also in 1970, a book that began as a contractual requirement and was hurriedly written. Despite the haste in which it was put together, *Practical Candleburning* has some moments of inspired genius. One of the biggest keys to the book's overwhelming success was the inclusion of spells from both the Christian tradition and the "Old Religion," a substitute term for Witchcraft. Today the use of the term Old Religion feels a bit comical, especially when all the spells in the book were freshly written by Buckland, but in 1970 Old Religion was common shorthand for religious Witchcraft, and a way to write about Witchcraft without using the term. By including two different

---

121. Buckland, *Witchcraft from the Inside*, 130. I am happy to tell you that this was one of my first Witchcraft books.

types of rituals, Buckland was setting his book up to appeal to the growing Witchcraft market and any Christians curious about candle magick.

Though brief, *Practical Candleburning Rituals* is also thorough. Most books dealing with magick in 1970 lacked context. In this short book, Buckland thoroughly explains how to prepare for magickal work on both a mundane and a spiritual level. This helps explain just why the book has been continually in print for over fifty years now and is one of Llewellyn's bestselling books ever! On a research trip of mine to the Llewellyn offices, Sandra Weschcke (Llewellyn's current owner) shared a smile with me and credited *Practical Candleburning* with keeping Llewellyn in business during the early 1970s. Though there was no doubt some exaggeration involved in that comment, the book has been tremendously successful. To date, it has sold over half a million copies and was later updated in 1976 and 1982.

Not surprisingly, the success of *Practical Candleburning Rituals* led to a sequel, *Advanced Candle Magick*, in 1996. Even though the title included the word *advanced*, Buckland's second stab at candle magick was still suitable for beginners as well. This time, though, he chose not to include separate spells for Christianity and the "Old Religion," and simply wrote his spells with only the vaguest inklings of deity.

Remembering Ray: Sandra Weschcke

There is so much to remember about Ray. I can still see him: his smile, his hugs, how sweet and kind he always was.

I first started hearing about Ray when Carl Weschcke and I started dating in 1971.[122] Llewellyn was a young company, and Carl was at the helm without a lot of staff to help. Ray was very important to Llewellyn right from the start. He was Carl's first influential author, and he helped pave the way for Llewellyn to become an important publisher of Wicca.

Back in the day, Ray's *Witchcraft from the Inside* and *Practical Candleburning Rituals* were our bestsellers, and *Practical Candleburning Rituals* still is! What a breakthrough these books were. Even today people talk about them as their first exposure to Wicca.

---

122. You'll read a lot more about Carl Weschcke in this book. Weschcke was the president and publisher of Llewellyn from 1961 until his passing in 2015.

I remember how proud Carl was when Ray wrote *Buckland's Complete Book of Witchcraft*. It was the hallmark of who Ray was, resulting in so much respect and accolades from both readers and reviewers. First published in 1986, our *"Big Blue"* is still selling strong in 2024.

Ray was a showman; he loved people, and he loved talking about his books at trade shows and giving free Tarot readings to booksellers who waited in long lines to see him. He frequently went with us to Book-Expo America and the International New Age Trade Show. People just loved him, and all of us at Llewellyn did too.

I will always remember Ray and hold him dear in my heart.

Sandra Weschcke *is the current president and treasurer of Llewellyn Worldwide. She was friends with Ray from 1971 until his passing in 2017.*

While writing *Practical Candleburning*, Buckland was also hard at work on what would become his third book, and one of the strangest titles in his vast catalog of works, *Mu Revealed* (1970). The fictional continent of Mu was first written about by British-American archeologist Augustus Le Plongeon (1825–1908), who believed that ancient Mayan civilization was related to both ancient Egypt and the lost continent of Atlantis. Le Plongeon's Mu was located in the Atlantic Ocean, and he equated it with Atlantis. Even in Le Plongeon's lifetime, serious scholars dismissed his theories, but they never completely went away and in the 1930s would become something of a phenomenon.

Beginning in 1926, English writer James Churchward (1851–1936) released a series of books on Mu that suddenly placed the continent in the Pacific Ocean and made it the cradle of humankind. In total, Churchward released five books on Mu from 1926 to 1935, each a little bit more outlandish than the last. However, Churchward claimed that his writings were based on actual written evidence, including stone tablets found in both India and Mexico. Churchward never provided much information about the Indian tablets, but he did link the Mexican tablets to archeologist William Nevin (1850–1937). Unfortunately for Churchward, Nevin documented all his digs, and there's no record there of any tablets from Mu (or anywhere else outside of Mexico). All of Churchward's work is littered with inconsistencies and fictitious sources, but that didn't stop his work from being continuously in print over the last ninety-plus years.

Buckland found Churchward's Mu fascinating and began writing a story about a fictitious archeological dig in the same area as Nevin's, but Buckland's (fictional) dig went deeper into the ground than Nevin's and turned up some previously undiscovered scrolls from Mu. Buckland meant for this project to simply be a lark, a farcical writing exercise, nothing more, nothing less. As Buckland plodded away on the project, he eventually came up with details about daily life on Mu, including the continent's religious proclivities and monetary system.

Some of Buckland's friends got in on the fun, too. Ed Fitch printed some signs with the name of the fake archeological expedition chronicled in the book and set them up around a construction site at the military base he was currently stationed at. Suddenly there was photographic "evidence" of the Mu dig. Ed Fitch also shows up as a character in the book. This version of Fitch is a university professor who helps decipher the scrolls found on the expedition.

As the project grew in scope, friends suggested to Buckland that he submit it to a publisher, in this case Warner Paperback Library. The acquisitions editor at Warner Paperback Library either didn't get the joke or simply didn't care and responded that they would be interested in the book with a couple of additions to it. Once the additions were made, Buckland was offered a contract and, according to Buckland, a $2,000 advance (about $16,250 in 2025 adjusted for inflation).[123] Buckland's initial response was laughter and to come clean with the publisher about the put-on. That didn't deter Warner Paperback Library, though; they simply added a clause to the contract that read "The Author agrees not to make any public statements, comments, etc., regarding his sources for this book and/or the authenticity of his material."

When *Mu Revealed* was released in 1970, the name on the book's cover was not Raymond Buckland, but Tony Earll. A longtime lover of anagrams, Buckland wanted to let all his potential readers in on the joke as quickly as possible; Tony Earll is an anagram for "not really."

As Tony Earll, Buckland also claimed that Mu was an abbreviation of the continent's true name, Muror, an anagram of "rumor." One of Buckland's old nicknames (in this case, Rudolph) shows up as Professor Hurdlop. Gerald

---

123. CPI Inflation Calculator, www.in2013dollars.com/us/inflation/1970?amount=2000.

Gardner also shows up in the book, this time as a researcher and not a Witch
or an anagram.

METRO-GOLDWYN-MAYER INC., 10202 West Washington Boulevard, Culver City, California 90230
Documentary Dept.

January 12, 1972

Mr. Tony Earll
c/o Buckland Museum
6 First Avenue
Bay Shore, New York

Dear Mr. Earll,

Your reply arrived the other day and I am certainly more
than pleased to have reached you. My reason for contacting you
now has doubled.

First, my own personal impression of MU and the story of
Kland sparked the possibility of a feature. This still exists.
If it is done, it would be with my own independant company, not
with MGM, and may be done in wide-16mm, for blow-up to 35mm.
Would you be interested in working on a script for such a pro-
ject, and/or advisor?

Second, MGM Documentary, with whom I am now associated,
is presently doing an hour show on the history of Man in the
New World-pre-Columbian. We have been unable to find anything
on Niven, Hurdlop, the digs you mention in your book, the
scrolls, or any relative material. Dr. Stirling and Eckholm,
who you mention also in your book, don't seem to have any information either. Could you shed some light on this? If these
things exist and can be got at, they should be in the show.
The show will air on ABC-TV April 17, 1972, so there is precious
little time. We have already shot all our footage at Teothuacan,
Tikal, Chichen Itza, etc.

Please write as soon as you can.

Sincerely yours,

Joseph Hugh Holsen

JHH/bj

Maybe Ray should have kept the Mu charade going just a little longer!

Mu Revealed attracted some attention after it was released. In his memoir,
Buckland writes that he received a letter from a major magazine offering to pay
all his expenses if he went on another Mexican expedition. MGM Studios (the
movie studio responsible for James Bond, among other films) also was interested in buying the movie rights to Tony Earll's story. Alas, once Buckland
came clean to both the magazine and MGM, he never heard from either source

again. Today, *Mu Revealed* occasionally shows up when believers in both Mu and the alleged lost Pacific continent Lemuria are written about.

Along with his ever-increasing presence in bookstores, Buckland was showing up in other spots, too. At New York's Fillmore East, he was a featured guest at the First Festival of the Occult Arts, a sign of the increasing interest in Witchcraft and the paranormal in the United States. The Fillmore gig resulted in Buckland meeting Abragail and Valaria (their pen names), two female Witches who were looking to start a mail-order occult supply store (which was pretty ambitious in 1970). In addition to their mail-order business, the Witches also opened a brick-and-mortar store in New York called the Witches Cauldron and went on to write the 1971 book *How to Become a Sensuous Witch*, notable for being the first ever book with an introduction written by Raymond Buckland (he also contributed a few spells to the project).

From 1970 to '72, Buckland became a frequent guest on college campuses. One event at Western Illinois University drew over two thousand people, and extra chairs had to be placed on the stage so people would have a place to sit![124] The biggest feather in Ray's cap might have been filling in for Muhammad Ali at a lecture at Canisius College, a Catholic university in Buffalo, New York. Apparently, Ali needed to bow out of the scheduled gig to train for an upcoming fight, and Ray filled his spot, moving his own previously scheduled spot up a few months.

The Bucklands were also showing up in more and more national periodicals, most notably *Cosmopolitan* and *Look* magazines. Raymond and Rosemary were usually featured with other occult practitioners (the *Cosmopolitan* article was titled "Hoodoo, Voodoo and You"), most often with Anton LaVey. In terms of visibility, the August 24, 1971 issue of *Look* might be the most iconic, but for all the wrong reasons. Instead of the Bucklands on the cover, readers were graced with the shaved head of Anton LaVey (head of the Church of the Satan) holding a human skull. The magazine's cover promises an article about how "Witchcraft is rising: East Coast white witches—West Coast black magic."

The magazine's article opens with several paragraphs about LaVey, at one point proclaiming that LaVey's Satanic Church is "the black side of Witchcraft."[125] Raymond is cast as LaVey's opposite, as "a bearded, bookish, British

---

124. This author's father is an alum of Western Illinois University and could have possibly been an attendee at this event!

125. Vachon, "Witchcraft Is Rising: East Coast White Witches, West Coast Black Magic," 40.

man who lives a comparatively unheralded existence in ... N.Y." Writer Brian Vachon writes that Buckland accuses LaVey of "giving witchcraft a bad name."[126] In contrast to the rather menacing image of LaVey on the magazine's cover, the Bucklands are featured in a full-page photo with Ray holding his horned helm and Rosemary looking quite demure in a flower print dress. In the article, one of the Bucklands describes the Craft as "a family religion, you see. It brings people together."[127] Despite a nude photo of the New York Coven sharing cakes and ale (tastefully shot so as not to expose any genitalia), the Bucklands are never portrayed in a sensationalist way. When compared to LaVey and the West Coast Witches profiled in the article, the Bucklands come across as wholesome.

Hollywood was also starting to call on Raymond Buckland, and in September of 1971, he flew out to Los Angeles to tape the nationally syndicated *Virginia Graham Show* for a Halloween episode. Buckland was especially looking forward to this taping because it would allow him an opportunity to meet legendary actor Vincent Price. Sadly for Buckland, Price was sick the day of the show's taping and was unable to appear, but this allowed Raymond the opportunity to open the show. Utilizing some primitive special effects, Buckland's disembodied head was the first thing to appear on the program, announcing that day's guests. Buckland wasn't the only Witch to visit the show that day either; he was joined by L.A.'s Louise Huebner (1930–2014) and the Sensual Witches Abragail and Valaria. Hilariously, Buckland watched his appearance on Graham's show on a showroom TV in a department store after slipping away from his mundane job. During the show, a store clerk apparently did a double take when he realized the guy watching TV was also the Witch on the television!

It's worth noting that in every television appearance he made, Raymond Buckland wore a business suit. He believed that it was his responsibility to look "normal" in public, and in his memoir, he complains about other Witches adopting "stereotypical images." In contrast to some of the other public Witches of the period, Buckland never wore a cape to a TV taping, and it may be why he was tapped to write another short book about Witch-

---

126. Vachon, "Witchcraft Is Rising: East Coast White Witches, West Coast Black Magic," 42.
127. Vachon, "Witchcraft Is Rising: East Coast White Witches, West Coast Black Magic," 42.

craft. That work, *Witchcraft Ancient and Modern,* was written in four weeks and also appeared in 1970. According to Buckland, his quickie book was contracted by HC Publishers to replace Leo Martello's *Weird Ways of Witchcraft,* which the public had interpreted as a personal diatribe against the Catholic Church. Witchcraft books sold well during this period, but Witchcraft books critical of Christianity were apparently problematic (and resulted in a lot of critical mail being sent to the publisher).

BERT I. GORDON PRODUCTIONS, INC.

3373 PATRICIA AVENUE

LOS ANGELES, CALIFORNIA 90064

tw 6-9117

reply to:
1041 No. Formosa Avenue
Los Angeles, California

September 30, 1970

Dr. Raymond Buckland
111 Timberline Drive
Brentwood, New York   11717

Dear Ray:

The time we spent together in my office Friday and at the restaurant was tremendously enjoyable as well as informative. The oral comments that were taped, as well as your notes pertaining to my screenplay really helped in authenticating the story.

Many many thanks for your invaluable help. I appreciate it immensely.

Sincerely,

Bert I. Gordon
Group III Productions

Despite Buckland's assistance, the film *Necromancy* was
apparently not an "honest" look at Witchcraft.

Thanks to his appearance on the *Virginia Graham Show*, Buckland was contacted by the producers of a soon-to-be-shot film titled *Necromancy*. Helmed by B-movie horror maestro director Bert I. Gordon (1922–2023) and starring the legendary Orson Welles (1915–85), *Necromancy* was about a cult leader desperate to bring his son back from the dead. Buckland writes that he was taken seriously as a consultant and even got some parts of the script changed, but the movie still didn't present Witchcraft in the best light. (Most of us aren't cult leaders trying to awaken the dead, for starters!) In addition to acting as a consultant, Buckland also appears on screen as a coven member and is listed in the credits as a "technical advisor." In the 1980s, *Necromancy* would eventually be released on video and renamed *The Witching*. (Despite the name change, the movie remained bad.) *Necromancy* would not be Buckland's last Hollywood gig, either. More were on the way, but most would also be equally forgettable.

As Buckland's public profile as a Witch grew, his relationship with Monique and Scotty Wilson began to change as well. In their first few years after initiation, both Raymond and Rosemary seemed to be quite close with the Wilsons. Their correspondence reveals two couples who seem to very much be friends. In one letter, the Wilsons' daughter refers to Ray and Rosemary as "Aunty Rowen and Uncle Robat,"[128] and by early 1965 the Wilsons had made the Bucklands the legal guardians of their daughter in the event of their death.[129] The Bucklands even vacationed a couple of times on the Isle of Man and helped out at the Witchcraft museum there while visiting. At one point, Monique even asked the Bucklands if they would be interested in helping her and Scotty run the museum full-time. This entreaty was immediately turned down by the Bucklands, and besides, Raymond was very much in the process of starting his own museum during that period.

Despite the level of familiarity between the two couples, there's also a level of deference on the part of Ray and Rosemary to the Wilsons. Monique was the "Witch Queen," and she had no reservations about telling the Bucklands (especially Raymond) what she expected of them. There are requests for the Bucklands to set up a lecture tour for her and chastisements for not writing back to potential initiates quickly enough. By 1967 their once robust

---

128. Morven, letter to Rosemary and Raymond Buckland, May 1, 1967.
129. Monique Wilson, letter to Rosemary and Raymond Buckland, January 13, 1965.

exchange of letters begins to wane, and vacations by the Bucklands to the Isle of Man became but a distant memory.

Rosemary cutting herbs on the Isle of Man

As Buckland's star grew in the United States, the Wilsons' star was starting to dim in the UK. Since becoming a public Witch, Monique had enjoyed a cordial relationship with the press, and articles about her were most often exceedingly positive. To put it simply, Monique was charming, and this endeared her not only to reporters but also to her neighbors on the Isle of Man. Unfortunately for the Wilsons, that cordial relationship with the press ended in 1969 when the tabloid paper *News of the World* printed an article alleging that the Wilsons' daughter, Morven, had participated in Witchcraft rites. The fallout from that article led to Morven being placed under the supervision of a probation officer to ensure that she was not a part of any Witchcraft rituals.[130]

(Most certainly, Morven had participated in Witchcraft rituals. Her taking of a Witch name confirms as much. As we've seen, the Bucklands' elder son, Robert, participated in rituals and in a limited capacity was given a modified form of initiation. Morven's level of participation in Witchcraft activities was probably similar.)

---

130. Hutton, *The Triumph of the Moon*, 340.

The negative press coverage of the Wilsons led to the couple being shunned by many in the Witchcraft community just when the Wilsons needed their extended community the most. When the court-ordered supervision of Morven ended, the Wilsons sold the Witchcraft museum on the Isle of Man in 1973 to Ripley's Believe It or Not for 120,000 pounds (the equivalent of about 1.9 million pounds or 2.3 million dollars in 2025). With the museum closed, the Wilsons moved to the city of Torremolinos on the Spanish coast and opened a café there. Monique Wilson didn't entirely retire after moving to Spain. She practiced the Craft for a few more years, eventually helping to establish a coven in Germany.[131]

Rosemary ready for flight

Monique Wilson died in 1982, when she was somewhere between fifty-five and sixty years old (the exact year of her birth is disputed). Scotty Wilson

---

131. Davis, *Monique Wilson & the Gardner Estate*, 2–3.

spent the last years of his life in the United States and died in the 1990s. As of this writing, Morven is still living and wants nothing to do with Witchcraft and refuses to discuss the subject or her parents' involvement in it. (I can't blame her.)

As for the contents of what was Gardner's Witchcraft museum, the museum's collection was first sent to a Ripley's museum in San Francisco. When that particular location closed, the collection was sent to St. Augustine, Florida. In the 1980s, the collection was moved into storage and eventually sold off, piece by piece. Much of the collection was purchased by the A&B Trading Company and then sold through ads in the back of magazines and eventually on eBay. Gardner's first attempt at a Book of Shadows, known today as *Ye Bok of Ye Art Magical*, was sold to Richard and Tamarra James, founders of the Wiccan Church of Canada, who also bought everything else from Ripley's that hadn't already been acquired.[132]

The selling of the Museum of Witchcraft and Magic made the Wilsons personae non gratae to many British Witches, and even today when I bring up the Wilsons, I'm met with disapproving looks. It's an absolute tragedy that the Wilsons sold Gardner's collection to Ripley's, but what choice did they have in 1973? The Witchcraft community was small at that time and not particularly organized. A campaign spearheaded through magazines and letters would have taken years to bear fruit and most likely would have failed anyway.

The Wilsons' time as public Witches certainly ended poorly, but many of us would not be here today without them. They actively sought to grow the Craft in the United States and had the foresight to make Raymond Buckland their ambassador in the New World. Today there are thousands of Witches who can trace their lineage back through Monique and Scotty Wilson. That's quite a legacy for a couple whose public time in the Witchcraft world lasted less than fifteen years.

· · · · · · · ·

Between Ray's lecture gigs, book writing, the fledgling museum, and several TV gigs, it's easy to forget that during this entire period he was still working for British Airways. That work had gone smoothly since becoming a

132. Davis, *Monique Wilson & the Gardner Estate*, 4.

part of the airline in 1963 and eventually resulted in a promotion that net-ted Buckland his own office and the freedom to come and go as he pleased. Despite how glamorous the world of professional Witchcraft can sometimes look, it didn't put much food on the table.

In addition to their public promotion of Witchcraft, the Bucklands were still running their coven in New York. Most of that time went smoothly, but a mishap in 1970 near Samhain almost burned down the Bucklands' place of residence. After setting up the coven's ritual space in their basement gath-ering place, Raymond went upstairs to join the rest of the circle for a glass of wine pre-ritual. While sitting in the living room, the entire coven heard a loud *bang!* They all just assumed it was a passing aircraft, but immediately upon opening the door to the basement, they were greeted by thick smoke.

Raymond proceeded to dash downstairs and discovered that an extra mattress stored in the basement had caught fire. He then ran back up the stairs to the bathroom, where the bathtub was still filled with water from pre-ritual baths. Over the course of several trips with a bucket, Buckland managed to put out the fire that was starting to lick the floorboards of the house. While extinguishing the fire, Buckland was most likely naked, as he was "dressed" for ritual. While Raymond fought the fire, the rest of the coven fought to put their clothes back on while Rosemary went to a neigh-bor's house to use a phone, as the fire had burned through the Bucklands' phone line.

The weirdness didn't stop there. When the fire department eventually showed up, the fire crew were all wearing tuxedos. Apparently the firefight-ers had been summoned while in the middle of a fancy event. Eventually the crew got the smoldering mattress out of the Bucklands' basement. When the Bucklands returned to the basement after the firefighters left, they were delighted to find that none of their ritual tools had been disturbed. And no rogue spell candles were to blame for the fire in the Bucklands' basement; their furnace had belched up a large chunk of glowing soot directly onto the mattress utilized by guests.

The Bucklands had managed not to lose their home in October of 1970, but change was definitely in the air. Buckland gave notice to British Airways in April of 1971 and decided to plunge full-time into the world of Witchcraft. That change would be one of many, and the early 1970s would be some of the most transformative years of Raymond's life.

Exercise 5: To Start a New Venture

Buckland's 1996 book *Advanced Candle Magick (ACM)* is much more thorough than its predecessor, *Practical Candleburning Rituals* (1970). More than just a collection of spells along with some fatherly advice, *ACM* veers strongly into ceremonial magick territory, with extensive use of magickal correspondences, many focusing on issues of timing, including specific moon phases and the use of planetary hours and days. There's also information about specific incenses and oils and what should go into the pre-spell bath. It's much more involved than Buckland's first book of candle magick, yet it remains accessible, if a bit more labor-intensive.

I picked this spell to start a new venture from *Advanced Candle Magick* for this chapter specifically because the late 1960s and early '70s began a time of drastic change for Raymond Buckland.[133] By 1970 he was no longer "just" a Witch and coven leader; he had become one of the most prominent spokespeople for Witchcraft in the entire world. That's a pretty big mantle to take on, but Ray wore it well. There was also the museum, which was certainly a new venture!

To Start a New Venture

Whether it be starting a new job, opening a business, starting a new life as a married person, or newly divorced, leaving your parents' home to be on your own, emigrating to a new land, being initiated into a new or different religion, there are many and various ways that some of us start new ventures. Here is a ritual that can make the transition go smoothly.

Timing

For seven days during the waxing cycle of the Moon

Day(s)

Saturday, Sunday, Monday, Tuesday, Wednesday, Thursday, Friday

Hour

Mercury

---

133. Buckland, *Advanced Candle Magick*, 195–200.

Candles

Astral for Petitioner; Day Candles as appropriate; Offertory: Brown (1) inscribed "Neutral," Yellow (1) inscribed "Confidence," Orange (1) inscribed "Encouragement," White (1) inscribed "Truth"

Incense

Myrrh or birch bark, dragon's blood, and juniper, or gum Arabic, lavender, and sandalwood

Oil

Cinnamon, myrtle, and olive oil for Brown Candle; cinnamon, clove, mace, narcissus, and storax, or cinnamon and patchouli for all others

Key Word

"Success"

Bath

Jasmine, lemon, lotus, and sandalwood

Breathe deeply and build your ball of protective light. While soaking in your ritual bath, meditate on the venture you are about to undertake. See it as a wonderful golden road stretching out before you, with incredible opportunities and the promise of great rewards. Enter the Circle in the hour of Mercury on a Saturday in the waxing cycle of the Moon. Stand, kneel, or sit before the altar. Light the incense. With the Oil, dress the Altar Candles and the Day Candle, while concentrating on the purpose of the ritual.

ALTAR SET-UP #14
TO START A NEW VENTURE

Light your taper; then from that, light the Altar Candles and the Day Candle. State your intent:

> *I am here to help [Name] set out upon a new road; a road to success. Here starts a new and exciting venture filled with opportunity. Let there be no regrets for the past as [he/she] faces the future, secure in the knowledge that all will go well.*

With the Awl,[134] inscribe the Petitioner's name on the Astral Candle, then dress the candle with Oil.

With your taper, light the Petitioner Candle and say:

> *This is [Name], who has the strength to overcome all negativity as [he/she] sets out to build a new life filled with promise. Let [his/her] spirit burn as surely as does this flame; a symbol of the inner strength that will prevail in all things.*

With the Awl, inscribe the Brown Candle with the word "Neutral." Dress it with Oil and say:

> *Here do I light the Lamp of Neutrality. This represents the past. Let the past be neutral so far as it affects the future, for here is the start of a new venture.*

With the Awl, inscribe the Yellow candle with the word "Confidence." Dress it with Oil, light it and say:

> *Here burns the confidence which [Name] has in [him/herself]. With a new purpose to life there is joy and determination. This flame burns steadily, reflecting that confidence.*

With the Awl, inscribe the Orange candle with the word "Encouragement." Dress it with Oil, light it and say:

---

134. Note: An awl is a tool used to write on candles. You could use a pin or needle here.

Encouragement burns ahead, drawing [him/her] forward to better and greater things. Anything is possible if you have the courage to try it. Encouragement is all you need and it is here in abundance.

With the Awl, inscribe the White candle with the word "Truth." Dress it with Oil, light it and say:

Truth is the light at the end of the tunnel. It burns for all to see. It is the foundation on which to build any new venture. Here it is in its rightful place as a part of what may be achieved. Truth burns brightly and strongly.

Take up the Censer and swing it, censing the whole area around the altar, while rhythmically repeating the Key Word "Success," and building up the energy to that focus. Replace the Censer. Say:

Now does [Name] set off on [his/her] new venture, steady in the knowledge that all will go well. [His/hers] is the path that leads to success.

Slowly move the Petitioner's Candle one-seventh of the way toward the Yellow, White, and Orange Candles, and say:

The way to success is straight and true, lined with opportunity and edged with love. Every step of the way [his/her] progress is watched over, each and every move planned for only good. Let the journey be enjoyed as it brings love and good fellowship into the way of the traveler. Start the new venture and enjoy the journey!

Sit for a while and picture the venture well under way, and bringing great joy and pleasure to the Petitioner. See him/her with no cares or worries, enjoying life to the fullest.

Extinguish the candles in reverse order and leave them in their positions. Start from those positions the next day, so that the Petitioner's Candle will be moved another seventh of the way to the right. In this way, by the end of the week it will meet, and touch, the Yellow, White, and Orange Candles.

The Buckland side of the family:
Ray's grandparents, father, and uncle

Ray's father, Stanley Buckland

Ray (*right*) with his brother, Gerard

Ray's mother, Eileen Lizzie Wells

The Buckland family (*Ray is on the left.*)

Young Bucklands at the beach (*Ray is on the right.*)

Gerard and Raymond on a walk with their mother

Ray (*right*) performing in *The Duke of Darkness* with friend Phil Mottram

I vant to be in your play!

The young thespian (*left*)

Count Rudolph and his Jass Men

* The Jass Men on vinyl

Uncle Charles
the magician

Ray out camping

A very dapper
Uncle George

Raymond Buckland (reluctantly) reporting for duty

* Ray and Rosemary near the beginning of their Witchcraft journey

* Scotty and Monique Wilson with Rosemary Buckland on the Isle of Man

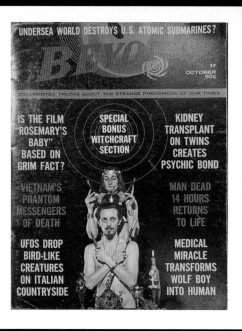

* Ray and Rosemary on the cover of *Beyond* magazine

* Buckland with a monkey skull (This is the version of Ray the world saw on *The Dick Cavett Show*.)

Ray often traveled with his ritual tools in a gun case, with his preferred weapons being his wand, sword, and athame.

Ray Buckland at Pan Pagan Festival 1980

* Ray Buckland and
Scott Cunningham

Ray with one of Tara's pet
snakes and a glass of wine

* Ray with English
High Priestess
Patricia Crowther

Tara and Ray at
their wedding

Tara and Ray in San Diego

* Barefoot Ray with his staff

Ray's ultralight aircraft

The pilot has been cleared for takeoff.

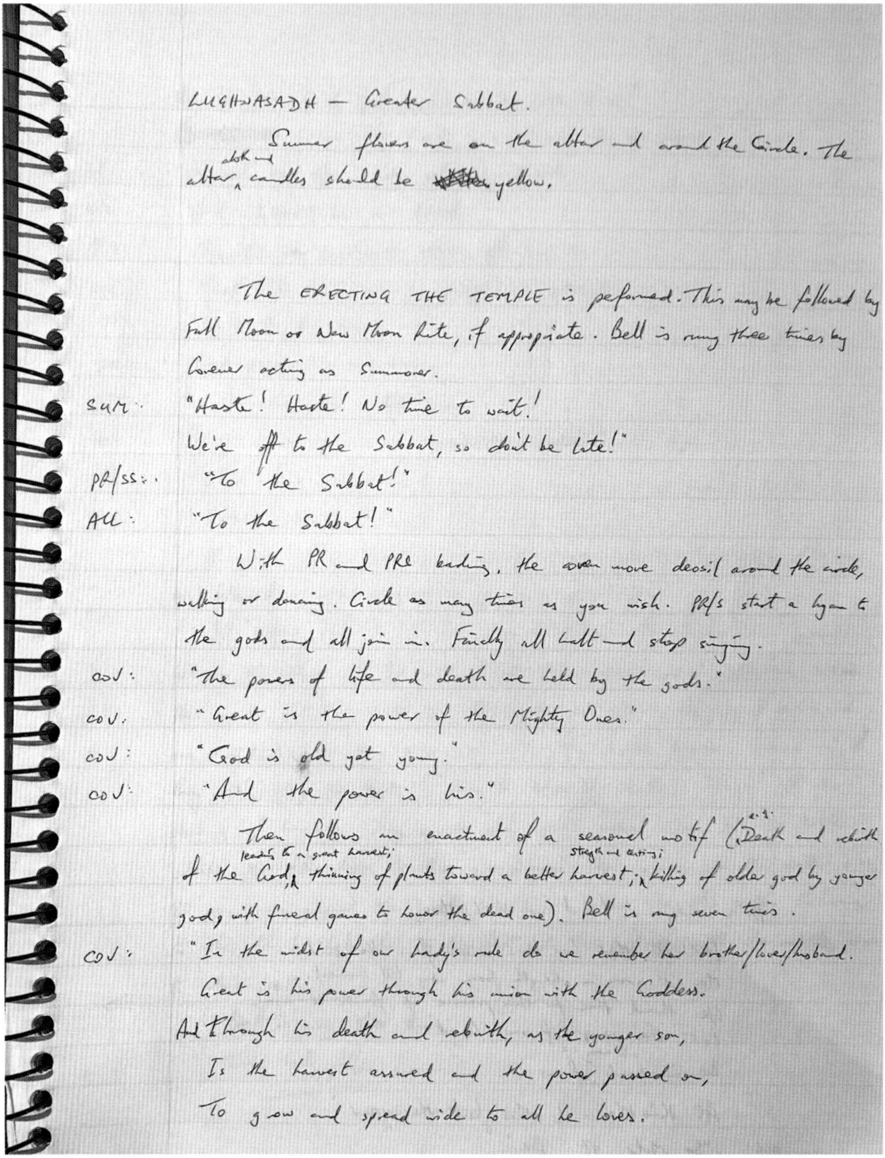

LUGHNASADH — Greater Sabbat.

Summer flowers are on the altar and around the Circle. The altar cloth and candles should be ~~[illegible]~~ yellow.

The ERECTING THE TEMPLE is performed. This may be followed by Full Moon or New Moon Rite, if appropriate. Bell is rung three times by Covener acting as Summoner.

SUM: "Haste! Haste! No time to wait!
We're off to the Sabbat, so don't be late!"

PR/SS: "To the Sabbat!"

ALL: "To the Sabbat!"

With PR and PRS leading, the coven move deosil around the circle, walking or dancing. Circle as many times as you wish. PR/s start a hymn to the gods and all join in. Finally all halt and stop singing.

COV: "The powers of life and death are held by the gods."

COV: "Great is the power of the Mighty Ones."

COV: "God is old yet young."

COV: "And the power is his."

Then follows an enactment of a seasonal motif (e.g. Death and rebirth of the God leading to a great harvest; thinning of plants toward a better harvest; strength and cutting; killing of older god by younger god, with funeral games to honor the dead one). Bell is rung seven times.

COV: "In the midst of our Lady's rule do we remember her brother/lover/husband.
Great is his power through his union with the Goddess.
And through his death and rebirth, as the younger son,
Is the harvest assured and the power passed on,
To grow and spread wide to all he loves.

* A page from what became the *Big Blue Book*

Scott Cunningham, Carl Weschcke, and Ray

Ray on the water

Ray (*right*) with his brother, Gerard

Early days at the farm: Ray with some baby goats

The man got even better-looking with age.

Ray (*middle*) with Dennis Carpenter and Selena Fox of Circle Sanctuary

Tara and Ray taking the dogs for a walk

Ray out for a
horse and buggy ride

Ray as master of ceremonies
at Lily Dale

Ray proudly posing
with *Dead for a Spell*

Ray out for a walk
with his dog Chico

Ray and Tara

Ray taking a nap and being watched over by guard dog Lupé

Ray cutting the ribbon at the reopening of the Buckland Museum of Witchcraft and Magick in Ohio

The Buckland Museum of Witchcraft and Magick in Ohio

All photos courtesy of Tara Buckland, except those marked with an asterisk (*). Thos photos are courtesy of the Buckland Museum of Witchcraft and Magick. Photo of Ra on the water courtesy of Gregory C. Ford. Photo of Ray with his staff and photo of Sco Cunningham, Carl Weschcke, and Ray Buckland both courtesy of Llewellyn Worldwide.

Chapter Six
From Gardnerian Witchcraft to Seax-Wica

The world of Witchcraft-related books was forever changed by the release of Paul Huson's (1942–present) *Mastering Witchcraft: A Practical Guide for Witches, Warlocks, and Covens* in 1970. Prior to Huson, Witchcraft books were generally about Witchcraft history, along with some insight into what Witches might do, but rarely were early Witchcraft books about actually *doing* Witchcraft. Some of those early books had snippets of Witch ritual. Gardner shares a little bit of a Yule ritual in his 1954 book *Witchcraft Today*, but never enough to really provide a complete portrait of Witch ritual.

While Huson's book was the first Witchcraft manual to be published by a mainstream press (G. P. Putnam's Sons) and remain in print for an extended length of time, the first book of Witch ritual was published in the spring of 1964 by Dumblecott Magick Productions, the vanity press of Charles (1895–1977) and Mary Cardell (1922–84). Charles and Mary Cardell are some of Witchcraft's oddest characters, and claimed to be brother and sister, despite being married. In the late 1950s, the Cardells had a falling-out with Gerald Gardner and the Gardnerian Witch community and began promoting their own version of the Craft. Their dislike of Gardner was so intense that they published his Book of Shadows in 1964 (shortly after Gardner's death) as the book *Witch* and attributed the book to "Rex Nemorensis." Not surprisingly, Dumblecott Magick Productions didn't have much in the way of distribution, and *Witch* is more of a footnote in Witchcraft history than a revolutionary movement.

What set Huson's work apart from that of the Cardells was that Huson's was easy to find. Certainly not every bookstore in the United States was carrying *Mastering Witchcraft*, but with a little legwork anyone interested in Witchcraft could track it down. And once they had found Huson's book, they were able to enter a world full of complete spells, with one chapter promising to spill the beans on "The Coven and How to Form One."[135] Huson's book mostly details various forms of magickal work, and much of that material is quite different from the Wiccan-Witchcraft that would be detailed in the books to come, but Huson really does share just what a coven is and how to form one circa 1970.

Huson doesn't provide a complete road map. Like Gardner before him, he only shares pieces of ritual, but there's just enough there so that anyone with a bit of creativity could easily fill in the rest of the blanks. Huson's book is a "how to do Witchcraft" book and not just an "about Witchcraft" book. By the time Raymond Buckland's first two books on Witchcraft were released in 1970 and 1971, he was already running behind.

As one of the leading public Witches in the United States, Sybil Leek attempted to put together her own how-to books but lacked the deft touch of Huson. Both her *Cast Your Own Spell* (1970) and *The Complete Art of Witchcraft* (1971) are long on history and ideas but severely lacking in easy practical application. However, the latter book is notable for including Doreen Valiente's *Charge of the Goddess* (published without attribution or permission, of course), the most well-known piece of Wiccan liturgy in existence. Like Huson, Leek was published by a mainstream press, and by the mid-1970s many of her books could be found on paperback spinners at the local grocery store.

Also published in 1971, Lady Sheba's (1920–2002) *Book of Shadows* was, after the Cardells' attempt in 1964, the first Book of Shadows ever published, and the first BoS to remain in print and be available for a substantial period of time. Born Jessie Wicker Bell, Sheba's *Book of Shadows* was not really her own. Though she claimed to be from a long line of Witches, she was initiated by an English Witch coven over the phone in 1970 and sent a copy of that coven's Book of Shadows. The BoS she received was heavily influenced by the

---

135. Huson, *Mastering Witchcraft*, 207.

Gardnerian one, and after receiving it, she promptly sent it to Llewellyn (the publishers of this book), who happily published it. (It's worth noting that Sheba's book also contained Doreen Valiente's *Charge of the Goddess*, just like Leek's.) An expanded version of Lady Sheba's *Book of Shadows* was released in 1972 as *The Grimoire of Lady Sheba*, again published by Llewellyn. Sheba most certainly broke an oath of secrecy by publishing the Book of Shadows given to her (bad), but her work had a huge impact on the Witchcraft movement in the United States (good).

In 2011 I was reviewing the ritual papers of a local Witch group established in the late 1960s in the San Francisco Bay Area. The rituals of this group were heavily influenced by Margaret Murray's work and the writings of Gardner, but the rituals themselves lacked the structure most of us are familiar with when encountering Wiccan-style ritual. The rituals of this group changed abruptly in 1971, and when I noticed the change, I muttered "Sheba!" under my breath. Sheba's "work" (in quotes, because it wasn't really hers) revealed just how to do Witch ritual. It was a big step!

Both the *Book of Shadows* and *Grimoire* completely lacked much context. Sheba simply presented what was in her BoS without much in the way of commentary. Some of what she shared was garbled and, even in the early 1970s, was clearly going against the prevailing trends in Witchcraft. The most glaring example of this is Sheba's placement of the summer sabbats, where she substitutes Rudemas for Beltane (Rudemas being the Christian Feast of the Cross celebrated May 3) and then gives Beltane as the name for the Summer Solstice.[136] (In fairness to Sheba, she is not the only person to use the word Rudemas, but Beltane for the Summer Solstice is another story!)

Sheba's books incensed Gardnerians but provided a road map for thousands of fledgling Witches. Today, Sheba's work feels quaint by comparison to the much better and far more thorough books that would follow, but that doesn't diminish its historical impact. Sheba's time in the Witchcraft zeitgeist would be short-lived, as 1973's *Witch* was her last book, and she mostly retired from public Witch life after that. One reason for her retirement was

---

136. Sheba, *The Grimoire of Lady Sheba*, 209 and 215.

no doubt the anger directed at her from many Witches over the publication of the BoS.

Not surprisingly, we can include Ray Buckland among the angry Witches of that period. Some of that dislike might have been because Buckland was aware of the problems in Sheba's story as soon as her book was published. In early 1967, Buckland was given a letter by a friend in Lansing, Michigan, who ran a small mail-order herb shop. The writer of the letter stated that they were trying to find Witches in the United States and was signed "Sincerely a Seeker, Mrs. Jessie Bell." A few months later, Buckland's contact in Michigan forwarded him a second letter from Bell. As with the first letter, Buckland declined to follow up on the inquiry. If Buckland had worked with Sheba, perhaps she never would have printed "her" Book of Shadows and grimoire.

Most of Buckland's ire at Sheba lies in her blatant disregard for the oaths she took to keep the workings of the Craft a secret, something Buckland had always taken (and would always take) very seriously. Sheba explained away her transgression by suggesting that the Goddess of the Witches had told her to share the BoS[137] and that, as an American, she wasn't bound by the "British Oath of Secrecy." Of course, the idea of an oath applying only to the seekers and/or initiates of a certain country is hogwash, but that didn't stop Sheba from attracting a large following, which included Carl Weschcke (1930–2015), the then president, owner, and publisher of Llewellyn.

By the time of Sheba's final books for Llewellyn, Buckland had written a small handful of occult-related books, but in some ways he was already behind the curve. Certainly Buckland's books in the early 1970s helped countless seekers, but people were starting to crave more than just information; they were more and more impatient to start the *doing*!

Initiation as a way to spread a religious movement might work in a country like the United Kingdom, an area less than the size of California, but it was always going to be a tough sell in the United States and Canada, where large cities are separated by hundreds and even thousands of miles. It doesn't help that Americans are rather impatient, too (something pointed out by Gerald Gardner in a letter to Ray dated November 8, 1962), but quite soon

---

137. Marquis, *Carl Llewellyn Weschcke*, 140.

Raymond Buckland would do more than just catch up to the first wave of how-to books. He would do them all one better.

• • • • • • • •

After leaving British Airways, Raymond Buckland wasted no time in moving on to his next venture: becoming a full-time Witch. The first step in that direction would come by turning the Buckland Museum of Witchcraft and Magick into a full-time operation. This was accomplished by moving the museum into a large Victorian rental in Bay Shore, on the South Shore of Long Island. Without any money to fix up the property, Raymond refinished the ground floor and painted the walls and trim. New display cases were purchased to make the place feel more like a museum instead of just a collection of artifacts in a basement.

The Buckland Museum of Witchcraft and Magick in Bay Shore, Long Island, New York

The museum opened on June 10, 1971, with admission costing one dollar for adults and fifty cents for children. Despite the museum never making much money, it did eventually bring in enough cash for Buckland to hire a receptionist, which was badly needed since Buckland was still actively lecturing around the country and doing radio and TV interviews. The museum had a small gift shop and, within half a year of opening, also began hosting lectures and workshops on a variety of topics beyond Witchcraft, including astrology, palmistry, Voodoo, and psychic development. The museum itself expanded during this time, too, as Buckland opened up the house's second floor and placed more exhibits there.

Media reaction in New York City to the museum's opening was quite positive. The museum made the local news and was even the subject of a one-hour documentary on a local station. The opening didn't make *The New York Times*, but it did make several other papers, including the *Long Island Catholic*, which wrote positively about the place. There were radio interviews, too, and a series of interviews with Barbara Walters for the TV show *Not for Women Only*, which would eventually air in October (of course) of that year. Later that year, Buckland was interviewed for *Scholastic Voice*, a magazine aimed at children, with six pages devoted to the museum.

A long list of Raymond Buckland's media appearances and mentions doesn't necessarily make for captivating reading, but it is illustrative of where America was in the early 1970s: in the midst of a growing interest in the occult, the unexplained, and Witchcraft. Not every media article was positive (as we have certainly seen!), and Satanists and Witches were often lumped together, but at least the media was talking to and recognizing people with beliefs outside the mainstream.

Perhaps the most memorable appearance by Raymond Buckland on mainstream television came on August 18, 1971, when Raymond Buckland appeared on ABC's *The Dick Cavett Show*. Cavett's show might have been number two in the ratings behind Johnny Carson's *Tonight Show*, but it was no slouch, and on the night Buckland showed up, Cavett also hosted actress Faye Dunaway and director Frank Perry, who were promoting the Western film *Doc*. Buckland was the last guest to take the stage that night, but he was given ten minutes of airtime, which was a pretty substantial chunk of the show's 45-minute run time (plus commercials).

Cavett mostly takes both Witchcraft and Buckland seriously on the show. Opening the segment, Cavett observes that "Witchcraft is coming back," making it worthy of conversation on a major broadcast network. Buckland himself is immediately charming as he settles in on the couch next to Cavett. Responding to a question from Cavett inquiring if he and Buckland had ever met, Raymond replies with a dry "not in this life so far as I know," earning several laughs from the crowd (along with a few groans).

For the most part, Buckland's interview goes down some fairly established paths: Witchcraft predates Christianity, Witches don't believe in the Devil, Witches don't do evil (bringing up his interpretation of the Threefold Law), and, most importantly, Witchcraft is a religion. Buckland strives to be nonconfrontational, attempting to find positive things to say about Christianity and Jesus. There's also a long segment with Ray explaining magick with poppets, a discussion that has not just Cavett interested but also Dunaway and Perry. The segment is positive but with a dash of sensationalism, which is about what one would expect on late-night television.

For those of us who grew up reading Buckland's books in the '80s, '90s, and beyond, his appearance on the show is surprising. Instead of a full beard, Buckland sports a light mustache and a Vandyke, and while his dark brown hair isn't long, it's not short either, and is combed backward, reaching just to his shoulders. He looks rather like a character from Shakespeare, which was probably the goal.

The museum's increased notoriety placed Raymond Buckland even more at the epicenter of the New York Witchcraft scene and brought new individuals into his life. No two had a more immediate impact than Judy (1939–2019) and Tom Kneitel (1933–2008), better known to many by their Craft names, Theos and Phoenix.[138] The Kneitels would go on to become some of the most influential Gardnerians in American history, and there are thousands of Witches today who trace their lineage not just through Gardner and the Bucklands but through the Kneitels as well. I don't like to use the word *enemies* to describe people, but let's just say that the later relationship between Raymond Buckland and the Kneitels was not a warm one.

Things started off well enough though. Buckland first met Judy Kneitel in October of 1971 when the latter paid a visit to the museum to ask about teaching classes there. In his memoir, Buckland writes that she introduced herself as an "astrologist" (a once common term for an astrologer), but she must have made a positive impression, since she began teaching at the museum in early 1972. She even helped with an exhibit, creating a "demon"

---

138. Clifton, *Her Hidden Children*, 24.

for a male mannequin dressed as a ceremonial magician. (Buckland named this figure Marvin the Magician, and he and his demonic companion were quite popular at the museum.)

On April 10, 1972, Rowen and Robat initiated Judy, who took the name Theos. Three weeks later, on May 1, her husband was initiated, taking the name Phoenix. During this period of time, there was an even bigger event happening in Raymond's life. He and Rosemary were in the process of breaking up and would be divorced by the end of the year. Depending on who you ask, either Raymond cheated on Rosemary or Rosemary cheated on Raymond. Not every relationship is destined to last for a lifetime. Sometimes things just don't work out.

In his memoir, Raymond accuses Rosemary of having an affair, but he also suggests that he might have been at fault simply because of the amount of time he was spending on the museum, lectures, and media appearances. Being two of the world's most recognizable Witches might also have made things more difficult. In his memoir, Buckland never portrays Rosemary as a villain, and he was always complimentary of her in his books.

Going hand in hand with the end of the Bucklands' marriage was Rosemary's decision to leave the coven and "retire" as a High Priestess. Rosemary must have been impressed by Judy Kneitel, whom she quickly elevated to the third degree and asked to lead the coven in her stead (though it's likely that Kneitel was not her first choice). Tom followed soon after his wife. And on November 17, 1972, leadership of what had been the Brentwood Coven passed to Theos and Phoenix, who quickly moved the coven's seat of operations to Commack, New York (also on Long Island).[139] With the passing of the baton (or sword), Rosemary and Raymond became "elders" of the coven. Though still there to provide advice, they would no longer serve an active leadership role. The downline of Theos and Phoenix would come to be known as the "Long Island Line" in Gardnerian Witchcraft. At the time of this book's writing, I feel comfortable stating that the Long Island Line is the largest line of Gardnerian Witchcraft in the United States (though I will say this is based entirely on personal observation, as I'm unaware of an annual Gardnerian census).

---

139. Lloyd, *Bull of Heaven*, 152.

The breakdown of Raymond Buckland's relationship with the Kneitels did not happen immediately after the transfer of coven leadership. In the early days after his divorce from Rosemary, Ray writes that he spent a lot of time with Tom and Judy and was quite grateful for it. He also still participated in rituals with the coven. In late 1972 and early 1973, he was most certainly "around." Raymond does not suggest that Rosemary was present when dropping in to see his old coven, but according to Tom Kneitel, Rosemary continued to act as an elder to the coven until 1985.[140] Whatever her involvement with the Commack Coven, it was most certainly behind the scenes. Her life as a public Witch, always quite limited to begin with, ended at this time.

The quick succession of the Kneitels resulted in the composition of the "Notes and Guidelines," an often-misunderstood document written by Theos and Phoenix and added to the Gardnerian BoS. Obviously I can't share the contents of "Notes and Guidelines" here (it's oathbound!), but it's essentially a set of instructions on how to run a Gardnerian coven. When historians write about "Notes and Guidelines," they often say that it was written by the Kneitels to fill the void in knowledge due to the departure of Raymond and Rosemary from the coven. But Ray always detested this explanation, mostly because he was "still around" during the period when "Notes and Guidelines" was written.

So what was the point of "Notes and Guidelines"? Sometimes people just like ideas spelled out plainly and to have written-down rules. There is most certainly precedent in the Gardnerian tradition for adding rules and instructions to the Book of Shadows. Gerald Gardner did it himself with the composition of a set of Craft laws known today as the Ardanes. Although Gardner claimed they were ancient, most everyone in his coven immediately knew they were not. "Notes and Guidelines" doesn't even claim to be ancient; the contents are simply labeled as notes.

I can tell you that the "Notes and Guidelines" are in my Book of Shadows. I can also tell you that I don't think about them very often or consult them with any regularity (and probably only once in my lifetime—while writing this book!). An article on the history of the Craft states that "Notes and

---

140. Lloyd, *Bull of Heaven*, 152.

Guidelines" have "hardened into rules and regulations" over the decades.[141] Poppycock! I have never met a Gardnerian who treats them as holy writ.

"Notes and Guidelines" is sometimes mentioned as one of the sources of the estrangement between Raymond Buckland and the Kneitels, which is why I mention it here. Reading Buckland's words on the matter, he clearly didn't like many of the Kneitels' additions to the Gardnerian Book of Shadows. In his memoir, Buckland recounts going through the BoS of a Gardnerian Priestess in Iowa initiated by Theos and Phoenix and "bringing it into line with the original" that he had received from Monique Wilson.

Today, many Gardnerians divide their BoS into sections, with each section highlighting the contributions of an individual Priestess or Priest. What Buckland received from Olwen would be called "core" today by some in the Gardnerian tradition, meaning that most of it came from Gerald Gardner. Subsequent sections would highlight contributions from individuals such as Rowen, Theos, and Phoenix. It's common practice for coven leaders to add to the BoS in the United States and to acknowledge their contributions (which is why some of us refer to our Gardnerian BoS as the "Forklift of Shadows"), but it's understandable that this might have bothered Ray back in the early 1970s, simply because there wasn't much precedent for it.

In his memoir, which is most often positive about *everyone*, Buckland pulls no punches when it comes to the Kneitels. He states that his eventual loathing of the couple stems from the Kneitels engaging in a "power trip":

> After a disagreement with me, Theos and Phoenix took off on what I can only describe as a great power trip. It seems they determined that they would be the "biggest and greatest" Gardnerians in the world. They stopped vetting those who wished to join the Craft and simply initiated anybody and everybody. It was said of them that if anyone happened to drive past their house very slowly, then they would run out and initiate them! In Volume 3 of Earth Religion News it was reported: "Fate magazine has been carrying classified advertisements for people to become Witches by Gardnerian Theos of L.I.... *Village Voice* has been carrying a similar ad but we are not sure if there is a connection. Promulgation is not supposed to be one of the tenets

---

141. Kelly, "The [American] Gardnerians, 1973–75."

of Wicca." Theos, it seems, wanted to be a "great" Witch Queen. (A Witch Queen, or Queen of the Sabbat, is a High Priestess who has had other covens hive-off from hers.) Theos set-out to have as many "daughter" covens as possible. And here was where her new rules came into play. Being uncertain of the people she had brought in, she stipulated that the new High Priestesses could not initiate anyone without her (Theos's) approval. This was patently absurd. If someone was of the caliber to be a High Priestess and have her own coven, she would most assuredly be competent enough to decide who she initiated. The Witch Queen was supposedly there only to give help and advice if and when needed, not to overrule.

Buckland sums up his feelings about Tom and Judy by writing that "more harm has been done to the Gardnerian movement in America by Theos and Phoenix than by anyone else, Wiccan, Pagan or Christian!"

Certainly the Kneitels initiated more Witches in their first eight years of running a coven than the Bucklands ever did in their first eight. Some of this is probably due to the reserved nature of Raymond and Rosemary when it came to initiates, and some of it is most likely the result of increased awareness and interest in the Craft. When it comes to the history and notoriety of Modern Witchcraft, 1974 was a far different era than 1964, due in large part to people like Ray Buckland writing about the Craft. I can't imagine too many Gardnerian Witches being comfortable with advertising a coven's existence in the pages of *The Village Voice*, but at the same time, shouldn't the Craft be at least somewhat accessible? There's a fine line between being a mystery tradition and being an unfindable tradition.

Most likely, just *how* the Kneitels had decided to run the New York Coven, once taking it over, played some role in the animosity between them and Raymond Buckland, but the anger probably runs deeper than Craft practices. The scars from Ray and Rosemary's divorce likely played a large role. It's human nature to choose a "side" in such instances, and choosing Rosemary over Raymond would have certainly cast Ray in the villain role. But there are two other factors that could have led to the estrangement: Craft politics and the acceptance of gays and lesbians in Gardnerian Witchcraft.

• • • • • • • • •

By the early 1970s, the Witchcraft world in both New York and the greater United States had expanded considerably. At one point the Gardnerian tradition was the only entry point into the Craft, but by 1972 there were at least a dozen magickal traditions in the United States and, with the ever-expanding number of traditions, more and more egos and pettiness.

Within the Witchcraft world, there has always been a desire to control the narrative. Many groups and individuals fancy themselves as arbitrators of just who is and is not a Witch. In initiatory traditions, this is taken a step further, with individuals arguing among themselves about just who is and is not a valid member of the tradition. These issues existed in 1972, exploded in the Gardnerian world in 1973, and continue to exist in the present day.

Just calling oneself a Witch is a political act. Embracing the term Witch often puts one on the margins of society, and for several decades after the emergence of Modern Witchcraft in the 1950s, being a Witch had serious repercussions. Witches lost children in custody battles, had their homes vandalized, and were fired from jobs because of their religious choices. Witchcraft is political in the greater sense of the word, but the Witchcraft world is also political on a smaller scale.

Today people often blame the internet for the various "Witch Wars" that play out in the magickal community, but Witch Wars have been a part of the Craft since Gardner first went public in 1951. Fifty years ago, arguments were waged in letter columns, while today they take place on social media. Localized Witch politics were just as prevalent in 1972 as they are today. The only difference is that more people take part in them now because there is an ever-increasing number of Witches.

The acceptance of the LGBTQIA+ community in Witchcraft circles fifty-odd years ago was more than a political issue for many in the Craft; it was also a theological consideration. Gardnerian Witchcraft is sometimes described as a "fertility religion," and the idea of male-female polarity was a prominent one in its early decades. The perfect coven was believed to consist of thirteen individuals: six female-male couples and a High Priestess (which has always felt odd since it makes for an uneven number of Witches!). Ritual tools were often gendered, with people deciding that, for whatever reason, a pointy knife contains male energy and a cup contains female energy. The focus on male-female polarity in initiatory Wicca often resulted in certain groups feeling left out, especially individuals from the LGBTQIA+ community. That's not to say that there were not gay individuals in initiatory Witchcraft traditions. According to an anonymous source, there were two gay men in Gerald Gardner's Bricket Wood coven back in the 1950s (and, yes, that coven is still active today). One of Buckland's very first initiates, Maverick, was a gay man, according to Buckland's memoir. Certainly there were covens accepting of gay and lesbian individuals in the Wiccan world, but not every coven was welcoming, and even if a coven was welcoming, sometimes a coven's ways of doing things were not.

According to Lois Bourne, one of Gerald's High Priestesses in the 1950s, Gardner himself was homophobic, and that's putting it mildly.[142] Bourne writes in her memoir that Gerald had a rather calm demeanor and never spoke ill of anyone, but that he had a "deep hatred and detestation of homosexuality."[143] She also writes that during a conversation Gardner once exclaimed, "There are no homosexual witches, and it is not possible to be a homosexual and a witch."[144] For many early Witches, homophobia came baked into the tradition.

There is another reason many Witches kept the gay world at arm's length in the 1950s and '60s: It was illegal in most places. Homosexuality became legal in England and Wales only in 1967.[145] In the United States, Illinois was the first state to legalize sodomy (1961), with other states following suit over the ensuing decades. On a national level, sodomy laws would not be ruled unconstitutional nationwide until 2003.[146] I don't think antigay rhetoric and exclusionary practices can be justified in any way, but the cultural context is worth pointing out here.

Janet and Stewart Farrar's *Eight Sabbats for Witches* (1981) and *The Witches' Way* (1984) are about as close to initiatory Wicca as one can get

142. Bourne, *Dancing with Witches*, 38.
143. Bourne, *Dancing with Witches*, 38.
144. Bourne, *Dancing with Witches*, 38.
145. UK Parliament, "Regulating Sex and Sexuality: The 20th Century."
146. ACLU, "Getting Rid of Sodomy Laws."

when working from a book. (Janet and Stewart were Alexandrian initiates, and their books are based on the Alexandrian Book of Shadows.) I think their work is at least somewhat representative of many Wiccan attitudes in the 1970s and into the early '80s. In *The Witches' Way*, the Farrars share their thoughts on gays and lesbians in the Craft, starting by sharing that they have gay friends, don't tolerate homophobia, and have had gay coven members. But they also write that their "concept of Wicca is built around natural maleness and femaleness of mind, body, and spirit."[147] It reads like an invitation that says, "You can come over if you want, but we don't really want you here."[148]

Despite one of the Bucklands' early initiates being a gay man, Raymond Buckland's early words on the subject of gays in the Craft in his written works were far from welcoming. In 1970's *Witchcraft Ancient and Modern*, Buckland wrote, "A 'gay witch' would be an absolute contradiction in terms. Being a religion of nature, the witch is very much heterosexual; there must be male and female, equal numbers of each, in a coven."[149] As we will see, this is not an attitude Buckland kept over the long term, and by 1973 he was firmly in the camp of gay ally.

Buckland's turnaround on the issue of gay individuals in the Craft was undoubtedly helped simply by knowing many gay Witches, or at least gay individuals sympathetic to Witchcraft. (As a Gardnerian of the 1960s and early '70s, Buckland likely would have still doubted the validity of Witches not initiated into the Gardnerian tradition.) The most prominent of those Witches was Leo Martello (1930–2000), but by 1972 Buckland had also made the acquaintance of Herman Slater (1938–92) and Eddie Buczynski (1947–89), owners of the Warlock Shop, one of New York City's first metaphysical stores aimed primarily at Witches. After its opening in 1972, the Warlock Shop became more than a store; it became one of New York City's busiest hang-out spots for prospective and practicing Witches.

● ● ● ● ● ● ● ●

---

147. Farrar and Farrar, *The Witches' Way*, 170.

148. Stewart Farrar passed away in 2000, and Janet is still with us. I don't believe either of them still held to these ideas by the end of the 1990s. The Craft changes and evolves, and so do the people within it!

149. Lloyd, *Bull of Heaven*, 199. This quote comes from Buckland's book *Witchcraft Ancient and Modern*, but I encountered it first in Lloyd's *Bull of Heaven*.

Though they were the owners of the Warlock Shop, neither Herman Slater nor Eddie Buczynski was an initiated Witch. Buczynski especially was eager to be an initiate and approached several different covens and groups. After at least two rejections, he eventually became an initiate of the New England Coven of Traditionalist Witches, run by Gwen Thompson (1928–86). (Thompson is best known for popularizing the "long version" of the Wiccan Rede, which she claimed was written by her grandmother.) Thompson and Buczynski shortly thereafter had a falling-out when Buczynski rejected Thompson's sexual advances. After this setback, Buczynski founded his own tradition, Welsh Traditionalist Witchcraft, which is still practiced today.

Despite forming his own tradition, Buczynski retained an interest in becoming a Gardnerian Witch and eventually approached Tom and Judy Kneitel about becoming an initiate, along with Herman. Until this time, the relationship between the owners of the Warlock Shop and the Kneitels had been quite warm, with the Kneitels even loaning Slater and Buczynski several thousands of dollars to keep the shop open during a difficult time (between two and three thousand dollars, depending on who is telling the story). To the credit of Slater and Buczynski, their debt was repaid promptly. Buczynski had also allowed the Kneitels to participate in his rituals. So his and Slater's rejection by the Kneitels must have been especially perplexing.[150] (Where was Raymond during this period? Without a High Priestess. He was not in a position to initiate anyone.)

Several months later, at the Warlock Shop, Slater and Buczynski meet Sira (Craft name), a New Jerseyite with an interest in Gardnerian Wicca. Sira begins corresponding with Kentucky's Theo and Thain, and shortly thereafter Sira flies to Louisville, Kentucky, and is initiated and then elevated to the third degree of Gardnerian Wicca on June 30, 1973, by Theo and Thain.[151] When Sira returns, she initiates both Slater and Buczynski, conferring upon them the third degree. Shortly thereafter, Buczynski forms his own Gardnerian coven with another of Sira's initiates.

None of this feels especially dramatic thus far, and it was rather commonplace for people to fly hundreds or even thousands of miles to be initiated into the Craft. "Quick" elevations were also a frequent occurrence during

---

150. The story of Buczynksi and the Kneitels is most thoroughly told in Lloyd's *Bull of Heaven*.

151. Lloyd, *Bull of Heaven*, 168.

this time period. But shortly after Buczynski formed his own Gardnerian coven, Judy and Tom Kneitel informed Buczynski and Slater that Theo and Thain were not in fact legitimate third-degree Gardnerians. The Kneitels also claimed that their assertion was backed up by Rosemary Buckland, who would have been Theo and Thain's initiator (and elevator).

Raymond Buckland, however, states that Theo and Thain were legitimate third-degree Gardnerians and had both been initiated and elevated to the third degree by himself and Rosemary. The claims by the Kneitels (and, by extension, Rosemary, though I have yet to find a public comment from her on the situation) that they were illegitimate third-degree Gardnerians was tantamount to calling Raymond Buckland a liar. There was no going back, and the relationship between Raymond Buckland and the Kneitels would never be mended.

The whole affair also set the New York City rumor mill into overdrive. One popular myth is that Theo and Thain had been initiated back in the mid-1960s but never elevated beyond the first degree. Buckland, due to his deteriorating relationship with the Kneitels, then flies to Kentucky and elevates Theo to the third degree in order for Sira to be elevated by Theo and her husband. It all sounds exhausting! The funniest addendum to this particular myth is the claim that Herman Slater financed Buckland's visit to Louisville. Slater was notoriously cheap, so it is extremely unlikely that he would have sprung for such a trip.

This brings up another question: Were Theo and Thain legitimate third-degree Gardnerians? I think it's safe to say yes. Buckland writes about the existence of a Kentucky coven in his 1966 pamphlet *Witchcraft...the Religion*. Certainly Rosemary would have known what was in that pamphlet and would have objected to the anecdote's inclusion if Theo and Thain had not been third-degree Gardnerians. At the end of the 1960s, Ed Fitch, too, mentions a Kentucky coven as existing, most likely a reference to Theo and Thain.[152]

While going through some of Buckland's written correspondence, I stumbled upon a small notebook full of Craft lore and the magickal names of all of Rowen and Robat's initiates. The entries for Theos and Thain include

---

152. Fitch, *A Grimoire of Shadows*, xv.

both their initiation and their elevation dates. According to Buckland's note-book, they were both initiated into the first degree on August 1, raised to the second degree on August 3, and then elevated to the third degree on August 5. These three rites occurred over just five days back in 1965. An entry for Theos provides a date for her first-degree initiation (spring of 1972), but the dates of her second- and third-degree elevations are blank, suggesting the Bucklands had yet to elevate her when the notebook was being written.[153]

Perhaps attempting to get the last word on the subject, Buckland writes in the 1974 edition of *Witchcraft from the Inside* that Theo and Thain were "two of the oldest (in terms of years in the Craft) leaders of the Gardnerian tradition" and the "two legitimate spiritual teachers of this tradition in America today."[154] Because of the reach afforded to him by his books, Buckland might have won the greater battle, but it was a different story in New York City. In order to quell the maelstrom, Sira was eventually initiated and ele-vated by the Kneitels, who didn't want anyone questioning the bona fides of her initiates.

Why all this drama about the initiation of two men in New York City? Certainly some of it was local politics; the Kneitels had become the hub of Gardnerian Wicca in New York City and perhaps did not want any com-petition. Michael Lloyd, in his incredible work *Bull of Heaven*, suggests that there might very well have been some degree of homophobia at play that kept Buczynski and Slater from being initiated as well. Slater and Buczynski were both flamboyantly gay, and one gets the feeling that in many Witchcraft cir-cles during that period, it was okay to be gay but not *too* gay. A less plausible theory for this mess is that Buczynski was not the best keeper of secrets, and the Kneitels, worried about the secrets of the Craft being disclosed, wanted to keep him from being initiated. (But after Buczynski was initiated, wasn't it too late anyway?)

As for the Kneitels, they most certainly had gay coven members in the 1970s. Tom Kneitel has said that "we trained, initiated, and worked with gay people right from the start. Sexual preference was never a factor in our

---

153. Buckland, untitled Craft notebook. Given that the entries are written in a variety of differ-ent ink colors, this notebook was likely written over the course of several years.

154. Buckland, *Witchcraft from the Inside*, 134.

decision as to whether to initiate."[155] In an interview with Leo Martello in 1973, Judy Kneitel suggested there was room for gay and lesbian individuals in the Craft, with caveats. To be a part of the coven, a prospective gay member would have to "establish a social rapport with our members" and have a working partner "of the opposite sex and [who] was otherwise suitable for membership." If these criteria were met, Judy said, there would be a "possibility" that they might be considered for initiation. She then adds that being gay is not an "affront to the Craft."[156]

In a 2004 email to author Michael Lloyd, Tom Kneitel states that the Bucklands "had never (and never would have)" initiated a gay Witch. Kneitel then suggests that such behavior was taught to them by Monique Wilson, who apparently was quite homophobic.[157] Kneitel's accusation is a strange one and is not backed up by the history of the Bucklands or Raymond's public words on the subject. Yes, Buckland danced around the issue in his early work, but that dancing would not last.

Buckland became quite public about acceptance of gays and lesbians in Wiccan spaces by 1973. In a letter from December of that year to *Earth Religion News* (Slater and Buczynski's Pagan newsletter), Buckland writes that the Craft had seen a "mellowing" in its approach to gay initiates, and that many Gardnerians and practitioners of other traditions were now willing to "accept individuals of whatever mind." He adds that what a person does outside the circle is their own concern and that being gay is "no more reason for exclusion from a Gardnerian coven than race or color." Perhaps the best part of the letter is that he states that this growing acceptance of gay Witches "is a good thing."[158]

• • • • • • • • •

The bickering and animosity between Buckland and the Kneitels would last for several years and often played out in the forum pages of Pagan periodicals. By random chance, I happened to pick up a copy of the Samhain 1975 issue of *Green Egg* magazine and was both delighted and horrified to find the Kneitels vs. Buckland feud in its pages. (I was delighted that I had stumbled

155. Lloyd, *Bull of Heaven*, 210–11.
156. Lloyd, *Bull of Heaven*, 210.
157. Lloyd, *Bull of Heaven*, 209.
158. Lloyd, *Bull of Heaven*, 210.

across something for this book, but horrified that I was given a ringside seat to their confrontation.)

In his letter in the "Forum" section, Tom Kneitel goes after Buckland for using the title "Doctor" and the honorific "PhD" in regard to the discipline of anthropology in some of his published works.[159] It is true that in many of his early works, Buckland used the title "Dr." and claimed to have a PhD in anthropology, both of which were clearly embellishments. (Buckland doesn't mention a college education in his memoir, and in later years he would mostly drop the honorifics from his book titles.) In his early books, Buckland tried to write as an academic outsider to Witchcraft and not a practitioner. Claiming false academic achievements was completely unnecessary, but in doing so, Buckland was most likely copying Gerald Gardner, who had done the same thing back in the 1950s. This doesn't make Ray's fudging of his academic achievements "right," but it does explain his reasoning.

It's one thing to call someone out for a falsehood and another to make it all so personal, which is clearly what Kneitel was doing in the pages of *Green Egg*. In his letter to the periodical, Kneitel himself states that Buckland had "in the past, used the title 'Dr.'"[160] Why bring up something from the past unless one is attempting to pour salt into old wounds? Kneitel then goes on to say that he had contacted King's College in London, Buckland's alleged university, and that the university had no record of awarding Buckland a degree in anything, or that Buckland had even enrolled at the university.[161]

Perhaps the most insulting part of the letter is Kneitel claiming that "certain statements he [Buckland] had made…gave me reason to question the depth of his knowledge about anthropology." The Kneitels and Buckland were most certainly friends at one point, and it seems obvious to me that they had most likely shared their backstories. Kneitel knew Buckland didn't have a PhD, so he wasn't suddenly questioning Buckland's academic credentials because of a questionable historical claim. (The Witchcraft books written in the 1970s are full of questionable historical claims.)

---

159. Kneitel, letter in "Forum," *Green Egg* magazine.
160. Kneitel, letter in "Forum," *Green Egg* magazine.
161. Kneitel was correct. Buckland did not attend King's College in London, but he did attend King's College School, a private school in Wimbledon. Ray's time at King's College School resulted in him earning the equivalent of a high school diploma in the United States.

Buckland's retort, in the same issue of *Green Egg* immediately following Kneitel's letter, is brutally funny in places and all at Kneitel's expense, but it doesn't do Buckland any favors either. While trying to explain his PhD, Buckland again states that he was a student at King's College, but that his doctorate is from "a nondescript little college in Sussex, which nobody has ever heard of," which of course doesn't really answer the question about Buckland's academic credentials.[162] Buckland also claims that Americans are "caught up" in the degree thing, but that in England no one really cares. Buckland also then makes a snide remark about Kneitel perhaps being a high school dropout. Neither Kneitel's education nor England's perception of academic credentials is particularly pertinent to the argument at hand though.

Buckland follows all that up by claiming that the use of "Dr." in his early books was not his decision but was the decision of the publisher.[163] There could be some truth to that, as certainly the honorific looks impressive on a book cover. As Buckland's stature as a Witchcraft writer grew throughout the 1970s, the title of "Dr." became less and less important and doesn't figure in many of his best-selling books of the period. Buckland can't resist embellishing, though, and writes that he had served on the "faculties of two universities and one college."[164] Certainly Buckland had lectured at some universities, but he was never on the faculty.

All of Buckland's questionable credentials show up in the 1975 edition of *Witchcraft from the Inside*. Though the honorific of "Dr." is left off the book's cover, the "About the Author" section contains all the disputed educational achievements. There's the studying at King's College, the PhD in anthropology, and the use of the title "Dr." with his name.

The shrewdest (and most accurate) thing written by Buckland in his follow-up to Kneitel is the observation that "it doesn't matter how many letters you have after your name—if your writing is no good it just doesn't get published!"[165] Buckland could have saved himself a lot of trouble by just sticking with that line of thought instead of invoking "nondescript" universities in Sussex. As Tim "Otter" Zell (now known as Oberon Zell), editor of

---

162. Buckland, letter in "Forum," *Green Egg* magazine.
163. Buckland, letter in "Forum," *Green Egg* magazine.
164. Buckland, letter in "Forum," *Green Egg* magazine.
165. Buckland, letter in "Forum," *Green Egg* magazine.

the *Green Egg*, mischievously notes after Buckland's letter, "By the way, what was the name of that 'nondescript little college in Sussex?'"[166]

Though there's no evidence that Buckland ever earned an advanced degree from an accredited university, he might have been conferred an honorary one. Hans Holzer writes in *The Truth About Witchcraft* that Buckland held a doctorate in philosophy, allegedly bestowed upon him by the Witchcraft museum on the Isle of Man![167] This information came from Mary Nesnick, which of course makes it suspect, but it seems like a very odd thing for someone to make up. Can a museum bestow an advanced degree? Not really, but there are plenty of degree mills out in the world, and I can imagine Monique Wilson *believing* that she had the authority to hand out an advanced degree.

Raymond Buckland's obituary in Britain's *The Telegraph* lists Brantridge Forest College as the origin of Buckland's degree, pointing out that Brantridge is listed as a "diploma mill" on various websites.[168] Again, Buckland never mentions any sort of university education in his memoir, nor are there any pictures or written material from his time at "university" in his archives. If Buckland had attended a university, there most likely would be written documentation confirming such an event.

Gerald Gardner once said that Witches were "consummate leg-pullers," and Buckland's claim to the title of Doctor is a pretty good example of this.[169] Buckland was clearly stretching the truth, but by the mid-1970s, such claims were mostly an afterthought. Buckland's exaggerated academic credentials drifted away after his first few books, and the bestsellers he had written by 1975 mostly forgo the use of the honorific "Dr." with this name. In 1979 Buckland did obtain a doctor of divinity degree from the Universal Life Church, an honor that can also be yours for the very low price of about $19.99!

• • • • • • • •

Despite the ugliness involving the Kneitels, Buckland, and Theo and Thain, Gardnerian Wicca in the United States would survive. Today the downline of the Kneitels is known as the Long Island Line, in honor of Tom and

166. Zell, editor's note in "Forum," *Green Egg* magazine.
167. Holzer, *The Truth About Witchcraft*, 86.
168. *The Telegraph*, "Raymond Buckland, Author and High Priest of Wicca—Obituary."
169. Gardner, *Witchcraft Today*, 23.

Judy's residence on Long Island. Neither Judy nor Tom ever wrote a Witch-craft book, so their influence on the Craft was limited to the area around New York City and the Gardnerian community. There are probably scores of Gardnerian Witches today who know the Kneitels only through their Craft names, Theos and Phoenix.

Do an online search for the Kneitels and you are more likely to get stories about Tom's time spent in the world of ham radio than anything involving Witchcraft. Tom Kneitel died at the age of seventy-five in 2008, and Judy passed away in May of 2019. Though their later interactions with Buckland were not positive, the Kneitels were both devoted to the Craft and did what they thought was best for the Gardnerian tradition.

While the Gardnerian community in New York City squabbled over who was and was not a proper third-degree initiate, Theo and Thain incorpo-rated their Gardnerian Craft as a "legal, non-profit religious corporation" in the state of Kentucky.[170] Today the Witches that trace their lineage back to them are known as the Kentucky Line of Gardnerian Witchcraft. Disputes between Long Island Line Gardnerians and Kentucky Line Gardnerians are also now nonexistent. Gardnerians don't "play nice" with everyone, but the Kentucky and Long Island lines are no longer engaged in a war over legit-imacy. Unlike the Kneitels, Theo and Thain eventually left the Witchcraft community, with sources telling me that Theo passed away in 2022 and that Thain identifies as a Catholic (in 2023) and is not interested in talking about Witchcraft.

In January of 1973, Raymond Buckland was America's best-known Gardnerian High Priest, but he wouldn't be by the end of the year. Due to his ugly falling-out with the Kneitels and the changing face of Witchcraft in the United States, Raymond Buckland would stop actively practicing the Gardnerian tradition and move on to new a phase in his life. It was time for Raymond Buckland to offer up something new and quite revolutionary for the Witchcraft world in 1974.

· · · · · · · ·

---

170. Buckland, *Witchcraft from the Inside*, 134.

In his memoir, Buckland states that his separation from the Gardnerian tradition was the result of things having "soured … by the events with Theos and Phoenix," but there was more to his discontent than personal disagreements. Some of his issues with the tradition stemmed from its rituals. Gardnerian sabbat rituals are not well fleshed out, and as Buckland notes, "You could take the May Eve Sabbat ritual and perform it any other time of year … and it would fit." Buckland believed that the sabbats "*should* be specific in their form." Buckland's dissatisfaction with the sabbat rituals in Gard Craft didn't mean he was through with Wicca, only that he was interested in creating a new form of Wiccan-Witchcraft. His break with the Kneitels and quest for something new led to the creation of a new tradition, Seax-Wica.

Seax-Wica is "Saxon Witchcraft," though there's not a whole lot of Saxon thought in Seax-Wica. For his new tradition, Buckland would use most of the language that had informed the Gardnerian path, Freemasonry, and the grimoire tradition. Buckland admits that his version of Saxon Witchcraft was not an attempt to "resurrect anything" or "to reconstruct the original Saxon religion." Instead, Buckland was using the Saxon culture as a "peg on which to hang everything." If the Gardnerian Craft was Celtic (which it really wasn't), then Seax-Wica would be Saxon (which it also wasn't).

Buckland's "Saxon peg" did provide his new tradition with two names for the Goddess and God. In order to better connect Seax-Wica to England, Buckland settled upon Woden and Freya as the primary deities of his tradition. Woden is the Saxon name of the sky god Odin, the king of the Norse gods, and the husband of the goddess Frigg. But because of the sexual connotations of the word *frig*, Buckland made Freya the primary goddess of Seax-Wica. In myth, Freya is the goddess of fertility, battle, and love and the counterpart of the god Freyr. Due to their similar-sounding names, Freya and Frigg have been conflated from time to time, but Buckland's primary reason for choosing Freya over Frigg was to keep chuckling in the circle to a minimum.

For many polytheists, this conflating of goddesses would be a serious transgression, but Buckland was never much of a polytheist. Instead, Buckland was very much a duotheist, seeing all the names of the various deities worshiped over the millennia as labels for *the* Goddess and God. This is a belief he would express in greater detail in his later works.

The rituals and beliefs of the Seax-Wica were publicly shared in Buckland's 1974 book *The Tree: The Complete Book of Saxon Witchcraft*. By the time of the book's publication, Buckland had been sharing his Saxon Witchcraft rituals for several months, and his impetus for getting the book published was his desire to be acknowledged as the author of the rituals. According to Buckland, there were already people in the United Kingdom planning to publish Buckland's Seax-Wica rituals and claim authorship. Considering the relative "youngness" of the rituals and the amount of time it takes to publish a book, I find this claim doubtful, but better safe than sorry. Instead of Llewellyn releasing the book, *The Tree* was published by Samuel Weiser, and at the time of this writing has now been in print for nearly fifty years.

Leaving behind the rituals of an established tradition for a tradition of one's own making is a rather big step and resulted in some rumors directed at Buckland, the most notorious one being that Buckland created the tradition as a joke. This allegation shows up in Margot Adler's *Drawing Down the Moon*, published in 1979, which helped that rumor to spread across the American Witchcraft world. In *Moon*, Adler suggests that Buckland, "rumor has it," created his new tradition "as a joke … in conjunction with a number of well-known and still practicing Gardnerian Witches."[171]

Margot Adler, who was a part of the New York Witchcraft scene and a Gardnerian, might have heard this rumor from (wait for it) Thomas Kneitel. In his memoir, Buckland shares a conversation he and Kneitel had about creating a "spurious" Witchcraft tradition:

> Tom and I once got into a discussion about the various jumped-up public Witches who claimed that their traditions were very ancient ones … yet they invariably consisted of large proportions of Gardnerian! We thought it would be funny to casually mention, somewhere, a tradition that we knew to be spurious and see how long it took before someone claimed ancient lineage in that tradition. We suggested things like Sumerian Wica, Etruscan Wica, or even something totally fictitious like "Saxonian" Wica. We didn't know what we meant by the word "Saxonian" (which was the point) and it was just one of several

---

171. Adler, *Drawing Down the Moon*, 93.

names thrown out and laughed at. We went no farther on the idea and I forgot all about it. Apparently, though, when I announced Saxon Witchcraft (Seax-Wica), Tom Kneitel remembered that evening of levity and assumed that I was following through on that suggested joke.

I once wrote that Buckland's *The Tree* was the first book ever written for Witches with no access to a coven; in other words, it was the first book ever written for *solitary* Witches. I was "corrected" by a self-styled Witchcraft elder, who assured me that *The Tree* was very much written for covens. The criticism directed at me was partially correct, as many of the rituals in *The Tree* are designed for covens. (The book contains no solitary Yule rituals, for instance.) But *The Tree* also offers the reader the opportunity to participate in a *dedication ritual* that confers all the benefits of initiation. Not only was this rather revolutionary material for a book, but it was also a revolutionary idea in most Witchcraft circles in 1974.

For a whole lot of good reasons, *The Tree* is often overlooked in discussions about early Witchcraft books. Lady Sheba's books will always be interesting to many because of the duplicity inherent in their publication. Over fifty years after the publication of Huson's *Mastering Witchcraft*, there is no book in the Witchcraft market quite like it. Today there are lots of books like *The Tree*, but in 1974 it was the first easily accessible ritual book that didn't violate any oaths (even Huson's work has bits from an oathbound Book of Shadows). *The Tree* is sometimes forgotten because it is not controversial.

By modern standards, there are also a lot of "weird" things in *The Tree* that aren't found anywhere else in Wiccan-style Witchcraft books. For the most part, *The Tree* is a pretty standard Wiccan text. There are rituals with circles, quarters, and deities, and Buckland uses the words *esbat* and *sabbat* and follows the established eight-spoked Wheel of the Year. But in an effort to differentiate his new tradition from Gardnerian Craft, he renames tools and adds new terms to his tradition that just don't exist outside of Seax-Wica.

In early Witchcraft traditions, a non-Witch was called a *cowan*, a term borrowed from Freemasonry that denoted a non-Mason. In Seax-Wica, a non-Witch is a *theow*. Once one has moved from being a theow to a person interested in Witchcraft, the seeker becomes known as a *ceorl*. Ceorls were the neophytes of the Craft; they were allowed to participate in rituals and be a part of the coven, and the idea of letting non-initiates into the coven certainly gave more people an opportunity to participate in Witchcraft. Despite the strangeness of the terms, the ideas behind them were solid.

In Seax-Wica, the initiated Witch was not called an *initiate*, but instead a *gesith*. Unlike the Gardnerian Craft, with its three degrees, there was only one initiation in Buckland's new tradition. A gesith was free to become a Priest or Priestess in the tradition, rotating positions that Buckland suggests the coven should vote on. The honorific "High" (as in High Priestess/Priest) could be used by a gesith only after serving two terms as the coven's Priestess or Priest.

What is really extraordinary about Buckland's system is that a self-dedicated Witch in the Seax-Wica tradition is seen as a gesith. For the first time ever in a tradition, a self-initiate could be confident that they were of equal standing with an initiate. If a solitary Saxon Witch joins a coven, they are accepted as a full member right away and don't have to go through the initiation process. Despite this rather new (and open) approach to the Craft, Buckland had trouble letting go of previously established patterns. He suggests that self-initiated gesiths, upon joining a coven, go through the cycle of theow, ceorl, and gesith. It's also possible that Buckland hoped that most of the initiates in his new tradition would get to experience an initiation ritual conducted by other Witches. Solitary rituals can be an entirely different experience from that of a ritual performed with others.

The hierarchy of a Seax-Wica coven was most likely inspired by Buckland's bitter feelings toward the Kneitels. In Seax-Wica, leadership in the coven would not solely be the responsibility of the High Priestess; now the High Priest would have equal standing. There would be no more arguments about who cast or didn't cast the circle. When describing the structure of the coven, Buckland was adamant that leadership involve both the Priest and the Priestess. No longer would the High Priest be "nothing more than a glorified Altar-boy."[172]

By making Seax-Wica public and available to anyone, Buckland's tradition was free of hierarchy. While it could be argued that Ray himself was at the top of the Saxon Witchcraft pyramid, anyone could start a Seax-Wica

---

172. Buckland, *The Tree*, 26.

coven and anyone was free to be a Priestess or Priest (and, with the blessing of the coven, become High Priest/ess). There would be no controversies
about degrees and who was and wasn't a Saxon Witch. The door was wide
open to anyone who wanted to enter the circle.

Buckland also did away with the idea of "working partners," most likely
to ensure autonomy for solitary practitioners and covens without a High
Priestess or Priest. If one part of the Priestess-Priest partnership is missing,
Buckland says the other ritual leader should simply perform both parts in the
ritual, pointing out that in Gardnerian Craft, the absence of a High Priestess
often means the cancellation of a ritual.

Despite this move away from the binary, Buckland still suggests that the
best covens have an equal number of male and female members. Ceorls preparing for initiation were encouraged to work with a teacher, most commonly
one of the opposite sex. (Doesn't it feel odd to read words like *ceorl*? It's not a
mystery to me just why these terms didn't catch on.)

Perhaps influenced by Herman Slater and Eddie Buczynski, Buckland
writes:

> It is not unknown for homosexuals, or lesbians, to work together
> exclusively as a Seax-Wican coven; or to blend quite happily with
> others.[173]

While this doesn't sound all that welcoming by modern standards, it was a
pretty big deal in 1974. Despite the rather inclusive-sounding language here,
Buckland also writes that

> it seems unlikely that a homosexual would be attracted to a religion
> which is definitely male-female based.[174]

In addition to the Priestess and Priest, there are other elected positions in
Seax-Wica, the most striking one being the *thegn*, or guard. The thegn begins
every ritual by blowing a hunting horn and brings a six-foot-long spear to
ritual and a large round shield to protect the other coven members. Less
striking is the position of *scribe*, who takes notes during coven meetings. The

---

173. Buckland, *The Tree*, 28.
174. Buckland, *The Tree*, 27–28.

number of covens that actually had a covener arrive at circle with a spear and a shield will never be known, but I'm guessing the answer is not many.

In a further effort to differentiate his new tradition from Gardnerian Craft, Buckland renamed the athame, dubbing it a *seax*. While *athame* is a made-up word, *seax* is actually an Old English word for knife! In Gard Craft, the athame traditionally has a black handle, onto which symbols are drawn. In Seax-Wica, the knife's handle can be any color and symbols are not required. These were small changes, but ones that made the Craft feel more accessible.

Despite words from the book (like *seax* and *thegn*) not catching on in Witchcraft circles, *The Tree* did have a long-term impact beyond the idea of self-dedication. In 1974, just what people would call the *sabbats* was still in flux. Lady Sheba's Wheel of the Year, for instance, consisted of Yule, Candlemas, Spring Rite, Rudemas, Beltane, Lammas, Autumn Equinox (Samhain),[175] and Hallowmas or Halloween. The astute reader will note that the Summer Solstice is called Beltane here, and Sheba gives Samhain as an alternate title for the Autumn Equinox.

Despite *The Tree* being a book about "Saxon" Witchcraft, Buckland gives the names of the four greater sabbats as the Irish-Celtic Imbolc, Beltane, Lughnasadh, and Samhain, and puts them on the calendar where we would expect them to be. His adoption of the Irish-Celtic names led to most Witches using those terms for the greater, or cross-quarter, sabbats going forward. Ironically, in choosing Lughnasadh over Lammas, Buckland forgoes the one greater sabbat that may have been celebrated by the Anglo-Saxons. (In 1974 most Witches did not have names for the equinoxes, and it wouldn't be until later in 1970 that terms like Mabon, Litha, and Ostara would start to become commonplace.)

Buckland also uses the term *cakes and ale* in *The Tree*. Previously, this mini celebration of thanksgiving found in most Witchcraft circles was referred to as *cakes and wine*. Both terms are still in use among today's Witches, but many of us (including this author) just prefer cakes and ale. Buckland's use of the term cakes and ale didn't suddenly lead to people pouring the wine out of their chalices, and many of us who use the term cakes and ale are more likely

---

175. That is not a mistake. Sheba lists the Autumn Equinox as "Autumn Equinox (Samhain)."
    Obviously, this did not catch on.

to use wine in ritual, but it did serve to popularize the turn of phrase, again demonstrating Buckland's influence on the greater Witchcraft community.

Remembering Ray: Alaric Albertsson

I became a gesith of Seax Wica in 1974, not long after *The Tree* was published. I don't think most people appreciate how revolutionary this tradition was. I have seen young people quote Ray out of context in a way that portrays him as homophobic, but nothing could be further from the truth. He wrote *The Tree* more than fifty years ago, at a time when gay people were still being electrocuted in a misguided attempt to "cure" them. Obviously some of his language is going to sound dated today. At that time, Wicca was a relatively safe space, but there were more than a few Wiccan homophobes who used the fertility argument to condemn and exclude gay people. Then Ray rolled out a new tradition that welcomed anyone who wanted to worship the old gods of England, a tradition that overtly welcomed gay people. It was both empowering and affirming.

The Seax tradition also challenged the ridiculous gatekeeping that prevailed at that time by introducing and embracing a self-dedication ritual. Ray discarded all of the hierarchy of Gardnerian Wicca. There are no degrees in Seax Wica. Either you are a gesith or you are not. And if you are, it does not matter if you have had an initiation or if you entered the tradition through self-dedication. There are no Elders, no Witch Queens. Every Seax witch is the equal of every other witch in this tradition. Ray himself declined any title or position other than a general acknowledgment that he was the *Faeder*, or founder, of the tradition.

The Tree brought one other thing to the Wiccan world that usually passes under the radar. After I became a published author, Ray Buckland and I often engaged in conversations either in person or by email, and during one of these chats, Ray told me that he had hoped the Seax tradition would revive the worship of Woden. As an Englishman, he was a descendant of a strong Anglo-Saxon heritage that was largely ignored in the early 1970s. The revival of the worship of Woden may have been one of his most notable achievements. Woden is revered today in Theodism, ADF Druidry, Fyrnsidu, and other forms of spiritual expression that otherwise bear little or no resemblance to Wicca. Most, if not all, of these Anglo-Saxon spiritual paths were influenced or inspired by Seax Wica.

When I lived in Pennsylvania, I was in a Seax coven, but now I am more likely to honor the Saxon gods in an ADF ritual with my local Druidic hearth or just raise a horn to them in a blót with my kindred. However, when I do practice Wicca, it is always in the Seax tradition— with modifications, of course. Ray encouraged Seax witches to adapt the rites to our needs.

I also maintain my ties with the greater Seax community. There are Seax witches all over the world. This is another reason why there are no Elders in our tradition. How would you enforce that? Anyone can pick up a copy of *Buckland's Book of Saxon Witchcraft* (the title that *The Tree* is now published under), perform the rite of self-dedication, and begin practicing the tradition. Anyone claiming to speak for the tradition just looks silly. I am probably one of the more widely known Saxon witches, and I am sure that there are countless Seax practitioners who have never heard of me. At one time, Ray tried to appoint an official spokesperson for the tradition, a steward to whom people could go with questions. This proved unsuccessful, and after the second attempt, the idea was abandoned. Ray told me that he decided Seax Wica had to sink or swim on its own merits. There could not be one spokesperson for the entire tradition.

This seemingly chaotic nature of Seax Wica is what I love most about it. My way of witchcraft may not be your way, but that does not mean you are doing it wrong, not when Ray Buckland himself has urged you "to adapt what I present to meet your own requirements" (page xiv).

While there is no shortage of Seax witches in the United States and England, the tradition seems to be especially popular in South America. I do not know why. Neither did Ray Buckland, although he was quite pleased by it. He often corresponded with Juan Espinoza, a leader in Peru's Seax community. There are active, thriving Seax covens today not only in Peru but also in Argentina, Chile, and Brazil.

My own relationship with Ray Buckland evolved considerably over the years. When I first discovered witchcraft in 1971, I was a huge fan of his *Practical Candleburning Rituals*, a book that I still recommend to people. A couple of years later, when *The Tree* was published, he became one of my heroes. It was another six years before I had the opportunity to meet him in person at the Pan Pagan Festival in 1980. I remember how courteous he was. But the turning point in our relationship was in 2009, when Llewellyn Worldwide released my first book, *Travels Through Middle Earth*. I was asked to speak at the Earth Warriors Festival, and one of the other speakers happened to be Ray Buckland. Somehow the two of us wound up in a corner together talking about his childhood in England and wondering what they were going to serve us for breakfast. I gave him a signed copy of my new book, and he gave me the best present imaginable, a signed copy of *Buckland's Book of Saxon Witchcraft*.

Again I was struck by the courtesy and respect he showed me.

Over the ensuing years, I often sought Ray's advice. He even helped me write the chapter on Seax Wica that I contributed to the 2014 anthology *Witchcraft Today: 60 Years On*. When Ray Buckland left our world in 2017, I lost a friend and mentor. He was the sort of man I aspire to be, kind and respectful to others. He was an inspiration.

Alaric Albertsson *is the author of* A Handbook of Saxon Sorcery and Magick *(Llewellyn) and* Travels Through Middle Earth: The Path of a Saxon Pagan *(Crossed Crow Books). He currently lives in Dubuque, Iowa.*

• • • • • • • •

While transitioning from Gardnerian Wicca to Seax-Wica, Raymond Buckland worked with several Pagan Way groups in the New York City area. Pagan Way groups were among the first "eclectic" Wiccan-style ritual groups, mostly utilizing the Outer Court materials devised by Ed Fitch. At one of those Pagan Way meetings, Buckland met Joan Taylor, and the two began dating in early 1973. By 1974 Taylor would become Buckland's second wife.

But the biggest change in Buckland's life was not a second wife, but his decision to move out of New York City. There were several factors that led to Buckland leaving, including the great responsibility of now raising his two boys on his own. In his memoir, he writes:

> I had been feeling a lot of loneliness after Rosemary left and, eventually, Joan moved into the house with me (she had been living at home with her parents). I felt that I needed to move away from Long Island and Joan agreed, wanting to go with me. I thought of the beautiful New Hampshire countryside, where our family had vacationed a number of times, and suggested it to Joan. The lease was about to run out on the museum and the landlord wanted to raise the already high rent. I thought it would be nice if I could buy a place in New Hampshire that had sufficient room on the same property for the museum.

The move to New Hampshire also prompted Buckland's marriage to Taylor; apparently, she would only move to New Hampshire if she and Buckland were at least engaged. Buckland was not particularly happy about the accelerated courtship, but he agreed anyway. Not surprisingly, Buckland's marriage to Taylor would be the shortest of his three marriages, and the least impactful on the course of his life.

Into the stocks with you! The Buckland Museum of Witchcraft and Magick
at Weirs Beach, New Hampshire

In April of 1973, Buckland and Taylor visited New Hampshire in search of a property to buy with enough room for them, the boys, and the museum. They eventually settled on a location at Weirs Beach, a small lakeside area within the northern part of the city of Laconia, New Hampshire. Their new house was not especially roomy, but it contained three bedrooms, a basement, and a lovely screened-in porch. There was also a two-story barn that Buckland used for storage and to host Witch rituals. The property's major selling point to Buckland might have been a "huge garage-type building" that could (and would) serve as the museum's new home. After the Brentwood house sold that spring, Raymond and Joan, along with the boys, set out for New Hampshire, and on July 20 of that year, Buckland's Museum of Witchcraft and Magick was once again open for business.

The Book Barn and a bit of the Sherwood Forest Archery Range at the Buckland Museum

Weirs Beach is a tourist area, so the museum was a natural fit; but unlike New York City, which is open year-round, the tourist season at Weirs Beach only lasts from Memorial Day to Labor Day. The tourist season just wasn't long enough to make the museum profitable, and shortly after the museum reopened, Buckland realized that he and Joan would have to get regular jobs from autumn through spring. It's hard to imagine a Witchcraft museum making a whole lot of money if it can't maintain regular hours near Halloween!

Despite the challenges posed by the museum's new location, Buckland really tried to make a go of it and soon expanded what was offered at the museum. Just outside the museum, Buckland set up stocks and a pillory, offering museum visitors a fun photo op. There was also Buckland's Book Barn, a secondhand bookshop located in the property's carriage house. He also added the Sherwood Forest Archery Range, mostly to give children something to do while their parents visited the museum.

The museum's ever-increasing number of things to do didn't help the bottom line all that much, but it did provide a few good stories. In his memoir, Buckland recounts a mother and son's experience at the archery range:

> On one occasion a mother with a young boy asked me if I'd show her son how to shoot. I took the bow and showed him how to knock the arrow. Then I showed him how to draw and sight (these were regular flat bows; not composites), and then I let fly. By the merest of chances the arrow flew down the range and imbedded in the bullseye, the gold in the very center of the target. I casually remarked, "There! Like that." Then I turned and walked away. It looked as though I shot like that all the time but, if truth be known, if I'd taken a second shot it could just as well have missed the target completely!

In his memoir, Buckland recounts meeting George Lutz (1947–2006) at his museum when it was located on Long Island. Lutz and his wife, Kathy (1946–2004), would become famous as the main protagonists of the 1978 book (and later 1979 movie) *The Amityville Horror*. According to Buckland, Lutz was especially curious about ghosts and asked a lot of questions about their nature and origin. Buckland then says he visited the home of the Lutzes at 112 Ocean Avenue a couple of times, which was the location of the alleged Amityville haunting.

While I believe it's possible that Lutz visited Buckland, the Lutzes did not live on Ocean Avenue while Buckland's museum was in New York. The Lutzes moved into the Amityville house in 1975, about a year after the house was the scene of a grisly murder. The murderer, Ronald DeFeo Jr. (1951–2021), killed all six members of his immediate family, including his mother, father, two brothers, and two sisters. Several psychic investigators did visit the Lutz home in the winter of 1975–76, and it's certainly the type of thing

Buckland would have been interested in doing, but he would have made the trip down to New York City from New Hampshire.

Buckland writes that he experienced "absolutely nothing" during his first visit to the Lutz home on Ocean Avenue. A follow-up visit with a psychic friend also resulted in nothing out of the ordinary. Buckland says other ghost hunters and psychics in the New York area reported the same lack of haunting. A few years later, Buckland was surprised and amused to see the Lutzes at the center of the whole *Amityville Horror* craze, believing that they had made up the entire ghost story. (Debate over whether or not *Amityville* was a hoax continues to the present day, and subsequent owners of the home have reported no hauntings of any kind.)

The new Buckland compound was a bustling place, especially in the summer, and was home not just to Ray, Joan, and the boys but also to several ghosts! Unlike the home on Ocean Avenue, Buckland did feel a ghostly presence in his new home. Shortly after moving into the house, Raymond and Joan got used to hearing heavy footsteps walk from the home's second floor down the stairs into the living room and then stop, when they were the only two individuals at home. Doors would occasionally slam for no reason, and after one such instance, Buckland noticed a man hurriedly walking toward the front door. Getting up to investigate, Buckland couldn't find the man, nor were there any cars or visitors around.

The Bucklands weren't the only people to experience ghosts at the new house. Joan's mom did as well. Ray's mother-in-law had woken up in the middle of the night and noticed a woman dressed in blue standing at the foot of her bed. The ghost looked at Joan's mom for a few moments and then slowly faded from sight. None of the ghost encounters were ever especially traumatic, and the family soon got used to their spectral visitors and made no effort to get rid of them.

As if two ghosts weren't enough, Ray and Joan soon had additional houseguests. Two friends of theirs who had fallen into a bit of a financial hole were soon living at the property at Weirs Beach, along with their three small children. The five extra roommates would stay with Ray and Joan for over a year. Luckily for everyone involved, Renny (Ray's youngest son) had moved back to New York City to live with his mother for a bit.

October of 1973 presented Buckland with another opportunity to talk about Witchcraft to a national TV audience. This time Buckland was a guest on *The Tomorrow Show with Tom Snyder*, a late-night talk show airing at 1:00 a.m. immediately following the *Tonight Show with Johnny Carson*. During this period, Snyder's show taped in Los Angeles in the same studio as Carson's *Tonight Show*, which allowed Buckland to spend a few moments sitting at Johnny's desk. Not surprisingly, Buckland's episode of *The Tomorrow Show* aired near Halloween, the time of year when the media tends to remember that Witches exist.

After several years of focusing exclusively on Witchcraft, Buckland found time for other pursuits while living in New Hampshire, one of which was Transcendental Meditation (TM). Buckland found the practice of TM "pleasant enough" but thought the practice's ethics were a bit lacking.

In addition to TM, Buckland also became involved with a Search for God study group during his time in New Hampshire. Despite the name sounding rather preachy, Search for God groups study the work of psychic Edgar Cayce (1877–1945). Although Cayce was a Christian, he was a firm believer in both reincarnation and the lost continent of Atlantis. Ray and Joan hosted the study group in their home, with most of their meetings focused on discussing Cayce's books and practicing group meditation. In addition to the study group, Buckland also spent a lot of time investigating past life memories (both his and those of friends) through hypnotic regression during this period.

It's a little jarring to think of one of the most famous Witches in the United States engaging in Transcendental Meditation and studying the works of a Christian psychic, but the religious and spiritual landscape of the 1970s was very different from that of today. Fifty-plus years ago, there just weren't a whole lot of opportunities to engage in occult and/or esoteric activities. For a lot of Witches of that era, dabbling in other practices was commonplace, and it certainly wasn't frowned upon. In an area like New York City, there were a fair number of Witchcraft and Pagan-related activities going on in the 1970s, but at Weirs Beach, New Hampshire? Buckland was simply taking advantage of the rather limited opportunities afforded to him at his new residence.

Despite his intense focus on Witchcraft during the 1960s and early '70s, Raymond Buckland had always been a bit of a polymath. A survey of his published works reveals a man with very broad interests and one who believed in the validity of a number of spiritual paths and esoteric pursuits. Buckland was always open to pursuing whatever interested him, even if that pursuit looked at Witchcraft with a degree of suspicion.

In 1973 Buckland was asked by HC Publishers to write a follow-up volume to *Witchcraft Ancient and Modern*. He came up with *Here Is the Occult* (1974), which focused on divination, Voodoo, Tarot, Black Magic, White Magic, Satanism, and, not surprisingly, Witchcraft. During the writing of *Occult*, the publisher asked Buckland to add a segment on exorcism, due to the popularity of the movie *The Exorcist* that year. Later that year, a friend of Buckland's arranged for Ray to meet with director William Friedkin (1935–2023), who had won an Oscar for his work on *The Exorcist*.

Friedkin was in the early process of creating a new stage version of *Macbeth* and wanted his Witches to be as authentic as possible. Buckland arrived on the West Coast armed with a tray of slides that he often used in lectures, and he gave Friedkin his usual Witchcraft talk, though this time in a small Hollywood office with an Oscar sitting on his audience's desk! Friedkin was impressed with Buckland's presentation and remarked, when it was over, that he wanted to make his Witches skyclad and have Lady Macbeth as the High Priestess of the Witch coven. Friedkin must have been a bit charmed by Buckland, as the director held Ray's hand and was led in a series of dances often used by Witches of the era.

The entire trip was paid for by Friedkin, including limousine service and a stay at the Beverly Wilshire Hotel. Buckland was paid $500 for his work, a significantly greater sum than the $200 initially promised when the trip was set up. Ever the self-promoter, Buckland used his meeting with Friedkin to share a screenplay he had been working on titled *The Third Day*[176] and credited to "Tony Earll."[177] Sadly for Buckland, Friedkin ended up passing on both the *Macbeth* project and the screenplay, but Buckland's 1974 adventure in Hollywood would not be his last foray into the movie business. There would be more opportunities in the years to come.

---

176. Lily St. Clair, letter to Raymond Buckland, March 4, 1975.
177. Lily St. Clair, letter to Raymond Buckland, June 30, 1975.

Many of Buckland's books during this period were on topics a bit beyond Witchcraft and the usual occult overviews. *Amazing Secrets of the Psychic World* (1975) was not just an overview of psychic phenomena but also an introduction to chakras, spirit communication, crystal gazing, and dozens of other practices. Unlike everything else Buckland ever wrote, this volume was an updated version of a previous book by British-American psychic researcher Hereward Carrington (1880–1958). *Psychic World* was published by Parker Publishing, a press that at the time focused exclusively on formulaic how-to books, even providing prospective authors with guidelines they were required to follow when producing their work.

Parker's guidelines are why Buckland's second book for the company begins with a rather emphatic "What This Book Will Do for You," promising that good health, love, money, and the ability to control others "can all be yours."[178] *The Magick of Chant-O-Matics* (1978) is the most oddly titled book in Buckland's catalog, and the one that most reads like a sensationalist self-help title. Nearly every chapter in the book is structured the same way. Chants are offered to fix a situation, along with personal stories relating how individuals such as "Tracy B." and "Billy K." used chants to get whatever their hearts desired. Some of the book's chapter titles read almost like infomercials, including one promising that you can "Protect Your Home and Family with the All-Enveloping Cover of Chant-O-Matics."[179]

Perhaps due to New Hampshire's more remote location, one consequence of Buckland's move there was that he did fewer personal appearances. There were still newspaper and media stories about Buckland and the museum during his time in New England, as well as several big opportunities such as consulting for Friedkin and the Snyder interview, but overall it was a less hectic travel schedule than he had experienced in New York. Much of this might also be related to a general cooling down of interest in the occult following the 1960s and early '70s.

There was also perhaps less time for unpaid work because Buckland was simply struggling to pay the bills in New Hampshire. It's easy to think of someone like Raymond Buckland working 24/7 on Witchcraft-related materials, but for most of Ray's life that was far from the case. In 1975 he helped

---

178. Buckland, *The Magick of Chant-O-Matics*, 3.
179. Buckland, *The Magick of Chant-O-Matics*, 12 and 211.

start Brothers Grimm Press, which, while sounding cool, focused mostly on printing menus and brochures for local businesses. At one point, to pay the bills, Buckland operated a folding press an hour away in Concord, New Hampshire, an especially horrific drive in the snow of a New England winter. One time Buckland got his hand stuck in the feeding mechanism and lost most of the skin on his fingers. Luckily for Buckland, he soon became the supervisor of the press's art department. Despite the TV shows and getting to hobnob with the occasional celebrity, the world of the working Witch is not always particularly glamorous.

I find Buckland's sojourn in New Hampshire to be one of the bleakest periods of his life. The museum was never going to be particularly profitable in an environment where it was only open for three and a half months a year, and then there were the (as Ray described it) "soul destroying winters" that he could never quite adjust to. So after just four years in New England, Raymond and Joan decided to move to Virginia Beach, Virginia, in December of 1977. At this point it was just the two of them, with Robert having joined the air force and Renny getting married. There was nothing keeping them from beginning a new chapter in their lives.

The move to Virginia Beach meant big changes in the life of Raymond Buckland, the most notable one being the end of the Witchcraft museum. Upon deciding to move south, Buckland sold the museum's display cases and put the exhibits and displays in storage. Over the next forty years, many of the items in storage would be either damaged or stolen, but the museum would eventually rise again.

Buckland's time in Virginia Beach was extremely unsettled. Over the course of four years, Raymond and Joan lived in four different locations, including two apartments during the first two months upon moving there. In 1979 they moved into a rental house located on a small island in the Chesapeake Bay. Buckland enjoyed living near the ocean, and he owned and piloted a small sailboat during this period, but the rental house was extremely damp. During the Virginia summers, many items in the house ended up covered in a layer of fine green mold! Buckland was forced to turn up the heat in the house to deal with the mold. Two years later, Ray and Joan would move into a different house owned by Joan's parents. At this point, Buckland was forty-six years old.

Virginia Beach did offer Raymond Buckland several creative outlets that were unavailable in rural New Hampshire. During his time in Virginia, he joined a writers' group, but perhaps most importantly, there were additional spiritual outlets. The Edgar Cayce Foundation's home base was in Virginia Beach, and Ray and Joan both spent a lot of time participating in the foundation's Association for Research and Enlightenment (A.R.E.), which focused on psychic phenomena and spirituality. During this period, A.R.E. was also home to one of the United States' most extensive metaphysical libraries, something that Buckland took full advantage of.

Despite the resources at A.R.E., the group was limited to mostly studying the work of Edgar Cayce, a constraint that didn't sit well with Buckland. Luckily, just down the road was the Association for Documentation and Enlightenment (A.D.E.), yet another Virginia Beach group interested in psychic phenomena. The biggest difference between the Cayce Foundation's A.R.E. and the A.D.E. was that the latter worked with living psychics; not surprisingly, Raymond Buckland soon found himself heavily involved with the group. The A.D.E. would change its name to the Poseidia Institute shortly after Buckland joined up (Poseidia being an alternate name for the lost continent of Atlantis), and he and Joan began teaching classes at the institute within eight months of moving to Virginia Beach.

In March of 1979, Buckland was appointed Director of the Education Center at Poseidia and was responsible for bringing in guest speakers and organizing workshops and lectures. Buckland also ran the organization's bookstore. During his time at the institute, Buckland became good friends with Michael Ragan, Poseidia's resident astrologer. Over the next few years, Ragan would accompany Buckland on several trips to Pagan festivals and events. Ragan himself would go on to found the Temple of Danann, a Pagan tradition inspired by Irish mythology.

Buckland's friendship with Ragan would lead to the establishment of a new press and mail-order business, Bell, Book and Candle of the Old Dominion, which sold a mixture of Witch essentials and various esoteric odds and ends. Wares ranged from ritual anointing oils and athames to books and Tibetan prayer wheels. There's a real sense of ambition to the products offered by Bell, Book and Candle of the Old Dominion. The business's "personal talismans" were personally engraved in bronze and blessed by a High

Priest (likely Ray). The company's brochure promised "individual attention guaranteed" for such custom orders.

Bell, Book and Candle of the Old Dominion also offered bachelor's, master's, and doctorate "degrees" from the Eugenia Institute of Metaphysics in a variety of categories, including arcane wisdom, philosophical occultism, and cosmic consciousness. In addition to degrees from the Eugenia Institute, there were also diplomas available from the New Christian Institute of New England. Obviously, nothing from Bell, Book and Candle of the Old Dominion was accredited, and the brochure's fine print did point out that certificates and diplomas were for "amusement only," but I can't help but wonder how many Witches once claimed degrees from Buckland's fictional schools. And at a price of fifteen to twenty-five dollars per certificate (the equivalent of about sixty-five to one hundred ten dollars in 2025), Buckland's wares were not cheap.

Bell, Book and Candle of the Old Dominion offering nearly everything!

Bell, Book and Candle of the Old Dominion did not have a brick-and-mortar location, but Buckland and Ragan often took their wares on the road and vended in the burgeoning Pagan festival scene. Many of those early events were skyclad (naked), and Buckland delighted in attending these events au naturel, perhaps because most Seax-Wica rituals required the wearing of ceremonial robes. During this period, Buckland also began to visit other Witches on the East Coast, and some of them had very different opinions from Raymond Buckland about just what Witchcraft and Wicca were.

• • • • • • • •

The most public Witchcraft-related group in the United States during the 1970s was the Church and School of Wicca, established by Gavin (1930–2016) and Yvonne Frost (1931–present) at the start of the decade. Unlike other Pagan and Witch groups of the era, the Frosts advertised their church in the pages of magazines and comic books, setting up a correspondence course for those interested in their group. Advertising the Craft in the early 1970s, especially in the context of a correspondence course, was seen as anathema by many during this period, with Buckland among the skeptical. Compounding matters even further, despite the Frosts claiming to be Wiccan, the Witchcraft they taught had very little to do with Wicca or any other established Witchcraft practice of the era.

In her book *Drawing Down the Moon*, an overview of Paganism and Witchcraft in the 1970s, Margot Adler felt it was necessary to list just how different the Wicca of the Frosts was from that of other practitioners in the 1970s. Unlike most Witches of that era, the Frosts were monotheists, did not identify as Pagan, and ignored the divine feminine. The Wicca of Gardner was exceedingly matriarchal, but Gavin Frost especially had no use for such ideas, calling matriarchy "a Marxist heresy."[180]

The most egregious of the Frosts' heresies during this period was the idea that children should have a ritualized first sexual experience at the start of puberty. Their 1972 book *The Witch's Bible* not only includes a ritual outlining such an event but also gives advice on how to make a phallus so that young women can practice coitus. In later editions of *The Witch's Bible*, the Frosts would include a disclaimer that everyone involved in these rituals should be over the age of eighteen, but that was clearly lacking in the book's first edition (and even with the disclaimer, it's all very unsettling and, as my acquisitions editor noted, "gross").

---

180. Adler, *Drawing Down the Moon*, 127–28.

Despite the Frosts holding beliefs very much at odds with the rest of the Witchcraft world, they were active participants in the magickal community from the 1970s into the early 2010s (though their attendance at events was often greeted with a great deal of controversy). In addition to their odd beliefs about the Craft, the Frosts often shared a narrative about the history of Modern Witchcraft that was very much at odds with the truth. At a lecture of theirs in the late 2000s, I was told that they (and not Raymond Buckland) were the first practitioners of Wicca in the United States and that Gavin himself had coined the term Wicca as a name for religious Witchcraft (despite the fact that Witches had been using the term Wicca with two *c*'s since the mid-1960s).

Over the course of the last twenty-five years, I have met a number of Witches who studied with the Frosts and have found many of them to be wonderful Witches. I have also met the children and grandchildren of the Frosts, and I think very highly of them. Gavin and Yvonne were also visitors to my own workshops and were most often pleasant, though Gavin tended to interrupt and remind people of his (alleged) importance. Despite my own misgivings about the Frosts, the couple was active in fighting for the religious rights of Witches and established the second Pagan-leaning (remember, by their own words they were not Pagans) church in the United States. Legacies are complicated, though I think the Frosts are more likely to appear in the footnotes of American Witch history than to headline a chapter.

Despite the problematic nature of Frostian Wicca, Raymond Buckland accepted an invitation to visit the Frosts in North Carolina in 1979. The purpose of the visit was to observe how the Frosts managed their Witchcraft correspondence course, as Buckland was thinking about creating a correspondence course of his own. Buckland (with Michael Ragan in tow) writes that the Frosts made their guests feel "welcome" and that the trip was overall a positive one. Buckland did confront the Frosts about their published rituals advocating for the sexual initiation of children, with assurances from Gavin that such material would be removed from future editions of *The Witch's Bible*, but Gavin did not live up to that promise.

Though Buckland disagreed with much of the material in the Frosts' correspondence courses, he was impressed by the organization displayed by Gavin and Yvonne. The Frosts were early adopters of computer technology, and by the late 1970s much of their correspondence course was computer-generated. Instead of individually going over the material submitted by their students, the Frosts set up "managers" to oversee the grading and critiquing of assignments. Managers were not allowed to come up with tailor-made answers to student queries. Instead, they were directed to search through a prearranged list of potential questions with corresponding answers. Questions not included on that list were ignored. Upon seeing how Gavin and Yvonne managed student questions, Buckland vowed that he would work with every student one-on-one and not rely on canned answers and outsiders to do his work.

The "Number One Witchcraft Course in the World"!

While putting together his Seax-Wica correspondence course, Buckland was traveling further afield and making more connections in the growing Pagan world. A trip to the Pan Pagan Festival in Indiana resulted in Ray striking up a friendship with Zsuzsanna (Z.) Budapest (1940–present), the founder of the Dianic Witchcraft tradition. During this period, he also met Atlanta's Lady Sintana (1937–2010), founder of the Ravenwood Church, one of the first tax-exempt Pagan groups in the United States.

Upon its debut, Buckland's "Home Study Course in Saxon Witchcraft" was an immediate hit and quickly became the best-selling product at Bell,

Book and Candle of the Old Dominion. The success was justified, too, as Buckland lived up to his pledge to grade every assignment himself and to generally be available to students. But the success of Buckland's first mail-order venture was due to more than just applying a personal touch (and being a rather famous Witch, which certainly helped!); his course was also thoughtful and well put together.

Buckland's correspondence course was created in an era before desktop publishing but still managed to look neat and professional. The pages of the course were created with an electric typewriter and feature several pictures interspersed throughout the text. The overwhelming majority of the illustrations were done by Buckland himself, including a rather flattering drawing of Gerald Gardner in the first lesson.

Gerald Gardner 1884-1964

Notice the striking portrait of Gerald Gardner in Buckland's correspondence course.

There were twelve lessons in the course, and students were expected to work through at least one lesson every two months. Unlike Buckland's *The Tree*, his correspondence course was more than just a collection of rituals and some vague instructions; it was an instruction manual about just *how* to do things. Each lesson was about fifteen to eighteen pages in length and included examination questions that had to be answered correctly (and then sent to Buckland) before a student was allowed to move on to the next unit.

Though most of the material in the course was broadly Wiccan, and was certainly capable of appealing to people outside of the Seax-Wica tradition,

Buckland was determined to lean into some of the quirks of his new tradition. Instead of including lessons on divination, herbal lore, and magick (which Buckland notes is the "old spelling" of the word *magic*), Buckland provides lessons on *hwata*, *lacnunga*, and *galdra*, all Old Norse words (or variations of Old Norse words) for those subjects. In a list of other contemporary Witchcraft traditions, Buckland even includes Algard (the tradition founded by Mary Nesnick), and in another passage he speaks rather favorably of both Sybil Leek and the Frosts, despite his sometimes chilly relationships with those individuals.

All of Buckland's work contains an immense amount of appreciation for Gerald Gardner, but Buckland can't help but include some criticisms of initiatory Craft. In the course's final unit, Buckland compares his Saxon sabbat rituals to those of an initiatory tradition, noting that in the ritual of the initiatory tradition it's impossible to tell what sabbat is being celebrated based on the words of the rite. Buckland writes that "the earlier quoted ritual, from the other tradition, could be said at *any* time of year and it would still fit in!" He then adds that this ritual of the other tradition "falls far short of the Saxon rituals."[181]

Ray's circle-casting drawing in his correspondence course

Buckland's Seax-Wica correspondence course was not cheap. Before receiving the first lesson, students had to pay a ten-dollar registration fee (thirty-five dollars in 2025 adjusted for inflation) and then ten dollars for each subsequent lesson. It was possible to pay for the entire course all at once, but there was no discount for doing so (though there was a discount for couples taking the course together). The full course cost a minimum of $130

---

181. Buckland, "Home Study Course in Saxon Witchcraft," lesson 12, page 3.

(about $450 in 2025 rounded up for inflation). While this might sound like a lot, keep in mind that Buckland was very much running a mom-and-pop shop, with minimal assistance and doing all the grading of the individual lessons. Those who paid for the entire course all at once and later had buyer's remorse were eligible to have part of their fee refunded.

I think Buckland really had the best interests of his students at heart with his correspondence course. He wasn't simply looking to cash a check; he wanted to get to his know students as much as was possible through a correspondence course. People registering for the course were encouraged to send in a photograph so that Ray could associate a face with the name on the study questions. He also made himself available to anyone interested in a Seax-Wica initiation. If you could get to Virginia, Ray would initiate you personally! If you couldn't get to Virginia, he was willing to go to you as long as his travel costs and accommodations were taken care of. (I would have paid $130 just for that honor!)

There is a bit of "hustle" to the promotional materials created by Buckland for his program. Certainly patrons got what they were promised, but Buckland really went for the hard sell once people expressed interest in the program. The introductory materials sent to students included breathless and anonymous testimonials about the power of Buckland's lessons. One student from Kansas exclaimed, "This course has saved my life, literally." My favorite comment is from a student in South Carolina, who wrote, "It has been said that anything can be improved upon, but to improve upon this course, at this time I don't know how."[182]

Individuals who chose not to participate in the Seax-Wica correspondence course after receiving their initial sign-up letter often got a second letter imploring them to reconsider:

At present nearly a thousand students are enjoying the course. They are from all age groups—our oldest student is in her eighties—and from many countries of the world. Won't you join them and start a new, exciting, and rewarding life?[183]

---

182. Buckland, "Home Study Course in Saxon Witchcraft," lesson 1, page 12.
183. Buckland, "Dear Friend" letter for the "Home Study Course in Saxon Witchcraft."

The correspondence course was only one part of a much larger and more ambitious plan of Buckland's. In *The Seax-Wica Voys* (a periodical for practitioners of Seax-Wica started in 1975 by Buckland) in October of 1982, Buckland shared plans for a pan-Wiccan seminary:

> The ultimate goal … is the founding of a true Wiccan *SEMINARY*—a recognized, respected, completely accepted college for the training of Wiccan Priests and Priestesses. I am not talking about a place to simply hold sporadic workshops, seminars, festivals, and the like. No, I mean a permanent *Wican* [sic] *college* with regular residential courses.

Buckland never came close to realizing his dream of founding a Wiccan seminary, but he did establish the Church of Seax-Wica later that year and affiliated it with the Universal Life Church in order to receive religious protections.

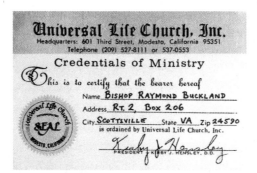

The Universal Life Church has its flaws, but it does offer legal protections.

• • • • • • • •

Buckland came face-to-face with his mortality in September of 1980 when he was diagnosed with a case of diverticulitis, an inflammation in the large intestine. Buckland originally believed that the abdominal pains he was experiencing were the result of some overly hot Cuban food, but after several days in bed with alternating hot and cold spells, a swollen stomach, and a temperature of 104 degrees, he realized that something quite serious was going on. Upon reaching the hospital, he was rushed into surgery and then spent over a week in the hospital. He was eventually released from the hospital with a colostomy bag and an appointment for a second surgery to remove either all or a large part of his colon.

When Buckland visited the hospital for his second surgery, he was told that the entire large intestine would have to be removed. He balked and asked that only the most infected portions of the colon be removed. His doctors warned against that course of action, mentioning that electing to have only a partial surgery could result in his malady coming back at any moment. Not wanting to live with a colostomy bag, Buckland ignored his physicians' advice. Buckland's decision would end up being the right one, as he never again had an issue with his colon, but it was a harrowing couple of months.

During this period, Buckland also got a magickal assist from hundreds of Witches and Pagans in the magickal community. That Samhain, the Magickal Childe's Herman Slater organized a Witch's ball at a New York discotheque. Slater's event featured music from several different Pagan performers, with Circle Sanctuary's Selena Fox (1949–present) in charge of the obligatory Samhain ritual (in addition to being a musical performer). Moments before the ritual was set to begin, Slater pulled Fox aside and asked her to come up with a healing rite for Buckland. When Slater made this request for an impromptu healing rite, he forgot to mention to Fox that Hans Holzer would be recording Fox's ritual. Fox recounts that when she started a chant for the healing work, she was surprised to see "a camera right in my face!"[184] Sadly, the footage of the healing ritual for Buckland (and of that entire night) is unavailable today, but the healing rite was certainly successful!

In his memoir, Buckland credits Joan with nursing him through his gastric adventures, but during this period of time their relationship was beginning to deteriorate. Shortly after moving to Virginia, Taylor went back to college and got a teaching degree. Her responsibilities in the classroom precluded her from joining Ray on the many trips he was taking to Pagan and magickal gatherings, both local events and those further afield. Joan was also less involved with the Craft and the small coven that she and Raymond had started upon moving to Virginia.

Raymond and Joan's marriage ended in the summer of 1982 after the couple shared a rather argumentative trip to the UK. Because of the difficulties

---

184. Fox, personal interview conducted on August 15, 2024.

in their relationship, Buckland had wanted to cancel the couple's planned trip, but he went along with it mostly to see his mother, who was then eighty-two years old. (In his memoir, Buckland mentions that at the time he didn't know how many more opportunities he would have to see his mother before she passed. She ended up living to be 101, another nineteen years!) Buckland took some time on the trip to visit his old childhood home and, not surprisingly, to chat with some UK Witches.

Things might have been tense between Buckland and many Gardnerian Witches in the United States, but that was not the case in the UK. While on holiday, he enjoyed a lovely visit with Patricia Crowther, one of Gardner's High Priestesses. Buckland also visited the Museum of Witchcraft and Magic in Boscastle, Cornwall. This visit sparked a long series of correspondence between Buckland and Cecil Williamson, the museum's founder. Williamson had been active in the Witchcraft world since the 1950s and was originally Gardner's partner for the Witchcraft museum on the Isle of Man before the two men had a bitter falling-out.

Buckland had also hoped to meet Doreen Valiente on this trip to the UK. Valiente was one of Gardner's earliest High Priestesses and wrote and revised much of the Gardnerian Book of Shadows after being initiated into the tradition. Even people unfamiliar with Valiente are probably familiar with her work, especially the *Charge of the Goddess* ("Once in the month, and better it be when the moon is full...").

In his memoir, Buckland recounts his meeting with Valiente:

> We went first to Brighton and attempted to visit with Doreen Valiente. I say "attempted" because I ended up talking to her through a locked door! Apparently she had been harassed a great deal by the local youth and had become overly cautious if not paranoid. She refused to believe that I was who I said I was, charging that I might be someone pretending to be me just to get in! It was rather sad.

Although this is most assuredly how Buckland perceived their interaction, the truth might be a bit different. In a letter to historian Philip Heselton, Witch Janet Farrar gives an alternate version of Buckland's meeting with Valiente:

There was one part of the year when nobody…was welcome at Doreen's house. When the World Cup was on, that was it! The door of the flat was locked and nobody got inside until the World Cup was over…We knew that was the one time you did *not* disturb Doreen Valiente. And unfortunately, poor Ray Buckland made the fatal mistake.[185]

Buckland's timing wasn't his only mistake; he showed up at Valiente's flat unannounced, and Valiente did not like unannounced visitors! Even if the World Cup hadn't been on, it's unlikely that Valiente would have answered the door for Ray. The visit was surely a disappointment for Buckland, but it makes for a rather amusing story.

Within four weeks of returning to the States, Buckland moved out of the house he shared with Taylor. Luckily for Buckland, Michael Ragan was also going through the process of a divorce and had space for a roommate. But Buckland wouldn't cohabit with his buddy Mike for very long. He had already met someone near the end of his relationship with Taylor, and that woman would turn out to be the absolute love of his life.

---

185. Heselton, *Doreen Valiente Witch*, 292. In case anyone questions Janet Farrar's version of these events, the Bucklands' trip in 1982 syncs up nicely with that year's World Cup.

Exercise 6: Protection

One of the things I've always appreciated about Raymond Buckland's writing is how easy he makes things. Today people write entire books about Witch bottles and other sorts of container magic, but Buckland makes creating a Witch bottle easy, and in less than nine hundred words! (The art of brevity is often underappreciated!)

I don't know if Buckland used a whole lot of easy Witch bottles in his personal practice, but considering some of the negativity he was dealing with back in the 1970s, it wouldn't surprise me. Perhaps someday, at the former site of the Buckland Museum of Witchcraft and Magick at Weirs Beach, someone will dig up a small glass jar filled with sharp objects and other nasty things! I've come to believe that Ray truly delighted in sharing magickal practices that could be done by just about anybody.

The following protection spell comes from *Buckland's Complete Book of Witchcraft*,[186] but a nearly identical version appears in lesson 9 of Buckland's Seax-Wica correspondence course. The only major differences between the two versions are the last paragraph of this exercise and the use of "he and she" (rather than just "he"), an early attempt at inclusivity and quite revolutionary for 1986, the year the *Big Blue Book* was published.

Protection

It is possible for the nicest person to have enemies. Some people may be jealous of you, misunderstand you, or just dislike the way you do your hair! Many people have said to me, "I do not need protection. I do not have any enemies." But there are the above-type "enemies" that you would not even know about. They may well be as sweet as pie to you, to your face, but be bitterly jealous, or whatever, behind your back. How do you protect yourself against their negativity? How do you protect yourself in case some warped individuals decide to work magick against you? You do not want to hurt them, but you certainly want to protect yourself.

---

186. *Buckland's Complete Book of Witchcraft*, lesson 11, page 239.

The best way is with a "Witch's bottle." This is an ancient defense, known throughout folklore. It is made on an individual basis. The idea is to protect yourself and, at the same time, *send back* whatever is being sent at you. You should never be the originator of harm, nor seek revenge, but you certainly can protect yourself.

To make a Witch's bottle, take a regular jar such as a 6-ounce instant-coffee jar. Half fill it with sharp objects: broken glass, old razor blades, rusty nails and screws, pins, needles, etc. When the jar is half filled with these objects, urinate in it to fill it. If a woman is preparing her bottle, she should also try to get some menstrual blood into it. Now put the top on the jar and seal it with tape. It should then be buried in the ground, at least twelve inches deep, in an isolated spot where it can remain undisturbed. If you live in a city, then it will be worth a trip out of town to find some remote spot to bury it.[187]

So long as the bottle remains buried and unbroken, it will protect you from any evil directed against you. This applies whether the evil is directed by an individual or by a group of people. Not only will it protect you, but it will also reflect back that evil on the sender(s). So the more he or she tries to harm you, the more he or she will be harmed by herself or himself.

Such a bottle should last almost indefinitely, but to be on the safe side I would suggest redoing the ritual once a year. With the present rate of housing development, you never know when your bottle may be dug up or inadvertently smashed.

---

187. Note: It's really not advisable in this day and age to bury any sort of bottle on private or public land without permission. If you don't have your own yard in which to bury a Witch bottle, ask a friend if you can use some of their yard.

Chapter Seven

Tara, San Diego & the *Big Blue Book*

Most Witches don't think of Witchcraft as a reincarnation cult, but the idea of reincarnation was inescapable in Wiccan-Witchcraft's early years and played a large role in Gerald Gardner eventually joining the Witch-cult. Upon meeting the New Forest Witches who would later initiate him, Gardner said that he was told by those Witches that "they had met me before," despite Gardner and the Witches having had no previous interactions in this lifetime. The Witches also allegedly said to him, "You belonged to us in the past.... Come back to where you belong."[188] Where Gardner belonged apparently was in the New Forest Coven.

In his own writings, Gardner repeats these ideas, suggesting that Witches will be born into their own tribe again after death. This process of reincarnation allows one to be with "those whom you loved, and loved you, and that you would remember, know, and love them again."[189] Many Witches talk of "coming home" after finding the Craft, suggesting that both those they meet in Witchcraft circles and the practice of Witchcraft feel familiar, despite both the individuals and the practice being new to them. Reincarnation among our own tribe also explains why so many of us instantly feel close to people who should otherwise be strangers.

Raymond Buckland would feel this sort of instant recognition on February 12, 1982. That day began innocently enough. Buckland was visiting Cleveland to appear on a local afternoon talk show, commonplace stuff for

188. Gardner, *The Meaning of Witchcraft*, 11.
189. Gardner, *The Meaning of Witchcraft*, 25.

one of the most famous Witches in America. That evening, after the interview, the local Pagan community threw a party in honor of Ray's visit. The party had a guest list, but the Pagan community was (and still is) small, making it easy for the occasional party-crasher to show up. The party-crasher that night was a young woman named Tara Cochran,[190] and she would change the course of Raymond Buckland's life.

Prior to the party, Cochran had been aware of Raymond Buckland. Cochran was a part of the Pagan scene in Cleveland and a reader of Witchcraft and New Age books. She had even made a point to watch Buckland's interview live that afternoon with a friend. While watching the interview, Cochran confessed to her friend that she wanted to meet Ray, suggesting that the two of them might have some sort of connection. Tara's friend knew just where Buckland was staying that weekend and that there was going to be a party in his honor that evening. That's where Cochran first met Buckland, and as Buckland says in his memoir, he "fell in love with her" that very night.

Over the course of the weekend, Buckland and Cochran spent as much time together as possible, with Cochran going to all of Ray's workshops and lectures over the next two days. Cochran even stopped by the Cleveland airport on her way to work on Monday morning to see Buckland off. Buckland and Cochran then began an ongoing correspondence through letters and long-distance phone calls (which back then could get plenty expensive!). When traveling, Buckland would arrange his flights with stops in Cleveland so that he and Cochran could steal an hour or two to be together at the airport. (This was, of course, back in the day when anyone could visit an airport gate, not just ticketed passengers.)

For Tara, there was something more to her relationship with Ray than "love at first sight." She truly believes they knew each other in a past life. Tara describes their past relationship as one shared between two friends, not two lovers. She also adds that they were both probably female in that past incarnation.

When she first set eyes on Ray, Tara says she felt a "stir and tingle," hinting at something that existed before they knew each other in this incarnation.

---

190. At the request of Tara Buckland, I have intentionally omitted a lot of personal material about her. This request was the result of the current political climate, one that is not particularly favorable to widowed Witches living in the Midwest.

In her words, they had "been together a long time" before physically getting together in 1982. In another case of something like premonition, Tara admits to having a boyfriend who looked like Ray during her college years in Scotland. She thinks her attraction to that boyfriend might have been in anticipation of meeting Ray a few years later.

Whether it was due to the influence of past lives or just sudden and inescapable love, Raymond Buckland and Tara Cochran quickly became inseparable. By August of 1982, Raymond and Joan had officially (if not yet legally) ended their relationship. Within a matter of weeks, Tara made the move to Virginia and began living with Ray, first in the bachelor pad Buckland shared with Michael Ragan and then in their own place. Instead of staying in Virginia Beach, the couple moved three hours west to Charlottesville, Virginia.

Upon arriving in Charlottesville in October of 1982, the two immediately began looking for new jobs. Tara, who had worked in the insurance industry when living in Cleveland, found work right away. It took Ray a little longer, but he eventually ended up working at the office of a real estate appraiser. Buckland enjoyed working in the appraisal office, and within a year had become a licensed real estate appraiser himself. During this time, Buckland developed a strong relationship with his boss, an ex-calvary officer in the US military. Buckland affectionately called his new boss "the Colonel." In 1984 the Colonel was looking to retire and would ask Ray to help run his business. It was an offer Ray would decline.

CA-R 3733   R. Cochran-Buckland
CERT. NO.   CERTIFIED APPRAISER

Let's see how much your house is worth!

A little over a year after ending his relationship with Joan, Raymond Buckland and Tara Cochran were handfasted at a Wiccan ceremony in Charlottesville. A second civil service wedding followed at a local Unitarian Universalist church, also in Charlottesville. Instead of Tara taking Ray's last name at their wedding, the two combined their last names, with each legally becoming a

Cochran-Buckland. Although Raymond would never change his name on the covers of his books, for many years he would give his name as Cochran-Buckland in all legal documents and even private correspondence. In promotional materials for Ray's workshops and lectures, the couple would list their enterprise as Cochran-Buckland Productions. (Eventually Ray would change his legal name back to just Buckland, because it was easier to negotiate government agencies with his original birth name.)

Remembering Ray: Tara Buckland

Ray and I were together for thirty-five years (married for thirty-four), and it was such an easy relationship. Ray was the love of my life. It's hard for me to say such things publicly, as I have always been a rather private person, but I am mustering the courage to speak of my very deepest feelings for the person I most love and admire. Ray was my greatest teacher. He taught me many things, but most of all he taught me how to love.

Looking back on my life B. R. (before Ray), I can see a pattern that led me to our eventual union. I do believe we are soul mates and were destined to meet and fulfill contracts in this life. I'm not going to belabor this; I just wanted to go on record as saying it.

I think I was twenty-seven and Ray was forty-eight when we met. As far as my parents were concerned, he was the absolute worst choice for a son-in-law that could ever be. He was twenty-one years older, twice divorced, a Witch, and (even worse than being a Witch) a penniless *writer* of weird books. By all accounts it was a marriage doomed to fail, yet we were together for thirty-five years—and despite my mother's dire predictions, they were extremely happy years.

I'd like to share a bit of Ray—his private side—with you. Most people in the Pagan community know him for his teachings within that realm, but I want to share the rest of him so you can get to know him a little better. In no particular order, I'm just going to list things as they come to me.

Even though Ray deeply loved his religion and loved writing about anything Pagan, he was first and foremost a *writer*. This was his opinion of himself, and I think it's a fair assessment. He loved to write anything and everything. Fiction, nonfiction, newsletters, poetry, personal letters—anything. In fact, we carried on our courtship through letters and had only met in person twice before he asked me to marry him! This may sound strange to some, but in writing, his natural shyness was overcome and he was able to express himself deeply. This quirky, letter-driven courtship was wonderful for us, but it only served to deepen my parents' conviction of some kind of nightmare scenario. My mother was convinced he'd "put a spell on me."

Ray was easygoing, nonjudgmental, and just plain fun to be with. He had an amazing sense of humor, and our marriage was full of corny jokes and laughter. He was also a natural peacemaker and always strived to reduce conflict whenever possible. The natural flip side of his easygoing nature was a proclivity to be a couch potato, and he was a very poor disciplinarian of children and small dogs.

Here's a funny dichotomy: Ray was a natural minimalist in his writing and his spiritual life. His words and his worship of the Gods were succinct and clutter-free. On the flip side, he was a disorganized pack rat. He saved everything! And he loved ritual simply because he loved theatre. Dressing up was so much fun for him.

Ray was deeply loving. He was emotive, and around the house he wore his heart on his sleeve. Sentimental to a fault, he adored all animals and nature and even kept stuffed animals on his bed and would get teary-eyed if I tried to remove them. Sometimes we would walk around the farm and he would get choked up just looking at all the beauty. I was in awe of his ability to be aware of, and absorb, the natural world, and I learned to see more deeply through his eyes.

He was an optimist! His glass was always half-full. He made the best of everything no matter the situation. He had a natural ability to brighten up himself and put a positive spin on anything—even when he was in the hospital with serious illness. I think some of this was his natural optimism, but some was also his bravery. I am such a chicken at times, so I often leaned on his bravery and rosy view of the world and of people.

Discerning! He was a Virgo; it goes with the territory! Yet he was able to not become overly judgmental or critical—except for one area. He could be extremely critical of Americans and their poor grammar, especially errors found in commercial advertising. One time he passionately announced that he would never *ever* buy a Ford vehicle again because of a grammatical advertising faux pas! (I'll put you out of your misery—the Ford slogan was "Go Further," which came out in 2012. The difference between *further* and *farther* is an ongoing grammatical quagmire.) Also, with his writing, he had no time for editors who thought they knew how to punctuate better than he did! I always found it humorous when this generally mild-mannered man would get agitated over grammar issues. I learned to avoid dropping the *-ly* ending on adverbs. Again, just another area where he taught me. (If you don't know what I'm talking about, here's an example. You should say "drive carefully," not "drive careful." THAT is now burned into me forever, along with many other grammatical laws of the Universe!)

He was an anti-establishmentarian, and this extended beyond just religious views. He was the supporter of the underdog in all things, including religion, downtrodden cultures (especially the Roma), and oddball people—really anything that needed support and a voice.

I knew this man inside and out. Our last twenty-seven years were shared on a remote farm, and we spent almost every day together. We shared our meals, walked miles every day, and sat on the couch in the evening and watched comedies, "costume-ers" (any historical show that involved great costumes), or murder mysteries while snuggling with dogs and each other. We talked about life and politics and religion and what happens after death. We joked and pulled pranks on each other and laughed ourselves silly. I just don't know what else to say other than I am immensely proud of all he accomplished—most especially his contributions to the modern Pagan movement. The only regret I have is that I never expressed enough just how proud I was of him. I hope he knows now.

Afternote: To anyone who wonders, I can attest that Ray is totally active on the Other Side. I have received positive, mind-boggling proof that life continues beyond "Earth School." In his death, I have found a deeper faith and strength and, most of all, a greater appreciation for him. Each moment is precious. Spend your moments well.

Tara Buckland *was married to Raymond Buckland for thirty-four years. She lives in Ohio.*

The stay in Charlottesville would be short-lived for the Cochran-Bucklands, but it would lead to Raymond participating in what has sometimes generously been referred to as a "movie." Shot in 1984 and finally released in 1989, *Mutants in Paradise* feels more like a film project designed for public access cable TV than an actual film, but it does contain a few minutes of Raymond Buckland playing a pipe-smoking psychologist. Buckland nods his head a lot during his bit part as Dr. Schrumpfen and gets in a handful of lines during his limited screen time. In true Hollywood fashion, Buckland believed that the "best bit" of his feature film debut ended up on the cutting room floor. (If you want to see Buckland as Dr. Schrumpfen, *Mutants in Paradise* can be found streaming online for free. Buckland enters the frame near the 33-minute mark.)

Tara and Ray at their wedding

Mutants in Paradise would be one of the last adventures Ray and Tara would have in Charlottesville, as by the time the movie had begun shooting, the couple had already decided to move to California, more specifically San Diego. Moving is an expensive undertaking, and the couple poured whatever they could into a moving fund, complete with a thermometer on the refrigerator to gauge their progress. Buckland credited the impending move to California as the reason that he never got to work on his Wiccan seminary idea and that he turned down the Colonel when the offer came up to run the appraisal office.

The Bucklands moved west on December 2, 1984, via airplane, a journey that was made easier for the couple when Ray's son Robert offered to transport their things to California in a U-Haul truck. While Ray and Tara got to California in a few uneventful hours, Robert had to deal with a rental truck that broke down on the highway several times on the cross-country trip. Luckily Robert had a friend with him who was towing Ray's car behind the truck. When the rental truck died on the highway, Robert and his friend would unhitch Ray's car from the truck and drive to the next town for assistance. After a week spent living in a hotel in San Diego, Ray and Tara moved into a second-story condominium just a few blocks from the beach.

San Diego would prove to be fertile ground for the Cochran-Bucklands, and during their time there, they would become close friends with Witchcraft author Scott Cunningham. Scott and Scott's father, Chet Cunningham, were also instrumental in convincing Raymond that he might be able to make a full-time living as a writer. That convincing would take several years, but ultimately they would make their case. In the meantime, the Bucklands would spend a lot of time with Scott Cunningham, both in professional and personal settings. If Ray was at a public Witchcraft event during the late 1980s, there was always a strong chance that Scott was nearby.

After not having a coven in Charlottesville, the couple got involved in group Witchcraft activities once more in San Diego. While Ray would never lead a large coven again, he and Tara, after getting established in California, did create a very small Seax-Wica group. The Bucklands also delighted in visiting the circles (and Witch-centric parties) of others in the area. After spending so many years creating and facilitating rituals, Raymond Buckland was more than happy to have others create ritual experiences for him and his new wife. There were also private rituals with just Tara and Ray, often in the hills around San Diego when the couple would go camping. Now completely free of winter, Ray's nemesis, the Bucklands were able to spend a lot of time outdoors and took advantage of their newfound circumstances.

But the move to San Diego wasn't all about ritual and camping trips; it also meant that the Cochran-Bucklands would have to find new jobs. Luckily for both Tara and Raymond, San Diego offered a vast array of interesting opportunities. Tara was the first to nab a job, becoming the office manager at a chiropractor's office in January of 1985. Dubbed "the Crystal Pope" by the Cochran-Bucklands, Tara's new boss utilized crystals while working on patients, and wasn't above asking for a little psychic advice now and again. Tara often sat in on patient sessions, meditating in a quiet corner to determine what ailed the patient. Two years later, she became the office manager at a local YMCA.

It took Raymond a little longer to find a job, but in May of 1985 he began working at Gateway Casting, a casting agency in San Diego. Before taking the job, Buckland had become friendly with the company's owner, who introduced Ray to actor John Carradine (1906–88). Carradine was Hollywood royalty, starring as Count Dracula in several iconic horror movies and playing the part of Preacher Casy in the screen adaptation of *The Grapes of Wrath* in 1940. By the time he died in 1988, Carradine had appeared in hundreds of films and television shows and had sired several sons who also went into acting. With both men sharing a love of Shakespearean actors, Buckland and Carradine became fast friends, paving the way for Buckland to join Gateway Casting, whose owners also managed Carradine's career.

While at Gateway, Buckland arranged casting calls and auditions. He also produced a trade newspaper for the agency, *Gateway Casting Gazette*. Buckland did just about everything for the *Gazette*, including creating the periodical's crossword puzzle. Buckland also oversaw an ad campaign that ran in both *Variety* and *The Hollywood Reporter* promoting Carradine for Emmy consideration in a children's afterschool special for television. (Carradine ended up winning that Emmy in September of 1985.) Gateway also allowed Buckland to don his old actor's hat and teach several acting workshops.

Sadly, Gateway didn't lead to any acting jobs for Buckland, but it did open the door for him to do some voice-over work in some children's stories and work in a recording studio. With Carradine, Buckland oversaw an audiobook recording of Bram Stoker's *Dracula*. Carradine and Buckland also recorded an audio version of English occultist Dion Fortune's novel *The Secrets of Dr. Taverner* for Llewellyn. Sadly, that recording was never released, with Buckland blaming ambiguity around the novel's copyright owner. Buckland also directed and interviewed Carradine for a VHS release about ghosts. Buckland's relationship with Carradine was both personal and professional, with Ray occasionally joining the actor for dinner but also driving the actor to various appointments in Southern California.

Buckland's most successful project with John Carradine was a reading of the Bible's New Testament for an audiobook. Carradine's Bible reading went on to win an International Angel Award from Excellence in Media, a Hollywood-based organization set up to improve the moral and ethical content of films, television, shows, books, record albums, and other forms of media. (The International Angel Awards were so unprestigious that there's barely a trace of them online, though I do have a picture of Ray holding his Angel Award.) When Carradine was unable to attend the group's award ceremony in Beverly Hills in February of 1988, Buckland went in his place. The ceremony allowed Buckland, an old movie buff, to meet Roy Rogers, Dale Evans, Burl Ives, Buddy Rogers, Della Reese, Jane Curtin, Dolly Parton(!), Iron Eyes Cody, and the original TV Lone Ranger, Clayton Moore.

Ray with his Angel Award

At the ceremony, Buckland accepted two Angel Awards, one for Carradine and one for himself as a producer! I'm guessing that Excellence in Media never checked up on Buckland to see that he practiced Witchcraft. With this particular award, Raymond Buckland became the only practicing Witch to win an award from a "family values" organization. All hail the power of the Craft!

The job at Gateway Casting also nearly led to a full-scale modeling career for Raymond Buckland. He went to several modeling auditions, including one for Marlboro cigarettes. At that audition Buckland was photographed wearing a fluffy turtleneck sweater while pretending to handle a large yacht. At the audition Buckland says "he puffed away like a veteran," though he was a non-smoker. Luckily for the Witchcraft world (I think), Buckland ended up not getting the gig and the test photos never ran anywhere. Buckland as a Marlboro Man might not have been the best look for Witchcraft in the 1980s.

Buckland did appear in a children's textbook produced for a Japanese audience in 1986. In *English as a Second Language*, Buckland can be seen checking in luggage at an airport, riding in an airplane, and driving a car. Buckland found the experience interesting, but sadly it didn't lead to any future modeling gigs.

Inspired by his change in surroundings, Buckland enrolled in a screenwriting class and began attempting to write for the silver screen. His first completed screenplay was a comedy titled *The Executive and Miss Kitty*. The screenplay was never produced as a film, but it was recorded, with Buckland narrating his work and a small cadre of actors portraying the screenplay's major characters. Buckland registered this first screenplay with the Writers Guild of America and eventually hired an agent, though none of Buckland's scripts were ever picked up by a studio.

Buckland did come close to selling a script on a few occasions. *The Wiitiko Inheritance*, about a man convinced he was turning into a cannibal, stayed with director Francis Ford Coppola for a long period of time before being returned. Wes Craven expressed some interest in *Conjure a Demon!*, which definitely seems like the kind of movie that was in Buckland's wheelhouse.

Nominally sticking with horror, Buckland wrote a Dracula vehicle for his friend John Carradine. *Positively the Last of Dracula* caught up with Carradine's interpretation of the vampire forty years after his initial portrayal but with a humorous twist. Unfortunately for Buckland, Carradine was in no condition to play a lead role by 1987, and he suggested that Buckland send the script to Vincent Price. Price also passed, having retired from doing horror-type films, but not before calling Buckland on the phone to compliment him on the script.

Working for Gateway got Buckland close to a lot of Hollywood types and was no doubt inspiring, but the job made it difficult to find time to write. Looking for something else that wouldn't take up so much time, Buckland found a job running a San Diego branch of a resume-writing service. He found this to be an extension of the fiction he was creating in his screenplays. Buckland helped build resumes for a little over nine months before moving into writing full-time. October of 1989 would be the last time Raymond Buckland ever held a mundane job; from here on out, writing would primarily pay the bills.

* * * * * * * *

The 1970s were a transformative decade for Witchcraft publishing. By the middle of the decade, it was possible to buy books full of complete rituals detailing the Wheel of the Year, along with some initiation and elevation rites. The work of writers such as Paul Huson, Sybil Leek, Lady Sheba, and Raymond Buckland allowed people to practice Witchcraft without having to start completely from scratch. But this first generation of how-to books often lacked context. Written rituals looked more like stage plays, and there was rarely any explanation for *why* the actions of a ritual occurred. Today the Wicca 101 book is taken for granted, but fifty years ago it didn't exist.

That began to change in the late 1970s. The first book that really felt like a modern Wicca 101 book was Doreen Valiente's *Witchcraft for Tomorrow* (1978). *Tomorrow* ends with a forty-page Book of Shadows that takes full advantage of Valiente's gifts as a ritualist and poet. There's also some practical advice about magick and information about the gods and the sabbats. Published by English publisher Robert Hale, Valiente's attempt at a 101 book did not have a large impact in the United States, with limited distribution playing a large role.

The second of the initial 101 books would have a huge impact not just on Witchcraft but also on women's spirituality and the burgeoning New Age movement. Published by Harper & Row in 1979, Starhawk's (1951–present) *The Spiral Dance* had no distribution issues and no problem finding an audience. Even when writing about history, Starhawk's prose reads like poetry. And in a radical departure from most easily obtainable Witchcraft books of the 1970s, Starhawk's Witchcraft is a mixture of not just Gardner-inspired Craft but also second-wave feminism, political activism, and the Feri Witchcraft of Victor and Cora Anderson. There was nothing like *The Spiral Dance* when it was released, and there's really nothing like it today, nearly fifty years later.

Despite the fine work of writers such as Valiente and Starhawk, there still wasn't a complete manual for Witchcraft in the style of Gerald Gardner on the market. Janet and Stewart Farrar had come close in their work, but their books often lacked the context that so plagued early Witchcraft books. Raymond Buckland saw an opportunity, and luckily for him, most of the material was already written.

· · · · · · · ·

Visit the Buckland Museum of Witchcraft and Magick in Cleveland, Ohio, and you'll run into what is likely one of the very few spiral-bound notebooks in the world housed in a plexiglass case. Museum curator Steven Intermill likes to tell visitors that this prized notebook is the original *Big Blue*, formally known as *Buckland's Complete Book of Witchcraft*. Intermill is only half-right though. While the 200-sheet green Norcom brand 5 Subject Notebook does contain some of *Big Blue*, it doesn't contain all of it.

One of the most famous notebooks in Witch history

The overwhelming majority of *Big Blue* comes straight from Buckland's original Seax-Wica correspondence course. In the introduction to *Buckland's Complete Book of Witchcraft*, Raymond states rather matter-of-factly in the introduction that *Big Blue* "is based on the very successful Seax-Wica seminary course" he had previously offered.[191] But there are differences between the two projects. For *Big Blue*, Buckland opted not to use the rituals he had written for his Seax-Wica correspondence course, and the earliest draft of these new rituals can be found in the spiral-bound notebook on display at the Buckland Museum. There is some other tinkering around the edges in Buckland's notebook that helped to transform the Seax-Wica course into a nondenominational Witchcraft primer, most notably the removal of the jargon that Ray created specifically for his new tradition.

As a historical document, Buckland's Norcom notebook is remarkable for revealing just how easily the new rituals came to Ray. Much of what is in the notebook ended up in the finished text of *Big Blue*, most often word for word. The notebook also contains a complete outline of what would become *Big Blue*, with Buckland noting when he would be quoting from his original study course and from some of his other books (most notably *Witchcraft from the Inside*). The questions conceived for *Big Blue* were also different from those included in the study course.

There are mistakes here and there in the notebook, of course. Certain words are scratched out, and in a few isolated cases entire paragraphs have wavy lines through them, indicating ideas that were, on second thought, unnecessary. Like many who write in spiral notebooks, Buckland mostly writes on the right-hand pages (writing away from the spiral binding), leaving the unused space on the left-hand pages for occasional corrections and brief sketches of ideas. As a writer myself, I was surprised to see how fully formed Ray's ideas were for this project right from the start.

Turning the Seax-Wica correspondence course into a book feels like a rather obvious choice, but the course was quite successful financially for Buckland, and putting much of the Seax-Wica material into a book would mean shutting down the course and taking a financial hit. But it would also free Buckland from having to grade the work of his students, leaving more

---

191. Buckland, *Buckland's Complete Book of Witchcraft*, xiv.

time for writing and other pursuits. To put it in perspective, individual lessons for the correspondence course were ten dollars each, while *Big Blue's* cover price was $12.95. (Today $12.95 sounds rather inexpensive, but rounded up for inflation that's the equivalent of about $37 in 2025. As of February 2025, *Big Blue* retails for $24.99.)

While in hindsight the publication of *Big Blue* feels like a no-brainer for Llewellyn, there were several employees at the publishing house at the time who expressed reservations. One of the criticisms was directed at the project's workbook form:

> I think maybe we should take a look at Buckland's Workbook and see if there's a way of livening it up. It is more like a grade school social studies book than a workbook for adults (that is fun and involves the person).
>
> He writes a chapter of text and then quizzes the reader. That's no fun.
>
> It should be more an actual workbook—ie participatory.... Not some silly quiz.... The way it is now, I think it will turn people off and certainly won't be very useful to anyone. The examination pages could very easily be dropped altogether and no one would know it. In fact it would make it less offensive.

The above critique was seconded by another Llewellyn employee who wrote:

> This is nothing more than Buckland's old self-study course—blah! It's over a decade old 1970! And most anyone who took the course is gonna be pissed when it shows up masquerading as something else.
>
> Its [*sic*] tedious & silly in its present form....
>
> This mess is a real disappointment to me. I was looking forward to it—but this is <u>very</u> different than what I was lead [*sic*] to expect. Blech! A real ripoff, Carl—you're gonna make a lot of Wiccans mad.

It's worth noting that these criticisms were directed at the earliest draft of the book, long before the book had been designed or edited. I've included these criticisms here because I find them personally interesting considering the book's later success. Ultimately, the lack of enthusiasm by some at Llewellyn for what would become the *Big Blue Book* wasn't shared by everyone in the company. The most important name at Llewellyn was clearly in Buckland's (and the book's) corner. That man was the company's president and owner, Carl Llewellyn Weschcke (1930–2015).

Though open to other people's critiques of potential books, Carl Weschcke had the final say on all projects. When Weschcke believed in a project, it would go forward, even if there was considerable pushback from some employees. Since acquiring Llewellyn, Weschcke had come to rely on his gut when deciding what to publish or, in some cases, not to publish.

Before the book's publication, Weschcke was especially bullish on *Big Blue*, writing to Buckland that he was sensing a "new growth in Wicca" and that he believed Buckland's book would "ride the crest of this new wave, and help broaden and sustain it."[192] (Weschcke was correct on both counts.) He goes on to write in bold type that *Buckland's Complete* "has a very big potential" and adds that "we know it will do well, and perhaps it will do super well and match PCB [*Practical Candleburning Rituals*] in number of copies sold."[193]

Ray and Carl at a booksellers convention. A poster for Ray's novel *The Committee* can be seen in the background.

---

192. Carl Weschcke, letter to Raymond Buckland, November 19, 1985.
193. Carl Weschcke, letter to Raymond Buckland, November 19, 1985.

What we now know (officially) as *Buckland's Complete Book of Witchcraft* was almost called something else entirely. In Ray's book proposal to Llewellyn, he gives the working title of *Ray Buckland's Complete Witchcraft Workbook*.[194] But Llewellyn never seemed completely on board with that title, and letters from early readers of the book use alternative names for the project, such as *The Witch's Workbook* and the *Complete Witchcraft Workbook*.[195] Reservations about using the word *workbook* led to several other titles being considered. At one point the book nearly had *Wicca* in the title and was going to be called *Wicca: Ray Buckland's Complete Book of Witchcraft*,[196] a title Ray calls "the best" in a letter to Weschcke.[197] Using the word Wicca in 1986 would have been a pretty radical move, as the term was not used as widely back then. Another proposed title was *Creating Your Own Reality: The Book of Witchcraft*, which sounds like a different book entirely.[198] After several months of indecision, Weschcke himself settled on the name of Buckland's magnum opus, dubbing it *Ray Buckland's Complete Book of Witchcraft*, with *Ray* eventually being removed, giving us the title we have today.[199]

One of the most striking things about *Buckland's Complete* upon publication was its sheer size, not necessarily in word count but in dimensions. Most Witchcraft-related books that Llewellyn published in that era were considerably smaller. Scott Cunningham's books were generally 6 by 9 inches, but *Big Blue* was a whopping 8½ by 11 inches! Even today, it's often one of the largest books in terms of length and width in the libraries of a great many Witches! The proposed size of the book concerned Llewellyn so much that they inquired with the book buyers for mall chains such as B. Dalton and Walden Books whether the book was going to be too big for the sellers' shelves![200]

---

194. Llewellyn Publishing Agreement with Ray Buckland, April 1, 1985.
195. Marion Zimmer Bradley, letter to Llewellyn Publications, August 24, 1986 (with a copy for Melita Denning and Osborne Phillips stapled to the letter).
196. Raymond Buckland, letter to Carl Weschcke, January 27, 1986.
197. Raymond Buckland, letter to Carl Weschcke, January 27, 1986.
198. Carl Weschcke, letter to Raymond Buckland, November 19, 1985.
199. Llewellyn internal memo, date unknown. The note reads, "An executive decision had been made by our fearless leader, Carl Llewellyn Weschcke, regarding Buckland's new tome. It is to be called RAY BUCKLAND'S COMPLETE BOOK OF WITCHCRAFT."
200. Carl Weschcke, Llewellyn internal memo, January 15, 1985.

One of Llewellyn's most pressing concerns with the book was never quite corrected: Nearly everyone who has picked up *Big Blue* thinks it looks like a workbook. When I picked up my copy in the early 1990s, it reminded me of the workbooks I had in elementary school. (The Llewellyn employee who brought up that critique was correct!) To address the "workbook-ness" of the work, Weschcke commissioned additional art from Buckland in order to make *Big Blue* look more like a "semi-coffee table book."[201] It's true that there's a lot of art in the book, most of it by Ray, but the two-column design of most of the pages simply gives the entire book a very workbook-like feel. The original Seax-Wica correspondence course lacked the two-column layout of *Big Blue* and, in my opinion, often looked more inviting, despite its use of traditional typewriter fonts. Buckland himself was "delighted" with the look and layout of the book, his only "quibble" being "the placement of the test questions."[202]

And those test questions! While some people working at Llewellyn clearly didn't like their inclusion in the book, a list of "questions to ponder" at the end of every chapter in Witchcraft books is now commonplace. While the queries in other Witchcraft books often come across as less clinical than Buckland's end-of-chapter "examination questions," they are basically the same thing. Every Witchcraft book that urges the reader to "keep a journal while working through this book" owes at least a small tip of the cap to Buckland.

Buckland's Complete Book of Witchcraft had a glorious rollout in 1986 over Samhain weekend. Instead of staying close to home for the book launch, Buckland (with Tara, of course) traveled to Minnesota's Twin Cities, where he was a guest on KSTP Channel Five's morning show that Friday (Samhain proper) and led workshops at a local bookstore the following day. Sunday was reserved for the book's official launch party at the home of the Weschckes. Buckland shared the spotlight that night with friends Scott Cunningham, whose *The Magic of Incense, Oils & Brews* shared a release date with *Big Blue*, and Donald Michael Kraig, who had just been named editor of Llewellyn's *New Times* magazine.

---

201. Carl Weschcke, Llewellyn internal memo, March 28, 1985.
202. Raymond Buckland, letter to Carl Weschcke, October 9, 1986.

Remembering Ray: Thorn Mooney

When I wrote my first book, *Traditional Wicca: A Seeker's Guide*, it was in large part because I felt that the climate surrounding Gardnerian Wicca (and initiatory Wicca as a whole) had shifted so much, especially in light of the many other styles of witchcraft that openly occupied the magical arena at the time. Those books we'd all been recommending for decades were no longer answering the questions that would-be witches were asking me, and it was cumbersome having to spend time countering outdated histories and critiquing past cultural assumptions through the lens of contemporary sensibilities. Why not just write a fresh take? When the publisher sent a copy of my book to Ray Buckland seeking an endorsement, I was totally mortified. This was *Ray Buckland*. Who was *I*? A Gardnerian fetus, freshly forged moon crown clenched in grubby hands like a toddler with crayons. Surely *the* Ray Buckland would have neither the time nor the inclination to read whatever I had scrawled. *Surely.*

I was floored when he wrote the loveliest, most sincere endorsement, right down to which section was his favorite, sending it directly to our shared publisher. I laughed, I cried, I called everyone I knew, and I still felt a little like throwing up.

And later, when he sent an email to ask why his own books weren't included in the suggested reading (keep in mind that *Traditional Wicca* was explicitly written to showcase younger voices in the movement), I was astronomically more mortified. How do you tell one of the great figureheads of your religion that you just…didn't *want* to? Nay, that you felt *obligated* to exclude him, just as you'd excluded the rest of the canon? You'd even made a joke to your publicist about how you weren't going to recommend a book that told seekers to forge an athame on their stovetop. But now your life was flashing before your eyes and you were *so sorry oh no what do I say.*

The truth is that you can admire and respect someone's influence and invaluable contributions while equally holding mixed feelings about pointing newcomers to their work. Being part of a young, fast-developing tradition like Wicca necessarily means living with a certain level of ambivalence about your own history. We're far enough away from the beginning to cherish the too-few stories about our founders but close enough that we can see their flawed humanity. I agonized over how to respond to that email for days. I called my initiators. I talked to my therapist. I texted sad faces to my editor.

And then Ray Buckland died, instantly absolving me. So it goes.

A minor, ridiculous story, but an absolutely magical one, made possible over the course of an enchanted life that I never could have imagined for myself when I cracked open my own first copy of *Buckland's Big Blue Book*. It's also emblematic of the sort of influence that Buckland had. In many ways, he was the bridge between two distinct generations of what has come to be called Wicca. On the one side, there is the secretive initiatory witch cult available to a select few intrepid explorers with both the gumption and the extraordinary luck to make their way into a coven. On the other side, there is the expansive, unbridled eclectic magic of the solitary practitioner, devouring books and experimenting with their own creativity. Lucky us, Buckland created maps to both.

Thorn Mooney *is a Gardnerian high priestess, author, and academic living in North Carolina. Her books include* Traditional Wicca: A Seeker's Guide *and* Witches Among Us: Understanding Contemporary Witchcraft and Wicca. *Visit her at www.thornthewitch.com.*

The talk of the launch party was a typo that had been found on *Big Blue's* back cover. Buckland's author bio states that Ray "spent many years *pubicly* defending the Old Religion." That word should obviously be *publicly*, but proofreaders miss things now and again! A dozen people looked over Ray's book before it was published, but no one noticed this rather embarrassing error. The mistake was quickly fixed starting with the book's second printing, making the "pubicly" sold first edition a collector's item!

There's an "everything and the kitchen sink" approach to the Craft in *Big Blue* that is absent from other Witch books of the era and even most Witch books of the present. There's history, theology, divination, astrology, meditation techniques, auras, dream interpretation, and two dozen other things crammed into the book's 250 pages. Not every subject is covered in depth, but the sheer scope of what is in the book is remarkable. When I was a young Witch, I felt pretty confident that anything I didn't know how to do was lurking somewhere in the pages of *Big Blue.*

Among the 101 books of the era, *Buckland's Complete* was certainly the most challenging. No other author of the period encouraged their readers to heat up a piece of iron on their kitchen stove in order to make their own athame! (I have friends who have used Buckland's instructions to construct their own athame with some success, and then there are people like me who think playing with a piece of glowing red metal in their kitchen is a recipe for disaster.) Not only does Buckland encourage some elementary blacksmithing, but he also encourages the Witches reading his book to make their own sandals and sew their own robes.

Despite Buckland's attempt to write a nondenominational book on Wiccan-Witchcraft, his personal biases do slip into the text from time to time. Since leaving the Gardnerian tradition, Buckland had really come to dislike certain elements of the Craft that he believed had evolved from the practice of ceremonial magick. He's not wrong. There are a whole lot of tools, practices, and even rites that come from medieval grimoires, but that shouldn't be surprising. Wiccan-Witchcraft isn't a 2,000-year-old mystery tradition; it's a modern practice that was inspired by traditions such as the ceremonial magick found in spell books and grimoires. Buckland's dislike of "ceremonial" elements is strong enough that he advises against the use of common ritual elements such as calling the "Guardians of the Watchtowers." Despite wands being ubiquitous among Witches, Buckland was not a fan of them, believing that wands were too closely linked to the ceremonial magick he wanted out of Witchcraft.

Much of what is in *Big Blue* was inspired by the Gardnerian Witchcraft that Buckland was initiated into back in 1963. That's not much of a surprise, as most Witchcraft traditions, especially in the United States, were influenced by Gardnerian Craft during this period. In certain parts of the book, you can see Buckland's appreciation for Gardner's Craft and, at the same time, his disdain for it, after his experience with the Kneitels. When writing about "Wiccan denominations," Buckland is protective of Gardner but adds that "there are also a large number of groups who call themselves 'Gardnerian' even though their Books of Shadows bear little resemblance to Gardner's original." Given Buckland's strong disapproval of people adding material to the Gardnerian Book of Shadows, it comes across as a swipe at Theos and Phoenix.

Since its publication in 1986, *Big Blue* has sold over half a million copies, making it one of the best-selling nonfiction Witchcraft books of all time. Despite its success, I'm unsure of how exactly to write about the book's legacy and impact on the Witchcraft world. *Big Blue* wasn't the first 101 book, and much of the material in its pages could be found in other sources, but for Witches growing up in the 1990s (and beyond), it was often a foundational text. It wasn't the only foundational text, of course. Some people preferred Scott Cunningham's *Wicca: A Guide for the Solitary Practitioner* or Silver RavenWolf's *To Ride a Silver Broomstick*, but *Big Blue* was always in the conversation. In the 1990s, every semi-well-read Witch I knew was familiar with *Big Blue*. For many Witches it is the title that began their love affair with Witchcraft or strengthened their practice beyond a few candle spells.

My own feelings about *Buckland's Complete* have fluctuated over the years. In my younger years, I respected the sheer amount of information in it and used it often as a reference book. As I've gotten older, I've found that many of the ideas in it do not resonate with me and are often vastly at odds with the contemporary Witchcraft community. Suggesting that "what names you use for your deities is a matter of personal preference" and that Woden and Cernunnos are the same being feels like an insult to polytheists. Your opinion may vary, of course, but this line of thinking is no longer a common one in Witch circles.

Outside of the theological quibbles, Buckland constantly draws me back in by just how pragmatic he is in *Big Blue*. When writing about Tarot cards, he suggests reading a book that offers interpretations of the cards and then follows that up by instructing the reader to "*put the book away.*"[203] In other words, familiarize yourself with some traditional interpretations, but trust yourself enough as a Witch to believe in *your* interpretation of things. Lessons like that stick with you and are why so many people are drawn to Buckland's work.

---

203. Buckland, *Buckland's Complete Book of Witchcraft*, 161.

I believe that *Big Blue* is one of the most significant Witchcraft books ever written, but I'm not entirely sure what its legacy is. It's not recommended to younger Witches with the frequency of some of the other 101 books of that era, but even today it remains a bestseller. It must still be resonating with people to be a perennial top performer on the Amazon charts. Due to its oversized dimensions and the prominent pentagram on its sky-blue cover, *Big Blue* might be the most recognizable Witchcraft book ever published. While all its contemporaries sport new cover designs, the cover of *Buckland's Complete* remains largely the same.

(The *Big Blue* cover is so iconic that it's instantly recognizable when it shows up on TV or in the movies. When my wife was first discovering the Craft back in high school, *Big Blue* made an appearance on a reality TV show featuring police officers that she was watching with her family. My wife's mother and stepfather were very anti-occult, and the appearance of Buckland's opus did not escape their gaze. My wife, who had checked out *Big Blue* from her local library, quietly went up to her room and hid the book in a dresser drawer. She returned it to the library the next day.)

If you've ever wondered how Buckland felt about people calling his *Complete Book of Witchcraft* by a variety of humorous names, well, he was completely on board. He quite happily called his book *Big Blue* and even found the more laborious *Uncle Bucky's Big Blue Book* both "amusing and complimentary." I think Buckland truly enjoyed all the attention he received from *Big Blue* and just how recognizable the book was.

Many successful Wicca 101 books spawn sequels, and while Buckland would continue to write Witchcraft books for the rest of his life, he never did attempt a direct sequel to *Big Blue*. However, *Buckland's Complete* did spawn an indirect sequel of sorts, a VHS production titled *Witchcraft: Yesterday and Today*. Just like *Big Blue*, *Yesterday and Today* sports a blue cover and a pentagram, and even the same font is used. Clearly the two projects were designed to complement each other.

Witchcraft: Yesterday and Today had its genesis in a letter Buckland wrote to Carl Weschcke in January of 1986:

> I was contemplating the fact that I used to take my many slides and travel all over the country lecturing at colleges and universities with

them. As you know, I did that for many years.... It occurred to me that there might well be a market (colleges, universities, libraries, as well as Pagans) if I were to put those slides onto video tape, together with commentary, of course. Just the slides would be a little static, but they could be intercut with some live action (you could get a group together to demonstrate rituals, for example) and with myself introducing, concluding, and perhaps also intercutting, **a la** Orson Welles or Vincent Price... sitting in a large ornate chair, or in front of a big bookcase or whatever. I think it could make a potentially profitable videocassette. Where else could people see the stuff from both my old museum and Gerald Gardner's....

[...]

Anyway, there's the idea for you to ponder.[204]

Buckland's *Witchcraft: Yesterday and Today* video would turn out much like it's described here, though it would take several more years to come to fruition.

(A humorous aside about the correspondence between Buckland and Weschcke: Many of Buckland's letters to Weschcke during this period include the temperature in San Diego at the time Ray was writing. Sharing San Diego's 72-degree temperature at the end of January to a person living in Minnesota feels especially cruel. In between pleasantries and the book business, Buckland was very much focused on getting Carl and his wife, Sandra, to move to the West Coast. Carl was often jealous of the weather but was happy to avoid California's much higher cost of living.)

Weschcke himself had been looking to get Llewellyn into the video business before Buckland approached him with the idea. At the time, Llewellyn was looking to rent out some of their building to a local cable company as a public access studio and production facility. Llewellyn was hoping that the proximity to such equipment would make video production easier for the publisher. Carl writes that he had "been attracted by the potential in Video [*sic*] for some time, but the costs are high and the marketing side is still problematic."[205]

---

204. Raymond Buckland, letter to Carl Weschcke, January 27, 1986.
205. Carl Weschcke, letter to Raymond Buckland, February 18, 1986.

Llewellyn's first foray into video would not take place in Minnesota, though, and it would not involve Ray Buckland either. Released in 1986, *Scott Cunningham's Herb Magic* unsurprisingly stars writer Scott Cunningham and focuses on the magickal properties of herbs. Most of the video was recorded at Taylor's Herb Gardens. At the time, Taylor's was one of the largest suppliers of herbs to nurseries and farmers in the United States.[206] Cunningham's project was overseen by deTraci Regula, who served as executive producer. Regula not only had experience working in Hollywood but also was a practicing Witch and part of the San Diego Pagan scene. She was good friends with Cunningham and would, in short order, also become good friends with Buckland.

Carl Weschcke saw Regula's potential as a director early on, and in a letter to Buckland in 1986, he mentions Regula as a possible director for the project.[207] Shortly after Buckland finished the screenplay for the video, Regula submitted a bid to Llewellyn to produce and direct the feature. By this time, Regula and Buckland had already been talking about the project, and in Regula, Buckland had a friend determined to bring his vision to life. Regula says that her involvement with *Witchcraft: Yesterday and Today* "came about organically but Llewellyn definitely wanted a very precise budget … for it."[208] Regula remembers the budget being in the range of about $3,000 (about $7,600 in 2024). A budget proposal sent to Llewellyn from Regula in July of 1989 lists the final cost for the entire project as $7,307 (about $18,500 in 2024 dollars).[209]

Given the video's tiny budget, it's not surprising that *Witchcraft: Yesterday and Today* is a rather simple affair. Most of the video features Ray in a sweater-vest and in pure professor mode. His history of Witchcraft, along with explanations of the sabbats, magick, and ritual tools, are intercut with scenes of a small coven performing ritual. In one of the video's more striking (and longest) scenes, a young woman dedicates herself to the Craft. The project was shot at just three locations: an old Victorian house in San Diego, Ray's

---

206. Lindner, "Kent Taylor 1944–2008."

207. Carl Weschcke, letter to Raymond Buckland, October 14, 1986.

208. DeTraci Regula, personal interview conducted on September 5, 2023.

209. DeTraci Regula, letter to Llewellyn, July 17, 1989.

friends' condominium, and Taylor's Herb Gardens. The video's cast consisted of Buckland and the coven of seven Witches.

The Witches in the movie were all local to San Diego and were actively involved in the Pagan scene there. Llewellyn didn't exert much control over the production, but Regula remembers that she "had to make sure that the people we chose to perform in it [the video] met with Llewellyn's approval.... They [Llewellyn] made it clear they wanted to approve the physical appearance of what we were using."[210] Photos were submitted, and the chosen cast proceeded as planned.

Having a limited cast was probably for the best, because it was a tiny production, with the cast and crew often working in tight spaces. Most shoots for the video had twelve to fourteen people in the room, and rehearsals for the video actually took place in the Bucklands' apartment. (At one of those rehearsals, a cast member was actually bitten by one of Tara's pet snakes. It was truly a production like no other!) The video was very much a family affair, too, with Tara Buckland composing the music (and performing most of it with Ray in studio) and Regula's mother doing the catering. Scott Cunningham was a constant presence, the production benefiting from his past experience with the herb video.

Just a couple of weeks before beginning production on the video, Buckland experienced a sharp pain in his back. He described the pain as "excruciating agony" and worse than what he had experienced ten years prior when dealing with his diverticulitis. Buckland ended up spending an entire week in bed, lying as still as possible to alleviate the pain. After Ray had endured a week of intense pain, Tara got him into a wheelchair and to a doctor's office. The diagnosis was not good: two herniated discs that would require surgery and most likely spinal fusion.

Buckland wasn't keen about the surgery and kept putting it off for months. During that time he visited a local chiropractor, who subjected him "to stretching and shock treatment and a variety of other stuff." Just getting onto his chiropractor's table was tortuous, and Buckland would scream his head off (his words, not mine) as he was eased onto the table. But Buckland made fast progress once he began his treatments and was soon walking

---

210. DeTraci Regula, personal interview conducted on September 5, 2023.

with the assistance of a cane. Just before the video shoot, Buckland boarded a plane for a speaking appearance in Michigan. He writes that he sat "glassy-eyed on the plane there and back." Anyone who has ever flown with back pain knows how taxing such flights can be. (Buckland also never had that spinal surgery; the chiropractor was enough.)

Regula says that Buckland's back issues did not really affect the video's production, and most people involved with the shoot were unaware that Buckland was dealing with intense pain while shooting. However, the lack of mobility does explain a lot about the video, most notably why Buckland is never in any of the ritual action scenes and why he doesn't move around very much. The majority of the video that features Buckland simply presents him sitting in a chair, his back ramrod straight.

If you've never seen *Witchcraft: Yesterday and Today*, you aren't missing out on all that much. The majority of the video features Buckland in professor mode speaking in what appears to be a library. Ray is personable yet serious (a little humor might have helped) throughout the film and is a deft narrator. Periodically the scene shifts to a group of Witches practicing ritual, though their appearances are mostly fleeting. Most of the action takes place indoors, but there are some rather joyous-looking scenes at Taylor's Herb Gardens. The video ends with Buckland sharing the Wiccan Rede, wishing the viewer well, and then picking up a copy of a Gerald Gardner's *Witchcraft Today* while the camera pans out. (The effect is more comical than scholarly.) The whole video wraps up in a little less than an hour.

The "library" that Buckland occupies for much of the video was completely fabricated. A lot of the books, tools, and decorative items came from Buckland's own collection, but Regula states that the set was very much a team effort. All the Pagans on set brought their own books and tools and magickal bric-a-brac and quickly turned an empty room into an impressive library. According to Regula, "You take five Pagans, and you have five carloads of stuff without any problem whatsoever."[211]

The film's small budget was used mainly to pay for the small crew, with one of the more major expenses being the rented teleprompter. Although few people who watch *Witchcraft: Yesterday and Today* in the present would find

---

211. De Traci Regula, personal interview conducted on September 5, 2023.

it groundbreaking, in one sense it was. *Yesterday and Today* utilized "an early digital teleprompter," Regula remembers, "one of the first computer-based teleprompters—previously it had been a camera shooting down on sheets of paper on a belt."[212] The two-person teleprompter crew were some of the only non-Pagans involved in the shoot. The film's other major expense was the videotape that was used, which cost the production about a dollar for every minute of videotape used.

The production schedule was tight, and the entire library sequence was shot over just three days in the old Victorian house. Due to the tight production schedule, Regula never got a chance to film any cutaway shots. During the video, there's a strange cutaway to a photo of Aphrodite against a fern, added only because there was a problem with the video of Ray during that sequence and there was nothing left to use to cover up the tape glitch. Llewellyn asked Regula to cut it out, "but there was nothing else to put there. If I'd just had a close-up of his hands!"[213]

There were other hiccups during production. The old Victorian house being used for the production was on a busy street, and the traffic noise easily bled through and into the house, interrupting production. The most notorious interruption was the sound of a stopped ice cream truck that kept playing and playing and playing its soundtrack over and over. Scott Cunningham wondered aloud if the ice cream truck was a front for drug dealers. Eventually the truck moved on and work on the video continued.

There were problems inside the house, too. The home's owner had a pet parrot that would frequently squawk in the middle of a shot. It was eventually discovered that placing a cover over the bird's cage resulted in the bird's silence. The darkness tricked the bird into thinking it was nighttime and time to go to sleep.

The condo used to film the self-dedication scene was owned by an elderly couple who were friends of Ray. They enthusiastically let him use their place because they were going to be out of town on a cruise during the filming. As luck would have it, the couple returned early from their cruise at 2:00 a.m., right in the midst of shooting. "Suddenly they're coming through the door," Regula remembers. "We had lights everywhere, cameras everywhere, we had

---

212. DeTraci Regula, personal interview conducted on September 5, 2023.
213. DeTraci Regula, personal interview conducted on September 5, 2023.

the maximum amount of Pagans for that evening."[214] It was quite the chaotic scene to walk into, perhaps made even more so because they were filming one of the movie's only two nude scenes.

Regula believes that the couple's early arrival home might have been planned and they might have been curious about the production. However, what they walked into was much more than they expected. Toward the end of the night, comments from the couple were being picked up on the audio equipment, expressing a lot of bewilderment and surprise. Regula and her crew tried to finish up as quickly as possible but still didn't leave until dawn.

While Regula was the director of the video, it's clear that Buckland had a large role outside of the script and his narration duties. In the outtakes section of the DVD release, Buckland can clearly be heard giving direction to the actors involved when staging the ritual parts. Regula has said that the production really was a true collaboration between Buckland, herself, and Scott Cunningham, who was there throughout the production.

Witchcraft: Yesterday and Today doesn't hold up particularly well thirty-plus years after its initial release (the original VHS version came out in 1990). The graphics look more like something from a home movie than a professional production, but there's still *something* captivating about the video. It's a time capsule of a different era of Witchcraft and was the only Witchcraft film at the time directed by a Witch, written by a Witch, and produced by a publishing house very much invested in Witchcraft. Those intangibles are why the video, at first on VHS and then DVD, has remained in print for over thirty years.

In 2005 Llewellyn rereleased *Witchcraft: Yesterday and Today* on DVD as *Witchcraft: Rebirth of the Old Religion*, with bonus features and an "update on Wicca" from Buckland. This time the production involved just the Cochran-Bucklands and Regula, and Ray opts for ritual-style dress instead of a sweater-vest. There's no teleprompter here either, just Buckland speaking off the cuff about the evolution of Wicca over the fifteen years since the original video. It's a rather impressive piece of extemporaneous speaking and shows just how much Buckland had been keeping up with the community he had done so much to help build.

---

214. DeTraci Regula, personal interview conducted on September 5, 2023.

Remembering Ray: Silver RavenWolf

From one RavenWolf to another—Raymond Buckland

The first time I spoke to Raymond Buckland, I was overwhelmed. My hand holding the phone receiver trembled so badly that I had to brace it against my body. Words escaped me. The excitement of finally meeting this extraordinary human being was more than my brain could process. I remember him laughing and saying, "Are you there? Have I lost the connection?" And when I finally stuttered my apology, he laughed with genuine kindness. I was and will always be a fangirl.

Over the next several years I had the privilege to interact with him on several occasions, including appearing together at several magical shops, participating in ritual, and enjoying dinners with my family when he came into town for the annual car show. I found him to be soft-spoken, intelligent, sincere, mischievous, and a delightful conversationalist with an incredible sense of humor. My children adored him. Our conversations ranged from Pagan politics to spirituality and the pursuit of embracing a daily spiritual lifestyle amidst our busy lives with so many varied interests. Raymond Buckland's influence on my life has been profound, and filling the role of High Priestess in ritual with him has been one of the high points of my Pagan life. But what can I tell you that no one else in this book can share?

Recently, I was in New Orleans aboard the riverboat the *Creole Queen* having the delightful chance to speak to author Thorn Mooney. I was telling her about this book and recounting a story or two of my interactions with Raymond Buckland when, for the first time, I spoke aloud of the most important lesson I had witnessed from this magnificent human being. Whenever I was with him, I would stand back and watch how he affected those around me. Whether he was signing books, conducting a seminar, or participating in ritual, individual after individual would walk up to him, sometimes clasping his hand, sometimes holding his arm, looking into his eyes, and thanking him for changing their lives. And every single time, person after person would turn and walk away with a huge, glowing smile.

At first, I stood there wondering what this was. How is he doing this? What is the reason for this type of adoring recognition? As I got to know him, I realized that Raymond Buckland was as genuine as you could get, that he genuinely cared about his readers, his initiates, and the general magickal community. His influence was not just in his writing and speaking, but in his sincere interactions with those around him. He exuded love to others. It wasn't what he was doing, but what he was *being*. His genuine care and influence on the magickal community was palpable, a force that could be felt by all.

It is amazing how one individual can affect a person in so many ways—a glittering web that connects us to the source through the words and actions of another. I was touched by his activities long before I met him, through his books and through the people he taught and associated with who became important in my own life: Ray Malbrough, Michael Ragan (whom our tradition of the Black Forest Circle and Seminary calls "Grandfather Ragan"), Lord Serphant of the Serpentstone Family, and so many more.

Raymond Buckland, often referred to as the Father of American Wicca, touched countless lives with his warm and approachable demeanor, deep knowledge, and genuine passion for the craft. His behavior was marked by kindness and openness, making him a beloved figure in the Wiccan and Pagan communities. Buckland's personality shone through his writings and teachings, where he combined wisdom with a touch of humor, making complex spiritual concepts accessible to all. His gifts as a writer, teacher, and spiritual leader inspired many to explore and embrace their own spiritual paths, fostering a sense of community and belonging among his friends, peers, and readers.

Through his books, lectures, mentorship, and personal interactions, Raymond Buckland's influence continues to resonate, positively impacting those who had the privilege to learn from him. I am grateful that I was afforded such a glittering gift. As an author? He taught courage and tenacity, navigating the seas of political Pagan discontent and holding his own against gossip, mistruths, jealousy, and misconception—something that can be incredibly difficult and personally debilitating.

Raymond Buckland rose above it all. To you … Mr. Buckland … Honor is the Law—Love is the Bond. You did it, and you did it well. Thank you.

Silver RavenWolf *(Pennsylvania) is a nationally recognized leader and elder of Wicca. The author of many books, including the best-selling* Solitary Witch, Teen Witch, *and* To Ride a Silver Broomstick, *Silver has been interviewed by* The New York Times, Newsweek *magazine, and* The Wall Street Journal.

• • • • • • • •

By the mid-1980s, Buckland had become a popular speaker at Pagan festivals and metaphysical bookstores. Promotional materials from Cochran-Buckland Enterprises shed light on the types of lectures Buckland was presenting during this period of time. Though capable of lecturing about a variety of topics (a chant-o-matic workshop would have been great!), Buckland narrowed down his offerings to three topics. All three of his lectures included good old-fashioned slideshows using a carriage-style projector.

Since Ray was always enchanted by history, two of his lectures were archival in nature. "Witchcraft Ancient and Modern" included all the historical material found in books like *Big Blue* and *Witchcraft from the Inside,* and one gets the feeling that Buckland could share such retellings completely from memory. His promotional materials point out that the lecture also includes "unique scenes of a Wiccan initiation."[215]

The other historical offering was "Gerald Gardner and the Beginnings of Modern Witchcraft."[216] Buckland's admiration for Gardner remained as strong as ever, even if he no longer actively practiced Gardnerian Craft. Most of the slides for the lecture came from Buckland's visits to Monique Wilson on the Isle of Man and highlighted Gardner's museum and its collection. The lecture also included images from Buckland's museum, with his promotional materials highlighting the museum's one-time location in New York. Today

---

215. Cochran-Buckland Promotional Materials, "Raymond Buckland Presents a Workshop."
216. Cochran-Buckland Promotional Materials, "Raymond Buckland Presents a Workshop."

we take such images for granted, but in 1987 this would have been a rare opportunity.

Drawing on Ray's work in books such as *Here Is the Occult* and *A Pocket Guide to the Supernatural*, "The Wide World of the Occult" was a two-hour overview of "Voodoo, Witchcraft, Ceremonial Magick, necromancy, folklore, ancient Egyptian beliefs, and fortune telling," which is a lot to jam into two hours![217] While Witchcraft was his life's work, I think Buckland loved to talk about other spiritual and magickal systems too. He was always far too curious intellectually to write and talk only about Witchcraft.

In addition to his two-hour lectures, Buckland advertised what he described as a workshop on "Beginning Witchcraft: The Basics" for covens and solitaries. This workshop was advertised as a three-hour program detailing beliefs, self-dedication, initiations, circle-casting, worship, sabbats and esbats, ritual construction, and working magick, specifically healing and divination magick. As a bonus, workshop attendees were given a "Certificate of Completion" at the end of the presentation. Buckland's ad copy appealed directly to solitaries who might want to start a coven. Participants were "encouraged to bring notebook and pencil."[218]

Given that the presenter was Raymond Buckland, prices for his workshops and lectures were quite reasonable. Lectures were $150 each, with the three-hour workshop priced at $250. Considering that Buckland was capable of filling a room, that cost was then divided among the participants (minus whatever the sponsoring organization was adding on top of Ray's fee).[219] For some people, the idea of a Witch charging $150 for a lecture is abhorrent, but the time and energy involved in a two-hour presentation is more than just the two hours of the actual lecture. There's the travel time involved, usually considerable since Buckland lived on the West Coast, and then there's the time needed to assemble the presentation, made more considerable by the use of slides (which back then were expensive to create). Frankly, I think Buckland would have been justified charging more than he did.

During this period, Buckland also participated in as many TV, radio, magazine, and newspaper appearances and profiles as possible. During his

217. Cochran-Buckland Promotional Materials, "Raymond Buckland Presents a Workshop."
218. Cochran-Buckland Promotional Materials, "Raymond Buckland Presents a Workshop."
219. Cochran-Buckland Promotional Materials, lecture fee structure.

time in New Hampshire and Virginia, he did noticeably fewer engagements than he had while living in New York, but they never completely went away. But in the latter half of the 1980s, Buckland's media profile began to grow once more. There were appearances on daytime talk shows such as *Sally Jessy Raphael* and profiles in prestigious newspapers such as the *Los Angeles Times*.

Buckland's appearance on the *Sally Jessy Raphael Show* was filmed on Monday, February 16, 1987, in St. Louis, Missouri. Buckland wasn't alone on the talk show either. For this appearance, he was joined by old friends Scott Cunningham and Selena Fox, along with Antiga, a Witch from Asheville, North Carolina. The show's crowd comes across as more curious than hostile, though (of course) one member of the studio audience thinks "it's all Satan." All four guest Witches look much like "normal" people, with Buckland in a blazer and Cunningham in a button-up shirt and tie.[220]

Despite not every member of the studio audience being sympathetic to Sally's four Witch guests, Raphael seemed to like the foursome. According to Selena Fox, during a commercial break during the taping, Raphael asked the Witches to perform a spell to improve her ratings! The entire 22-minute show comes across as a positive portrayal of Wicca, especially rare in 1987.

There was also an appearance on the syndicated television series *Secrets and Mysteries* in 1989. Hosted by Irish actor Edward Mulhare (1923–97), who was best known for a recurring role on the TV show *Knight Rider*, *Secrets and Mysteries* documented paranormal and "mysterious" historical events. Not surprisingly, Buckland appeared on the episode about the "black art" of Witchcraft. Despite producing only sixteen episodes and airing for only two years, the series would go on to have a long second life when it was released on VHS, where it stayed in print until 2001.

Some of Buckland's increased media presence was no doubt the result of *Big Blue*'s runaway success. Though never quite a *New York Times* bestseller, *Big Blue* did well in the book marketplace and appeared on several smaller bestseller lists put together by book wholesalers. With *Big Blue*'s provocative cover and presence in most mall bookstores, Buckland's profile as an author

---

220. You can watch the video for yourself on YouTube thanks to the Buckland Museum's YouTube channel: "Ray Buckland, Selena Fox, Scott Cunningham on Daytime Television." Be warned, though, that the sound gets super terrible by the end of the video.

was greater than ever. But there was another reason for Buckland's rising media star during this period: the Satanic panic.

Beginning in the late 1970s, large groups of Americans began to believe that an organized Satanic conspiracy was running rampant throughout the United States and spreading their beliefs through heavy metal music and role-playing games such as *Dungeons & Dragons*. These Satanists were believed to have infiltrated the very fabric of American society, including civic groups, schools, and, perhaps most notably, preschools. Accusations of sexual abuse leveled at child daycare centers made front-page news in the United States, and despite absolutely zero physical evidence, innocent people served lengthy jail sentences all due to mass hysteria. (The most famous of these cases was the McMartin Preschool trial, which lasted for seven years and ruined the lives of the accused.)

There has never been an underground network of Satanists targeting children (or anyone else) in the US, but reality didn't matter during the Satanic panic. If you were somehow connected to the "occult," you were a suspect and the subject of curiosity. People have always been interested in Witchcraft, of course, but in the 1980s public Witches were seen as even more scandalous. And despite not being involved in any Satanic conspiracy or groups, Witchcraft was made an issue in child custody cases, and most certainly people lost jobs because of their spiritual beliefs. Satanic panic had real consequences.

The original purveyors of Satanic panic were fringe Christian groups, but in the age of Ronald Reagan, they found a natural audience in the newly emboldened "Moral Majority." As the fervor over Satanic conspiracy grew, the media picked up on the craze and quickly realized that it was good for TV ratings. Anything that smacked of the occult or the unknown, and might rile up viewers and listeners, was suddenly in demand. Buckland's increased public profile rightly benefited from this phenomenon.

Buckland was either the perfect figure to speak up for Witches during the Satanic panic or the last type of person you would want representing Witches. For practicing Witches, Buckland was a great ambassador. One of his core beliefs had always been "Witches don't even believe in the Devil," so what better candidate was there to repudiate accusations of Witches being involved in a Satanic conspiracy? Of course if you were the media, Raymond Buckland, with his professorial ways and three-piece suits, might have been a disappointment. While his short beard might have given off an occult vibe, Buckland's disarming nature and infectious sense of humor always made him likable in public forums.

Remembering Ray: Selena Fox

Note from Jason Mankey: In the course of writing this book, I conducted a Zoom interview with Circle Sanctuary's Selena Fox in August of 2024. Here are some of her thoughts about Ray from that conversation. Portions have been edited for clarity.

• • • • • • • • •

I first connected with Ray Buckland in the 1970s. It's possible that we met at the last Gnosticon (1976), and we had postal connections beginning in the 1970s and that might have also been how we first started connecting. I had the opportunity to work with some other groups and festivals back in the 1970s, and in 1980 I was in charge of publicity for what was then called the Pan Pagan Festival. At that time I was reaching out to elders from around the country and I thought it was really important for Ray to be part of that event. A year later he was at the first Pagan Spirit Gathering in 1981.

One of the commonalities I had with Ray was that we were both creating additional pathways for people to become a Witch (and/or a Pagan) that were outside of the traditional coven-based initiation system. There was some controversy regarding the self-initiation path of Seax-Wica and our Circle Craft, and we were getting some blowback about the whole concept of self-initiation. We felt that through our own work with the Craft, it [self-initiation] was really appropriate and would be helpful to others, and a lot of people really connected with that type of path.

Ray was willing to experiment, and not just with what was established. His creativity was just fabulous! I really think that Ray, myself, and others were part of what I call "redecorating the halls of religion." We allowed some different ways of practicing religion and spirituality to become more known and accessible.

We were both doing media during the so-called Satanic panic because we both thought that someone had to be out and public to counter the misinformation. Was that the safest thing to do back then? No, but we got opportunities to share correct information about the positives of nature religion and Witchcraft in particular. During that time, the Craft was being demonized and people were intentionally sharing misinformation. I do think we put out some information that changed attitudes in a positive way. It's hard to tell what the ripple effect is from anything you do, but I'm really thankful that Ray and I were a part of that journey.

Because he was one of our guest speakers at Pagan Spirit Gathering, he would come in early for the event, allowing time for the guests and organizers to just hang out. I'm just really thankful that part of my life journey was being able to be with Ray. We had some fun times, and I'm just really thankful that our lives intertwined.

At the core, the Ray I knew had a very loving and healing presence. It was not a put-on; it was genuine. He really was a guiding light.

Rev. Selena Fox *is senior minister and high priestess of Circle Sanctuary, a Nature Spirituality church, Pagan resource center, and nature preserve with a worldwide Ecospirituality ministry that includes networking, publishing, education, environmental preservation, counseling, events sponsoring, and other work.*

Considering the climate at the time, it's surprising how drama-free most of Buckland's public appearances were in the 1980s. But that all ended in October of 1987 when a series of lectures he was scheduled to deliver in Minneapolis, Minnesota, were canceled. Ray was originally scheduled to speak at Many Voices, a New Age center in Minneapolis, but the demand to see him was so great that his appearance was moved to a local YWCA hall. The change in location meant a higher-profile event, and this is when the trouble started.

"Christian" fundamentalists began threatening both the event organizers and the local YWCA. Shortly thereafter, both the New Age center and Llewellyn (located just outside of Minneapolis) began receiving threatening phone calls. Demonstrating just how courageous they were, the fundamentalists involved in the harassment were all anonymous. Individuals who experienced the misfortune of answering the fundamentalists' calls were treated to exhortations such as "You're going to burn for this!" and "May the blood of Jesus spill on all of you."

With tensions high and the threat of violence real, the YWCA and the New Age center felt forced to cancel Buckland's scheduled talks. Shortly thereafter, he was invited to write an editorial for the *St. Paul Pioneer Press Dispatch* newspaper. Ray regarded this letter so highly that he included it in his memoir:

> Religious discrimination, bigotry, and suppression of freedom of speech are rife in the Twin Cities. I am an author and lecturer. I have had more than a dozen books published, have lectured at universities across the country, and have been interviewed by the likes of Dick Cavett, Barbara Walters and Tom Snyder. Yet because of a group of "Fundamentalists" I was denied the right to lecture in Minneapolis on October 16 and 17, 1987.
>
> Many Voices, a local New Age bookstore, had invited me to the Twin Cities to give two lectures and a workshop. The events were to be held at the YWCA, which was booked many months in advance. Part of my presentation was to deal with "Witchcraft," apparently a buzz word to some. Actually I prefer the more correct "Wicca," the original root word. A group of "Fundamentalists" (typical of their species, they manage to remain anonymous) complained to the YWCA, making such a fuss the booking was summarily canceled, leaving the promoters (and myself) very much out of pocket and disappointing many who were looking forward to the lectures.
>
> The problem here is that the action was taken on misinformation. The Fundamentalists are still living in the Dark Ages, with visions of Wicca as being Satanism and Devil-worship. Nothing could be further from the truth. In actual fact the Wicca do not even believe in the Devil, let alone worship him. Wicca is a very positive, nature-oriented religion. Its one law is to harm no one. The Fundamentalist might learn something from [those in Wicca, as] Wicca always has a very tolerant attitude toward all other religions, believing that there are many paths that lead to the center—no one path being right for all.

Wicca is recognized as a religion by the federal government; witness the inclusion of it in Department of the Army Pamphlet No. 165–13 "Religious Requirements and Practices of Certain Selected Groups—A Handbook for Chaplains." There are many Wiccan Churches operating in a number of states, all accepted by the IRS and other federal agencies.

To ask a fundamentalist about a Witch is tantamount to asking a Nazi about a Jew. They are certainly entitled to their opinions but they should not be allowed to force those opinions on others. To suppress the freedom of speech is to encourage and perpetuate ignorance. In twenty-five years of public speaking (including at Roman Catholic colleges and high schools, Methodist churches, etc.) I have never before been denied an audience.

The Twin Cities is the home of Llewellyn Publications, probably the biggest and certainly the most respected publisher of New Age works in the world.

I therefore find it a sad reflection on the Twin Cities and, especially, on the YWCA—an organization I have strongly supported in the past—that they should condone, if not encourage, religious discrimination and intolerance.

—*Raymond Buckland, Ph.D., D.D.*

• • • • • • • •

Living in San Diego and increased royalty payments allowed Raymond Buckland to indulge in long-simmering interests. As a former member of the Royal Air Force, Ray had always had an interest in flight but found very few opportunities to engage in it. Back in 1973, he had joined his then father-in-law, Ray Taylor, on a few flights in Taylor's Cessna 170, a small single-engine aircraft with room for four. During this time, Buckland also helped Taylor construct a Steen Skybolt, a small plane with one seat, designed for aviation hobbyists. Financial considerations prevented Ray from being able to buy his own aircraft or even take flying lessons, but he was so excited about the possibility of flight that he joined the Experimental Aircraft Association that year and remained a member for the next twenty-five years.

In 1989 Buckland began looking into ultralight aircraft and started visiting a small airport outside of San Diego named Perris Valley as part of his
research. Ultralight aircraft are designed for the aviation hobbyist and do not
require a pilot's license or a vehicle inspection and are limited to an empty
weight of 254 pounds (excluding some safety devices) and just one occupant.
In addition to being small planes, they are also limited to a maximum of five
gallons of fuel and a top speed of 5 knots per hour (about 65 miles per hour).
An ultralight aircraft can reach heights of 9,900 feet (about 3,000 meters)
and has a range of about 130 miles (which is why many ultralight pilots strap
a gas can to their plane—so they have enough fuel to get back to their starting point).

Although the term *ultralight aircraft* implies a small and sleek plane, the
reality is something entirely different. There are ultralights that resemble a
streamlined conventional personal plane, but most ultralights are assembled
from kits and look like a go-kart with wings. The original ultralights were
hang gliders with small engines, but over time they gained more maneu-
verability and, perhaps most importantly, landing gear, making takeoffs
and landings much easier. Though most ultralight aircraft fly out of small
airports, one could conceivably take off and land in a large backyard (and
many ultralight pilots do!). Most ultralights contain a parachute that can be
deployed in case of an emergency to bring both the pilot and the plane safely
to the ground.

During his visits to Perris airfield, Buckland came into contact with
the United States Ultralight Association, which offered lessons and an
organization-issued license. As Buckland writes in his memoir, "Anyone with
any sense—and I counted myself among them—took training and obtained
an ultralight pilot's license." Training took place in a plane similar to an ultralight but with two seats (the two seats made it too heavy to officially be an
ultralight). Just the idea of flying an ultralight plane delighted Buckland, and
he joined the local San Diego Ultralight Association and became an active
member even before his first training flight.

Buckland's first flying lesson took place on January 24, 1990, and lasted
an hour. The flying lessons continued over the next nine months in a variety
of conditions to prepare Buckland for whatever circumstances he might find
himself in while flying. The training itself was quite rigorous, and some days

he would take off and land twenty times in an hour. In late June of that year, Buckland's instructor decided that Ray was "ready to solo," and Buckland began flying by himself for the first time. In September, Buckland passed a written exam and received his ultralight certification.

Buckland's early flying days were spent renting a vehicle from the airfield, but he, along with a friend, eventually bought a personal ultralight vehicle. With airplane ownership came additional concerns, such as maintenance. After installing a new propeller on his Cobra ultralight, Buckland and his plane's co-owner noticed some wear and tear on the bolts holding the gears that turned the propeller in place. After the parts were replaced, overseen by an engineer who worked at the airport, Buckland took the ultralight up for a flight and almost died. He wrote about the experience in the association's newsletter in April of 1991:

> I flew around locally, west of the field, for about ten minutes reveling in the perfect flying weather. I decided to fly across to the east, to the flat area behind the hill at the back of the strip. I also thought it would be a good idea to do an easterly approach to the strip, to see what it was like. I knew I had the place to myself. I came in from the west, around the tree, and lined up with the strip. I wasn't planning on touching down; just trying the approach. I therefore eased-on the throttle to climb up and continue over the hill. I had hardly reached treetop height when there came the ominous whirl of an engine disconnected from the prop!… I immediately put the nose down, cut the engine and kept straight ahead. There was no runway left; nothing but uphill rough ground. At least I was to the left of the tree and over the ditch. Although the ground ahead was very rough, it was pretty well clear of rocks, so I just put it down there. I hit fairly hard—probably because it was an uphill grade—and ran forward. Then my nosewheel dug into a soft spot and came up against a root, tipping me up. So there I was, hanging in my harness but alive.

The engineer who had assisted Buckland had installed weaker parts than what was required, and those parts disintegrated while Ray was in the air. Though the situation was precarious, Buckland found the experience a valuable one, because he now knew he could trust himself to keep calm in an emergency situation.

Buckland's interest in flying wasn't limited to the trips he took in his ultralight, and he became increasingly active in San Diego's flight community. In 1989 he became the secretary of the San Diego Ultralight Association, overseeing the group's newsletter, which he turned into a sixteen-page monthly magazine with photographs. He held that position for nearly four years.

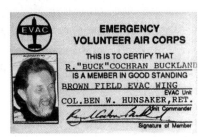

EMERGENCY
VOLUNTEER AIR CORPS

THIS IS TO CERTIFY THAT
R."BUCK"COCHRAN BUCKLAND
IS A MEMBER IN GOOD STANDING
BROWN FIELD EVAC WING
EVAC Unit
COL.BEN W. HUNSAKER,RET.
Unit Commander
Signature of Member

"Buck" was a nickname of Ray's during this period.

Ray's most rewarding work was as part of the Emergency Volunteer Air Corps (EVAC), a part of the Experimental Aircraft Association. Inspired by the 1989 San Francisco earthquake, EVAC was established to help local officials in times of emergency. Because ultralights don't require a lot of room to take off and land, there was the potential that ultralight vehicles could be useful in performing emergency rescue operations and surveying damage from natural disasters. Buckland became the public relations director for the San Diego unit of EVAC and became affiliated with the San Diego County Office of Disaster Preparedness.

As his local EVAC unit's resident writer and video star, Buckland wrote, produced, directed, and edited a video on how ultralight vehicles could assist in emergency situations. Ray also served as narrator and star, visiting a variety of local airports and interviewing several local officials. When the video was finished, it was shared with other regional EVAC chapters. To many of us, Raymond Buckland was a famous Witch, but to members of the ultralight community, Raymond Buckland was a minor celebrity—the guy in the video.

Exercise 7: A Handfasting Rite

Raymond Buckland and Tara Cochran were married on August 25, 1983, in Charlottesville, Virginia, at the local Unitarian Universalist church. The two would remain married until Ray's passing in 2017. Terms like *soulmate* and *twin flame* are often overused in our society, but most certainly Tara and Ray shared a very special connection. Though Raymond Buckland's most visible partner over the course of his life as a public Witch was ex-wife Rosemary, he shared more of his life with Tara than with his previous partners. It's impossible to read the handfasting vows that are included in the *Big Blue Book*[221] and not think of them as expressing Ray's feelings for Tara.

● ● ● ● ● ● ● ● ●

This rite should be performed during the waxing of the Moon. The altar may be decked with flowers and flowers strewn about the Circle. If the coven normally wears robes, for this rite it is suggested that the bride and groom at least be skyclad; preferably the whole coven.

It is traditional in the Seax-Wica for the bride and groom to exchange rings. These are usually gold or silver bands with the couple's (Craft) names inscribed on them in runes. These rings rest on the altar at the start of the rite. The priapic wand is also on the altar.

The Erecting the Temple is performed. Priest and priestess kiss.

Covener: "There are those in our midst who seek the bond of handfasting."

Priestess: "Let them be named and brought forward."

Covener: "…(groom's name)…is the man and…(bride's name)…is the woman."

Bride and groom move forward to stand facing priest and priestess across the altar—bride opposite priest and groom opposite priestess:

---

221. Buckland, *Buckland's Complete Book of Witchcraft*, lesson 8, 137–39.

Priestess (to groom): "Are you … (name) … ?"

Groom: "I am."

Priestess: "What is your desire?"

Groom: "To be made one with … (bride's name) … , in the eyes of the gods and the Wicca."

Priest (to bride): "Are you … (name) … ?"

Bride: "I am."

Priest: "And what is your desire?"

Bride: "To be made one with … (groom's name) … , in the eyes of the gods and the Wicca."

Priestess takes up sword and raises it high. Priest hands priapic wand to bride and groom. They hold it between them, each with both hands.

Priestess: "Lord and Lady, here before you stand two of your folk. Witness, now, that which they have to declare."

Priestess replaces sword on altar, then takes her athame and holds the point of it to groom's chest. Groom repeats the following, line by line:

Priestess: "Repeat after me: 'I, … (name) … , do come here of my own free will, to seek the partnership of … (bride's name) … . I come with all love, honor, and sincerity, wishing only to become one with her whom I love. Always will I strive for … (bride's name) … 's happiness and welfare. Her life will I defend before my own. May the athame be plunged into my heart should I not be sincere in all that I declare. All this I swear in the names of the gods.* May they give me the strength to keep my vows. So mote it be.'"

Priestess lowers her athame. Priest then raises his athame and, in turn, holds it to the breast of the bride. She repeats the oath, line by line, after him:

Priest: "Repeat after me: 'I, … (name) … , do come here of my own free will, to seek the partnership of … (groom's name) … . I come with all love, honor, and sincerity, wishing only to become one with him whom I love. Always will I strive for … (groom's name) …'s happiness and welfare. His life will I defend before my own. May the athame be plunged into my heart should I not be sincere in all that I declare. All this I swear in the names of the gods.* May they give me the strength to keep my vows. So mote it be.'"

Priest lowers the athame. Priestess takes up the two rings and sprinkles and censes both. She hands the bride's ring to the groom and the groom's ring to the bride. They take them in their right hands, remaining holding the priapic wand with their left hands.

Priest: "As the grass of the fields and the trees of the woods bend together under the pressures of the storm, so too must you both bend when the wind blows strong. But know that as quickly as the storm comes, so equally quickly may it leave. Yet will you both stand, strong in each other's strength. As you give love; so will you receive love. As you give strength; so will you receive strength. Together you are one; apart you are as nothing."

Priestess: "Know you that no two people can be exactly alike. No more can any two people fit together, perfect in every way. There will be times when it will seem hard to give and to love. But see then your reflection as in a woodland pool: when the image you see looks sad and angered, then is the time for you to smile and to love (for it is not fire that puts out fire). In return will the image of the pool smile and love. So change you [sic] anger for love and tears for joy. It is no weakness to admit a wrong; more it is a strength and a sign of learning."

Priest: "Ever love, help, and respect each other, and then know truly that you are one in the eyes of the gods and of the Wicca."

All: "So mote it be."

Priest takes priapic wand from couple and replaces it on the altar. Bride and groom each place ring on the other's finger and kiss. They then kiss priest and priestess across the altar, then move deosil about the Circle to be congratulated by the others.

Then shall follow the ceremony of Cakes and Ale followed by games and merriment.

*Names used for the gods may be inserted here.

Chapter Eight

Romani & Scottish Roots

San Diego, with its proximity to Los Angeles, provided Raymond and Tara Cochran-Buckland with a variety of opportunities that simply weren't available in Virginia. One of the most interesting perks was the opportunity to hobnob with Hollywood's rich and famous. One of the individuals to become a good friend of the Bucklands during this period was cinematographer (and future Oscar winner) Dean Semler (1943–present) and his wife, Anne (or, as the Bucklands referred to her, Annie). This time, Gateway Casting had nothing to do with the Cochran-Bucklands hanging out with Hollywood elite. Tara Buckland and Annie Semler simply struck up a friendship, and before long, the two couples began spending time together.

Although Dean Semler is probably not a name familiar to most moviegoers, he has had a long and illustrious Hollywood career. A native Australian (as is Anne), Semler rose to Hollywood prominence after shooting the second and third *Mad Max* movies starring Mel Gibson. Semler would go on to shoot such films as *Cocktail* and *Young Guns* and would earn an Oscar for cinematography for Kevin Costner's 1990 film *Dances with Wolves*, and since that time he's never really stopped working. Semler has dozens of movie credits and has even stepped into the director's chair. In 1988 Semler invited the Bucklands to visit an active Hollywood shoot, though sadly the movie he was filming that day was the forgettable *K-9* starring Jim Belushi. (Ray still raved about the experience though!)

There's probably no topping a Hollywood movie shoot, but the Cochran-Bucklands had plenty of interesting things to share with the

Semlers, and not just discussions about Witchcraft! One evening when the Semlers came over for dinner, Tara cooked up a pot of rabbit stew, a traditional Romani dish. According to Raymond, twenty years later Dean Semler was still talking about that stew.

Tara's stew led to further discussions about the Roma and inspired Ray to write a treatment for a movie he titled *Spell of the Gypsy*. Semler took an interest in the project, and in the early months of 1990, Raymond and Dean Semler got into serious discussions about the production. Despite the word *spell* in the movie's title, *Spell of the Gypsy* was a love story, again illustrating how comfortable Buckland was branching out from his occult roots. Over the next year, the project got serious enough that Buckland wrote a full screenplay for *Spell* and produced both a standard storyboard and a video storyboard.

Like all of Ray's attempts at Hollywood success, *Spell* was never produced, and Semler moved on to other projects. The only real silver lining to the whole experience was that both Ray and Tara got to be photographed with the Oscar that Semler won for *Dances with Wolves*. Raymond Buckland wouldn't be remembered for *Spell of the Gypsy*, but he would be remembered for several books with the word *gypsy* in the title.

Buckland was comfortable with the word *gypsy* in a variety of circumstances. He uses the word in screenplays, books, and his memoir. He used the term in both his public and his private life and was happy to identify his Romani heritage with the term. Today the word *gypsy* is recognized by most individuals as a slur (the term *gypped*, as in being cheated, comes from the word), and as a writer I can tell you that it's uncomfortable to use. *Gypsy* is a complicated word, and even today there are some in the Roma community who continue to use it. I've made the choice in this book to mostly avoid the term unless I'm directly quoting Ray or referencing one of his works that uses the word.

• • • • • • • •

After the success of *Big Blue*, both Llewellyn and the reading public most likely expected Raymond Buckland to write more books specifically about Witchcraft. *Big Blue* is a rather comprehensive book, but there's always *more* that can be written on the subject of Witchcraft, and who better to do it than Ray? But Raymond Buckland had no interest in cashing in on his recent literary success. Instead, he looked to his family roots and decided to write about his Romani heritage.

The origins of the Roma people are in northern India, but the Roma were displaced by a series of Muslim invasions into the area during the eleventh century. As a result, many Roma were taken prisoner and forced into modern-day Turkey. Later, other Romani groups migrated into various parts of Europe, including what is now England, Wales, and Scotland. Europeans mistakenly called the Roma *gypsies*, believing they were from Egypt due to their dark skin, and the term has been with us ever since.

Despite looking very English, Buckland very much had Romani blood flowing through his veins. In the early 2000s, Raymond had his DNA tested, and the most dominant ethnic group in his DNA population matches was Romani.[222] Buckland's grandfather (Herbert Alfred Buckland) was Romani and had spent much of his early life living in a *vardo*, the traditional horse-drawn wagon favored by the Roma that also doubled as a home. Vardos are not just living spaces; they are practically pieces of art. Vardos are often brightly painted and contain highly decorative wood carvings. The Buckland vardo was eventually donated to the Kenwood House museum in London and put on display for a period of time.

Raymond inside a traditional vardo

---

222. DNA Tribes Genetic Ancestry Analysis, "Part C: Your High Resolution Global Population Match Results."

But life in the vardo was not for Herbert Alfred Buckland, and he became the first of the Buckland Roma to settle into a house without wheels. This must have been a big step for Herbert, as he was the patriarch of his particular branch of the Buckland family. Herbert eventually became an insurance agent, but he shared the ways of the Roma with his sons and later his grandsons, despite his now sedentary lifestyle.

Buckland writes in his memoir that "in Rom life, if a male Romano marries outside the Rom…then the wife, although accepted into the tribe, is often treated very badly by her mother-in-law, if not the whole tribe." Buckland wrote that line in reference to his mother, who came from outside the Roma, noting that his mother was often picked on by his grandmother, Nana. Nana's antagonism toward her daughter-in-law might have been related to Eileen Buckland's ethnic origins, or perhaps Nana Buckland just had a permanently sour disposition.

Raymond wrote that local merchants "lived in fear of her [Nana's] wrath" and that Nana would often walk across busy streets without a care in the world, resulting in drivers slamming on their brakes and honking their horns. When young Raymond and his family moved into Nana's house after the death of Herbert, Buckland recounts being one of the few people who would happily sit with his grandmother for extended periods of time. Young Raymond got along well with Nana Buckland and was "one of the few who did."

Buckland's grandmother may have also inspired Ray's love of divination and Tarot:

> I can hardly remember a time when she didn't have the cards in her hands. She loved to play the popular games, such as whist and even poker, but as often used the cards to read to friends and neighbors; to tell fortunes. In those days it wasn't easy to find tarot cards and, like many Gypsies, Nana had made her own deck. She had taken a regular poker deck as the Minor Arcana and had then drawn and painted designs on blank cards to make up the Major Arcana.

There were also moments spent with Grandfather Herbert that may have played a role in Ray's interest in magick and the occult:

Although, due to the war, I had got to spend little time with my grandfather, I very much enjoyed what time I did have with him. He was full of stories of Gypsy life and often demonstrated Rom ways to me. I remember one time when he and I had taken a walk down to the banks of the River Thames and were standing watching a young boy fishing. We watched for the longest time, with no apparent activity. Finally my grandfather asked the boy "Caught anything yet?" The boy shook his head in disgust.

After a moment's thought my grandfather asked "Would you like me to catch one for you?" The boy looked at him in disbelief but, with a sigh, handed over his fishing pole. My grandfather cast into the river and within less than three minutes pulled out a large fish.

Catching a fish isn't necessarily a magickal act, but it's easy to imagine the hold such a display might have had on the mind and imagination of a young lad. It certainly would have made Grandfather Herbert appear magickal.

There is one other incident from Ray's childhood that suggests some sort of magickal ability on the part of Herbert Buckland:

Grandad had a hothouse at the bottom of his garden, filled with a variety of plants and flowers. In one corner a sturdy grapevine grew up, to trail back and forth across the glass roof of the house. It used to bear wonderfully big black grapes, I recall. Apparently Grandad had "Gypsied" it from the famous grapevine at Hampton Court Palace. In other words, although you weren't allowed to touch the famous vine (dating from the time of King Henry VIII, and these days separated from the public by glass), Grandad had "somehow" managed to come home from a visit with a healthy clipping in his pocket! My father later grew a beautiful vine from a clipping taken from Grandad's. Uncle George grew another and, many years later, my brother Gerard grew one at his home as did his daughter.

Herbert Buckland wasn't the only Buckland patriarch whom Ray credited with magickal abilities due to his Romani heritage; he saw that power in his father, Stanley, as well. During the war, a neighbor of the Bucklands kept several racing greyhounds (illegally) in a small pen. One day one of the greyhounds found its chain-leash wrapped around its leg, resulting in a deep cut. The dog, angry, scared, and in great pain, snapped and gnashed its teeth at anyone who tried to help. But the dog's agitated state did not stop Stanley Buckland. Ray's father tackled the problem by putting on a pair of thick leather gloves and going into the pen, speaking quietly to the dog, and assuring the canine that all would be okay. This time the dog didn't snap, and Stanley was able to unwrap the chain from the dog's lead. He then dressed the wound and patted the dog on the head.

Buckland's first book on Romani magickal tradition was initially titled *Gypsy Fortune Telling* (1988), illustrating Buckland's comfort with the word *gypsy*. This book was begun just as *Big Blue* was being released, and it was almost named something else. In his proposal to Llewellyn, Buckland's proposed title is *Gypsy Dukkerin'*, dukkerin' being a Romani term for fortune-telling.[223] This was not a title that Carl Weschcke and the crew at Llewellyn were happy with, and with some reluctance Buckland agreed to change the title to *Secrets of Gypsy Fortunetelling*.[224] The change in title was done to make the subject of the book clearer, but it also left the door open for future "Secrets of" books if Buckland desired to go that route.

Fortunetelling might be the best of Buckland's three early Romani magick books, helped to a large degree by days spent in the company of Nana Buckland while she read Tarot. But Buckland consulted more than just his childhood memories for the project. There were also extensive calls to his mother to inquire about all the things her husband's family did that might have been influenced by their Romani heritage. Buckland also consulted a Romani man who restored vardos in Hampshire, England. Buckland writes that this gentleman helped him "fill-in a lot of gaps in my knowledge of Romani lore."

The *Fortunetelling* book was launched at the American Booksellers Association (ABA) convention in Anaheim, California, in May of 1988. To promote the book's launch, Llewellyn arranged for Raymond to give Tarot readings at the event instead of doing a traditional book reading and/or signing. Taking inspiration from his latest book, Raymond attempted to recreate the deck his grandmother had used, using playing cards for the Minor Arcana and drawing his own Major Arcana cards. Buckland's readings were

223. Raymond Buckland, letter to Carl Weschcke, March 25, 1988.
224. Carl Weschcke, letter to Raymond Buckland, April 7, 1988.

a hit at the convention, and the folks at Llewellyn were so impressed with Buckland's homemade deck that they immediately asked him if they could publish it!

Upon getting home from the convention, Buckland went to work making large-scale artwork for the deck, and Llewellyn subsequently published *The Buckland Gypsy Fortunetelling Deck* at the very end of 1988 (a nearly unheard-of turnaround time for such a project). Much of the reason for the quick turnaround time was the simplicity of the deck. The Minor Arcana were truly just regular playing cards, with the only stylizations appearing on the kings, queens, princes (for jacks), tens, and aces.

Buckland's *Gypsy Fortunetelling Deck*

The Major Arcana in Buckland's deck are more stylized, but there's a simplicity there too. Instead of depicting imposing and esoteric figures, Buckland's Major Arcana cards feature scenes from everyday Romani life. There are horses pulling vardos and individuals gathered to eat and to cook dinner. The Major Arcana are numbered 1 to 22 instead of the usual 0 to 21, and the images on the Buckland deck do not correspond to the "traditional" images established by the Rider-Waite-Smith deck.[225] Instead of including elaborately rendered images of the Major Arcana, Buckland's deck features simpler drawings; for example, a picture of "just a horse" serves as a Major Arcana image. The deck also lacks any titles on the Major Arcana cards; instead of there being a title on the card, like "The Hermit," there is simply a number. After being released as a stand-alone deck, it was later repackaged to include Buckland's *Fortunetelling* book.

Perhaps the oddest of Buckland's series of Tarot decks and oracle cards was *The Buckland Gypsies' Domino Divination Deck* (1999). Like playing cards, dominoes began being used for divination shortly after their creation in the twelfth century. Early dominoes were often nearly indistinguishable from playing cards, as both could be made using paper, ceramic tiles, or bones.

Buckland's *Domino Divination Deck*

Buckland's *Domino Divination Deck* didn't utilize actual dominoes at all, but instead was a deck of cards. Each card contains a series of dots (or, in some cases, one dot or no dots) representative of a traditional domino tile. For example, a card might contain a square of four dots next to one dot. This

---

225. First published in 1909 by the Rider Company, the Rider-Waite-Smith is the most popular Tarot deck in the world, and many modern Tarot decks have adopted its correspondences. The deck was designed by occultist A. E. Waite and illustrated by Pamela Colman Smith, then both members of the Independent and Rectified Rite of the Golden Dawn.

would be a domino containing a four on its left-hand side and a one on its right. In addition to the domino symbol, each card contains an explanation of the card's meaning and the day of the week the card is associated with. There was also a small booklet included with the deck. The cards didn't stay in print for very long, but the contents of the deck's book were repackaged, with extra material, as *Buckland's Domino Divination: Fortune Telling with Dominoes and the Game of Dominoes* and published through Pendraig in 2010. This time, the term *gypsy* was wisely left off the cover.

In 2001, thirteen years after the *Fortunetelling Deck*, Buckland would release a more traditional Tarot deck. Teaming up with artist Lissanne Lake (1956–present), who did all the illustrations, *The Buckland Romani Tarot: The Gypsy Book of Wisdom* features full-color artwork on every card and Tarot correspondences as established by the Rider-Waite-Smith deck. As an example, Buckland's Death card is the traditional number 13 and features a burning vardo with a haunting spectral figure holding a scythe in the background.

Buckland's *Romani Tarot*

In this deck, Buckland substitutes Romani words for the four traditional suits, dubbing his suits *koros*, *koshes*, *bolers*, and *chivs*. Most versions of the deck that have been published over the years include English translations of the Romani words, letting the Tarot reader know that koros are cups, koshes are staves, bolers are wheels, and chivs are knives.

Taste in Tarot decks is rather subjective, but I find *The Buckland Romani Tarot* to be a very pretty deck. Many reviewers are critical of Lake's artwork, but I find it on par with many of the decks published during this time period. Apparently, my feelings about the deck are not the norm, because *The Romani Tarot* went out of print rather quickly. Over the years it has been reprinted by other publishers, and the Kindle version is available if reading cards on your phone is your thing, but physical copies of the deck are hard to come by and are expensive, often costing hundreds of dollars.

Secrets of Gypsy Fortunetelling had been a strong seller, so Buckland decided to follow that volume up with another book on Romani magick. As a writer intent on paying the rent, Buckland picked the ever-popular subject of love magick as a focus. It was also at this point that Buckland realized "Secrets of" could turn into a very lucrative series of books, and while coming up with *Secrets of Gypsy Love Magick* (1990), he began to imagine other volumes in the series.

Love Magick is essentially a collection of spells inspired by Buckland's Romani heritage, and despite the title, it features a broad range of spells. While there is a lot of love magick in the book, there are also spells "For Peace at Someone's Death" and "To End Sibling Rivalry." Perhaps these can be related tangentially to "love," but for all practical purposes *Love Magick* is essentially just a spell book.

Perhaps the most disappointing of Buckland's Romani-related material is 1990's *Secrets of Gypsy Dream Reading* (a second edition was released as *Gypsy Dream Dictionary*), which could have just been called *Buckland's Guide to Dream Reading*. Like most of Buckland's Romani books from this period, there are very few footnotes or citations, and it's impossible to know just where he's getting his information.

All three of Buckland's *Romani Magick* books are small volumes, and not one of them is over two hundred pages. None of them dive all that deeply into the history of the Romani people or their magickal practices either. The first two are mostly just spell books with a bit of Romani gloss, and the third is a dream dictionary. There's nothing wrong with either of those things, as

Buckland was writing for a general audience, but anyone expecting context and history might have been disappointed.

Check out that belt buckle!

Eight years later, though, Buckland would write a much more comprehensive book about Romani culture, history, and magick. *Gypsy Witchcraft and Magic* (1998) reads like a true labor of love for Raymond Buckland. *GW&M* is more than just a spell book; there's plenty on Romani history and culture, too. In Buckland's earlier work on Romani themes, it feels like Romani culture is mostly just a pegboard on which to hang a bunch of spells, but in *GW&M* it truly feels like the Romani are being celebrated.

GW&M is lavishly illustrated by Llewellyn standards. There are the usual decorative illustrations common in Llewellyn books of the 1990s and sketches detailing specific goings-on in various spells, but the thought put into the book goes deeper than that. There are pictures of Buckland standing next to a vardo and even pictures of authentic Romani dress. The most striking images are on a glossy insert featuring photographs taken in the early 1900s of everyday English Romani families. These extra touches simply connect the reader to the Romani in a way that Buckland's early books on the subject do not.

GW&M is a huge improvement over Buckland's previous work on the subject, but it does suffer from some of Ray's personal biases. The biggest bias in the work is Buckland's attempt to connect Romani thought and practice to both Modern Witchcraft and Paganism. Though many Romani today (and back in 1998) self-identify as Christians and Muslims (religious beliefs vary greatly among the Romani), Buckland can't help but hint that the Romani are all practicing some sort of organized Witchcraft in secret. In a chapter on Romani religion, Ray writes that "wherever the Gypsies rested in their travels, they would adopt—at least outwardly—the religious beliefs of their immediate neighbors."[226] Being from India, the Romani certainly practiced a non-Abrahamic faith before moving into Europe, but that doesn't make them all still "secret Pagans" five hundred years later.

At the end of that same chapter, Buckland attempts to connect the Romani to Wiccan-Witchcraft:

> Whether or not any Gypsies shared Wiccan beliefs, we do not know. There is no doubt that there is much similarity between the two groups. Witches had a vast knowledge of herbs, for example. Gypsies had similar knowledge.... They had a closeness with nature that the witches also possessed, and may even have worshipped the same deities under different names.[227]

---

226. Buckland, *Gypsy Witchcraft and Magic*, 10.
227. Buckland, *Gypsy Witchcraft and Magic*, 19.

Buckland's author photo from *Gypsy Witchcraft and Magic*

Considering that Wicca didn't exist five hundred years ago, it's very unlikely that the Romani possessed a whole lot of Wiccan beliefs. Like most groups, the Romani practiced (and practice) folk magick along with various forms of divination, but I'm not sure that makes the two groups overly similar. I feel like maybe I'm being harsh toward Buckland here, as one gets the feeling that Ray wants all this to be true *so badly*, even though connections between Wiccan-Witchcraft and Romani magickal practice are very unlikely. I'm sure Buckland, like most of us, wanted the various parts of himself in complete agreement with one another, in this case Buckland the Rom and Buckland the Witch.

Perhaps the oddest tangent in GW&M is a chapter devoted to "Gypsy Shamanism." As Buckland believed shamanism to be a universal practice at the root of all religions, it's not surprising to find him trying to connect the cultural traditions of the Romani to shamanism, but it makes for uncomfortable reading in the 2020s. Buckland does have a source for the Romani shamanism he's writing about, a man Buckland describes as "an old Gypsy shaman" living in an "ancient upturned boat under some trees."[228] But the shamanism shared by Buckland's shamanic informant has a definite whiff of the neo-shamanism of Michael Harner (1929–2018), complete with the requisite "power animals" common in books on the subject.

My quibbles with the book are only a small part of GW&M's actual contents. The vast majority of the book's pages are filled with spells and folklore from Romani culture(s) around the world. And as a spell book, GW&M does its job effectively. It's also much clearer in this volume where the spells on the printed page are actually coming from—namely, actual Romani in England and various printed sources.

Buckland's Romani books also resulted in a couple of new workshops he took on the road. "Gypsy Fortunetelling" was an obvious workshop to present, and besides, there was a fortunetelling deck and a book to promote! More surprising was a workshop on "Gypsy Shamanism" first shared long before *Gypsy Witchcraft and Magick* was published. The material Buckland shares on the subject of Romani shamanism is a scant five pages in GW&M; oh to be a fly on the wall for an hour-long presentation on the subject!

228. Buckland, *Gypsy Witchcraft and Magic*, 162.

With the exception of *Secrets of Gypsy Dream Reading* (now titled *Gypsy Dream Dictionary*), all of Buckland's books on Romani magick are now out of print at Llewellyn. However, much of the material in those books can be found in *Buckland's Book of Gypsy Magic: Travelers' Stories, Spells & Healings* published by Red Wheel/Weiser in 2010. Given the later publication date, one might expect to see *Romani* in the title instead of *Gypsy*, but old ways of speaking are hard to give up, and so are words that might possibly sell books. (It's also possible that even by 2010, the publisher was *still* not aware of the offensive stereotypes related to that word.) *BBoGM* also has a very striking picture of Ray dressed in traditional Romani garb in the "About the Author" section. (I swear the man got better-looking with age.)

Buckland's appreciation of Romani culture was very real; after all, it was very much his culture! Because of Ray's appearance, I sometimes come across people critiquing Buckland for writing books about Romani magick. Buckland's books about Romani practices aren't perfect, but the story he was telling was very much at least partly his own. He was a man who was proud of his heritage and the continuing legacy of the Romani people. Buckland's fascination for and appreciation of his Romani heritage did not lessen with age, either, or when he picked up other interests (which we will get to shortly). Certainly this exploration of his cultural heritage sold some books, but they weren't exploitative. If it had been just about "selling books," certainly there were far more sensational subjects to write about.

Around the same time Buckland began researching his Romani roots, he became intrigued by Tara's ancestors, the Scots. Both Tara and Ray entered this world through an unlikely source: traditional dance. Shortly after moving to San Diego, the couple found themselves in Balboa Park and just happened to stumble upon a performance by the Royal Scottish Country Dance Society. Intrigued by the performance, the couple joined the society and soon began taking dance lessons. The Royal Scottish Country Dance Society would become a large part of Ray and Tara's lives, with the couple becoming a part of the society's dance exhibition team. As members of the dance team, the Cochran-Bucklands performed all over Southern California and were even featured on television a handful of times.

Tara and Ray partying in hippie attire

Tara's Scottish roots go back to the traditional Scottish clans, in Tara's case, Clan Cochran. As a male marrying into the family, Raymond became an accepted part of the clan, eventually becoming the West Coast representative of Clan Cochran. Both Cochran-Bucklands represented Clan Cochran at the Highland Games in San Diego, operating a booth promoting Clan Cochran. This also enabled Ray to proudly wear the Cochran tartan, which he did both at dancing performances and at official Clan Cochran events. In his memoir, Buckland comments on just how "friendly" and welcoming the Royal Scottish Country Dance Society was to Tara and him. The Cochran-Bucklands enjoyed dancing so much that they ended up becoming a part of the English Country Dance and Song Society, too. The Bucklands would spend many of their holidays in San Diego with friends they met through their dancing experiences.

· · · · · · · ·

One of the more interesting projects Buckland worked on during this period was *The Book of African Divination*. This was not a project conceived of by Buckland, but a work-for-hire arrangement through Llewellyn. *The Book of*

African Divination: Interpreting the Forces of Destiny with Techniques from the Venda, Zulu, and Yoruba began as an oracle deck for Llewellyn, drawn by artist Kathleen Binger and based on West African (Cameroonian) spider divination. As is the case with most oracle decks, Binger was asked to provide a companion book to go along with her deck. She eventually submitted a small thirty-two-page booklet, which just wasn't big enough for Llewellyn. Llewellyn then suggested that Binger contact Buckland to write a book to accompany her deck.

Buckland dove into the project with his usual level of excitement and produced a small book touching on various types of African divination, the meanings of the cards in the deck, and some sample readings. Llewellyn was apparently quite happy with the results but ultimately rejected the book and deck. Having signed a contract, Buckland and Binger were paid a "kill fee" to pay them for their time.

While Buckland was quite proud of the work he did on *The Book of African Divination*, even back in 1990 Llewellyn realized that a book on African culture written by two individuals of European descent was perhaps not a good idea. With their Llewellyn contract void, Buckland and Binger were free to shop the project to other publishers, eventually ending up at the publisher Inner Traditions. *African Divination* remained in print for several years, and today sells for hundreds of dollars online and has become a little-known curio in the bibliography of Raymond Buckland.

· · · · · · · ·

Appendix A in the first edition of *Buckland's Complete Book of Witchcraft* includes a list of the various Witchcraft traditions in existence at the time of the book's writing. When the book was released in 1986, most of the traditions listed in that appendix would have been familiar to readers active in the burgeoning Witchcraft scene, except for one: Pecti-Wita. Buckland's entry on Pecti-Wita describes a solitary Witchcraft tradition originating in Scotland:

> A Scottish Solitary tradition passed on by Aidan Breac, who personally teaches students in his home at Castle Carnonacae, in Scotland. The tradition is attuned to the solar and lunar changes, with a balance between the God and the Goddess. Meditation and divination play a

large part in the tradition and it also teaches several variations on solitary working of magick. Information is not generally available and Mr.
Breac (who, as of this writing, is about ninety years old) is not seeking
further students.*

The entry also includes a cryptic footnote(*) stating that Ray was in touch
with Aidan Breac and hoped to be allowed to "present the Pecti-Wita teachings to a larger audience" in the near future.[229]

There is nothing in Buckland's memoir about Aidan Breac, nor have I
come across any correspondence between Buckland and Breac. Over the
years, Buckland took many trips back to the island of his birth, and on one of
those trips he could have made Breac's acquaintance. Alternatively, Buckland
and Breac could have been engaged in ongoing written correspondence that
is now lost. The anonymity of Breac (Buckland is the only Witchcraft writer
to mention him) makes Breac a bit of an enigma. When Pecti-Wita is mentioned in some online forums, there are commentators who like to suggest
that Aidan Breac might have been a fictional creation of Raymond Buckland.

The idea that Aidan Breac is a fictional character feels like a bit of a
stretch, though it's perhaps not completely out of the question. When Buckland first mentions Breac in the pages of the *Big Blue Book*, the reference is
fleeting and is buried in one of the appendices at the end of the book. The
idea that Buckland would make up an entire tradition and include it in
the *Big Blue* is just nonsensical to me. Buckland's entry on Pecti-Wita also
includes some biographical information, such as Breac's age and alleged location. Again, these feel like odd details to make up. Perhaps Aidan Breac was
an anagram (a favorite game of Ray's) or simply a nom de plume to ensure an
individual's privacy. As we will see, Buckland also (cleverly) hid the location
of Aidan Breac as well!

Five years after the release of *Buckland's Complete Book of Witchcraft*, Raymond Buckland would document the Witchcraft (or, in this case, the *Wita*)
of Aidan Breac in his 1991 book *Scottish Witchcraft: The History and Magick
of the Picts*.[230] There are dueling areas of emphasis in the title and subtitle of

---

229. First edition of *Buckland's Complete Book of Witchcraft*, 228.
230. Later printings were retitled *Scottish Witchcraft and Magick: The Craft of the Picts*, though
the book's contents remained unchanged.

this book, leading one to wonder whether it is a book about Scottish Witch-craft or Pictish Witchcraft. The Picts were forerunners of the Scots, but the two groups of people are very different. With the title and subtitle chosen (by both Ray and Llewellyn, since authors typically don't have final say over titles), the book feels like it's trying to appeal to different audiences: people curious about Scotland and those who think that some sort of really ancient lineage is the only way to confer legitimacy in Witchcraft. Is this a book about the Scots or the Picts?

In the introduction to *Scottish Witchcraft*, Buckland provides a little more detail as to the location of Aidan Breac. This time around, Breac's location would not be Castle Carnonacae, but the counties of Ross and Cromarty (or Ross-shire and Cromartyshire, to use their Scottish names). The previ-ously mentioned Castle Carnonacae is not written about, probably because Castle Carnonacae is not a real castle in Scotland, nor is Carnonacae even a real location in Scotland. Instead of being a place, Carnonacae is allegedly the name of a tribe of ancient Britons. In Claudius Ptolemy's (c. 100–c. 70 CE) *Geography*, the mathematician includes a long list of all the groups liv-ing in Great Britain. One of those groups, said to reside in what today is northwest Scotland, were the Carnonacae, not coincidently in the area of the current-day counties of Ross and Cromarty.[231] Castle Carnonacae, then, was a Buckland joke and a veiled reference to Breac's location. (It's likely that Breac, who was close to ninety years old when the *Big Blue Book* was pub-lished, wanted to keep his location something of a secret.)

Buckland would provide additional details about Breac in the second edi-tion of *Buckland's Complete Book of Witchcraft*, which was first published in 2002. The book's biggest revelation was that Breac was "born and raised in a hereditary Craft family on Priest Island."[232] Buckland has now given us a real location for Breac! But alas, while Priest Island is a real island off the west coast of Scotland, it's also uninhabited, and has been uninhabited for a very long time. Breac is also described in the second edition of *Big Blue* as being descended "from the Carnonacae tribe of Picts," and I can't help but

---

231. Thayer, "Book II, Chapter 2: Location of Albion Island of Britannia."
232. Second edition of *Buckland's Complete Book of Witchcraft*, footnote in the "Acknowledgments" section.

wonder if one of Buckland's friends had caught his "Carnonacae" joke in *Scottish Witchcraft* and called him out on it.[233]

It's possible that *Scottish Witchcraft* was released in 1991 because Buckland was waiting for Breac's passing before writing about the Scotsman's tradition. On the dedication page in *Scottish Witchcraft*, 1989 is given as the year of Breac's passing. There is a long history of "keeping silent" in Witchcraft, and sometimes death opens the door to write about traditions and practices that have otherwise been kept secret. If Breac was trying to keep his identity a secret (perhaps one of the reasons for the Castle Carnonacae joke), such worries would have mattered less after his death. It might also be why Buckland shares an actual true description of the area Breac lived in.

Ray Buckland with staff

233. Second edition of *Buckland's Complete Book of Witchcraft*, footnote in the "Acknowledgments" section.

As the subtitle of *Scottish Witchcraft: The History and Magick of the Picts* suggests, the book isn't just about Scotland. Buckland writes that the tradition of Adrian Breac dates back to the time of the ancient Picts. During the time of the Roman Empire, the Picts were known as fearsome (and painted) warriors, but not much else is known about them. The Picts ceased being a separate group of people by the end of the tenth century CE after intermarrying with the Scots and Gaels, who were then also living in what would become Scotland. Buckland's suggestion that Pecti-Wita is thousands of years old isn't all that surprising, since it's the type of claim he had been making about Witchcraft traditions since he began publishing in the 1960s. But by 1991, one can't help but think Buckland might have started to know better. (And if Pecti-Wita were actually thousands of years old, it would be literally groundbreaking since so much is unknown about the ancient Picts.)

Near the end of *Scottish Witchcraft*, Buckland admits that the Gaelic, Norse, and Saxon cultures influenced the Pecti-Wita tradition, an admission Buckland was forced to make after a fellow author pointed out the abundance of Norse and Germanic words in the book.[234] In addition to the Norse and Germanic influences, there are also several contemporary references that suggest modern influences on "Pecti-Wita." That begins, of course, with the word Wita as a synonym for Wicca, with Wita becoming commonplace only after Gerald Gardner. If someone is going to try to make their tradition sound ancient but also make it sound unique, Wita is not a bad choice. Buckland's Pecti-Witans also use tools that closely resemble the tools found in Wicca. A staff is substituted for the sword, and a dirk for the athame (a knife is a knife!), but all these tools essentially function the same way they do in more well-known versions of Wiccan-Witchcraft.

---

234. Buckland, *Scottish Witchcraft*, 201.

Buckland celebrating "Bealltainn" in *Scottish Witchcraft*

Once Buckland gets past the claims of the Pecti-Wita tradition being thousands of years old, there is a lot of genuine Scottish folklore in the pages of *Scottish Witchcraft*. But there is also a lot that just feels like Wicca with a new cultural gloss applied, similar to Buckland's books on Romani magick. It's hard to find fault with Buckland here, as this was pretty common in Witchcraft books in the 1980s and '90s, with various authors dressing up eclectic Wicca with folklore from a particular ethnic group. While most authors probably should have known better by 1990, back then there was a sincere belief that Wiccan-style Witchcraft was thousands of years old, and that its practice was close to universal, especially among the peoples of Europe.

In a radical departure from Buckland's other Witchcraft books, *Scottish Witchcraft* also contains twenty pages devoted to wilderness survival. (While reading this section of the book, I thought I was reading an old Boy Scout manual.) Instead of a more traditional initiation ritual, the Pecti-Wita initiation ceremony "must surely be the seven days spent out in the wild, living off the land."[235] To this end, Buckland offers instructions on building a shelter,

---

235. Buckland, *Scottish Witchcraft*, 176.

starting a fire with sticks, catching trout with one's fingers, and plucking the feathers from game birds. (The seven-day initiation period in the wild may very well be why I have never encountered a Pecti-Witan before.)

Some of the odd tonal shifts in *Scottish Witchcraft* might be because it was a book Raymond Buckland didn't really want to write. During the early 1990s, Llewellyn was publishing a lot of "ethnicity specific" books on Wiccan-Witchcraft. The most well-known of those books are 1990's *Celtic Magic* and *Norse Magic*, both by D. J. Conway (1939–2019). If *Scottish Witchcraft* was meant to be similar to the two Conway books in question (which contain very little "Norse" or "Celtic" folklore), then we all owe Raymond Buckland a huge debt of gratitude. Despite my quibbles, Buckland's book is far superior to and more original than Conway's volumes.[236]

In a letter to Carl Weschcke at Llewellyn in 1992, Buckland admits that he was tired of writing Witchcraft books and that *Scottish Witchcraft* was something Llewellyn requested him to write:

I don't want to write just Wiccan material; more accurately I don't want to write any more Wiccan books. I very much want to write other stuff; humorous as well as serious, fiction as well as fact. Let's face it, I've already written five fairly major books on the subject. I did manage to make something of a break away from Wicca with the three Gypsy books but got snagged back when I was asked to write *Scottish Witchcraft*.[237]

Despite not really wanting to write it, *Scottish Witchcraft (and Magick)* remains one of Buckland's most successful books. As of 2021, it was on its twenty-first printing, and it also remains a useful book for anyone looking to connect their Witchcraft practice to Scotland. Unlike Buckland's foray into Romani traditions, *Scottish Witchcraft* was a one-off. Having done his service to Aidan Breac (and Llewellyn), Buckland would move on to other writing adventures, one of which would introduce his work to an entirely new audience.

---

236. D. J. Conway was a talented writer, and *Celtic Magic* was my first Witchcraft book as an adult, but both *Celtic Magic* and *Norse Magic* contain a lot of questionable historical material.

237. Raymond Buckland, letter to Carl Weschcke, May 18, 1992.

Exercise 8: Power Raising

One focus in *Scottish Witchcraft* is solitary practice, which Buckland says is how the tradition was conventionally practiced. Buckland had dabbled in solitary Witchcraft before in his previous books (both *The Tree* and *Buckland's Complete* have sections on it), but *Scottish Witchcraft* was truly about Witchcraft away from a coven. Buckland's Witchcraft progressed from a Craft minus anything but coven work to a practice where solitary Craft work wasn't just acknowledged but was embraced.

Raising energy in solitary practice can be challenging, but Buckland makes it sound easy in *Scottish Witchcraft*.[238] The one thing I've taken from Buckland's writing more than anything else is how he takes difficult magickal ideas and techniques and makes them accessible. Power raising is one of the bedrocks of magick, and Buckland shares how to do it well in just a couple of paragraphs.

Power Raising

I have discussed the inner power we all possess in most of my previous books on Witchcraft. It is something which everyone has within them, but which some can bring out more strongly than others. The Polynesian word *mana* is sometimes used for this power. Aidan Breac used the Scottish word *maucht* (pronounced "maw-kt," or "maw-cht" with a guttural "ch"), meaning energy, or power. Your *maucht* is what is responsible for those flashes of ESP you sometimes experience; for causing someone in a crowd to turn and look at you when you want them to; for creating a situation that you desperately desire to be there. The power given off by sacred objects and holy sites can also be described as *maucht*. *Maucht* is the power underlying all forms of magick. It is the means by which sickness is cured…or caused. It is like electricity, for example, in that it is simply a "power," and the operator can decide whether to use that power for good or evil.

---

238. Buckland, *Scottish Witchcraft*, 85–87.

How can you generate the power? The secret seems to be in working yourself up to *ekstasis*, or "ecstasy"; in "getting out of yourself." This is so in virtually all forms of magick found around the world, not just in Pictish magick. In Gardnerian, and similar forms of Wicca, this *ekstasis* is induced by dancing. Starting slowly and then gradually working up in a fever pitch causes the blood to course through the body and, in turn, generates the power needed to perform the magick.

In the PectiWita dancing can also be done, though it is not essential. If you are to dance, then there is no set form to it; no choreographed set of steps. It is free-form. It is more of a movement with a regular, rhythmic beat.

To practice, find a recording of a good, steady, rhythmic drum beat. There are many good Haitian drum recordings, Amerindian rhythms, African drums, and the like (see *Bibliography*). Or you can stick with the Scottish theme and go with the beat of some rousing Highland reel. I'd suggest avoiding the strathspeys (too slow) and the jigs (too "jumpy"). The main this is, to get the "feel" of moving to a strong, hard beat; to be able to move around with a small area, in a freeform style of dance/movement. Listen for the emphases to the rhythms. Bang your feet onto the ground in time with those strong beats. Then practice doing it without the recorded music.

With practice—and some will need more than others—you will be able to really work yourself up into a sweat, swinging around to the beat that is in your head. And this is the start of "getting out of yourself." In Chapter Eleven I give more details of actual dance steps you might try.

To achieve the same pitch of excitement without actually dancing can be done. Try it sitting in a chair, or on the ground. Listen to that same exciting music and let your body just sort of move/rock with the beat. By rocking and moving your arms and tapping your feet, clapping your hands, it is possible to work up to much the same state of *ekstasis* as is done by actually dancing around.

Chapter Nine
Doors to Other Worlds (& Ohio)

One of the world's largest occult movements began in the winter of 1848 in Hydesville, New York. There, in a log cabin, the family of John and Margaret Fox were subjected to a series of "knocks" or "raps" that had no known human origin. The knocking sounds seemed to coalesce around the couple's two youngest daughters, Kate (Katherine) and Maggie (Margaretta), then aged fifteen and twelve, respectively.[239] Over the course of that winter, the Fox family learned to communicate with the entity making the noises, who revealed himself to be a peddler who had been murdered in their house. As tales of the spirit spread around Hydesville, the Foxes' neighbors descended upon the log cabin to communicate with the spirit. A year later, now living with Leah, their older sister, Kate and Maggie Fox shared the phenomena around them with paying customers and became the world's first public spirit mediums.[240]

Ghosts have been around for millennia, most likely since people first began conversing around a fire at night, but until the Fox sisters, no one had ever actively communicated with the souls of the dead over an extended period of time. As the story of what happened in Hydesville spread across the United States (and later the world), Spiritualism (the belief that the living can indeed communicate with the dead) spread with it. The Fox sisters

---

239. Or they might have been eleven and fourteen. The Fox sisters changed their story several times over the years to sound younger than they actually were.

240. The saga of the Fox sisters can be found in *Talking to the Dead: Kate and Maggie Fox and the Rise of Spiritualism* by Barbara Weisberg.

were the first public mediums, but they were far from the last, and by the end of the 1840s the United States was home to perhaps hundreds of mediums. While many of those individuals were truly gifted with the ability to speak to those who had passed on, many others were charlatans and phonies looking to make a quick buck.

During the time of the Fox sisters, the idea of spirit mediumship was taken seriously by universities and scholarly societies. Mediums were "tested" to see if the sounds and other phenomena manifesting around them were being produced by human means. The Fox sisters were tested early on, with no reported signs of trickery. Not surprisingly, much of the American public embraced Spiritualism, as not only could the living now communicate with dead relatives, but Spiritualism was also proof that the soul survived death. Following the American Civil War (1861–65), many people needed such comforts more than ever.

Despite scholarly studies of spirit mediums, there were many who looked upon Spiritualism and its mediums (who were most often female—misogyny definitely played a role here) with skepticism. That skepticism reached fever pitch in 1888 when Maggie Fox, with her sister Kate alongside her, confessed that the knocking sounds that defined her work as a medium had been produced by cracking her big toe. It should be noted that Maggie was paid $1,500 (the equivalent of about $48,000 in 2025) for her confession. Maggie recanted faking the raps just one year later, and despite standing near Maggie during her confession, Kate never confessed to faking anything.

The popularity of Spiritualism waxed and waned over the following decades, but the practice, and its influence on American society, continued. Many of America's earliest Spiritualists were also abolitionists, and many more were suffragettes. The latter is especially not surprising considering just how many women worked as spirit mediums. Spiritualism provided financial opportunities to women in a society where few others existed. The popularity of Spiritualism also led to the establishment of Spiritualist retreat centers and churches, both of which still exist today.

Spiritualism is no longer a word we hear with much frequency, but it is still very much an ongoing tradition. Any time a group of people get out a Ouija or spirit board, they are engaging in a Spiritualist practice. Trance mediumship has been practiced since the 1840s and is still common today.

Mediums are all over reality TV, and they also write books and are most certainly a part of our celebrity-obsessed culture. Even if the word Spiritualism isn't used all that much anymore, the actual practice is more commonplace than ever.

Raymond Buckland had been exposed to Spiritualism as a young boy thanks to his Uncle George, and while it was never a big part of Buckland's Witchcraft practice, there were moments when he dabbled in it. Psychic mediumship was commonplace in the work of Edgar Cayce, and at the Poseidia Institute, Buckland was responsible for scheduling psychics and mediums for visits to Virginia Beach. Most of us who practice Witchcraft or follow what is thought of as an occult path have at least brushed up against a spirit medium or two. Spirit communication is often all around us, even if we don't always call it that. It was no different with Buckland.

In June of 1990, the Bucklands paid their first visit to a bona fide Spiritualist community. Located just north of San Diego, Harmony Grove was established in 1896 to "further the teaching of spiritualism as a religion, philosophy, and science."[241] During the Cochran-Bucklands' first visit to Harmony Grove, they attended an "Old-Fashioned Open Circle" and were not impressed. In his memoir, Buckland writes:

> It (the séance) was in red light and I'm afraid the medium did not impress either of us. She was demonstrating direct voice (which is where Spirit speaks through the medium). It was supposedly a little black girl named Topsy (!), who was a regular with this medium. The "little girl" voice was so painfully artificial—and stereotypical—that we couldn't take it seriously.

Despite being unimpressed, the Cochran-Bucklands returned just a few weeks later, and several times after that.

They must have eventually had a positive experience at Harmony Grove, because by September of 1990, they began sporadically attending a Spiritualist church in San Diego. Church attendance did not mean that Raymond Buckland suddenly believed in the validity of every medium who came his way. With his background in both theater and Witchcraft, Buckland was

---

241. Harmony Grove Spiritualist Association, "HGSA Beginnings."

very sensitive to fakes. "Transfiguration séances," where the medium's face allegedly transforms into spirit images from across the veil, were a particular source of ire for Buckland. Mediums who engage in this kind of performance often sit with a red light projected up onto their face and then start changing their facial expressions. Due to the light, and the attendees' willingness to believe, the face of the medium might actually look to be physically changing. As Ray writes in his memoir, "By tipping his head very slightly and pursing his lips, he [the medium] created a shadow...that could be mistaken for a moustache!" Buckland marveled at the gullibility of people who could believe such (at least to him) obvious trickery.

For Buckland, the séance with a flashlight under the chin was a game he played as a boy in England on camping trips and on Guy Fawkes Night. The only difference between what he did as a kid and the séance experience was the red paper taped over the lens of the flashlight. Harmony Grove was not the only place where Buckland encountered mediums whom he believed to be fraudulent; trickery was present as well at a variety of Spiritualist communities whose standards Buckland expected to be much higher.

Buckland had also had very genuine transfiguration experiences in Witchcraft circles, giving him a benchmark to compare future transfiguration experiences to. At his Gardnerian initiation, he saw Monique Wilson transform from "a forty-something-year-old woman into a girl of eighteen or so." Buckland also adds that the transfiguration of Monique Wilson occurred in good candlelight, no red light effects needed. There were similar experiences in later circles, with Priests and Priestesses taking on new forms to his eye.

As a lifelong chronicler of the unexplained, Buckland also saw a clear difference between "psychic mediums" and "spirit mediums." At the Spiritualist church he attended in San Diego, he once encountered two neophyte mediums still in training. These two young mediums were able to provide details about the person they were reading for but no details from spirit. A good spirit medium with a true connection to a departed soul will be able to share specific names and events unknown to anyone but the recipient of the reading and the spirit they are communicating with. Having ESP (extrasensory perception) is not the same as communicating with the dead.

Back in the 1950s, Buckland had engaged in some limited form of spirit communication. There was some automatic writing, a bit of trance mediumship, and, not surprisingly, the Ouija board, but it was a practice he had given up once he moved to America. Now forty years later, he found himself once more ready to speak with the souls of the dead. It all began by accident at Samhain in 1990. Buckland's reentry into Spiritualism began rather mundanely, with Ray telling a story in flickering candlelight about how the Romani had invented fire, all while his pet rats sat perched on his shoulder. When the story was over, Buckland let out a deep breath and relaxed for a bit with the other dozen or so guests at the party. And then, rather nonchalantly, he announced that he was going to give some readings as a spirit medium.

Ray with his pet rats perched on his shoulder

The pronouncement surprised both Ray and Tara and was completely unexpected. After his unforeseen announcement, Ray began doing readings for those around him. He remarks in his memoir that the readings "were absolutely accurate on everything I said about the connecting spirit." Despite his accuracy, Buckland began panicking after his first half-dozen readings and cut off the proceedings, to the disappointment of those whom he had not yet done a reading for. Worried about making a fool of himself, Buckland quickly wondered if his initial accuracy had simply been beginner's luck.

There are many different ways of communicating with the spirits. Buckland described himself as "clairvoyant" and "clairsentient." As a clairvoyant, Buckland could see a spirit in something resembling physical form. If Buckland saw a spirit near you, he could describe it in such a manner that its identity would become known to you. Buckland was able to communicate with spirits because he was clairsentient, meaning he could sense the ideas that a particular spirit might be trying to get across to the living. Buckland was able to sense the emotions of the spirits, and was given visual clues when that wasn't enough. Many mediums are clairaudient, which means they can hear the voice of spirit (which would obviously make spirit communication much easier), a gift Buckland lacked.

With this new insight into his psychic and magickal abilities, Buckland would begin an incredible third act as a writer and a teacher. While many of you reading this book might know Raymond Buckland primarily as a Witch, there is an entirely different group of people who know of Ray through his work as a Spiritualist and medium. Certainly there is some overlap between those communities, but the two are also very different in some ways. And in the coming years, Ray would run into some issues in the Spiritualist community for being a Witch (but that part of the story will come later).

In 1991 Raymond Buckland sat down to write what might be the other defining book of his career, *Buckland's Book of Spirit Communications*, also known as the *Big Red Book*. But much like the *Blue Book*, it would take several years (not until 2004) for *Big Red* to turn into the workbook familiar to readers today. *Spirit Communications* actually began its published life with the title *Doors to Other Worlds: A Practical Guide to Communicating with Spirits* when it was published in 1993 and was actually not much larger than a mass-market paperback (just 5¼ by 8 inches!)

Inspired by his newfound (or perhaps rekindled) love of Spiritualism, Buckland felt called to write about the subject. *Doors to Other Worlds* is an ambitious book and a bit more than the expected how-to volume. Not only does Buckland attempt to share just how to communicate with the dead through a variety of means in *Doors*, but he also shares the history of Spiritualism and tackles the subject of frauds in the Spiritualist community. When writing the book in 1991/92, Buckland was more of an outsider in the Spiritualist world, and as a result was quite comfortable being critical. By Llewellyn's standards, *Doors* is lavishly illustrated, with several pencil drawings from Ray along with many (mostly blurry) archival photos. There are also several photos of a fairly nondescript Ray in a short-sleeve collared shirt (complete with glasses in a case in the left breast pocket) and khaki pants modeling a couple of the techniques written about in the book.

Writing about Spiritualism was not just something that excited Ray; this was also an opportunity to take a step away from Witch books. Buckland very much saw *Doors* as a way to reach an entirely different audience and begin a new chapter in his writing career. In a letter to Weschcke, Buckland calls *Doors* a "departure" and a "complete break from what I've been doing."[242]

As a now full-time writer, Buckland was also hopeful that a book with a broader appeal than his usual Witchcraft-related volumes might make more money. He admits to wanting a "goodly size advance for it [the book], if possible."[243] Part of that search for a larger advance and a new writing start also led Ray away from Llewellyn. Buckland was hoping to sign with a more mainstream publisher for *Doors*. (In his letter, Buckland says that the work was being considered by HarperSanFrancisco.[244])

Ultimately, Buckland's Spiritualism book did not end up with HarperSanFrancisco or any other mainstream publisher, and Buckland found himself once again under contract with Llewellyn. However, Llewellyn, much like Buckland, was looking to broaden their market, too. After contracting *Doors*, Carl Weschcke wrote to Ray that he appreciated

the Spiritualism book not only as another Buckland book, but because it is a quality book in a subject area at the edge of our more established lines—which is the way we've been structuring our growth. While it seems possible to keep publishing every Wicca, Astrology, Magick, etc. book that we want, adding to the subjects we publish without going far afield (beyond our "mission") allows us to grow and become more important to the market while adding stability that only variety can provide.[245]

---

242. Raymond Buckland, letter to Carl Weschcke, May 18, 1992.
243. Raymond Buckland, letter to Carl Weschcke, May 18, 1992.
244. Raymond Buckland, letter to Carl Weschcke, May 18, 1992.
245. Carl Weschcke, letter to Raymond Buckland, July 4, 1992.

During the course of his long writing career, Buckland wrote for nearly a dozen publishers, but his relationship with Llewellyn was always the most successful of those collaborations (and equally so for Llewellyn—many of their best-selling Witchcraft and magick books have "Buckland" on the cover).

Weschcke kept his word, and much of the promotion designed for *Doors* was aimed directly at the Spiritualist market, a new frontier for Llewellyn in 1993. There were mailings to Spiritualist churches and to Spiritualist camps such as Harmony Grove. Promotional copies also found their way into the hands of practicing spirit mediums. Even the endorsements for *Doors* (mostly) featured authors outside the world of Witchcraft, the only exception being Buckland's old friend (or is that frenemy?) Hans Holzer, described on the back cover as a "noted author and parapsychologist."

Doors to Other Worlds was successful upon publication, but not in the same way as the *Big Blue Book*. From 1993 to 2003, it went through a modest eight printings, making it a success for Buckland and Llewellyn during that period but not the kind of success that makes a book iconic. Part of the reason for the book's solid but not spectacular initial run might be traced to the name. *Doors to Other Worlds* sounds more like a guide to transdimensional travel or communicating with deity than a book about spirit mediumship. The book's cover probably didn't help much either, simply featuring a set of slightly ajar double doors with light emanating from behind them. To be the blockbuster it deserved to be, *Doors* needed to be marketed as something more than just another book about talking with spirits.

In 2004 a second edition of *Doors* was released, this time dressed up to resemble *Buckland's Complete Book of Witchcraft*. Instead of having a pentagram, the cover featured a heptagram (seven-pointed star), and instead of being blue, the cover was red. The dimensions of the book were now more in line with *Big Blue*, and so was the layout. *Doors to Other Worlds* had morphed into a workbook, complete with new examination questions at the end of every chapter. Like the *Big Blue Book*, the cover for the *Big Red Book* was sparse, featuring only the title, now *Buckland's Book of Spirit Communications*, with Ray's name neatly at the bottom.

Despite the cosmetic changes, the differences between *Big Red* and *Doors* are minimal. *Red* contains everything in *Doors*, though much of the material is in a different order from how it was first presented. Ray's original draw-ings were replaced with drawings from Llewellyn's art department in *Spirit Communications*, though most of the photographs remain, including the ones of Ray in his button-up shirt. The biggest additions to the spruced-up vol-ume are biographies of famous mediums at the end of every chapter, some of which feature contemporary mediums (and have not always aged well).

It's easy to look at *Big Red* and see a book attempting to capitalize on the success of a previous volume, but the previous volume was Ray's, too! Raymond Buckland as a professor instructing his students had always been a good role for him, and there's just something about the formula that works. It's a shame the book wasn't released in its current format back in the early 1990s, as it seems like such an obvious choice. But Ray was trying to separate himself to at least a small degree from his reputation as "just a Witchcraft writer," and a book that closely resembled his most famous (and visually dis-tinct) work was not going to help with that.

* * * * * * * *

San Diego, California, had been good to Raymond and Tara Cochran-Buckland. They had dozens of friends and a full social calendar in South-ern California, but San Diego was not a place conducive to owning a home, especially on a writer's income. After several years in townhouses and apart-ments, the Bucklands decided they really wanted a house, and maybe even more than that. When discussing their move, Ray was open to a lot of places, but a return to New England and its "soul crushing" winters was an emphatic "never again."

After careful consideration, the couple decided to move to Ohio. In Ohio they would be close to Tara's parents, and centrally located too, making it easy for Ray to get to speaking gigs by car. Real estate prices in Ohio were also much more manageable, and in Ohio the Bucklands could dream big when it came to property. Saying goodbye is never easy, but it's easier when there's a world of possibility in front of you.

The couple's first six months in Ohio were spent in Millersburg, a village with a population of about three thousand people. It was a completely differ-ent world for the Bucklands, but a writer can write anywhere. Millersburg, located about a hundred miles from Cleveland in North Central Ohio, served as a base while the Bucklands looked for a larger property, hopefully something they could turn into a farm. After several properties fell through, the Bucklands purchased a small ten-acre farm with an old unfinished house near Glenmont, Ohio, on 1992's Winter Solstice (most certainly a good omen). Over the next several years, they would purchase additional adjoining land, eventually owning a nearly thirty-acre parcel. Raymond and Tara Cochran-Buckland would live on that piece of property for twenty-seven years.

It's odd to think of Raymond Buckland, famous Witch and spiritual medium, as a farmer, but that became a large part of his identity after moving to Ohio. The Bucklands mostly raised livestock, primarily sheep, but also some chicken, geese, and ducks, with Tara doing the majority of the work, leaving Ray free to write. Raising sheep is intense work, as is the emotional toll of sending animals you've raised to the slaughterhouse. Due to the difficult nature of the work, the Bucklands eventually abandoned the sheep-raising enterprise but kept the farm.[246]

In addition to raising livestock, the Bucklands also took in several rescue horses and had a few Shetland ponies that helped with work around the farm. The Bucklands would load the ponies up with klibbers (pack saddles for ponies) and wander their property searching for firewood to brighten the Ohio winters. There were afternoons and evenings spent wandering with the ponies while picking up trash on local roads. There was also a cart for pony rides, especially fun when the grandkids came to visit.[247]

Life at the farm was challenging but rewarding, but the Bucklands' more remote location did present some obstacles. Doing anything away from the farm required a rather long drive. Tara lamented that simply going to a yoga class was a fifty-minute drive one way. Saddened by the lack of a writers club in Glenmont, Ray started his own, and soon he had a dedicated group meeting at his house weekly to discuss writing projects. (They would eventually move to a local coffee shop and continue meeting until Ray's death in 2017.)[248]

Upon moving to Ohio, Buckland gave up flying ultralight aircraft, but he still found time to tinker with motorized vehicles. For much of his time in Ohio, Buckland worked on developing a three-wheeled automobile. The

246. Tara Buckland, personal interview conducted on November 6, 2023.
247. Tara Buckland, personal interview conducted on November 6, 2023.
248. Tara Buckland, personal interview conducted on November 6, 2023.

"Buckland Manx" utilized an old Honda motorcycle engine, and Buckland went that route because of an earlier car he had owned that was also powered by a motorcycle engine. At times the Manx looked like a cross between the front half of a roadster and the back half of a motorcycle. Other prototypes included a half-go-cart, half-motorcycle hybrid and a Manx whose body resembled that of a Volkswagen Beetle. The Manx never got beyond being a hobby, but Buckland had fun with it.

Taking the Manx out for a test drive

Naming his car the Manx was also a tip of the cap to Gerald Gardner. The Manx are an ethnic group who originally resided on the Isle of Man, the home of Gerald Gardner's Witch museum. It was also on the Isle of Man that Raymond Buckland spent several summers in the '60s vacationing with Rosemary and the kids and staying with Monique and Scotty Wilson. Living on the farm, Buckland had quite a lot of room to tinker with things and take his Manx out for test drives.

• • • • • • • •

The world's largest Spiritualist community can be found in southwestern New York on the shore of Cassadaga Lake. Today known as Lily Dale, the community was founded in 1879 as the Cassadaga Lake Free Association and served as a summer camp for Spiritualists. (Imagine an adolescent summer camp but for adults, and all about talking to the spirits of the dead.) The Cassadaga Lake Free Association changed its name to the Lily Dale Assembly in 1906, after it grew from a collection of tents into a village with several hundred permanent structures. At its height, Lily Dale had its own firehouse and post office, and even today it is home to several hotels.[249] In addition, Lily Dale also serves as the headquarters of the National Spiritualist Association of Churches, one of the largest Spiritualist church organizations in the United States.

Old Victorian houses crowd the narrow streets of Lily Dale, gardens dot the landscape, and the entire town is surrounded by an old-growth forest. The town was even home for a time to the original Hydesville cabin of Kate and Maggie Fox, which was moved to the property in 1916. In 1955 the original Fox cabin burned to the ground, and today a replica can be found on the grounds, along with a museum housing several artifacts that once belonged to the Fox sisters. Lily Dale is well situated, and not just because of its picturesque location. Just twenty-six miles down the road lies the Brushwood Folklore Center, home to several Pagan events every year.

The hamlet of Lily Dale hosts about 250 permanent and semipermanent residents, but every year during the summer, the size of the community swells as over thirty thousand tourists descend on the town annually.[250] The overwhelming majority of those tourists visit Lily Dale to do one thing: take advantage of the town's dozens of spirit mediums. And for many years, one of those mediums was Raymond Buckland.

Lily Dale would also serve as the venue for Buckland's final film appearance, 2010's *No One Dies in Lily Dale*. Premiering on July 5, 2010, on the premium cable channel HBO, *No One Dies in Lily Dale* follows several visitors around Lily Dale as they seek closure and mourn the loss of loved ones. Buckland appears in the movie near the 48-minute mark and gets about two and a half minutes of screen time.

Many of the mediums in the film are shown giving readings and appear in extended segments. Buckland, however, just randomly shows up in the

---

249. Leonard, *Talking to the Other Side: A History of Modern Spiritualism and Mediumship*, 221.
250. Durn, "To Join This Community of People Who Speak to the Dead, Prepare to Be Tested."

documentary, sitting serenely at a picnic table with Cassadaga Lake behind him. At this picturesque spot, Buckland is approached by two young women with questions about Lily Dale. In the short segment, Buckland comes across as friendly and knowledgeable. There is also something refreshingly authentic about Buckland during his limited camera time, a feeling echoed by the young women in the film who say, "I really enjoyed talking to him," as they walk away from Ray.

The Raymond Buckland in the film is very much the same Raymond Buckland who inhabits his books. There is the ever-present belief that there is a thread connecting most of the world's spiritual traditions. In his *Lily Dale* segment, Ray links the practice of talking to spirit mediums to similar rites found in Voodoo, pointing out that both traditions seek to connect the living with the spirits of the dead. Ray never saw any competition or disagreement between the worlds of magick, Witchcraft, and Spiritualism, despite many others feeling differently.

Echoing some of the criticisms of spirit mediumship that can be found in *Buckland's Book of Spirit Communications*, Ray responds affirmatively to a question inquiring whether there are fake mediums. "Absolutely," he answers and then points out that "just because something can be done in a fake way doesn't mean that all of it is done in that way." He counsels that there are always fakes and the only way to separate the truth-tellers from the frauds is to personally evaluate the information given to you by a medium.

Ray's Corvette parked at Lily Dale in 2012

Buckland's presence at Lily Dale was not without controversy. Most Spiritualists identify as Christians, and there were many at Lily Dale who were uncomfortable with a Witch working among them. While there are many Spiritualists who believe in Witchcraft-adjacent ideas, such as reincarnation, Pagan deities are an entirely separate matter. Buckland never dealt with outright hostility at Lily Dale, but for many in the Spiritualist world, Buckland's spiritual beliefs clearly came from a much different place.

Buckland did more than just read for clients at Lily Dale; he was an active part of the community and often hosted various events there. Playing master of ceremonies allowed the old performer in Buckland to shine, and his MC performances were peppered with jokes:

> How many of you are here at Lily Dale for the first time? Welcome. We have a wonderful evening of entertainment for you tonight. I'm absolutely delighted to have been asked to host the show. Mind you, I was lucky to get the job. One of the Lily Dale mediums insisted she could bring through Johnny Carson to do it. The only problem with that is that he'd insist on bringing Ed McMahon with him.[251]

There were also more reflective moments in his public appearances, such as when he lamented that winter was that "long dead period when we sit around waiting for the new Lily Dale season to start."[252] Lily Dale was a "home away from home" for Buckland and an opportunity to put his myriad different skills to use.

Though the years after Buckland's move to Ohio were focused primarily on writing, Ray still found time to teach workshops and classes, and many of those took place at Lily Dale. Never one to worry about upsetting the apple cart, Buckland wasn't afraid to share many Witchcraft-related ideas in his classes. In a workshop called "Unconventional Forms of Spirit Communication," Buckland dared to bring up "forbidden" tools such as crystal balls and Tarot cards. Despite their taboo status at Lily Dale, Buckland believed there was "really no good reason *not* to use them."[253]

---

251. Raymond Buckland, *Opening Monologue.*
252. Raymond Buckland, *Death and Dying.*
253. Raymond Buckland, *Unconventional Forms of Spirit Communication.*

Buckland's arguments for using such tools were logical. In defense of crystal balls, he wrote in his lecture notes:

> Crystal balls … used by "crass fortunetellers" … should never be associated with Spiritualism … But things like trumpets [should] still [be] acknowledged …[254] A medium is expected to see clairvoyantly … without any physical aid. Yet if that medium gazes into a crystal ball in order to focus her attention … what's wrong with that?[255]

In Buckland's mind, anything that helped a medium achieve focus was fair to use, even if the perceptions of some of those items were less than favorable. Not surprisingly for someone who liked to make things accessible, Buckland was all in on people using Ouija boards from discount stores.

Buckland was also a proponent of using Tarot cards for spirit mediumship, a tool not then allowed in Lily Dale (though they were allowed at some other Spiritualist camps). Buckland's method for using Tarot cards for spirit readings was to let the dead know that the entire deck was theirs to communicate with and then turn over the cards and "see what strikes most strongly," and then interpret those cards. It's a shame that Buckland never developed these ideas more concretely in print form. Not every Witch has a spirit board sitting in their living room, but most of us have a Tarot deck or two.

Buckland did not see much difference between psychic mediums and spirit mediums, finding that both forms of mediumship allow people to tap into something greater than their conscious self. The vehicle used most likely depends on personal circumstances and preferences. In the *Big Red Book*, Buckland makes a note of this, writing:

> Rather than mediums, specifically, we are finding a veritable plethora of "psychics" who read tarot cards, palms, runes, crystal balls; who chart horoscopes, do healing using a variety of methods, and even use talking boards and tip tables.[256] The psychic has replaced the medium in many ways.[257]

---

254. Trumpets are used to amplify the disembodied voices of spirits during séances.
255. Raymond Buckland, *Unconventional Forms of Spirit Communication*.
256. Table tipping is a very popular form of otherworldly communication in Spiritualism.
257. Buckland, *Buckland's Book of Spirit Communications*, 198–99.

Buckland also built a workshop around this idea titled "Who's Who and What's What." Presented in 2007, Buckland's workshop was designed to "demonstrate how the veil between the practices of medium and psychic can grow thin and even disappear under certain conditions."[258]

By the time Buckland started presenting workshops and doing readings at Lily Dale, he had already written *Doors to Other Worlds* (1993) and was an accomplished spirit medium, but past accolades don't matter at Lily Dale. All mediums at Lily Dale are vetted and tested by their peers before being allowed to do readings on site. Buckland's testing was conducted by the Morris Pratt Institute, and he received his Educational Course of Mediumship certification on April 18, 2006. During Buckland's time at Lily Dale beginning in the early 2000s (there is some dispute about *exactly* when Buckland began doing readings there), he most likely read for hundreds if not thousands of people. Buckland stopped doing workshops and readings at Lily Dale only because of health concerns starting in 2015. If Buckland were alive today and in good health, I have no doubt that he would still insist on spending a few weeks each summer on the shores of Cassadaga Lake.

Today a small part of Buckland's spirit still resides at Lily Dale year-round. In honor of the "Spiritualist Witch," the community dedicated a bench on the premises in Buckland's honor. On the back of that bench are the words "A great teacher and a friend to all." That sounds like a fitting epitaph for Ray.

• • • • • • • •

Though Buckland did not write any future "classics" after moving to Ohio, he was extremely productive, writing for multiple publishers in a variety of genres. Buckland continued his long association with Llewellyn in the new millennium by writing *Signs, Symbols, and Omens: An Illustrated Guide to Magical and Spiritual Symbolism* in 2003. *Signs* is notable for a number of reasons. Twenty-plus years after its initial publication, it remains a bestseller for Llewellyn, and as of 2024, it is in its twentieth printing. But most importantly, the book features signs and symbols drawn by Ray himself. Despite

---

258. *The Observer*, "Well-Known Author Ray Buckland to Be Guest Speaker."

Ray's rather significant artistic skills, most of his work done for major publishers featured the artwork of others.

Buckland also had books published in the new century by his longtime colleagues at Samuel Weiser (who had published *The Tree* back in 1974). Most notable was *The Weiser Field Guide to Ghosts* (2009), which might have been better served with the title *Raymond Buckland's Field Guide to Ghosts!* Weiser also reprinted much of Buckland's Romani material after it was taken out of print by Llewellyn. *Buckland's Book of Gypsy Magic* (2010, Samuel Weiser) contained material from four previously published Buckland books dealing with Romani magick.

Despite telling Llewellyn publisher Carl Weschcke back in the early 1990s that he wanted to get away from writing Witchcraft books, Buckland returned to the genre in the early 2000s. Some of that consideration might have been financial. The early 2000s marked a high point for the sales and profitability of Witchcraft books, but Buckland's own practice had changed since *Big Blue*'s publication fifteen years prior, inspiring him to write about Witchcraft again. *Wicca for Life* (2001) and *Wicca for One* (2004), both published through Citadel Press, were books representative of where Raymond Buckland was on his path in the early 2000s. By 2001 Buckland had been a Wiccan practitioner for nearly forty years, which certainly sounds like "Wicca for life" to me.

Buckland had opened the door for solitaries back in the 1970s, but *Wicca for One* ended up being Ray's first (and only) book designed exclusively for solitary practitioners. *Wicca for One* was representative of Ray's personal journey, too. After a long period of working with others, Buckland's Wiccan practice had become mostly a solitary and private affair by 2004. While today many Witches start out as solitary practitioners before moving to coven work, Buckland's journey unfolded in the opposite way.

During this period Buckland also wrote some "encyclopedic" works for Visible Ink Press, a publisher known for producing compendiums on various subjects. Sticking with what he knew best, Buckland wrote volumes for the publisher focused on Witchcraft, fortune-telling, and spirit communication, beginning in 2001 and continuing in 2003 and 2005. All three books were some of the longest works of Buckland's career, with *The Witch Book* being over 600 pages long! *The Fortune-Telling Book* and *The Spirit Book* were comparatively shorter, at only 500-plus pages per book. In an interview published a little over a year before his death, Ray would list the three books he wrote for Visible Ink among his favorite titles.[259]

Buckland titled his unpublished memoir *So Little Time*, and the last twenty years of his life really felt that way in terms of the man's writing. Buckland churned out books during the last seventeen years of his life at a nearly unprecedented rate. In addition to the more mainstream publishers written about above, Buckland also wrote for occultist Peter Paddon's (1964–2014) Pendraig Publishing. Buckland's work for Pendraig consisted of reworked material previously published by Llewellyn that had gone out of print. Pendraig was a small operation, but by 2010 even small publishers were able to get authors prominently featured on websites such as Amazon and offer secure distribution into bookstores. The 2000s saw Buckland working hard to keep most everything he had ever written in print in some form.

Some of that desire to have "everything in print" (and generating income) was no doubt motivated by changes in the publishing landscape. For a brief period of time from the early 1990s through the very early 2000s, it was possible for a Witchcraft author to make a good living writing books and doing public appearances. But by 2010, book piracy was making it more and more difficult to maintain a steady income. Even for an author as popular as Raymond Buckland, piracy was an ongoing concern and a problem that made his back account much smaller than it had previously been.

Changes in the publishing world might have also played a role in Buckland's desire to test the waters of self-publishing in a substantial manner. Buckland had always flirted with self-publishing. Buckland's first "book," the pamphlet *Witchcraft … the Religion*, was published by the Buckland Museum. (This pamphlet was a work Ray was so fond of that he often had it included on the "Other Books by Raymond Buckland" page that graced most of his printed work.) But Buckland's first foray into self-publishing was a one-off. There was no desktop publishing in the 1960s, and self-publishing much beyond a pamphlet was prohibitively expensive. Besides, Buckland had begun writing for mainstream publishers shortly thereafter, with a great deal of success.

---

259. Ward, "An Interview with Raymond Buckland, American Wicca Pioneer."

As the 1980s rolled around, Buckland once more dipped his athame into the world of self-publishing, establishing Taray Publications at the start of the decade. Named after both Tara and Ray, Taray Publications focused on reprints of Witchcraft books in the public domain and books that lacked an American publisher. Books from Taray looked more like pamphlets than books (they lacked spines, for example, and much in the way of cover art), but they were another revenue source and shared some Craft history that might otherwise have been out of print or unavailable to the average reader. By the time *Big Blue* was released, Taray had ceased to be an active entity, as the Bucklands were far too busy to oversee a small publishing house.

In 1995 Raymond Buckland once more stepped into the fringes of self-publishing, releasing *Ray Buckland's Magic Cauldron* through Galde Press. Buckland had initially pitched *Magic Cauldron* to Llewellyn in 1992, but as the book's material consisted mostly of previously written material over the last thirty years, the publisher did not have any interest. Undeterred, Buckland connected with Galde Press, by then the publisher of the seminal occult magazine *Fate*. *Magic Cauldron's* cover features a rather devilish-looking drawing of Ray's head suspended over a cauldron. The effect is either striking or comical depending on your point of view, but at least the book found its way into print. *Magic Cauldron* failed to cause much of a stir, but Buckland would work with Galde Press again.

In the 2000s, Buckland would step firmly into the self-publishing world, establishing Buckland Books as an outlet for his work that was unable to find a home at a conventional publishing house. Buckland's plans for his new publishing arm were originally quite ambitious. The centerpiece of the enterprise was to be a series of books called "Buckland Doorway To," on various esoteric topics. Capitalizing on the Buckland name and writing about topics that had previously been bestsellers for the man should have been a winning combination. Profit margins are much higher for creators, especially if that creator has an established brand, but self-published books lack the reach of a conventionally published book.

After releasing a few reprints designed to appeal to Lily Dale visitors, the Buckland Books enterprise got off to a promising start with *Buckland Doorway to Candle Magic* (2007), capitalizing on Buckland's previous success with candle magick books. But a short sixty-page volume selling for $12.95 did not end up tempting very many readers. If Buckland had waited a few more years to roll out the Buckland Doorway To series, he might have done quite well. Short books on occult topics are hot sellers on e-readers, and considering Buckland's reach and reputation, he could have been a real trailblazer in that arena, but alas, he was probably a bit ahead of his time. While Buckland announced other Doorway To volumes on topics such as psychic protection, spirit communication, healing, divination, scrying, Tarot, and ritual construction, none of them ever made it into print.

Instead of releasing new titles in the Buckland Doorway To series, Buckland Books became an outlet for much of Ray's previously unpublished fiction. Going back to his school days, Buckland had been writing fiction for decades, but he didn't officially publish a full-on novel until 1993. As chance would have it, Llewellyn was looking to expand beyond their usual Witchcraft and occult titles and had decided to make a move into the realm of occult fiction. Buckland's novel *The Committee* was the publisher's first fiction novel. Ray described it as a "psi-techno thriller." *The Committee* revolves around a group established by the US government to overcome psychic threats, definitely playing into Ray's wheelhouse. A follow-up novel, *Cardinal's Sin*, was published in 1996, featuring many of the same characters.

Buckland wouldn't release another fiction book until 2008's *The Torque of Kernow*, a fantasy novel that was listed as a release from Galde Press/ Buckland Books. Parts of *Torque* were written over a decade and a half earlier, with Buckland originally starting the process in the early 1990s. Other writing projects led to *Torque* being shelved before Buckland found the time to finish up the project.[260] Buckland had high hopes for *Torque*, with follow-up volumes also set in the land of Kernow. But like so many self-published fiction books, the novel failed to find an audience and the series ended after one book.

Buckland didn't have much luck in the fantasy genre, but he would do much better in the world of historical mysteries. Through Buckland Press (renamed Queen Victoria Press), he received positive notices for *Churchill's Secret Spy*, a thriller set in World War II. Buckland would realize his dream of writing successful fiction for a major publisher with the publication of the

---

260. Melanie Harris, "Author Interview: Raymond Buckland."

first volume in the Bram Stoker Mystery series, *Cursed in the Act* (2014), through Berkley/Penguin publishers. As the title suggests, Bram Stoker was one of the novel's principal protagonists along with stage manager Harry Rivers. Set in the late nineteenth century when Stoker was the manager of London's Lyceum Theatre, *Cursed in the Act* allowed Buckland to mix history, mystery, and a touch of the esoteric to generally positive reviews.

A second Bram Stoker Mystery (*Dead for a Spell*) followed shortly thereafter, but Berkeley/Penguin passed on a previously contracted third volume. Even with that bit of disappointment, the experience was a positive one for Buckland, allowing him to visit mystery writer conferences and mingle with both fans and fellow authors (many of whom Buckland was a fan of). Mystery conferences helped Buckland meet both Peter Lovesey (1936–present), best known for his Sergeant Cribb and Peter Diamond books, and Ann Cleeves (1954–present), creator of the character Vera Stanhope.[261] The Stanhope character eventually got her own television series, *Vera*, which ran from 2011 to 2025 on Britain's ITV.

Buckland would release a third Bram Stoker book (*A Mistake Through the Heart*) in 2015 through Buckland Books. The following year, he would release three books in the Penny Court Enquirers series, again set in Victorian England. The first two books were grounded in the mundane, but in the third book, *Deadly Spirit*, Buckland couldn't resist adding some Spiritualist twists to the mystery mix. The Penny Court Enquirers would be Buckland's last traditional fiction books, but before his passing in 2017, he released a collection of the cartoons he had drawn over the years, titled *Laff with Olaf and Others*. Ray really did try to "release it all" before his passing later that year.

Outside of his books, Buckland is most famous in Witch circles for bringing the Gardnerian tradition to the United States and for establishing Seax-Wica. Both endeavors involved circling with a variety of different individuals, but over the last thirty years of his life, Buckland described his spiritual path as "solitary" and avoided the use of specific labels. While acknowledging that Seax-Wica was still a part of his life, he was also comfortable drawing from "a variety of beliefs and practices."[262]

---

261. Tara Buckland, personal interview conducted on November 6, 2023.
262. Ward, "An Interview with Raymond Buckland, American Wicca Pioneer."

But Buckland's practice was not quite as solitary as he liked to make it out to be. On the Buckland farm, he and Tara had set aside a small glade for spiritual purposes. There among a small clearing in the trees, the couple built several personal altars and installed a two-foot-tall goddess statue. A glimpse into their private spiritual retreat can be found in the outtakes part of the DVD *Witchcraft: Rebirth of the Old Religion* from 2005. Ray also kept a personal altar in the couple's home. According to Tara, Ray grew even closer to the gods later in his life, and as his health declined, he found great comfort in their presence.[263]

Ray also worked with a couple of other Ohio Witches from time to time. After participating in a book signing at a Witch shop called the Cat & the Cauldron, in Columbus, Ohio, Buckland initiated the store's owner, Kat Tigner, into the Craft. In 2005 Buckland would join Tigner in starting a new coven, the Temple of Sacrifice, which followed an Egyptian pantheon.[264] Tigner, along with her friend Toni Rotonda, would be a part of Ray's inner circle for the rest of his life, though most of his practice would continue in a solitary vein.

Despite Buckland ceasing to actively practice the Gardnerian tradition in 1973, his initiatory path was still on his mind during the last ten years of his life. While looking through some of Buckland's personal correspondence, I stumbled upon a list made by Ray chronicling all thirty-five initiations he had participated in as a Gardnerian High Priest.[265] The list contains the legal names of all of his and Rosemary's initiates, along with Craft names and initiation dates. Buckland may have left the Gardnerian tradition, but he clearly still had an attachment to the Witchcraft he had first been exposed to in the 1960s and to those he and Rosemary had initiated.

In published interviews, Buckland was always effusive in his praise for Gerald Gardner and spoke in mostly reverent terms when asked about Gardnerian Witchcraft. But the same cannot be said for specific people in the tradition, most notably Theos and Phoenix. In one of the last interviews conducted with Ray before he died, Buckland was still smarting from his falling-out with the Kneitels back in the early 1970s. Buckland was always

263. Tara Buckland, personal interview conducted on November 6, 2023.
264. Ward, "Buckland Museum Poised to Reopen in Midwest."
265. Raymond Buckland, "From the Desk of Dr. Raymond Buckland."

adamant that he had followed the Book of Shadows he had been given "to the letter," while Theos and Phoenix made "a LOT of changes … erroneously attributed to me."[266] He then concludes his critique of the couple by saying they "probably did more harm to Witchcraft than did the whole of the Christian persecutors back in the Middle Ages!"[267] Forty-five years feels like a long time to hold a grudge, but Buckland had been fielding complaints and questions about his decision to leave the Gardnerian tradition for decades, making it hard to completely move on from that period of his life. Despite his dislike for Theos and Phoenix, Buckland retained his admiration for the Gardnerian tradition and its founder.

Remembering Ray: The Legacy of Seax-Wica

For many Witches, the *Big Blue Book* remains Raymond Buckland's crowning achievement, but there are still many Witches today who see the establishment of the Seax-Wica as Ray's most notable contribution to the Craft. Often overlooked in the laundry lists of traditions that accompany Witchcraft books, Seax-Wica is still very much an ongoing tradition, and one that is now practiced worldwide! In addition, there are many Seax-Witches today who find that the tradition is easily adaptable, helping to create a space for everyone in the circle. I think Ray would be proud of how his creation has grown and changed over the last fifty or so years.

Saxon Witchcraft as Inclusionary Heathenry

I must admit the first time I picked up a copy of *Buckland's Book of Saxon Witchcraft* I was underwhelmed and set it aside as yet another rehash of Wiccan belief. After having climbed degrees in an Alexandrian lineage of practice, I was disenchanted with Wicca due to its emphasis on power structures, secrets, and gendered polarity. I found a spiritual center in a solitary practice of Saxon paganism, which many would consider a branch of modern Heathenry.

---

266. Ward, "An Interview with Raymond Buckland, American Wicca Pioneer."
267. Ward, "An Interview with Raymond Buckland, American Wicca Pioneer."

Heathenry falls victim to many of the same issues as Wicca: infighting over "correct" reconstruction of antiquated practices, power struggles centered on proving mystical authenticity, and the looming shadow of pagan hate groups that operate just outside the city. It seemed obvious that, as we sought to form a progressive Saxon pagan group, we would need to purposely sideline any quest for reconstruction in favor of a contemporary practice. Woden and Freo clearly lent themselves to this endeavor, and as we began to materialize those values important to us, we quickly realized that many of the same elements were already included in a dusty text that I had read some two years earlier.

Seax Wica provides a clear and simple working structure that encourages adaptation to meet the needs of your community. While we have not replicated *The Tree*, we have adapted much of its contents to further integrate elements of Saxon history, anthropology, and Old English where possible. We emphasize Buckland's intent that all who participate in ritual are to be acknowledged as equals—and to this end have done away with the priestly role entirely.

Any attendee may volunteer to take ritual responsibilities (save for roles such as Thegn) when or if they feel comfortable to do so, encouraging participation and learning by doing. Self-initiations are honored; however, group-specific initiation is encouraged to weave Wyrd effectively with our greater whole. To that end we have carved a large wooden disk as a shield, a mobile altar of practice and physical manifestation of egregore and combined will. It is only fitting then that magical names of the initiated be inscribed on its back.

Gender has always been a touchy subject in British Traditional Wicca, with limited inclusion of LGBTQIA+ participants and gendered concepts of the divine. While Buckland supposed that homosexuality was the result of reincarnation from a different gender, the root of his meaning was still radical—that queer people have a place within Seax Wica. We enact this through a contemporary lens as *radical inclusion*—that all peoples regardless of ethnicity, gender, sexuality, age, and ability should have equal opportunity to participate. It is telling then that our membership is largely queer. We continue to honor Woden and Freo as written but no longer seek them as a divine gendered pair. Instead, they manifest as the great Cat and Crow, common animals within the cityscape that remind us that enchantment and magic need not be rare or exotic. They hold the high seat as patrons of our combined craft, and each member is free to participate in additional groups, faiths, and pantheons as they see fit.

While acts of radical love were poignant and revolutionary at the time of writing [2023], we have adapted to a post-COVID-19 world—we do not kiss after each ritual action, and we are content to provide our own vessels from which to receive communal cakes and ale. Similarly, the Sabbats and their respective names have been altered to more closely reflect the Anglo-Saxon year.

Seax Wica has proved fertile grounds from which our small community has grown. I would be lying to say it has been without conflict, from both traditionalist and racist elements within our city. But when a seal breaches in the river next to our circle, as we laugh and share stories with full bellies or lie beneath the canopy of trees finding runes in their branches—I cannot help but be thankful for what we have created. Buckland was a pioneer in American Paganism, championing a vision of accessible Craft open to all peoples. My once pristine copy of *Buckland's Book of Saxon Witchcraft* no longer collects dust on my shelf, but is loved and worn as it passes between hands of those eager to learn. And while our workings have taken their own character, we must credit Raymond Buckland for his clear working structure that continues to inspire us today.

Fennis Reed (Ácholt Inhíred) *is an amateur naturalist residing in Sacramento, California. They coordinate a Seax Wica coven and find solace in practical acts of sorcery and living animism.*

Seax-Wica in Argentina

My name is Santiago Gennari and I will tell you about my experience in the Seax-Wica tradition. I am from Buenos Aires, Argentina, and some know me in the tradition as Wulfnoð, which means Bold Wolf in Old English.

The Seax tradition was presented to me by the gift of the gods when I was looking for a Wiccan tradition with which I identified and that gave me the necessary basis to be able to practice it in a solitary way. To find that the Book of Shadows of the tradition (*The Tree*, 1974) was available to the public was a surprise, and the fact that it was in Spanish was an added value, since at that time I did not know any English.

The Seax tradition provided the possibility of self-development; the practitioner, when they saw it prudent, could make a dedication and take an oath to the tradition and the gods. Raymond himself put it this way:

> Although still a branch of the Mystery Religion of the Wicca the *Seax-Wica* do not have an Oath of Secrecy *per se.* They have a "Rite of Self-Dedication," which serves a similar, though not identical, purpose. This means that their rites *are* available for study. It means that those searching for the Craft *can* have ready access to at least one branch, or tradition, of it.[268]

Therefore, anyone can have access to the tradition and practice freely on equal terms within it. That caught my attention because in the Wiccan traditions in general, one must go through a coven initiation and a process of degrees. But here anyone who fulfilled the Manifesto of the tradition was considered a Gesith (person who performed the rite of dedication or was initiated into a coven) until they proved otherwise.

Therefore, the tradition, as I say, is self-cleansing of people who wish to place themselves in positions of authority over others. Raymond himself indicated that he was in the same position as any another Seax practitioner, and that we simply recognize him as *Fæder*, for being the Father of the tradition.

The Saxon tradition of Witchcraft allowed me to adapt the rites to my own needs, something totally acceptable as long as we do not modify the pattern of rites of *The Tree* and we maintain the use of the names of the gods of the Anglo-Saxon pantheon. For example, after a few years of practice and understanding, I was able to adjust the rites to my geographical area (Southern Hemisphere), something so important in witchcraft.

---

268. Buckland, *The Tree*, 4.

All this made me live and experience my practice in a more meaningful way, know my own abilities, and work on my personal and spiritual growth in relation to the virtues of the gods. And in relation to this, by manifesting the attributes of the gods, I had a feeling of personal empowerment, responsibility, and the ability to manifest my desires and goals through will and Saxon Witchcraft.

Recently, although my practice is still mainly solitary, I decided to create a meeting place for those interested in the tradition in Argentina, the Seolfor Mōna coven, from the Old English *silver moon*, in reference to my current place of residence on the banks of the Rio de la Plata and because silver is a symbol of the goddess of Seax-Wica. Undoubtedly, guiding other seekers, or *Theows*, is a source of great satisfaction. So is meeting many practitioners from other countries and exchanging opinions about the tradition.

Therefore, I can say that Fæder Ravenwolf (Uncle Buck) was and continues to be a great teacher and sage through his legacy to modern witchcraft, which changed the lives of many of us and, in my case, brought a tradition with its own identity. Thank you, Fæder! Long live Seax-Wica!

Seax Gesith Wulfnoð *is an Argentinian Witch.*

Well, You Adapt!

Frigesfolc, named for the folk of the goddess Frige, was formed in Pittsburgh, Pennsylvania, in the late 2010s. We would meet on the full moon to honor Woden and Frige as our primary deities and to celebrate Mona, god of the Moon. We also held sabbat rituals to observe the ever-changing Wheel of the Year and did workings together when the need would arise.

When we began, we followed the traditions written in our Book of Shadows that had been passed down to us from the Seax Wiccans before us. Over time, the needs of our coven began to shift and we explored making some adaptations. As a coven of queer witches, some of the traditional male and female roles just didn't work for us. For example, it was tradition that the Priest called the wermenn (males) into the circle, followed by the Priestess calling in the wifmenn (females). What do you do when you have folks attending rituals who don't fit neatly into the gender binary? Well, you adapt!

We shared the Priest and Priestess roles among those of us who had taken our oaths to the coven, and we called each other into the circle based on who was leading the ritual. It was an easy way to make our space more inclusive—both for ourselves and for our guests, who also tended to defy the gender binary. Pagan spaces evolve and change, and it was important to us to be actively welcoming to our communities.

Another tradition we altered was the "cakes and ale" portion of the ritual. To ensure that folks in recovery could attend without compromising their sobriety, we replaced the ale with rose lemonade. This became our special tradition just because we found the rose lemonade on sale one day and it became a habit.

When making these adaptations, use your creativity! I have an autoimmune disorder that requires me to avoid gluten. That puts a damper on the cakes! Instead, we started the tradition of sharing dark chocolate among ourselves and with Woden and Frige.

Through these changes, we held true to the spirit of gathering with our kin to honor the deities we hold sacred. Where there is room to welcome more into the arms of Seax Wica, there is room for change.

Diane Dahm *is a practicing witch.*

In 2016, clips of Raymond Buckland performing a stand-up comedy routine began to make the rounds on social media. Despite Ray's celebrity, the clips never attracted a wide audience (even today most of them have accumulated less than a thousand views), but for Witchcraft history nerds like me, they are irresistible. Despite most people becoming aware of Buckland's return to comedy only in 2016, he had been sporadically posting stand-up routines to his YouTube channel since 2014.

All the stand-up videos were recorded at amateur comedy nights in the Hotel Millersburg in Millersburg, Ohio. (The Hotel Millersburg is about a twenty-five-minute drive from the Buckland farm.) The amateur nights were held twice a year, with Buckland being one of the organizers. In the videos, Buckland looks quite dapper, always in a bowler hat and a button-up shirt, with dress pants and nice leather shoes. Depending on the weather, he also sports a sharp-looking vest or jacket. The Millersburg Hotel was not an optimal venue for comedy, as the stage was tiny and barely up off the floor, but the crowds (and Buckland) didn't seem to mind.

Despite his advancing age and some health issues post-2015, Ray appears spry and his voice is strong. In most of the videos Ray can be seen glancing at notes that appear to be written on a business card. He might not have had all his routines memorized, but there's still a great deal of confidence in his appearances. Having spent decades in front of audiences, Ray never appears nervous or anxious in his performances as a stand-up comedian.

I'm forever indebted to Ray for spending much of his life as a professional Witch (many of us wouldn't be here today without his work), but the comedy stuff really makes you wonder what might have been. Ray is genuinely funny, and while some of my younger friends will complain that Buckland's routines are heavy on the dad jokes, they still evoke laughter. In the videos, there are times when Buckland has his audience absolutely howling.

Most of Buckland's material is rather benign, but his set of mother-in-law jokes definitely has some bite. Here are a few jokes from that routine:

My mother-in-law is very much like a Slinky. You remember the Slinky? It's a toy that's really of no earthly use to anyone but really puts a smile on your face when you push it down the stairs.

My mother-in-law is one of these people, she puts toilet paper on the seat, even in the dining room.

Our clock fell off the wall.... If it had fallen just a minute before, it would have hit my mother-in-law on the head. That damn clock was always slow.

She does enjoy Social Security sex, though. That's a little bit once a week but not enough to keep you happy.

She's asked me actually if I will be her sexual advisor, at least I think that's what she meant. Her actual words were "when I want your fucking advice, I'll ask for it."[269]

Most of Buckland's jokes are short, with a quick punch line, and would have worked nicely in a joke book:

I used to work at a fire hydrant factory, but there's never anywhere to park near there.

Don't you hate when your foot falls asleep during the day? You know the damn thing is going to be up all night.

This morning I got up and said to my wife, "I'm going for a walk this morning." She said, "How long will you be gone?" I said, "The whole time."[270]

I just finished reading *Lord of the Rings* again. That's about the tenth time I've read it. I guess that's what they call hobbit-forming.[271]

Buckland's hobbit joke resulted in several groans from his audience, but also some laughs.

Ray was also capable of putting together longer material:

Did you ever wonder where farts go? Seriously, I mean, everybody farts and some fart all through the day, right? All through the day and people all over the world fart. You ever wonder where those farts go? I was looking at a scientific magazine the other day, *Scientific American* I think it was, and it said that farts, it's really hot air, so they tend to rise and go up to the stratosphere really. And you know what you've got up there, you've got the ozone layer, and just above that apparently is the fart layer. And this is why we need to really preserve the ozone layer. Now you can see where I'm going with this. I mean, if we get rid

269. Buckland, "Raymond Buckland Stand-Up: My Mother-in-Law."
270. Buckland, "Raymond Buckland Stand-Up #4."
271. Buckland, "Raymond Buckland Stand-Up #5."

of the ozone layer, those farts are going to come back and there is no guarantee that they will go to the original owners.[272]

The last twenty-six years of Buckland's life were perhaps not as groundbreaking as the thirty-year period that began upon his arrival in the United States back in 1962. However, Ray got to spend two and half (mostly) healthy decades doing all the things he loved: writing, being outdoors, performing, working on cars, and sharing his gifts with the world. He also got to spend that time doing those things with the woman he loved more than any other.

Raymond and Tara Buckland spent twenty-six years in Ohio, twenty-five of them on the farm they shared together. As an author, part of me feels like I've shortchanged this part of Ray's life compared to the number of words I spent on other stages in his life in previous chapters. But in the course of writing this chapter, I went back to Buckland's unfinished memoir and read the header to that work's last (and unfinished) chapter, "Part 7: Cars and Spiritualism (1991–Present)," which made me think that perhaps I wrote this chapter very much as Ray might have.

---

272. Buckland, "Raymond Buckland Stand-Up #4."

Exercise 9: Finding Your Spirit Guide

I don't know the name of Raymond Buckland's spirit guide, but I feel confident that he had one. To do all the things that Ray did during his lifetime, I have to think there was some sort of higher power pushing him along. Ray fervently believed in *the* Goddess, and it's possible that she was his lodestone, first helping him find his way into the Wica, and then to Tara, and finally onward to Ohio and Lily Dale.

In the section "Finding Your Spirit Guide" in lesson 5 of *Buckland's Book of Spirit Communications*, Ray provides a meditation to help others meet their own spirit guides.[273] Ray approaches the finding of spirit guides with an all-encompassing spirit, offering several different scenarios as to what a spirit guide might ultimately be.

· · · · · · · · ·

We all have a spirit guide, whether we are aware of it or not. Many Christians think in terms of a "guardian angel," perhaps even identifying it with one of the Christian angels or archangels, or one of the saints, and can accept the concept in those terms. As a Spiritualist and potential medium, it is a good idea to make contact with your guide. There is an easy way to do this, which is through a meditation journey.

Begin by making sure you are quite secure (unlikely to be interrupted), and sit in a comfortable, straight backed, meditation chair.... There are two main ways you can take this journey. You can carefully read through what follows and get it firmly in your mind, then you can repeat it to yourself (it doesn't have to be word-for-word; just get the general feel of it) and follow through with the suggestions as you give them to yourself. Or you can first read the written journey on to a tape recorder and then, when you are ready, simply play it back and follow through on the suggestions. Either way can be effective. The choice is yours. Here is the journey:

---

273. Buckland, *Buckland's Book of Spirit Communications*, lesson 5, 54–56.

You are walking along a country lane. The sun is shining down and you feel warm and happy. There's an open field on your left and a large woods on your right. You can hear birds singing in the trees and a gentle breeze wafts against your face. You see, ahead of you, a small path that leads off to the right, into the wood. Take that path. It leads at a slight downwards slope, winding in amongst the trees. You can see the sun up above, shining down through the branches and creating a wonderfully warm and comforting environment. Small animals, such as squirrels, rabbits, and chipmunks, peek out at you as you go on your way. You catch an occasional glimpse of a baby deer through the trees.

The angle of descent gradually steepens, and you come to a cliff edge. You are not very high up; in fact, no higher than the tops of the trees on the ground below the cliff. You see that someone has cut large steps into the face of the cliff and these lead down to the wooded ground below. You go down the steps. It's an easy descent and you feel safe and secure as you go down. At the bottom you cross the short expanse of grass to go, once more, in amongst the trees.

As you move on, you soon become aware of the babbling of a brook. The sound gets louder as you approach it. As the path makes a turn to the right, you see the brook ahead of you; its busy waters rushing over and around small and large stones. The path you are on follows along the side of the brook and you walk along it, noticing how the water swirls and eddies as it goes on its journey. Other small streams come in to join it and gradually it swells until it becomes a small river. As you walk on, beside it, you enjoy occasional glimpses of fish in the river, and of a duck or two that lands on the water then takes off again.

A large tree has fallen and stretches across the river, its upper branches on the far bank. Take the opportunity to cross over; jump up onto the tree trunk and walk across. You feel firm and secure, knowing you will not slip or fall. On the other side, you notice a large number of wild flowers growing in amongst the trees and underbrush. There is another path—you were obviously not the first to cross by the fallen tree. Follow along the path and notice the flowers and, again, the animals and birds.

Ahead of you the trees start to thin and you come out of the wood into a field. Stop and stand with the wood behind you. Fields stretch away to the horizon ahead of you. Off to the left you can make out high mountains, and to the right you can see the wood curving around and off with more fields beyond. But in front of you, in the middle of the field at whose edge you stand, there is a circle of standing stones. Each stone stands nine or ten feet tall. There are a number of them forming this circle… great granite monoliths. They look older than time; as if they have stood here for century upon century. Count how many there are.

Move forward into the ring. You feel happy, warm, and comforted, as though the stones are guardians surrounding you and keeping out all negativity. Walk into the very center of the circle they form and sit down on the grass. You are aware of the warmth of the sun and the sound of the birds. Again you feel that gentle breeze on your cheeks. Close your eyes for a moment and breathe deeply. Breathe in the wonderful, positive energies of this sacred place.

As you sit there quietly, you become aware of another person joining you. Keep your eyes closed. This person has come up from behind you and now moves around to face you. It is a good presence; a comforting one. It is your personal guide. It is the doorkeeper who has watched over your progress for many years. Don't yet open your eyes, but stand up and reach out your hands and take those that are offered. Feel them. Feel the warmth and love that comes from them.

Now open your eyes and see your guide. Is it a man or a woman? Young or old? What is he or she wearing? Everything about this guide. Ask by what name you should call him or her and greet them appropriately. Ask if they have any special message for you.

Know that this stone circle is your "special place." You can come here at any time, knowing that you can meet with your guide, or anyone else you wish, and be perfectly safe and secure. You can ask all you *wish to know of your guide. No one else can come here without your permission.*

When you have finished speaking with your guide, bid him or her goodbye and say that you will meet again very soon. Then turn and walk out of the circle, back toward the woods.

Retrace your steps, going back to the river and across the fallen tree trunk. Follow back along the path until it parts company with the stream. Go up the steps in the cliff and head out of the wood again, back on to the country road. Know that you have had a unique journey, but that you can repeat it any time you wish.

Find yourself back in your meditation chair; breath[e] deeply and relax, as you prepare to come back to your normal surroundings. Follow the steps I've previously given, for coming out of meditation. In other words, go through your body from the top of your head down to your toes, feeling your muscles awakening, feeling fresh and energized, ready for anything you want to tackle. Finish by opening your eyes and, after a couple of minutes of reorientation, stand up and feel good.

Chapter Ten
Immortality

Steven Intermill was bored.

It was April at the Christmas Story House Museum in Cleveland, Ohio, and Steven, the museum's curator, was having trouble concentrating. Steven liked his job at the Christmas Story House, but he dreamed of running a museum dedicated to something he was truly passionate about. Thinking about things that he was passionate about brought to mind "Witchcraft," and then another question: "Whatever happened to the Buckland Museum of Witchcraft and Magick?"

Buckland's museum had ceased being a truly active entity in the fall of 1977 when Ray set out to Virginia from New Hampshire. Before leaving New Hampshire, Buckland sold all the display cabinets for his museum but packed up the artifacts and took them with him to Virginia. In Virginia, they were moved into a storage unit and then eventually into Ray's garage, where he got the chance to look over the collection once again. But there was no place for the museum in Virginia, and when Raymond and Joan divorced in 1981, the museum items went back into storage. When Raymond and Tara Cochran-Buckland moved to California, the collection went with them, ending up (you guessed it!) in another storage unit. When Raymond and Tara moved to Ohio, the contents of Raymond's museum followed, only to end up back in another storage unit and then eventually the barn at the Buckland farm. Periodically during this period, Raymond would share some items from the collection at lectures and author events, but with over five hundred pieces, the collection was too unwieldy to travel with. For twenty-two years the collection mostly gathered dust and was spoken of strictly in the past tense.

Renewed interest in the museum during the mid-1990s nearly led to Ray Buckland selling the collection to the owner of a Witch shop in Las Vegas. The original plan was to reconstitute the museum in Las Vegas, but a suitable and, most importantly, affordable site couldn't be procured. Undeterred, the Las Vegas shop owner interested in Ray's collection began formulating plans to reopen the museum in the Dominican Republic! Due to his long-standing love of Vodou and Haiti, Ray thought this was a great idea.[274] According to Tara Buckland, this idea got well beyond just the planning stages and permits were being looked into. But in the end, Ray and Tara just didn't feel comfortable with the person looking to reopen the museum, and the plan was scrapped.[275]

But then in 1999, Raymond Buckland made the decision to sell the museum collection to Michael (Monte) Plaisance and his wife, Tolia-Ann, of Houma, Louisiana, near New Orleans. Buckland believed that New Orleans was the perfect city to house a Witchcraft museum. The Plaisances didn't have much of a connection to Buckland or the traditions he was a part of. (There are websites claiming the Plaisances were Gardnerians, but that is inaccurate.) Instead, the Plaisances had their own Witchcraft tradition, the Church of Thessaly, a home-grown Hellenic Witchcraft tradition. The Plaisances sent Buckland a deposit for the artifacts from the museum, agreeing to pay the rest of the agreed-upon price at a later date after the museum had opened. Buckland actively promoted the Plaisances' plans for a new Buckland museum and spent time in New Orleans raising money for the project. Given the magickal history of New Orleans and the Plaisances' connections to the city and the occult community, it all felt like a perfect fit, until it wasn't.

Five years after selling the collection, the Buckland Museum of Witchcraft and Magick reopened in the French Quarter of New Orleans in late 2004, but it didn't stay open for long.[276] Within a year, this new version of the museum closed. The collection was packed up yet again, with Plaisance then suggesting that charging admission to view the collection was tantamount to "blasphemy":

---

274. Both Haiti and the Dominican Republic are located on the island of Hispaniola.

275. Tara Buckland, Zoom interview conducted on February 4, 2025.

276. Ward, "Buckland Museum Poised to Reopen in Midwest."

The museum, although it was a pleasure to own and operate, just did not generate the amount of interest needed to succeed in comparison to the amount of work both I and everyone who helped put into it. The museum, to myself and to many others, is filled with religious artifacts that are important to the history of pagan religion and as such, I felt that profiting from the exhibition of these items was tantamount to blasphemy and also degraded the sacredness of these artifacts. Because of these conflicts of interest in myself, I opted to pack the museum up and store it away until I could find a way to fund it without having to charge for admissions.[277]

In 2008 Buckland sued Monte Plaisance for the return of the Buckland Museum collection for not paying the remainder of the agreed-upon selling price. In a 2017 interview with *The Wild Hunt*, a Pagan news outlet, Buckland claimed that "he [Plaisance] did not come through with the money (forcing a lawsuit), misplaced many of the artifacts, and badly treated or even destroyed others."[278] Rumors circulated that many of the items in the collection had been sold or given away as gifts.[279] Plaisance has publicly stated that "all of the items that were part of the original purchase agreement were present and accounted for when I returned the collection," though as of this writing the allegations persist.[280] For his part, Plaisance claimed that after "some discussion" with Buckland, he and his wife facilitated the return of the collection, a claim disputed by both Buckland and the available evidence (most notably the lawsuit filed in court).[281] Plaisance last commented on his time with the museum collection in 2016, and in that statement he announced his "complete and total withdrawal from the pagan community and the Wiccan religion."[282]

In 2009 possession of the museum's pieces was given to Velvet Rieth, also in New Orleans. Rieth was known for her charity and good works, volunteering in soup kitchens and homeless shelters in New Orleans, and for being active in the Louisiana Pagan community. She began a Pagan prison ministry

277. Pitzl-Water, "Taking Back Buckland's Collection."
278. Ward, "Reboot of Buckland Museum Set for Apr. 29."
279. Kagan, "Welcome to the Pagan Con Artist Gallery."
280. Plaisance, "Full and Unedited Statement on the Buckland Museum."
281. Pitzl-Water, "Taking Back Buckland's Collection."
282. Pitzl-Water, "Taking Back Buckland's Collection."

in 1996 and published a Wiccan book for children in 2007. Rieth hoped to establish another museum to house the Buckland collection, again in New Orleans. But until the space could be acquired, Rieth took parts of the collection to Pagan events so others could appreciate them.

Shortly after taking control of the collection, Rieth began dealing with symptoms of Pick's disease, a malady similar to Alzheimer's. Due to her illness, Rieth would be unable to find a new home for the Buckland Museum. Rieth passed away in early 2016 surrounded by her immediate family. Despite Rieth being unable to reopen the museum, Buckland credited her with helping to preserve the collection: "Rev. Velvet Reith [sic], and her helpers, were instrumental in rescuing the collection and started the job of restoring it."[283]

In June of 2015, the collection returned once more to Ohio, and Raymond Buckland placed the museum's artifacts in the hands of Toni Rotonda and Kat Tigner, old friends of his who had both circled with him and been a part of his last coven. After nearly thirty years of movement, the collection was not in good shape (despite the work of Rieth and her friends). Kat and Toni described the condition of the collection in 2016 to *The Wild Hunt*:

> When we originally received the collection from New Orleans in July of 2015, the items were not carefully packed or labeled in any way. There were large foot lockers filled with what could only be described as chaos. We had no idea who (and in some cases, what) these items belonged to, or their relevance to the museum. Many of the items were in pieces (in separate foot lockers), broken, or missing. It was very disheartening. Thankfully, because of Ray's extensive record-keeping (thank the gods!), we were able to identify, catalog, and restore many of the artifacts.[284]

Remembering Ray: Toni Rotonda

I have many fond memories of Raymond Buckland, most of which are filled with laughter and bring a smile to my face. Ray had an incredible sense of humor, and whether you were attending his shows as a

283. Ward, "Reboot of Buckland Museum Set for Apr. 29."
284. Ward, "Buckland Museum Poised to Reopen in Midwest."

stand-up comedian or just sitting around his kitchen table having a cup of tea, his stories had a way of drawing you into his world. His comedy and wit always left you in good spirits.

However, there is one story…

Years ago, before the Buckland Museum opened in Cleveland, Ohio, my High Priestess, Kat, and I would drive up to Glenmont, Ohio, to visit with Ray and Tara Buckland. We were collecting information about the artifacts that were going to be displayed in the Buckland Museum. We really enjoyed these trips. We would spend the two-hour ride home laughing, excited about the information we had collected and writing down more questions for the next visit.

Ray was extremely meticulous about his records and archives. He kept everything. He would always be ready with what he wanted to cover with us for the day. This particular day, Ray had us come out to the large detached garage that served as a workshop and storage. He had a long table filled with white boxes and stacks of black three-ring binders. He already had the chairs set up for us. He sat in the middle, while Kat was on his left and I was on his right. Ray began with a box filled with newspaper articles and correspondence letters. Everything he pulled out of the box had a memory or backstory. There was always so much information, so I made sure to record everything.

Ray placed one of the three-ring binders in front of him and opened it. This particular binder had a collection of old photos from his original museum on Long Island. Each page was a plastic sleeve filled with photos of artifacts or museum display cases that he had put together. Every page that was turned brought up a different emotion. Some brought laughter with a shared story, and some a quiet smile as he would touch the image on the page. He would turn to one of us and ask, "Is this still there?" A relieved smile would follow when we answered, "Yes, it's there. We still have it." Kat and I were grateful to have this special time with him.

The next page flipped, he stared at the image on the photo. He took us to a time in the early 1960s when he and his family were struggling financially. Monique Wilson had just initiated Ray, and she was putting a great deal of pressure on him to get the Gardnerian tradition started in the United States. The photo on the page was of his grandparents' candelabra that he had brought with him from England.

The photo reminded him of a difficult time. They had just sold the family car to be able to afford the trip to the Isle of Man. Monique's letters were becoming increasingly demanding, and Ray recalled not knowing what to do. The beautiful candelabra in the photo had once been covered with multiple layers of paint, and he told us of taking on the tedious task of removing the stubborn layers. While working on this, he contemplated his future and what he should do. Should he just forget all this and give up this path?

He was confused and stressed and began to doubt himself. He said, "I asked the Goddess to help me. I asked her to give me a sign as to what I should do." He continued to scrub the paint from the old candelabra. He said he noticed something shining through the paint. It was some kind of figure. Right then and there, peeking out from under the paint, was the face of the Foliate Man (the Green Man). This was his sign! He couldn't believe it. It was right there in front of him.

Even now, over fifty years later, his face lit up with excitement while he told us this story. We were excited too! "Well, the Goddess answered!" Kat said. Ray was quiet, then his expression changed. While gently touching the photo, he dropped his head and began to cry.

I shut my camera off.

I do not know what he was thinking about at that moment. This was a side of Ray I had never seen before. It saddened me to see my Spiritual Father in such a vulnerable state while reflecting on his life. We had shared so many laughs together that I had forgotten about the painful sacrifices he had made long ago to choose this path. We all have made sacrifices to follow a Pagan path, but because of individuals like Raymond Buckland, it has become much easier for us to learn, experience, and live this path.

Ray, Kat, and I sat in silence for a moment. Kat put her hand on Ray's shoulder and leaned down in front of his bowed head. She said, "We thank you, Ray. The world thanks you for what you've done." Ray brushed the tears from his face and nodded with his head still down.

Ray's old family candelabra, as it was displayed at the Buckland Museum of Witchcraft and Magick in Bay Shore, Long Island, New York

The drive home was quiet that night. No talking or laughter like usual. Just silence and reflection. Kat and I never spoke about it. We didn't need to. It was a private moment between Ray and the Goddess, whom he had spent his life serving.

Every morning I say a prayer of gratitude. I thank Her every day. Today I thanked Her for giving Ray that sign.

Tonita "Toni" Rotonda *is the High Priestess of the Temple of Sacrifice Coven in Columbus, Ohio, and is the current owner of the Buckland Museum of Witchcraft and Magick. Her dedication to the Craft led her to the restoration and preservation of Raymond Buckland's collection of Witchcraft and occult items. Along with her spiritual pursuits, Toni restores Victorian homes and works with rescue animals.*

It's near this point that the bored and curious Steven Intermill enters the picture. On April 11, 2016, Intermill sends a note to Ray asking what had happened to the Buckland Museum. Buckland excitedly sends a follow-up email, and a few weeks later, in early May, Intermill hears from Toni Rotonda, the owner and caretaker of Buckland's Museum collection. After some discussion on the phone, Intermill sets off for Columbus, Ohio, to view the collection with his then coworker Joshua Dickerson (today Dickerson is the owner of the Christmas Story House).[285]

Toni Rotonda and Raymond Buckland going through museum items

At the time of Intermill's visit, most of the collection was still packed up, and Rotonda spent most of the visit rifling through storage boxes and presenting Intermill with items to look at. Rotonda was immediately impressed with Intermill's understanding of Witch history; Intermill was one of the first people to view the collection in a long while who really knew who all the early players were in Modern Witchcraft. After viewing the collection, an excited Intermill called up his wife, Jillian Slane, to discuss the idea of bringing the Buckland Museum back from hibernation. Slane appreciated Inter-

285. Steven Intermill, personal interview conducted on December 6, 2023.

mill's enthusiasm but cautioned her husband not to sign any papers or make any commitments he would be unable to keep.[286]

The rainy drive back to Cleveland from Columbus was an eventful one for Intermill and Dickerson. A motorcycle just ahead of the pair on the highway suddenly began weaving and then flipped over on its side. Intermill and Dickerson immediately pulled over to check on the motorcycle driver, with Intermill urging the bike-rider to stay still until help could be summoned. Another car pulled over and quickly called 911, dispatching an ambulance to the scene. The accident "shook" Intermill and Dickerson, and Intermill couldn't help but wonder if his visit to the Buckland collection had played a part in the accident he had just witnessed.[287]

In an interview with me in 2023, Intermill admitted that when "you mess around with occult forces, things pop in your head," and on the day of the accident, Intermill had shared those feelings with Dickerson.[288] Dickerson, though, refused to take the bait and didn't believe that the objects Buckland had spent much of his life caring for were cursed or imbued with negative energy. Instead, Dickerson saw the accident as a positive, a reminder from the universe that "you gotta live life how you want to live it. Who knows what's going to happen and what's going to get thrown at you?"[289]

In June of 2016, Intermill paid another visit to Columbus to view the Buckland collection, this time with Slane, herself an extremely accomplished museum curator. Though initially excited for her husband, Slane had trouble visualizing what a new iteration of the Buckland Museum might look like. Intermill says Jillian couldn't picture his vision for the collection until the couple came across an old medical astrology poster housed in a piece of Plexiglas. For whatever reason, she was able to clearly see that poster as a centerpiece on a museum wall.[290]

Despite Steven and Jillian's initial excitement about reopening the Buckland Museum, things moved slowly for the rest of 2016. That would change on November 8, 2016, Election Day in the United States. Before

---

286. Steven Intermill, personal interview conducted on December 6, 2023.

287. Steven Intermill, personal interview conducted on December 6, 2023.

288. Steven Intermill, personal interview conducted on December 6, 2023.

289. Steven Intermill, personal interview conducted on December 6, 2023.

290. Steven Intermill, personal interview conducted on December 6, 2023.

the election, Intermill says the couple were "teetering on this idea [of reopening the museum], back and forth." But after Trump got elected, the couple were "so freaked out that we had to do something, something for the Goddess." That "something" was reopening the Buckland Museum.[291]

Before work began on reopening the museum, Intermill and Slane journeyed to Millersburg, Ohio, to catch one of Ray's stand-up comedy nights, where they also met up with Toni Rotonda. It was that evening when Buckland, Rotonda, and Intermill officially decided that "yes, we are going to reopen this museum."[292] Rotonda would retain ownership of the collection, while Intermill would lease the collection and be responsible for displaying it along with Slane and running the day-to-day operations of the museum.

Though Buckland was not in the best of health on the night when he first met Intermill, Intermill was still in awe of Ray's presence. According to Intermill, Ray "had that rizz. You could tell he was chill because he was a baller. If he was standing in a crowd of five people, he was the one you noticed. There was something about him like that."[293]

Reopening the Buckland Museum presented the couple with a lot of challenges, the most notable one being a lack of money. As Intermill puts it, "I had no start-up capital. I didn't have any money."[294] The new museum's first home would be a back room of A Separate Reality record store, an arrangement helped out by Intermill's friendship with the store's owner. The back room wasn't in the best of shape, and Intermill and Slane had to clean up the space and repaint it.

A lack of start-up funds also meant there were no display cases for the museum's items. Luckily for Intermill, the local natural history museum that Slane worked at was looking to unload a bunch of cases. With no way to transport or store the cases on his own, Intermill took advantage of his position at the Christmas Story House Museum, using the museum's van to pick up the cases and then storing them in the museum's archives. He justified the move by giving half of the display cases he picked up to the Christmas Story House.

291. Steven Intermill, personal interview conducted on December 6, 2023.
292. Steven Intermill, personal interview conducted on December 6, 2023.
293. Steven Intermill, personal interview conducted on December 6, 2023.
294. Steven Intermill, personal interview conducted on December 6, 2023.

The Buckland Museum of Witchcraft and Magick was officially scheduled to reopen on the evening of Saturday, April 29, 2017, but in the week
leading up to it, Intermill came down with a major cold. With Intermill inca-
pacitated, the major work of getting the collection ready for visitors fell to
Rotonda and Slane, who spent most of that Thursday and Friday making
final preparations for the reopening. Intermill describes the last few days
before the museum's reopening as "not a good scene."[295]

**Ray at the newly reopened Buckland Museum of Witchcraft and Magick
housed in a back room of A Separate Reality record store**

But the reopening itself? That was a very good scene. Not surprisingly,
Ray was there to cut the ribbon for the grand reopening, and he was joined
by hundreds of friends! Intermill had expected "maybe twenty people," but a
viral article about the museum on the website Dangerous Minds had sparked
a lot of interest in the museum's opening and its founder.[296] Intermill says
there were "people from states away" and a line down the street to get in at
the opening, all to see a small collection of Witchcraft-related items and
to possibly meet the man behind them, Raymond Buckland. "There were
people from states away with the idea that they had to meet Ray Buckland"

295. Steven Intermill, personal interview conducted on December 6, 2023.
296. Dangerous Minds, "New Witchcraft Museum Features Occult Artifacts Once Owned by
    Aleister Crowley."

that night, explains Intermill.[297] And those who did see and meet Ray were greeted by a spry older gentleman with a serious "bop to his step."[298]

Much of that bop was thanks to just how great everything looked at this new iteration of the Buckland Museum. "Steven, this is the best the collection has ever looked on display," an excited Buckland said to Intermill that night.[299] Intermill thinks some of that praise was due to "the real serious cabinets" the exhibits were displayed in, but some of it came from just how serious the museum's new caretakers were about the collection.[300] It's also worth mentioning again that Intermill and Slane are museum professionals and know just how to display and exhibit objects of historical significance.

Nearly two years later, in 2019, the Buckland Museum of Witchcraft and Magick would have a second grand opening in a new location, just a mile and a half from the record shop that previously housed the museum. This time the museum would be the building's sole tenant, allowing Intermill to supplement the museum's admission fees with souvenirs and Witchcraft-related books and tools. Today the Buckland Museum of Witchcraft and Magick houses not just the original items procured by Raymond Buckland but also an ever-growing collection of Witchcraft-related objects from around the world. Many of the items in the museum have been donated by famous Witches (and some not-so-famous Witches too—the museum is home to one of my magick wands), and the museum has been instrumental in preserving not only Buckland's legacy but valuable pieces of Witchcraft history as well.

Today, in 2025, the Buckland Museum of Witchcraft and Magick remains a popular tourist destination. Google "Buckland Museum" and you'll come across dozens of articles featuring Intermill and Slane sharing their excitement about the museum. If you get a chance to visit the museum yourself, you'll see many of Ray's working tools and the original draft of *Big Blue*. Buckland's museum is one of the man's most enduring legacies, and thanks to Rotonda, Intermill, and Slane, it is in truly great hands.

The "bop in Buckland's step" in April of 2017 was especially extraordinary considering the physical challenges Buckland had been facing over the

---

297. Steven Intermill, personal interview conducted on December 6, 2023.

298. Steven Intermill, personal interview conducted on December 6, 2023.

299. Steven Intermill, personal interview conducted on December 6, 2023.

300. Steven Intermill, personal interview conducted on December 6, 2023.

previous two years. On August 4, 2015, Buckland suffered a major heart attack while battling pneumonia. The heart attack was severe and sudden enough that he had to be transported by helicopter to a local hospital. Once there, Buckland spent several days attached to a breathing tube. He spent a week in the hospital before returning home, his physical condition much diminished.[301]

Buckland worked hard to get back in shape after his heart attack, walking two miles most days and exercising for an hour daily. Many of his stand-up performances currently online were recorded after the 2015 heart attack, and the work Buckland did to get back in shape is readily apparent. But at age eighty, Buckland was mostly slowing down. The time of personal appearances and lectures was largely over.

A collection of Ray's hats and part of his library in his office on the farm in Ohio

Raymond Buckland ended this incarnation on Wednesday, September 27, 2017. Earlier in the week he had been having some breathing problems and had been admitted to a local hospital. Buckland had a known issue with his heart's mitral valve and was awaiting experimental surgery on it when he passed. Tara describes her final moments with Ray this way:

---

301. Ward, "An Interview with Raymond Buckland, American Wicca Pioneer."

[Ray] was feeling pretty good otherwise and excited that all his test results could be accessed on his iPad with a special password from the hospital.... That was the last thing we talked about. Shortly after that, he got up to go to the bathroom and turned to a nurse who was busy doing something-or-other and said: "Oh hey, I feel a strange fluttering" and then he collapsed.... It was basically an instantaneous and painless death.[302]

Raymond Buckland cast a long shadow over both the American Pagan and Spiritualist communities. During his lifetime he undoubtedly met thousands of people, and through his books, he connected with hundreds of thousands more. In the wake of his death, tributes and remembrances were plentiful. Raymond Buckland's passage was both noted and mourned by the communities he had served in life.

Ray's office just a few years before his passing. On the whiteboard behind his desk, you can see the storyboard for his 2014 novel *Cursed in the Act.*

Buckland felt no fear at his passing. Due to his experiences as both a Witch and a spirit medium, he firmly believed in the immortality of the

---

302. Tara Buckland, email communication on February 3, 2025.

soul. I imagine he died with some regrets, most notably not getting more time with Tara in this lifetime, and then there were all the other books he was undoubtedly planning to write. But long before his passing, Raymond Buckland had already achieved a type of immortality. As long as there are Witches, his name will be remembered.

. . . .

In September of 2021, I visited Salem, Massachusetts, for the first time. For my wife and me (and a couple of friends), this marked our first major outing since the start of the COVID-19 pandemic the previous year. Our visit occurred a few days after the Autumn Equinox, and while the temperature was quite warm, fall was definitely in the air. For years we had been told to visit Salem in October, but we found late September to be plenty busy. We walked shoulder to shoulder on the streets of Salem with the hordes of fellow tourists, and every store we visited was full of people. We were later told that the number of tourists in town that September weekend was equivalent to the usual October Samhain-related crowds.

For many Witches, visiting Salem is something akin to a religious pilgrimage. While not every tourist who visits Salem is a Witch or a Pagan, many are, and even those who aren't are at least sympathetic to magickal practices. While Witch shops can be found throughout the entire city, the greatest concentration of them can be found on Essex Street, home to many of Salem's most famous and popular attractions. On Essex Street you'll find the famous (or infamous) statue of actress Elizabeth Montgomery, who played Samantha Stephens on the television show *Bewitched*. It's also on Essex where you'll find the city's most popular (and lucrative) witchy bookstores.

While I was in Salem, I spent a lot of time in those bookstores mostly looking for my own books, but in between those triumphs and disappointments I began to notice something else: Most every store carried *Buckland's Complete Book of Witchcraft*. And most stores did more than just carry the *Big Blue Book*; those shops had dozens of copies on the shelves. There was one store I visited with fifty copies of Buckland's masterwork on display. Most Salem shops keep one or two copies of the books they stock on their shelves, not cases of one title. Buckland was the exception.

I would have expected titles similar to *Big Blue* (such as Silver Raven-Wolf's *To Ride a Silver Broomstick* and Scott Cunningham's *Wicca: A Guide for the Solitary Practitioner*) to also have entire shelves dedicated to them, but that just wasn't the case. And the covers of both RavenWolf's and Cunningham's books have been redesigned over the past ten years to appeal to a new audience. *Buckland's Complete* looks nearly the same as it did forty years ago; it's still a large blue book with a big pentagram on the cover. The only difference between the original version I own and the latest edition is a banner on the bottom of the cover proclaiming "The Classic Course in Wicca for 25 Years." Classic indeed!

Any question about Ray's immortality and legacy disappears after a trip to Salem. His work still occupies pride of place in much of the town. Witchcraft books have never been particularly profitable, but Raymond Buckland has a legacy in print that most writers could only dream of. Not only have many of his books been continuously in print for decades, but they have also educated, consoled, and enlightened hundreds of thousands of readers. They have also been translated into a dozen languages. If a community, regardless of location, has self-identified Witches, they probably have Buckland books nearby. Raymond Buckland might be the most read contemporary Witch author of the last sixty years. That's an achievement.

But Buckland did more than write books. When I visit with other Gardnerian Witches, his name always comes up. The vast majority of us in the United States trace our lineage directly through Ray (and Rosemary). Things might have ended poorly for Buckland in the Gardnerian tradition, but many of us within that tradition still look at him as a guiding light and a figure worth emulating. I'd argue that Ray's legacy was secure when he brought Gardnerian Wicca to the United States in 1963. That act alone conferred a degree of immortality that most other Witches will never achieve.

Buckland's fingerprints are on more than just Gardnerian Wicca, too. Through his books and interviews, he popularized the use of the Irish-Celtic names for the greater sabbats and introduced the Pagan world to the idea of the Threefold Law of Return. He also created an entirely new tradition and provided a space for solitary practitioners and the uninitiated. And like the best Witches, Buckland always found room for change and growth in his practice and believed that the Craft had room in the circle for everybody.

Raymond Buckland might not have created the modern Witchcraft world as we know it today, but he was instrumental in its construction.

Ray Buckland in Victorian dress for a séance in 2009

Buckland might never show up on lists of the world's most famous Spiritualists, but I would argue that he provided more people with the tools to contact the dead than did his more famous twenty-first-century peers. Buckland didn't write books about living with the spirits; he wrote books to teach others how to live with the spirits. Buckland's contributions to Spiritualism are greater than many of the mediums who have ended up on reality TV shows. Those mediums might be famous for a period of time, but a legacy survives only if it is passed on to others. Buckland always shared his passions in ways that allowed others to adopt them if they chose to do so.

Over the course of writing this book, I made the decision not to psychoanalyze Ray while writing about him. Many biographies are full of needless editorializing in an attempt to figure out a subject's motivations. But because we are near the end, allow me a bit of self-indulgence for a moment. I once believed, while writing this book, that Ray's biggest goal in life was to become famous. He clearly enjoyed hobnobbing with celebrities and being on stage, and after he discovered Witchcraft he went public with that fact rather quickly, and did so during an age when there were very serious repercussions for practicing an alternative faith tradition.

But toward the end of his life, Ray was perfectly content on the farm, writing the books he loved and spending his days with Tara and the grandchildren. During that long period of contentment, Witchcraft was at the height of its popularity and there were all sorts of things Buckland could have been doing to cash in on the Craft's newly prominent place in society and his long association with it. But he didn't. Instead, he simply continued to write about the things he was passionate about, unconcerned with what the rest of society might have been excited about in the moment.

I don't think Ray was concerned with celebrity at all. Instead, he was simply an extremely passionate man who spent a lifetime chasing down the things he loved. And the things he loved were Spiritualism, Witchcraft, art, the unexplained, the occult, combustion engines, music, and performance. Ray wanted to share those passions with as many people as possible, and I would argue that he did a pretty damn good job of it. And if there wasn't an outlet for sharing the things he loved, he'd start one. Sometimes that resulted in Witchcraft museums on Long Island, and other times it resulted in open mic comedy nights in Millersburg, Ohio. I'm not sure it mattered either way to Raymond Buckland.

As an author, I often wonder what people will take with them from the books I've written. In this particular case, I worry that all anyone will care about is that maybe Buckland (perhaps) didn't meet Gardner and that Buckland wasn't a PhD. I'm sure there will be people who talk about those things, but what I want people to take from this book is Buckland's love for the things he was passionate about. Ray could have done dozens of things, but he chose to focus on the things he loved so that others might love them in return. I think that's a life well lived.

Closing Thoughts & Acknowledgments

I mention in the introduction to this book that I am not a biographer. I think there are likely hundreds more stories featuring Raymond Buckland that could be told in a volume such as this one. I spend very little time writing about Lily Dale, for instance, while it's possible that the Spiritualist community there might be able to write a whole book just about Ray! But as this book is called *High Priest*, I chose to spend most of these pages writing about Ray's life as a Witch and his influence on Wiccan-Witchcraft. In many ways this book is a starting point and not an ending for those looking to know more about Ray Buckland.

In the course of researching this book, I did encounter several people who did not like Ray. That's understandable; not everyone is universally loved, and I'm sure Ray had bad days and most certainly his departure from Gardnerian Wicca was not an amicable one. But I made a conscious decision not to write a gossipy book or write about allegations that could not be substantiated.

And now for the thank yous … First of all, I want to thank Tara Buckland for entrusting me with this project. Tara is one of the brightest souls I've ever met, and when I think about her, I can't help but smile. Tara, thank you for your kindness and willingness to answer my many (many) varied questions about Ray.

Speaking of answering questions, both Toni Rotonda and Steven Intermill answered a lot of questions! If you've gotten this far in the book, you know that Steven is the director of the Buckland Museum of Witchcraft and Magick in Cleveland, Ohio, and Toni is the caretaker and owner of Ray's collection and the museum. Both are fine people and have helped me in dozens of different ways during the writing of this book. Steven (along with his wife, Jillian) has also become one of my favorite people in the universe to grab a drink with. Thank you for your hospitality while poking around the museum! And Toni, when I met you at Pagan Spirit Gathering back in 2019, I just knew that we were going to end up working on a project together! This book would not have been possible without the two of you.

It usually takes me about six months to write a book, but this book took over two years! I'm extremely thankful to Elysia Gallo, my editor at Llewellyn, for her patience and understanding during the trials and tribulations that occurred while writing what you now hold in your hands. There were COVID cases, canceled trips to Lily Dale, and half a dozen other things that made this book more challenging than most. While I will probably never work on a project like this again, I'm glad I got this one opportunity to try something different.

Also at Llewellyn, thank you to Sandra Weschcke for opening up the vaults and letting me dig through Ray and Carl's correspondence over the years. My absolute favorite part of this book was discovering how *Big Blue* developed, and I only got to share that with you all because of Sandra's kindness and generosity. Also know that after ten books at Llewellyn, I'm still tickled and delighted every time I release a new one. That crescent moon on the spine means the world to me.

Thanks to all the contributors who made this book better. You all captured a side of Ray that I was unable to. It is much appreciated. Special thanks to Ivo Dominguez Jr. for doing Ray's chart. There is no one I trust more with astrological matters than Ivo.

I started this book project just about the time I started giving my Wednesday nights to the Witch's Movie Coven (live stream and podcast!). Patti Negri, Heather Greene, Courtney Buckley, Richard-Lael Lillard, Rob Cohen, and Christine Roth have truly become the other coven in my life. Thank you all for the texts that keep me up at all hours of the night and for the camaraderie and friendship we share. And to my "other" coven, I love you all! We are celebrating over thirteen years as a group as I write this!

I absolutely treasure my friends and colleagues in the Pagan writing community. Thorn Mooney is not just one of my favorite people in the world, but also one of the smartest people I know. Thanks for always being available when I had a question. I love to complain while writing a book, and no one heard more complaints from me than Phoenix LeFae, Gwion Raven, Laura Tempest Zakroff, Astrea Taylor, and Mat Auryn. You are all terrific friends and sounding boards. There are a bunch of other people I feel like I should thank in this category, too, but the page count for this book is already really high. If we share whisky at festivals, just know that I love you and that I should have included your name here.

My friends Callie and Fermin Coto encouraged me to write this book back in the early days of the COVID-19 pandemic. I wouldn't have done this without your prodding or perhaps all those bottles of wine you shared during the course of that very long year.

As always, this project would not have been possible without my wife, Ari. We have been married for over twenty years now, and together for nearly twenty-seven! In another ten years, we will have overtaken Tara and Ray in relationship longevity! (A worthy goal, I believe.) Ari, you own my heart, now and forever.

I remain humbled that people read my work and actually seem excited about it. If you are one of those people, I probably owe you the most thanks of all.

Bright Blessings,
Jason W. Mankey
July 2024

A Chronological Buckland Book List

Raymond Buckland began his writing career in 1966 with the publication of *Witchcraft ... the Religion* and continued writing until his death in 2017. That's fifty-one years—an incredibly long time to spend at any vocation! Because of the length of Ray's writing career, creating a definitive list of all his titles is a daunting task. Many of his earlier books have been repackaged and republished, and several of his works have been retitled over the decades.

There is also the vexing problem of just what, exactly, constitutes a book. Many of Ray's later nonfiction works are more like pamphlets than traditional books. But if Ray said it was a book, I tried to include it in this list. Titles that have been reprinted can be found under their original publication title, and I make a note of volumes that have been extensively updated in later editions. This list also includes all the divination decks that have Ray's name on them, along with his forays into video. I'm sure I've missed a book or two along the way, as Ray wrote so many of them, especially in the last few years of his life.

The Chronological Buckland Bibliography

Witchcraft ... the Religion. Buckland Museum, 1966.

A Pocket Guide to the Supernatural. Ace Books, 1969. 2nd ed. 1975.
    Reprinted by Queen Victoria Press in 2017.

Mu Revealed (writing as Tony Earll). Warner Paperback Library, 1970.

Practical Candleburning Rituals. Llewellyn, 1970. 2nd ed. 1976. 3rd ed. 1982.

Witchcraft Ancient and Modern. HC Publishers, 1970. Later published by Queen Victoria Press in 2017. (Sometimes the title of this book is given as *Ancient and Modern Witchcraft*.)

Witchcraft from the Inside. Llewellyn, 1970. 2nd ed. 1975. 3rd ed. 1995. Reprinted as *Witchcraft Revealed* by Queen Victoria Press in 2016.

Here Is the Occult. HC Publishers, 1974. Republished in 2009 by BookSurge Publishing.

The Tree: Complete Book of Saxon Witchcraft. Samuel Weiser, 1974. Republished as *Buckland's Book of Saxon Witchcraft* in 2005.

Amazing Secrets of the Psychic World (with Hereward Carrington). Parker/Prentice Hall, 1975.

The Anatomy of the Occult. Samuel Weiser, 1977.

The Magick of Chant-O-Matics. Parker/Prentice Hall, 1978.

Practical Color Magick. Llewellyn, 1983. 2nd ed. published as *Color Magick: Unleash Your Inner Powers* in 2002.

Buckland's Complete Book of Witchcraft. Llewellyn, 1986. 2nd ed. 2002.

Secrets of Gypsy Fortunetelling. Llewellyn, 1988.

The Buckland Gypsy Fortunetelling Deck. Llewellyn, 1988. 2nd ed. published as *Gypsy Fortunetelling Tarot Deck* in 1998.

Witchcraft: Yesterday and Today (VHS). Llewellyn, 1990. Released on DVD as *Witchcraft: Rebirth of the Old Religion* in 2005.

Secrets of Gypsy Dream Reading. Llewellyn, 1990. Published as *Gypsy Dream Dictionary* in 1999.

Secrets of Gypsy Love Magick. Llewellyn, 1990.

Scottish Witchcraft: The History and Magick of the Picts. Llewellyn, 1991.

The Book of African Divination (deck, with Kathleen Binger). Inner Traditions, 1992.

Doors to Other Worlds: A Practical Guide to Communicating with Spirits. Llewellyn, 1993.

The Committee (novel). Llewellyn, 1993.

Ray Buckland's Magic Cauldron. Galde Press, 1995.

The Truth About Spirit Communication. Llewellyn, 1995.

Advanced Candle Magick: More Spells and Rituals for Every Purpose. Llewellyn, 1996.

Cardinal's Sin (novel). Llewellyn, 1996.

Gypsy Witchcraft and Magic. Llewellyn, 1998.

The Buckland Gypsies' Domino Divination Deck. Llewellyn, 1999. Reprinted as *Buckland's Domino Divination* by Pendraig in 2010.

Coin Divination. Llewellyn, 2000.

The Buckland Romani Tarot. Llewellyn, 2001.

The Witch Book: The Encyclopedia of Witchcraft, Wicca, and Neo-paganism. Visible Ink Press, 2001.

Wicca for Life. Citadel Press, 2001.

Cards of Alchemy. Llewellyn, 2003.

Signs, Symbols & Omens: An Illustrated Guide to Magical and Spiritual Symbolism. Llewellyn, 2003.

The Fortune Telling Book. Visible Ink Press, 2003.

Buckland's Book of Spirit Communications. Llewellyn, 2004.

Wicca for One. Citadel Press, 2004.

Mediumship and Spirit Communication. Buckland Books, 2005.

The Spirit Book: The Encyclopedia of Clairvoyance, Channeling, and Spirit Communication. Visible Ink Press, 2005.

Death, Where Is Thy Sting? Buckland Books, 2006.

Face to Face with God? Buckland Books, 2006.

Ouija–"Yes! Yes!" Doorway Publications, 2006.

Buckland's Doorway to Candle Magic. Buckland Books, 2007.

Dragons, Shamans, and Spiritualists. Buckland Books, 2007.

The Torque of Kernow (novel). Galde Press/Buckland Books, 2008.

The Weiser Field Guide to Ghosts: Apparitions, Spirits, Spectral Lights, and Other Hauntings of History and Legend. Red Wheel/Weiser, 2009.

Buckland's Book of Gypsy Magic. Red Wheel/Weiser, 2010.

Buckland's Domino Divination. Pendraig, 2010. Previously published as *The Buckland Gypsies' Domino Divination Deck* by Llewellyn in 1999.

Golden Illuminati (novel). Pendraig, 2010.

Solitary Séance: How You Can Talk with Spirits on Your Own. Llewellyn, 2011.

Atomic Sunrise (novel). Galde Press, 2012.

Paranormal Poetry: A Chapbook of Poetry, Strange and Unusual. Buckland Books, 2013.

Churchill's Secret Spy. Queen Victoria Press, 2014.

Cursed in the Act: A Bram Stoker Mystery (novel). Berkley/Penguin, 2014.

Dead for a Spell: A Bram Stoker Mystery (novel). Berkley/Penguin, 2014.

The Liberty Squadron (novel). Galde Press, 2014.

A Mistake Through the Heart: A Bram Stoker Mystery (novel). Buckland Books, 2015.

One Clue at a Time: A Penny Court Enquirers Mystery (novel). Buckland Books, 2016.

The Noble Savage: A Penny Court Enquirers Mystery (novel). Buckland Books, 2016.

Out of This World: A Collection of Science Fiction Short Stories. Queen Victoria Press, 2016.

Deadly Spirit: A Penny Court Enquirers Mystery (novel). Queen Victoria Press, 2016.

Laff with Olaf and Others (cartoons). Queen Victoria Press, 2017.

Ouija Connection to Spirit: The Talking Board and How to Contact the Spirit World. Queen Victoria Press, 2017.

Fletcher's Folly: A Gothic Romance Mystery (novel). By Eileen Lizzie Wells (Raymond Buckland). Queen Victoria Press, 2017.

Raymond Buckland's Alchemy Coloring Book: Color the Cards of Alchemy. Queen Victoria Press, 2017.

Additional Contributions

Aradia, Gospel of the Witches. By Charles G. Leland. Buckland Museum, 1968. Introduction by Raymond Buckland.

Ghosts, Spirits, and Hauntings: Am I Being Haunted? Edited by Michael Pye and Kirsten Dalley. Includes an essay by Raymond Buckland called "Talking to Ghosts."

Grandfather's Advice. By Carroll Wright. Edited by Raymond Cochran-Buckland. Bailey Printing, 1984.

Bibliography & Further Reading

One of my favorite things about writing a book are all the other books and materials I get to read while doing so! A lot of the material in this bibliography will be inaccessible to the average reader (though you never know, maybe Llewellyn will let you look at some old office memos?), but if you are a Pagan/Witch history nerd, you will still find several titles here that might interest you. I love so many of these books and resources that I can't help but comment on some of them! As always, happy reading!

—Jason W. Mankey, July 1, 2024

ACLU (American Civil Liberties Union). "Getting Rid of Sodomy Laws: History and Strategy That Led to the Lawrence Decision." June 26, 2003. https://www.aclu.org/documents/getting-rid-sodomy-laws-history -and-strategy-led-lawrence-decision.

Adler, Margot. *Drawing Down the Moon*. Beacon Press, 1986. 2nd ed. Originally published in 1979. Adler's book was the first serious look at Paganism in America. If you want to know what kind of world Buckland's *The Tree* was released in, this book will give you a pretty good idea.

BabyNamesPedia. "Robat—Meaning of Robat." Accessed February 2025. https://www.babynamespedia.com/meaning/Robat.

Bourne, Lois. *Dancing with Witches*, Robert Hale, 2006. Originally published in 1998.

Bradley, Marion Zimmer. Letter to Llewellyn, August 24, 1986. A copy of the letter was included for Melita Denning and Osborne Phillips.

Buckland Museum. "Ray Buckland, Selena Fox, Scott Cunningham on Daytime Television." YouTube video, November 24, 2021. Video of Raymond Buckland, Scott Cunningham, Selena Fox, and Antiga on the *Sally Jessy Raphael Show* filmed on Monday, February 16, 1987, in St. Louis, Missouri. https://www.youtube.com/watch?v=myPScLwdxIg.

Buckland, Raymond. *Advanced Candle Magic: More Spells and Rituals for Every Purpose.* Llewellyn, 1996.

Buckland, Raymond. *Buckland's Book of Gypsy Magic: Travelers' Stories, Spells & Healings.* Red Wheel/Weiser, 2010.

Buckland, Raymond. *Buckland's Book of Spirit Communications.* Llewellyn, 2004. Originally published in 1993 as *Doors to Other Worlds: A Practical Guide to Communicating with Spirits.* Also known as the *Big Red Book.*

Buckland, Raymond. *Buckland's Complete Book of Witchcraft.* 2nd edition, revised and expanded. Llewellyn, 2012. Originally published in 1986. I own the 18th printing from 1994!

Buckland, Raymond. "Dear Friend" letter for the "Home Study Course in Saxon Witchcraft" (Buckland's Seax-Wica correspondence course). Buckland Museum collection.

Buckland, Raymond. *Death and Dying.* Undated text file.

Buckland, Raymond. *Doors to Other Worlds: A Practical Guide to Communicating with Spirits.* Llewellyn, 1993. Republished as *Buckland's Book of Spirit Communications* in 2004. Also known as the *Big Red Book.*

Buckland, Raymond. "From the Desk of Dr. Raymond Buckland." Personal note, undated.

Buckland, Raymond. *Gypsy Dream Dictionary.* Llewellyn, 1999. Originally published in 1990 as *Secrets of Gypsy Dream Reading.*

Buckland, Raymond. *Gypsy Witchcraft and Magic.* Llewellyn, 1998.

Buckland, Raymond. "Home Study Course in Saxon Witchcraft." 1981. This was Buckland's Seax-Wica correspondence course.

Buckland, Raymond. "I Live with a Witch. *Beyond* magazine, October 1968.

Buckland, Raymond. Letter in "Forum." *Green Egg* 8, no. 74 (November 6, 1975). I knew this letter existed, but I did not expect to see it show up in the mail of the Buckland Museum on one of the days I was visiting! But there it was.

Buckland, Raymond. Letter to Carl Weschcke, January 27, 1986.

Buckland, Raymond. Letter to Carl Weschcke, October 9, 1986.

Buckland, Raymond. Letter to Carl Weschcke, March 25, 1988.

Buckland, Raymond. Letter to Carl Weschcke, May 18, 1992.

Buckland, Raymond. Letter to Monique Wilson, March 14, 1963. Buckland Museum collection.

Buckland, Raymond. Letter to Monique Wilson, May 15, 1963. Buckland Museum collection.

Buckland, Raymond. Letter to Monique Wilson, exact date unknown 1. Buckland Museum collection.

Buckland, Raymond. Letter to Monique Wilson, exact date unknown 2. Buckland Museum collection

Buckland, Raymond. Letter to Monique Wilson, October 23, 1963. Buckland Museum collection.

Buckland, Raymond. Letter to Monique Wilson, exact date unknown 3. Buckland Museum collection.

Buckland, Raymond. Letter to Monique Wilson, November 13, 1963. Buckland Museum collection.

Buckland, Raymond. Letter to Monique and Scotty Wilson, June 4, 1964. Buckland Museum collection.

Buckland, Raymond. Letter to Monique and Scotty Wilson, August 4, 1964. Buckland Museum collection.

Buckland, Raymond. Letter to Monique and Scotty Wilson, June 2, 1965. Buckland Museum collection.

Buckland, Raymond. Letter to Monique and Scotty (and Yvette) Wilson, February 4, 1966. Buckland Museum collection.

Buckland, Raymond. *The Magick of Chant-O-Matics.* Parker/Prentice Hall, 1978.

Buckland, Raymond. *Opening Monologue.* Undated text file.

Buckland, Raymond. *Practical Candleburning Rituals.* 4th ed., revised. Llewellyn, 2018. Originally published in 1970.

Buckland, Raymond. "Raymond Buckland Stand-Up: My Mother-in-Law." YouTube video, March 12, 2014. https://www.youtube.com/watch?v =IS-EUXJK_hE&t=198s. I think Ray's mother-in-law bit is genuinely funny, but it's also kind of mean! I find most of Ray's stand-up pretty funny, but as I noted in the text, some people will groan that he's mostly telling dad jokes.

Buckland, Raymond. "Raymond Buckland Stand-Up #4. YouTube video, March 25, 2015. https://www.youtube.com/watch?v=D8VrbYt2yRA.

Buckland, Raymond. "Raymond Buckland Stand-Up #5." YouTube video, November 7, 2015. https://www.youtube.com/watch?v=Y76Nb9L23 F8&t=2s.

Buckland, Raymond. *Scottish Witchcraft: The History and Magick of the Picts.* Llewellyn, 1991. Later printings were retitled *Scottish Witchcraft and Magick: The Craft of the Picts.*

Buckland, Raymond. *Solitary Séance: How You Can Talk with Spirits on Your Own.* Llewellyn, 2011.

Buckland, Raymond. *The Tree.* Samuel Weiser, 1974. This book was republished by Weiser in 2005 as *Buckland's Book of Saxon Witchcraft.*

Buckland, Raymond. *Unconventional Forms of Spirit Communication.* Undated text file.

Buckland, Raymond. *Wicca for One: The Path of Solitary Witchcraft.* Kensington Publishing, 2004.

Buckland, Raymond. *Witchcraft from the Inside.* 2nd ed. Llewellyn, 1975. Originally published in 1970, and the 3rd edition in 1994.

Buckland, Raymond. *Witchcraft: Yesterday and Today.* VHS. Llewellyn, 1990. Later released on DVD as *Witchcraft: Rebirth of the Old Religion* in 2005.

Buckland, Raymond. Untitled Craft notebook. Exact dates unknown.

Buckland, Rosemary. Letter to Monique Wilson, exact date unknown. Buckland Museum collection.

Buckland, Rosemary. Letter to Monique and Scotty Wilson, December 5, 1966. Buckland Museum collection.

Buckland, Tara. Email communication on February 3, 2025.

Buckland, Tara. Personal interview conducted on November 6, 2023.

Buckland, Tara. Zoom interview conducted on February 4, 2025.

Carson, Jo. *Celebrate Wildness: Magic, Mirth, and Love on the Feraferia Path.* Natural Motion Pictures, 2015. Feraferia is one of the most interesting home-grown American Pagan traditions. Worth reading up on!

Clifton, Chas S. *Her Hidden Children: The Rise of Wicca and Paganism in America.* AltaMira Press, 2006. An overlooked and vital text for those interested in the earliest days of American Paganism.

Cochran-Buckland Promotional Materials. Lecture fee structure. No date provided.

Cochran-Buckland Promotional Materials. "Raymond Buckland Presents a Workshop." No date provided.

Collins Online English Dictionary. "Rowen." Accessed February 2025. https://www.collinsdictionary.com/us/dictionary/english/rowen.

CPI Inflation Calculator. https://www.in2013dollars.com.

Dangerous Minds. "New Witchcraft Museum Features Occult Artifacts Once Owned by Aleister Crowley." April 28, 2017. https://dangerous minds.net/comments/new_witchcraft_museum_features_occult _artifacts_once_owned_by_aleister_crow.

Davis, Morgan. *Monique Wilson & The Gardner Estate.* GeraldGardner.com. Accessed February 2025. http://www.geraldgardner.com/Monique _Wilson.pdf. I have met Morgan Davis a few times, and when I gush that I am a fan of his work and website, he usually laughs me off and swears up and down that I must be joking. I am not joking!

DNA Tribes Genetic Ancestry Analysis. "Part C: Your High Resolution Global Population Match Results" for Raymond Buckland, April 30, 2008. Provided by Tara Buckland. While Ray took his DNA test back in 2008, today's tests are ever more accurate.

Durn, Sarah. "To Join This Community of People Who Speak to the Dead, Prepare to Be Tested." Atlas Obscura. December 7, 2021. https://www .atlasobscura.com/articles/spiritualism-medium-test-lily-dale.

Farrar, Janet, and Stewart Farrar. *The Witches' Way.* Phoenix, 1984.

Fitch, Ed. *A Grimoire of Shadows.* Llewellyn, 1996.

Fox, Selena. Personal interview conducted on August 15, 2024.

Gardner, Gerald. *High Magic's Aid.* I-H-O Books, 1999. First published in 1949.

Gardner, Gerald. Letter to Raymond Buckland, exact date uncertain, 1962. Perhaps the coolest thing about this project was holding a letter typed and signed by Gerald Gardner in my grubby little hands, not something I ever expected to happen in my lifetime.

Gardner, Gerald. Letter to Raymond Buckland, November 8, 1962.

Gardner, Gerald. *The Meaning of Witchcraft.* Magickal Childe, 1991. Originally published in 1959. Magickal Childe was the publishing arm of Herman Slater's Magickal Childe store. Herman is in this book!

Gardner, Gerald. *Witchcraft Today.* I-H-O Books, 1999. Originally published in 1954.

Grimassi, Raven. *Encyclopedia of Wicca and Witchcraft.* Llewellyn, 2000. Raven was one of the nicest Witches I ever had the privilege of meeting. He also lived in San Diego when the Cochran-Bucklands lived there.

Harmony Grove Spiritualist Association. "HGSA Beginnings." Accessed February 2025. https://harmonygrovespiritual.org/beginnings.

Harris, Melanie. "Author Interview: Raymond Buckland." SFX, December 14, 2008. https://www.gamesradar.com/author_interview_raymond_buckland.

Heselton, Philip. *Doreen Valiente Witch.* The Doreen Valiente Foundation in association with the Centre for Pagan Studies, 2016.

Heselton, Philip. *Witchfather: A Life of Gerald Gardner, Volume 1: Into the Witch Cult.* Thoth Publications, 2012. Heselton is Gardner's premier biographer.

Heselton, Philip. *Witchfather: A Life of Gerald Gardner, Volume 2: From Witch Cult to Wicca.* Thoth Publications, 2012.

Hoffman, Lisa. "The Witch Next Door." *New York Sunday News,* October 27, 1968.

Holzer, Hans. *The Truth About Witchcraft.* Pocket Books, 1971. Originally published in 1969.

Holzer, Hans. *The Witchcraft Report.* Ace Books, 1973.

Huson, Paul. *Mastering Witchcraft: A Practical Guide for Witches, Warlocks, and Covens.* Perigee Books, 1980. Originally published in 1970.

Hutton, Ronald. *The Triumph of the Moon: A History of Modern Pagan Witchcraft.* 2nd ed. Oxford University Press, 2018. Originally published in 1999. For twenty years, I overused the original edition of *Triumph.* Today, I similarly abuse the second edition. I met Professor Hutton in 2022, and he knew who I was. I nearly died of embarrassment.

Intermill, Steven. Personal interview conducted on December 6, 2023.

Internet Movie Database (IMDb). "The Army Game (1957–1961): Full Cast and Crew." Accessed February 2025. https://www.imdb.com/title /tt0149416/fullcredits/?ref_=tt_cl_sm.

Kagan, Susan R. "Welcome to the Pagan Con Artist Gallery." Nolawitch, LiveJournal. August 10, 2008. https://nolawitch.livejournal.com/76176 .html.

Kelly, Aidan. "The [American] Gardnerians, 1973–75." Patheos. Last updated November 12, 2012. https://www.patheos.com/blogs/aidan kelly/2012/11/the-american-gardnerians-1973-75.

Kelly, Aidan. *A Tapestry of Witches: A History of the Craft in America, Volume I.* Hierophant Wordsmith Press, 2016. There are parts of Kelly's book that are wrong, but it still has some good information in it.

Kneitel, Thomas. Letter in "Forum." *Green Egg* 8, no. 74 (November 6, 1975).

Knowles, George. "Raymond Buckland." Controverscial. Accessed February 2025. https://www.controverscial.com/Raymond%20Buckland.htm.

Leek, Sybil. *Diary of a Witch.* Signet Books, 1968. One of my dream jobs is editing an anthology of Sybil Leek's long-out-of-print works.

Leonard, Todd Jay. *Talking to the Other Side: A History of Modern Spiritualism and Mediumship.* iUniverse, 2005.

Lindner, Kelly E. "Kent Taylor 1944–2008." *HerbalGram.* The journal of the American Botanical Council. Accessed February 2025. https://www .herbalgram.org/resources/herbalgram/issues/79/table-of-contents /article3313.

Llewellyn. Internal memo, date unknown.

Llewellyn. Publishing Agreement with Ray Buckland, April 1, 1985.

Lloyd, Michael. *Bull of Heaven: The Mythic Life of Eddie Buczynksi and the Rise of the New York Pagan.* Asphodel Press, 2012. My love for this book is absolute. I think it's one of the five best books on American Witch history ever published.

Long, Max Freedom. *Discovering the Ancient Magic.* 1936.

Mankey, Jason. *Transformative Witchcraft: The Greater Mysteries.* Llewellyn, 2018. Probably my favorite of all the books I've written.

Marquis, Melanie. *Carl Llewellyn Weschcke: Pioneer and Publisher of Body, Mind & Spirit.* Llewellyn, 2018. Melanie's biography of Carl Weschcke is masterful! If you enjoyed this book even a little, you should read Carl's story.

McGrady, Mike. "Suffolk's Secret Witch." *Newsday,* October 30, 1965.

Observer, The. "Well-Known Author Ray Buckland to Be Guest Speaker." October 20, 2007.

Pitzl-Water, Jason. "Taking Back Buckland's Collection." *The Wild Hunt,* November 10, 2008. Archived, no longer online. I am indebted to Manny Tejeda Moreno, *The Wild Hunt's* current editor-in-chief and publisher, for pulling up this article for me.

Plaisance, Michael (Monte). "Full and Unedited Statement on the Buckland Museum." *The Wild Hunt,* July 2016. http://wildhunt.org/wp-content/uploads/2016/07/Full-and-Unedited-Statement-on-The-Buckland-Museum.pdf.

Randolph, Vance. *Ozark Magic and Folklore.* Dover Publications, 1967. Originally published in 1947 as *Ozark Superstitions.*

Regula, deTraci. Letter to Llewellyn, July 17, 1989.

Regula, deTraci. Personal interview conducted on September 6, 2023.

Sheba, Lady. *The Grimoire of Lady Sheba.* Llewellyn's centennial edition. Llewellyn, 2001. Originally published in 1972. Sheba was either the best or the worst thing to ever happen to the Craft. The truth probably lies somewhere in the middle.

Sheba, Lady. *Witch.* Llewellyn, 1973.

St. Clair, Lily. Letter to Raymond Buckland, March 4, 1975. Buckland Museum collection.

St. Clair, Lily. Letter to Raymond Buckland, June 30, 1975. Buckland Museum collection.

St. Clair, Margaret. *Sign of the Labrys.* Dover, 2016. Originally published in 1963 by Bantam Books.

Telegraph, The. "Raymond Buckland, Author and High Priest of Wicca —Obituary." October 20, 2017. https://www.telegraph.co.uk /obituaries/2017/10/20/raymond-buckland-author-witch-obituary.

Thayer, Bill. "Book II, Chapter 2: Location of Albion Island of Britannia (from the First Map of Europe)." *The Geography of Claudius Ptolemy.* Dover, 1991. This website is an annotated version of a public domain publishing of Ptolemy's *Geography.* https://penelope.uchicago.edu /Thayer/E/Gazetteer/Periods/Roman/_Texts/Ptolemy/2/2*.html.

UK Parliament. "Regulating Sex and Sexuality: The 20th Century." Accessed February 2025. https://www.parliament.uk/about/living -heritage/transformingsociety/private-lives/relationships/overview /sexuality20thcentury.

Vachon, Brian. "Witchcraft Is Rising: East Coast White Witches, West Coast Black Magic." *Look* magazine, August 24, 1971.

Ward, Terence P. "Buckland Museum Poised to Reopen in Midwest." *The Wild Hunt.* July 27, 2016. https://wildhunt.org/2016/07/buckland -museum-poised-to-reopen-in-midwest.html.

Ward, Terence P. "An Interview with Raymond Buckland, American Wicca Pioneer." *The Wild Hunt,* June 1, 2016. https://wildhunt.org/2016/06 /an-interview-with-raymond-buckland-american-wicca-pioneer.html. Terence did a lot of great work during his time with *The Wild Hunt.*

Ward, Terence P. "Reboot of Buckland Museum Set for Apr. 29." *The Wild Hunt,* April 20, 2017. https://wildhunt.org/2017/04/reboot-of -buckland-museum-set-for-apr-29.html.

Weisberg, Barbara. *Talking to the Dead: Kate and Maggie Fox and the Rise of Spiritualism.* HarperSanFrancisco, 2004. This is a very fun book on one of America's great occult exports. If you are interested in Spiritualism, the abolitionist movement, and/or women's rights, you'll find something of interest in this book.

Weschcke, Carl. Llewellyn internal memo at Llewellyn, October 10, 1983.

Weschcke, Carl. Llewellyn internal memo, January 15, 1985.

Weschcke, Carl. Llewellyn internal memo, March 28, 1985.

Weschcke, Carl. Letter to Raymond Buckland, November 19, 1985.

Weschcke, Carl. Letter to Raymond Buckland, February 18, 1986.

Weschcke, Carl. Letter to Raymond Buckland, October 14, 1986.

Weschcke, Carl. Letter to Raymond Buckland, April 7, 1988.

Weschcke, Carl. Letter to Raymond Buckland, July 4, 1992.

Wicker, Christine. *Lily Dale: The True Story of the Town That Talks to the Dead.* Harper San Francisco, 2003. Sadly, Wicker doesn't talk about Buckland in her book about Lily Dale, but Ray would most certainly have known many of the people she did write about. There's not much history in Wicker's book, but it does provide an interesting portrait of several Lily Dale mediums.

Wilson, Monique. Letter to Raymond Buckland, February 26, 1963. Buckland Museum collection. I think Monique Wilson's story is one of the sadder chapters in modern Witch history. Today Monique Wilson is much maligned in many Witch circles, but many of us would not be here without her choice to initiate Ray back in 1963. The selling of Gardner's museum and collection was a tragedy for the Witchcraft community, but I also think Wilson had very few options.

Wilson, Monique. Letter to Raymond Buckland, June, 5, 1963. Buckland Museum collection.

Wilson, Monique. Letter to Raymond Buckland, July 28, 1963. Buckland Museum collection.

Wilson, Monique. Letter to Raymond and Rosemary Buckland, October 28, 1963. Buckland Museum collection.

Wilson, Monique. Letter to Rosemary Buckland, September 13, 1963. Buckland Museum collection.

Wilson, Monique. Letter to Rosemary and Raymond Buckland, September 13, 1963. Buckland Museum collection.

Wilson, Monique. Letter to Rosemary and Raymond Buckland, January 13, 1965. Buckland Museum collection.

Wilson, Monique. Letter to Rosemary and Raymond Buckland, May 24, 1965. Buckland Museum collection.

Wilson, Morven. Letter to Rosemary and Raymond Buckland, May 1, 1967. Buckland Museum collection.

Wynne, Gregory. "They're Witches, Just Ask 'Em." *Long Island Press*, October 31, 1965.

Zell, Tim Otter. Editor's note in "Forum." *Green Egg* 8, no. 74 (November 6, 1975).

Photo & Art Credits

Black & White Photos and Art in the Book

Page 10: Stanley Buckland, courtesy of Tara Buckland

Page 10: Eileen Lizzie Wells, courtesy of Tara Buckland

Page 12: Young Raymond Buckland, courtesy of Tara Buckland

Page 14: Certificate of Merit for Raymond, courtesy of Tara Buckland

Page 16: Stan Buckland's business card, courtesy of Tara Buckland

Page 17: Ray's Uncle George Buckland, courtesy of Tara Buckland

Page 19: Ray's early business card, courtesy of Tara Buckland

Page 20: Ray Buckland with ventriloquist dummy, courtesy of Tara Buckland

Page 23: Ray Buckland's natal chart, courtesy of Ivo Dominguez Jr.

Page 28: Program for *The Scarlet Pimpernel/Thieves' Carnival*, courtesy of the Buckland Museum of Witchcraft and Magick

Page 29: Ray with his trombone (*center-left*) and Count Rudolph's Syncopated Jass Men, courtesy of Tara Buckland

Page 31: Ray looking dapper in uniform and sporting quite the mustache, courtesy of Tara Buckland

Page 36: Ray's Rudolph Cartoons business card, courtesy of Tara Buckland

Page 39: Ray's Uncle Charles the ventriloquist, courtesy of Tara Buckland

Page 45: Original art from excerpt of *Solitary Séance*, courtesy of Llewellyn Worldwide. From *Hands: A Pictorial Archive from Nineteenth Century*

Sources, Jim Harter, editor (Dover Publications 1985). Border from Art Explosion.

Page 50: Gerald Gardner headshot, courtesy of Llewellyn Worldwide

Page 57: Monique Wilson in Priestess regalia, courtesy of Llewellyn Worldwide

Page 76: Method of Binding photo from *Buckland's Complete Book of Witchcraft*, drawing by Ray Buckland, courtesy of Llewellyn Worldwide

Page 96: Raven-tressed Rowen (Rosemary), courtesy of Llewellyn Worldwide

Page 99: Ray Buckland's horned helmet, courtesy of Llewellyn Worldwide

Page 102: Altar setup photo from *Practical Candleburning Rituals*, courtesy of Llewellyn Worldwide

Page 107: Hans Holzer, Wikimedia in the public domain

Page 108: Margaret St. Clair, Wikimedia in the public domain

Page 119: Raymond Buckland's magickal tools, including Rosemary's cuff, courtesy of the Buckland Museum of Witchcraft and Magick, photograph by Jason Mankey

Page 123: Sybil Leek, courtesy of Llewellyn Worldwide

Page 136: Letter to Tony Earll, courtesy of the Buckland Museum of Witchcraft and Magick

Page 139: Letter to Raymond from Bert Gordon, courtesy of the Buckland Museum of Witchcraft and Magick

Page 141: Rosemary cutting herbs, photograph by Ray Buckland, courtesy of Llewellyn Worldwide

Page 142: Rosemary on a broom with a Witch hat, courtesy of the Buckland Museum of Witchcraft and Magick

Page 147: Altar setup for the Start a New Venture candle spell in Buckland's *Advanced Candle Magick*, courtesy of Llewellyn Worldwide

Page 155: The Buckland Museum in Bay Shore, courtesy of the Buckland Museum of Witchcraft and Magick

Page 182: The Buckland Museum of Witchcraft and Magick at Weirs Beach, courtesy of the Buckland Museum of Witchcraft and Magick

Page 183: Book barn and archery range at the Buckland Museum, courtesy of the Buckland Museum of Witchcraft and Magick

Page 191: Bell, Book and Candle of the Old Dominion catalog, courtesy of the Buckland Museum of Witchcraft and Magick

Page 194: Raymond Buckland home study course pamphlet, courtesy of the Buckland Museum of Witchcraft and Magick

Page 195: Photo of Ray's Gerald Gardner drawing from the Seax-Wica course, courtesy of the Buckland Museum of Witchcraft and Magick

Page 196: Photo of Ray's circle-casting drawing from his Seax-Wica course, courtesy of the Buckland Museum of Witchcraft and Magick

Page 198: Ray's Credentials of Ministry card from the Universal Life Church, courtesy of Tara Buckland

Page 207: Ray's Certified Appraiser card, courtesy of Tara Buckland

Page 211: Tara and Ray at their wedding, courtesy of Tara Buckland

Page 214: Ray with his Angel Award, courtesy of Tara Buckland

Page 217: Ray's Norcom brand 5 Subject Notebook, courtesy of the Buckland Museum of Witchcraft and Magick, photograph by Jason Mankey

Page 220: Ray Buckland and Carl Weschcke at a booksellers convention, courtesy of the Buckland Museum of Witchcraft and Magick

Page 246: Ray's Emergency Volunteer Air Corps card, courtesy of Tara Buckland

Page 253: Raymond inside a vardo, courtesy of Tara Buckland

Page 257: Buckland's *Gypsy Fortunetelling Deck*, courtesy of Llewellyn Worldwide

Page 258: Buckland's *Domino Divination Deck*, courtesy of Llewellyn Worldwide

Page 259: Buckland's *Romani Tarot*, courtesy of Llewellyn Worldwide

Page 261: Buckland in Romani gear with large belt buckle, courtesy of Tara Buckland

Page 263: Buckland's author photo on the steps of a wagon, courtesy of Llewellyn Worldwide

Page 266: Tara and Ray partying in hippie attire, courtesy of Tara Buckland

Page 270: Ray Buckland with staff, courtesy of Llewellyn Worldwide

Page 272: Ray Buckland celebrating Bealltainn, courtesy of Llewellyn Worldwide

Page 281: Ray with pet rats on shoulder, courtesy of Tara Buckland

Page 287: Ray driving his Manx, courtesy of Tara Buckland

Page 289: Ray's Corvette at Lily Dale in 2012, courtesy of Jason Mankey

Page 319: Ray's family candelabra, courtesy of Toni Rotonda

Page 320: Toni Rotonda and Raymond Buckland going through boxes, courtesy of Toni Rotonda, photograph by Kat Tigner

Page 323: Ray in front of display case at the reopening of the Buckland Museum in 2017, courtesy of the Buckland Museum of Witchcraft and Magick, photograph by Steven Intermill

Page 325: Ray's hats and books in his office on the farm, courtesy of Tara Buckland

Page 326: Ray's office on the farm with storyboard, courtesy of Tara Buckland

Page 329: Ray Buckland in Victorian dress for a séance in 2009, courtesy of Gregory C. Ford

Eight photos of Ray with Carl Weschcke and Scott Cunningham at the end of the book, courtesy of Llewellyn Worldwide

Color Insert Photos

Color photos are listed here in the order they appear in the insert.

The Buckland side of the family: Ray's grandparents, father, and uncle, courtesy of Tara Buckland

Ray (*right*) with his brother, Gerard, as young children, courtesy of Tara Buckland

Ray's father, Stanley Buckland, courtesy of Tara Buckland

Ray's mother, Eileen Lizzie Wells, courtesy of Tara Buckland

The Buckland family (*Ray on left*), courtesy of Tara Buckland

Young Bucklands at the beach (*Ray on right*), courtesy of Tara Buckland

Young Gerard and Raymond on a walk with their mother, courtesy of Tara Buckland

Ray (*right*) performing in *The Duke of Darkness* with friend Phil Mottram, courtesy of Tara Buckland

Ray, the young thespian (*left*), courtesy of Tara Buckland

Ray dressed as a vampire, courtesy of Tara Buckland

Count Rudolph and his Jass Men, courtesy of Tara Buckland

The Jass Men on vinyl, courtesy of the Buckland Museum of Witchcraft and Magick

Ray out camping, courtesy of Tara Buckland

Uncle Charles the magician, courtesy of Tara Buckland

A very dapper Uncle George, courtesy of Tara Buckland

Raymond Buckland reporting for duty, courtesy of Tara Buckland

Ray and Rosemary near the beginning of their Witchcraft journey (close-up shot), courtesy of the Buckland Museum of Witchcraft and Magick

Scotty and Monique Wilson with Rosemary Buckland on the Isle of Man, courtesy of the Buckland Museum of Witchcraft and Magick

Ray and Rosemary on the cover of *Beyond* magazine, courtesy of the Buckland Museum of Witchcraft and Magick

Ray with his ritual tools in a gun case, courtesy of Tara Buckland

Buckland with a monkey skull, courtesy of the Buckland Museum of Witchcraft and Magick

Ray Buckland in ritual garb at Pan Pagan Festival 1980, courtesy of Tara Buckland

Ray Buckland and Scott Cunningham, courtesy of the Buckland Museum of Witchcraft and Magick

Ray with pet snakes and a glass of wine, courtesy of Tara Buckland

Ray with English High Priestess Patricia Crowther, courtesy of the Buckland Museum of Witchcraft and Magick

Tara and Ray at their wedding, courtesy of Tara Buckland

Tara and Ray in dancing clothes in San Diego, courtesy of Tara Buckland

Barefoot Ray with his staff, courtesy of Llewellyn Worldwide

Ray sitting in his ultralight aircraft, courtesy of Tara Buckland

The pilot has been cleared for takeoff (Ray sitting in airplane), courtesy of Tara Buckland

A page from what became the *Big Blue Book*, courtesy of the Buckland Museum of Witchcraft and Magick

Scott Cunningham, Carl Weschcke, and Ray, courtesy of Llewellyn Worldwide

Ray on the water, courtesy of Gregory C. Ford

Ray (*right*) with his brother, Gerard, sitting on a sofa, courtesy of Tara Buckland

Ray with some baby goats, courtesy of Tara Buckland

Ray in sweater with arms crossed, courtesy of Tara Buckland

Ray (*middle*) with Dennis Carpenter and Selena Fox of Circle Sanctuary, courtesy of Tara Buckland

Tara and Ray taking the dogs for a walk, courtesy of Tara Buckland

Ray out for a horse and buggy ride, courtesy of Tara Buckland

Ray in suit as master of ceremonies at Lily Dale, courtesy of Tara Buckland

Ray proudly posing with *Dead for a Spell*, courtesy of Tara Buckland

Ray with dog on lap, courtesy of Tara Buckland

Older Ray and Tara with heads touching, courtesy of Tara Buckland

Ray taking a nap with dog, courtesy of Tara Buckland

Ray cutting the ribbon at the reopening of the Buckland Museum of Witchcraft and Magick in Ohio, courtesy of Tara Buckland

Interior of the Buckland Museum of Witchcraft and Magick in Ohio, courtesy of Tara Buckland

Index

To Write to the Author

If you wish to contact the author or would like more information about this book, please write to the author in care of Llewellyn Worldwide Ltd. and we will forward your request. Both the author and the publisher appreciate hearing from you and learning of your enjoyment of this book and how it has helped you. Llewellyn Worldwide Ltd. cannot guarantee that every letter written to the author can be answered, but all will be forwarded. Please write to:

Jason Mankey
⅘ Llewellyn Worldwide
2143 Wooddale Drive
Woodbury, MN 55125-2989
Please enclose a self-addressed stamped envelope for reply,
or $1.00 to cover costs. If outside the U.S.A., enclose
an international postal reply coupon.

Many of Llewellyn's authors have websites with additional
information and resources. For more information,
please visit our website at http://www.llewellyn.com.

Ray with his good friends Carl Weschcke and Scott Cunningham in the late '80s